LINCOL

P9-BZK-693

THE FONTANA ECONOMIC HISTORY OF EUROPE

General Editor: Carlo M. Cipolla

There is at present no satisfactory economic history of
Europe—covering Europe both as a whole and with
particular relation to the individual countries—that is
both concise enough for convenient use and yet full
enough to include the results of individual and detailed
scholarship. This series is designed to fill that gap.

Unlike most current works in this field the *Fontana
Economic History of Europe* does not end at the outbreak
of the First World War. More than half a century has
elapsed since 1914, a half century that has transformed
the economic background of Europe. In recognition
of this the present work has set its terminal date at
1970 and provides for sixty contributions each
written by a specialist. For the convenience of students
each will be published separately in pamphlet form
as soon as possible. When all the contributions have
been received they will be gathered into six volumes
as The Fontana Economic History of Europe. A
library edition will also be available.

THE FONTANA ECONOMIC HISTORY OF EUROPE

The Fontana
Economic History of Europe
Volume 1

The Middle Ages

Editor Carlo M. Cipolla

Harvester Press/Barnes & Noble
By agreement with Fontana Books

This edition first published in 1976 by
THE HARVESTER PRESS LIMITED
Publisher: John Spiers
2 Stanford Terrace
Hassocks, Nr Brighton
Sussex, England
and published in the U.S.A. 1976 bu
HARPER & ROW PUBLISHERS, INC.
BARNES & NOBLE IMPORT DIVISION
10 East 53rd Street, New York 10022.

The Middle Ages
This edition first published in 1976
by The Harvester Press Limited
and by Barnes & Noble
By agreement with Fontana

First published in paperback in 1972
by Fontana Books

© Carlo M. Cipolla 1972, 1976
© J. C. Russell 1969, 1976
© Jacques Le Goff 1971, 1976
© Richard Roehl 1970, 1976
© Lynn White Jr. 1969, 1976
© Georges Duby 1969, 1976
© Sylvia L. Thrupp 1971, 1976
© Jacques Bernard 1971, 1976
© Edward Miller 1970, 1976

The Harvester Press Limited
ISBN 0 85527 159 0
Barnes & Noble
ISBN 0–06–492176–X

Printed in Great Britain by Redwood Burn Limited
Trowbridge, Wiltshire
Bound by Cedric Chivers Limited, Portway, Bath

All rights reserved

Contents

63663

General Introduction

When introducing a new work, it is customary to point out that it is sorely needed and will fill a wide, important gap. Actually, whether there is a gap in the literature available in any field and whether a new book adequately fills it, is up to the reading public to decide. It must be admitted however that both the publisher and the editor of this work felt that there was a great need for a comprehensive and up-to-date economic history of Europe.

The plan of the work follows traditional lines. Chapters have been assigned to topics such as population, agriculture, manufactures, trade, technology and entrepreneurial activity. This categorisation crosses with another, which divides the history into three chronological periods: the Middle Ages (900–1500), the early modern period (1500–1700) the period of industrialisation (1700–1914) and the contemporary scene (1920–1970). The first part of the Middle Ages has been left out because the work is devoted essentially to explaining the emergence of the modern industrial world.

All forms of division are arbitrary. When one is adopted, the distortions and biases that may derive from it must be made clear and, if possible, corrected. Chapters dealing with agriculture, trade, technology, finance and the like tend to emphasise unduly the factors that operate on the supply side. Therefore, chapters on the levels and patterns of demand have been inserted to correspond to each of the three chronological periods of our story. I am not at all convinced that these restore the balance sufficiently, but certainly the potential imbalance has been noticeably corrected.

For the two most recent periods (1700–1914 and 1920–1970) the treatment though following the pattern just outlined is also enlarged by an exposition of the industrial development of individual countries, each country being

8 *General Introduction*

treated as a special case. This essentially means that the same subject has been studied twice but from different angles. When single countries were analysed, the dividing criterion for the individual chapters was the state as a political unit. Obviously, industrial development did not always or even frequently coincide with the boundaries of political entities. Within each country there were rapidly growing regions and stubbornly stagnant areas. Some countries were more homogeneous than others. England was a fairly homogeneous area. At the other end of the spectrum Italy was, as Prince Metternich said, a 'geographical expression' with dramatic internal contrasts. Admittedly, to use and compare national averages for such different cases is not a sensible or a meaningful operation. Piedmont and Sicily are in many ways less compatible than England and Scotland: yet conventionally Italy is treated as a statistical entity while figures cited for England are carefully qualified as omitting Scotland and Ireland. Moreover national averages tend to conceal the subtle mechanisms which favour internally some regions at the expense of others and which are such an essential element of the process of development.

In ordinary textbooks and general treatises on economic history, the analysis of the process of industrialisation is generally made with reference to England, France, Germany and, occasionally, Russia. The no less interesting experiences of other countries are all too often left aside. Therefore, we have made a point of including in our story also the cases of Scandinavia, the Low Countries, Switzerland, the Habsburg Empire, Italy and Spain.

In keeping with my statement that all partitions of a subject are arbitrary, I must further point out that economic history in itself is a partition, and a most arbitrary one. It has been adopted for convenience of analysis and academic training. But life has no such compartment; there is only history. What we call economic and social history can be understood only if we take into full account the work done in other arbitrary partitions, such as the individuated histories of ideas, collective psychology education, science, technology, medicine, warfare. It is fashionable nowadays to talk of capital-output ratios, production functions, marginal returns and the like. But interesting as it is to deal with such tools and to measure some of these variables, the real problem of understanding history is a much more interesting and at the same time a much more elusive one. The real problem is understanding the human reality that is behind those variables and makes them what they are.

I find it trivial to distinguish between 'new' and 'old', 'qualitative' and 'quantitative' economic histories. Such distinctions simply serve to perpetuate academic quarrels. The fundamental distinction is between good economic history and bad economic history, and this distinction depends neither on the kind of symbolism used nor on the number of statistical tables inserted. Instead it depends on the relevance of the questions raised, the quality of the material collected to answer the questions, and the choice and the use of the analytical method, which must be suited both to the questions raised and to the material available.

C. M. CIPOLLA

The Origins
C. M. Cipolla

Our story begins in the impoverished Europe of the eighth and ninth centuries. People were few. High fertility was matched by high mortality. Violence, superstition, and ignorance prevailed. Economic activity had fallen back to low levels and to primitive forms. It was the golden age of monasticism, because people dreamed of peaceful oases where they could wall themselves away from the sinful world and its sinful inhabitants and pray for a better life in a better world. On an economic level, the manorial organisation reflected the same attitude of distrust of outside elements. It is traditional to view the self-sufficiency of the early medieval manor as a consequence of the lack of trade. But trade never ceased completely, and it is easy to argue that the causal relationship was neither so simple nor so one-directional. The lack of trade was itself a result of the self-sufficiency of the manor. When a document of the time warns that 'all things necessary. ought to be made on the manor so that it would not be necessary to buy or borrow them outside the manor,' it does not exclude the possibilities of obtaining the necessities from the market; it simple stresses the desirability of not becoming dependent upon the market. The market was unreliable and gave no assurance of providing necessities regularly. Trade relations both over long and short distances were irregular and unpredictable. It was inconceivable that a community could live on commercial activity without engaging directly in agriculture for the daily necessities of life. Those who knew of the existence of Venice regarded it as an abnormally strange, utterly inexplicable phenomenon, and the extensor of an eleventh century document reported with wonder: 'That nation does not plow, sow or gather vintage.'[1]

1. 'Et illa gens non arat, non seminat, non vindemiat.' *Instituta Regalia et Ministeria Camere Regum Langobardorum*, parag. 4, in MMGGHH, *Scriptores* 30, part 2, pp. 1450-7.

During the Dark Ages, most of the people were serf-peasants. Of the few craftsmen, some were itinerant workers, but most were part-time craftsmen and part-time serf-peasants who divided their time between tilling their plots of land and producing crude artifacts for the community or for the landlord, and they shared the destitute lives and poor living conditions of the serf-peasants. There were also itinerant merchants, but this group was far from being homogeneous. There were petty peddlers who covered relatively small areas attempting to sell their poor merchandise in the villages or at the weekly markets. Bigger merchants operated over long distances, often across the borders of countries, carrying with them silk or highly ornate cloth, objects made of ebony or of ivory, religious relics, jewellery and slaves. These merchants appeared mostly at the large fairs held at different times in different localities. Between these two types of merchants were other, intermediate, types. But all merchants, regardless of the size of their business, shared some common characteristics. Their position on the social ladder was low. They were itinerant, virtually rootless vagabond people, and they were looked upon suspiciously by everyone. The Church damned them because their lives were devoted to the pursuit of material gains, a sinful thing according to the clergy. Local administrative officials regarded them with distrust, fearing constantly that these roving adventurers would turn out to be spies of the enemy or wicked thieves. The common people also held suspect these strangers who often had no homes and no land, men who moved to and from strange places, often with strange merchandise, indulging in black marketeering, usury, and God knew how many other sinful activities.

The surviving documents of the period are unfriendly to the merchants. Liutprand of Cremona reports that the merchants of Verdun castrated young children and sold them as slaves on Moslem markets. A text from the Meuse region, dating from the first quarter of the eleventh century, shows two merchants talking as they pass a church: one suggests that they go in to pray, but the other refuses,

saying he does not want to take his mind off business. A
passage in the text of *The Miracle of St. Foy* tells of a merchant
of Auvergne enriching himself through illicit speculation in
the wax used to make candles for the pilgrims who flocked
to the shrine of St. Foy of Conques. The chronicler Alpert
of Metz describes the merchants as tough men (*homines duri*),
who scorn the law unless it happens to favour their own
side. They are heavy drinkers, and the only people they
admire are those who can tell indecent stories in a loud
voice and incite them to laugh and drink. With the money
they make, they hold vulgar banquets at which they become intoxicated.[2] Such ideas were not totally absurd.
Only tough characters dared travel about in the forested,
troubled, insecure Europe of the Dark Ages. Only greedy
adventurers dared face all the hardships of a dangerous,
itinerant life for the sake of pecuniary gain. Only un-
scrupulous men would so openly defy the moral condemnation of the Church and enter a profession held in low
social esteem.

The clergy and the warlords ruled society and controlled
most of its wealth. The cultural traits of these two groups
moulded society and directed its performance. Their
respective ideals were to pray and to fight. Neither
group sincerely despised wealth. On the contrary, they
cared for Mammon as much as everybody else did, if not
more. But it was inconceivable for members of the two
ruling groups to spend their lives in the production of
wealth. Wealth had to be produced by the lower orders,
the serfs. The 'betters,' the clergy and the warlords, had
the right to take over all or part of this product while
devoting themselves to the noble activities of praying and
fighting, the acknowledged ends of society. Production was
a means. Devotion and gallantry were the ends. Social

2. On all that precedes cf. E. Sabbe, 'Quelques types de marchands
des IXe et Xe siècles, in *Revue Belge de Philologie et d'Histoire* 13 (1934),
pp. 176-87, and F. Vercauteren, 'The Circulation of Merchants in
Western Europe from the 6th to the 10th Century: Economic and Cultural Aspects,' in S. L. Thrupp (ed.), *Early Medieval Society* (New York,
1967), pp. 185-95.

esteem and reward were given to those who were successful in pursuing the noble ends, not to those who were successful in providing the vulgar means.

There was no conscious denial of practicality. Quite the opposite. One must merely be aware of what was meant by 'practical.' The most practical thing for the clerks was to pray for the salvation of their souls and, if possible, also for the salvation of the souls of their friends. The most practical thing for the knights was to show strength and valour. For both clerks and knights it was practical to exploit those who produced wealth. Education was not despised, but the concept of education was also peculiarly suited to the prevailing ideals of the two ruling groups. The knights despised or, in the best cases, had no interest in literary education, which they left to the clergy. As a group of Goths allegedly told Queen Amalasunta, 'Letters are removed from manliness, and the teaching of old men results for the most part in a cowardly and submissive spirit.'[3] The knights respected education which added to their strength and valour-training in horsemanship, in hunting, in tournaments. Given their goals, this was a good and practical education indeed. For their part, the clergy cultivated literary and musical education, for this allowed them to read the holy texts and to sing in church.

The lower orders acquiesced in their inferior social status and passively accepted not only their low position on the social ladder but also the prevalence of the cultural values of the ruling groups. The acceptance of the one implied the other. Moreover, they had no higher or nobler sets of values to oppose to those of the rulers. Gallantry and devotion seemed indeed worthier ideals than the vulgar desire of simply wanting something more to eat, to wear, or to spare.

Manorial organisation was not conducive to high levels of productivity. But, given the general conditions and the prevailing cultural traits of the time, it was possibly the best kind of arrangement. As a matter of fact, a number of important technological innovations were adopted between

3. Procopius, *Gothic War* 1, 2.

the seventh and the tenth centuries—the heavy plough appeared, the three-field rotation system, new methods for harnessing horses, and improved integration of agriculture and herding. The net result of these and other changes, coupled with the end of the major invasions, must have been an increase in agricultural productivity, especially after the end of the ninth century. Whether this growth in agricultural productivity was in itself sufficient cause for the development that took place after the middle of the tenth century is open to dispute. But there is no doubt that it was a necessary condition.

It is impossible to define causal relationships; all that we can do with a fair degree of confidence is describe the major trends. After the middle of the tenth century the population grew all over Europe. In the long run, no bottlenecks appeared in the economic system. Land was plentiful, and the capital necessary for development was slowly, though painfully, created. Production grew in every sector. It is customary to refer mostly to the growth of long distance trade with occasional, though not always pertinent, reference to Venice, the Crusades, and the spices, and these were undoubtedly spectacular developments. But perhaps more important was the growth of local trade and craftsmanship. Although this is not the place to discuss all these movements in detail, it is necessary to point out that an essential aspect of the process of development, its 'cause' as well as its 'effect,' was the rapid growth everywhere in the number of people who practised some trade or some kind of craft. Their numbers grew both in absolute terms and in relation to other groups, and they grew also in wealth.

In the North, these people usually clustered around a castle or an abbey, wherever geophysical-political conditions favoured communications and exchanges.[4] In the South, the natural gathering points were what remained of the old Roman towns. In their wake all sorts of people flocked towards the growing urban centres: fugitive serfs, uprooted adventurers such as that multilingual *pannosus*

4. See H. Pirenne, *Medieval Cities.*

mentioned by Liutprand in his *Antapodosis*,[5] and especially in Italy also members of the lesser nobility.[6] What brought people to the towns were the growing opportunities available in the urban centres rather than any worsening of the economic situation in the countryside. People left the country because they thought that in the towns there were better opportunities for economic and social advancement, and this belief made them intolerant of the slow mobility of the rural world. *Stadtluft macht frei* was said in Germany: the air of the town makes one a freeman. In more than one way this movement resembles—as far as motivations and feelings are concerned—the migration of Europeans to America during the nineteenth century. In both cases there was some hope of moving to a better world, a more open society, and fuller economic opportunities.[7]

It is generally admitted that whether it was a question of the resurgence of a town amid decayed Roman ruins in the South or of the first beginnings of a town life in the North, the emergence and growth of the new urban centres represented a revolutionary turning point in western history—something that gave to that history its unique and peculiar character. The roots of all subsequent developments including the Industrial Revolution and its products can be traced to the urban development of the Middle Ages.

Towns, however, existed elsewhere in the medieval world, in China as well as in the Byzantine Empire. Large cities seem to have been proportionately more numerous in China than in Europe until the nineteenth century, and until the eighteenth century urbanisation may have been higher.[8] Constantinople enclosed a surface of about 3,500 acres when Paris measured 20, Tournai 30, and Milan 283.[9] Towns had existed also in the more distant past, ever

5. H. Pirenne, 'Un prétendu drapier milanais en 926,' in *Studi Medievali* N. S. 1 (1928), pp. 131-3.

6. E. Sestan.

7. C. M. Cipolla, *Clocks and Culture* (London, 1967), pp. 17-18.

8. R. Murphey, 'The City as a Center of Change: Western Europe and China,' *Annals of the Association of American Geographers* 44 (1954), p. 354.

9. R. S. Lopez, *The Birth of Europe* (New York, 1967), p. 131.

since the Neolithic Revolution: in most ancient Sumer as in Egypt. No culture had actually identified itself with the city as thoroughly as had classic Greece and Rome. If the town of Medieval Europe gave to European history a unique character and determined an historical course so peculiarly different from that of other societies, it is obvious that the medieval city must have been something essentially different from the towns of other areas or other times.

The difference was not in the professional composition of the town dwellers. The towns of Medieval Europe had merchants, craftsmen, and professional people, but also a large population of priests, nuns, and monks, plus a number of landlords. On the other hand, the towns of ancient Egypt, classic Greece and Rome were largely inhabited by tradesmen, craftsmen, money changers, lawyers, judges, teachers, doctors and the like, and this sort of people was more numerous in towns than in the villages. Similarly, in China, Ching-te-chen was the site of the Imperial Potteries. Shanghai, long before becoming a treaty-port under foreign domination, was the leading commercial hub of the Yangtze Valley. Canton was the consistent focus of foreign trade. Chunking, Chengchow, Hankow, Hsiagtan, Soochow, and Wuhu were all developed commercial centres. When we compare the medieval town with the towns of other areas and other times we find a broad similarity both in the professional composition of the population as well as in urban functions. Yet there was an essential difference.

In the towns of the classical world as in the towns of China the merchant, the craftsman, the doctor, and the notary never acquired a socially prominent position. Even when they acquired wealth, they acquiesced in an inferior social position: they passively accepted a low position on the social ladder and, at the same time, the prevalence of the cultural values of the ruling groups. The rural ideals of the upper classes permeated the whole society, and as the landed gentry dominated both the countryside and the towns socially, politically, and culturally, powerful elements of cohesion obliterated the differences between the urban and the rural world. The town was not an organism in itself, but rather an organ within the broader context of an urban-rural continuum.

The story of the European city after the tenth century is totally different. In medieval Europe the town came to represent an abnormal growth, a peculiar body totally foreign to the surrounding environment. The essence of the change was pinpointed by a perceptive member of the feudal order, the German Otto von Freising. When describing the Italian towns who fought against the emperor Frederick Barbarossa the Redbearded, one of the last champions of the feudal order, Otto remarks: 'They do not disdain to give the girdle of knighthood or honourable positions to young men of inferior station and even workers of the vile mechanical arts, whom other peoples bar like the pest from the more respected and honourable circles.'[10] How right he was, the conservative bishop. And yet he was too simplistic in depicting the new social order that had emerged in the towns. As Professor Lopez once wrote, the democracy of the municipal government was not and had no desire to be equalitarian and total.[11] In the Communes it was not absolute majority that was sought after, but rather according to the definition given at the beginning of the fourteenth century by Marsilio of Padua, the 'general agreement of the worthiest part.' *Stadluft machts frei*. There were no serfs in the towns. All were free. All were equal. But some were more equal than others.

The medieval city was dominated politically, socially, and culturally by the merchants and the moneychangers —as all textbooks of economic history teach—and also by the pharmacists, the notaries, the lawyers, the judges, the doctors, and the like. It was this composite social group that from the beginning had been the driving force of the emergence of towns as independent bodies, and which was also behind the brotherhoods, the *conjurationes* with which the burgher's emancipation had begun. They were the

10. Otto von Freising, *Gesta Frederici*, II, 12 in *Scriptores Rerum Germanicarum* 54 (G. Waitz, ed.), (Hanover-Leipzig, 1912), p. 116.

11. R. S. Lopez, *op. cit.*, p. 270.

predivites—the very wealthy ones—over whom a conservative of the calibre of Lambert von Hersfeld gave vent to his wrath when he described the rising of Cologne of 1074. They owed their high social position to their wealth, but not to wealth alone. In China too, and in the towns of ancient Greece and Rome there had been many wealthy merchants and craftsmen. Yet the wealthy Chinese, Greek, and Roman tradesman never succeeded in imposing themselves socially nor did they succeed in overthrowing the sets of values of the landed gentry. The reasons why the wealthy burghers succeeded where their Chinese, Greek, and Roman counterparts failed are not easily explained. Undoubtedly the medieval burgher prospered in an environment in which the state practically did not exist. Establishing the city as an independent corporate entity with well-differentiated adminstrative organs, the burgher actually gave birth to the modern state as we conceive it. The medieval burgher was also favoured by the coexistence of several major centres of feudal power. In more than one case the burgher took advantage of the rivalry among them, playing one against the other, the king against the barons, the bishops against the king. Moreover, towns grew mostly because of immigration. Those who left the countryside for the towns were leaving behind or actually fleeing from an environment toward which they had nothing but feelings of hostility. Thus the rebellious mood of the towns was constantly refuelled while growing wealth and success gave to that mood overtones of boldness and pride.

This leads us to the crucial point. The wealthy Chinese tradesman faced an entrenched landed gentry which might have acted as all entrenched social classes do but whose sets of values and ideals were embodied in a philosophy of high ethical value. It was not easy for a merchant to challenge the Confucian ideals of the scholar-officials. Similarly in Greece and in Rome the landed gentry identified itself with sets of values and ideals derived from highly developed and sophisticated philosophies. The burgher of the medieval town was not dwarfed by imposing cultural structures standing in his way. The claim to pre-eminence of the lay baron rested on his skill in tournament and his bloody passion for war. Even when reinterpreted by minstrels in terms of gallantry and chivalry, the sets of values of the lay feudality were not of a kind to command much respect once the society had begun to move out of a very primitive state. The burgher of the medieval town was more often than not a merchant, but no longer was he the tough adventurer of the Dark Ages. He had slowly developed into a relatively cultivated person who took pride in contributing to the erection of a beautiful public building, to the opening of a school or hospital, to the general prosperity and greatness of his town. Looking at what he and his fellow burghers were accomplishing, he felt deeply in his bones that they were 'the betters.' One perceives this feeling of pride in the buildings that they erected as well as in writings such as the following description of fourteenth century Florence by the merchant Giovanni Villani:

'It was estimated that in Florence there were some 90,000 mouths divided among men, women and children . . . and it was reckoned that in the city there were always about 1,500 foreigners . . . We find that the boys and girls learning to read numbered from 8,000 to 10,000, the children learning the abacus and algorism from 1,000 to 1,200 and those learning grammar and logic in four large schools from 550 to 600 . . . We find that the churches then in Florence and in the suburbs were 110 and . . . 30 hospitals with more than 1,000 beds to receive the poor and the sick . . . The workshops of the guild of wool and woollen merchants were 200 or more and they made from 70,000 to 80,000 pieces of cloth, which were worth more than 1,200,000 gold florins. And a good third of this sum remained in the land as the reward of labour, without counting the profit of the entrepreneurs. And more than 30,000 persons lived by it. The *fondachi* of the guild of importers of transalpine cloth were some twenty, and they imported yearly more than 10,000 pieces of cloth, worth 300,000 gold florins . . . The banks of money-changers were about eighty . . .

The association of judges was composed of some eighty members. The notaries were some six hundred. Physicians and surgeons, some sixty. Apothecaries, some hundred.

'There were in Florence 146 bakeries . . . Every year the city consumed about 4,000 oxen and calves, 60,000 mutton and sheep, 20,000 she-goats and he-goats and 30,000 pigs. During the month of July some 4,000 *some* of melons came through Porta San Friano . . .

'Florence within the walls was well built, with many beautiful houses, and at that period people kept building with improved techniques to obtain comfort and richness by importing designs of every kind of improvement. They built parish churches and churches of friars of every order, and splendid monasteries . . . And it was such a wonderful sight when foreigners, not accustomed to cities like Florence, came from abroad . . .'[12]

The story of the relationship between the burghers and the Church is more complex. All the money bequeathed to the Church by wealthy merchants proves that the merchants continued to nourish strong feelings of guilt in the face of the moral preaching of the Church and the intelligentsia— notaries, judges, doctors, apothecaries—did not challenge the ideals and the values of the Church. But by laying the foundations of the secular state, the burghers made possible a compromise by which they exerted power on the sphere that mattered to them, leaving to the Church control over spiritual matters. On the other hand, the Church proved very accommodating. The moral condemnation of mercantile and banking activity was progressively softened. More than that, the members of the clergy who grew up and lived in towns came to share the value system of the burghers:

'The population increases every day . . . In the city, including the suburbs, there are ten hospitals for the sick . . . Every sort of the poor people, except the lepers,

12. G. Villani, *Cronica*, Book XI, Chapter XCIV. Engl. Transl. in R. S. Lopez and I. W. Raymond, *Medieval Trade in the Mediterranean World* (New York, 1955), pp. 69 ff.

for whom another hospital is reserved, are received there, and they are kindly and bountifully restored to health, bed as well as food being provided. Also, all the poor needing surgical care are diligently cared for by these surgeons especially assigned to this task; the latter receive a salary from the town . . . There are in this city alone 120 doctors of both laws . . . The notaries are more than 1,500 . . . The experts in medicine, who are popularly named physicians, are twenty-eight. The surgeons of different specialties, indeed, are more than 150, among whom are a great many who, obviously being excellent physicians, have derived from the ancestors of their family the ancient traditions of surgery. The professors of grammatical art are eight. They supervise crowds of pupils . . . The teachers of the elements of reading and writing indeed number more than seventy. The copyists surpass the number of forty. Indeed there are three hundred bakeries in the city . . . The shopkeepers who sell at retail an amazing amount of goods of all kinds, doubtlessly are more than a thousand. The butchers number more than 440. There are more than eighteen fishermen for all kind of fish . . . The hostelries giving hospitality to strangers number about 150.' The smiths who outfit quadrupeds with iron shoes number about eighty, and this indicates the multitude of horsemen and horses . . . More than 150,000 cartloads of firewood are certainly burned every year in the city alone. . . .'[13]

This is a thirteenth century description of Milan. In it we find the same tone, the same outlook, the same philosophy, the same approach as the fourteenth century description of Florence. They give every appearance of having been written by the same author. But they were not. The Florentine report was written by a merchant, Giovanni Villani, the Milanese report by a friar, Bonvecino da Ripa.

13. Bonvecinus de Rippa, 'De Magnalibus urbis Mediolani,' ed. by F. Novati, in *Bullettino dell'Istituto Storico Italiano* 20 (1898), pp. 67-114. English translation in Lopez and Raymond, *op. cit.*, pp. 60, ff.

The fourteenth century report on Pavia written by another friar, Opicino de Canistris, is exactly of the same kind. The town burgher had prevailed, and his outlook and philosophy had commanded respect and infected all sorts of townspeople and all avenues of urban activity. Thus the towns stood, with all the pride and self-assurance that old woodcuts betray when they show the skylines of the cities, as coherent islands of a new culture. There is absolutely nothing alien to us in the descriptions of Florence and Milan that I quoted previously and in other similar descriptions that I have not quoted. A nineteenth century Londoner describing London or a twentieth century American describing New York would not have written much differently from Bonvecino or Giovanni because our culture is the direct descendant of theirs, born within the walls of the medieval cities, the product of the social revolution that saw 'young men of inferior station and even workers of the vile mechanical arts, whom other peoples bar like the pest' reach 'the girdle of knighthood or honourable positions.'

To understand the economic history of Western Europe from the twelfth century until the Second Industrial Revolution, we have to explore a great number of variables and accomplishments in the fields of technology, agriculture, trade, public and private finance, manufactures, and so on. We can, if we want, calculate yield ratios, capital output ratios, productivities, and the like. But at the very heart of the matter, there lies the cultural fact of those compact societies of burghers who were so proud of what they were doing and who thought that they were 'the betters' because they did what they did.

1. Population in Europe 500-1500

J. C. Russell

Demography is concerned with the various phases of the study of population: the numbers of persons in geographical areas of differing sizes, the distribution of settlements of geography and size, the divisions by age and sex, the percentage of population by marriage, fertility and birth rate, expectation and death rate, and migration. Medieval population shared many of the characteristics of people in all history: at birth about 105 boys to 100 girls appear, most children are born to woman aged eighteen to forty-two although younger and older women bear a few, few people live to be a hundred, cities tend to have more female than male inhabitants: these are among the more common characteristics. Medieval population also shared in characteristics peculiar to preindustrial cultures: expectation of life of about thirty years at birth and indeed until nearly the teenage years, earlier deaths for women and thus a high sex ratio (that is, of men to women), relatively low density of population and small size of cities. Sharing very largely in a Christian culture it was monogamous.

Despite a unity of geography and time, the population varied considerably in size. It experienced near the beginning (A.D. 542-700) and again near the end (1348-1500) plagues which reduced the population well down to fifty per cent in the first half century of epidemics and kept it low for another century. Between 700 and 850 and again between 950-1050 (depending upon the part of the continent) and 1300 there were periods of rapid population increase, at least by preindustrial standards. Just before the plagues and again between 850 and 950-1050 population rose only slowly or not at all. These were general trends: there were local variations of importance.

THE EVIDENCE

Demographic evidence is most valuable when it includes

a high proportion of population and is properly recorded. For the first half of the Middle Ages the best are surveys of monastic holdings in France, such as that of Abbot Irminon's polyptyque of St. Germain-des-Prés (Paris) of about 819 and similar documents of St. Remi of Rheims and St. Peter of Marseilles. Irminon's survey divides population by households or families with about 3·6 persons to the unit. St. Peter's survey gives the age of many of the children. All show a high sex ratio. The Abbot's data seem inclusive for several parishes and indicate their size. .

Italian evidence for most of the population of some cities and even of country districts becomes important in the fourteenth and fifteenth centuries. Florence had a census of mouths (*bocche*) and heads of families (*poste*) in 1380 which enables an index to be set up for their relationship, about 4·2 *bocche* to the *poste*. Florence also recorded baptisms by sex in the period. In 1402 similar person-family surveys were made of some villages in the Romagna. Treviso in 1384 divided its population for survey into these groups: males older than fourteen years, younger males, religious, women and servants showing the usual superior numbers of women expected of cities. However, a second survey twelve years later would show that the first was very defective. In the fifteenth century several other general surveys occurred in Italy. In demography as in other phases of life Italy was a leader in the Middle Ages.

From Iberia come surveys of scattered Pyrenean villages in the later Middle Ages and from Castellon de la Plana in 1438: from France a survey of 1471. Ypres had partial lists of most of its inhabitants in 1412, 1431 and 1437 and Fribourg in Uchtland (German Switzerland) in 1444-8. The evidence about the practically total surveys of Nuremberg in 1449, Nördlingen in 1459 and Strasbourg in 1473-7, when published in the nineteenth century astonished scholars by their small size. In general the tendency has been to reduce estimates in all phases of medieval population. Size of household varied from 3·5-7 of Castellon de la Plana and Ypres to 4·14-5·5 of the German cities. From some of them as well as from earlier surveys some estimates of the percentage of married persons is available.

A second type of evidence, of head tax (*chevage*) or lists of those liable for military service apparently began in Italy, although few of them remain. In the later fourteenth century, it was very popular in northern Europe: in England of 1377, in the Low Countries, France and Germany. Generally including those above age fourteen, it should include about two thirds of the population (if the women were included). The English households, marked in many returns, present about 2·4 adults or 3·5 persons to the household. Here, as with all taxes, the problem of the exempt and the nonpayer enters.

By far the most widespread source, coming from nearly every part of Europe, was the tax based on households or houses. Here the number of persons to the unit is vital. If names are given, the percentage of women in the lists furnish a clue: the more women the lower the average number to the house or household. If nonpayers because of poverty are included, the coverage is obviously better. Occasional data (such as the number in murdered households in England) are helpful. Great collections, such as the Domesday Book of 1086 in England, the 1328 list of hearths in France, the Peter's Pence returns for Poland and Scandinavia, supply a quantitative, if somewhat tentative base for estimate of population.

This type of tax data is available for many cities as well as for countryside. The money tax lists of the fourteenth century often list the *pobres* and *nichils* who did not pay. A common form was the hearth tax which appeared frequently, especially in France, Italy and the Low Countries. There, however, it came eventually to be a tax unit with less and less relation to actual numbers, so that it must be used with care. Even more care is required of lists of 'burgesses' who often constitute only about 60% of the adult men of a city. Evidence gives some estimate of population and area of about 150 cities, largely towards the close of the Middle Ages. From these the density of population of cities can be inferred.

The use of city size to estimate population is encouraged

by a knowledge of the history of urban development in the Middle Ages. What is best, of course, is a first rate geographic study of a city, such as that of Sauvaget for medieval Damascus.[1] However, many studies do give rough ideas of the building of new walls and thus one may follow the size of cities. The collections in the *Deutsche Städtebuch*, edited by E. Keyser, provide a remarkable body of such information. The medieval city seldom had large open places except in front of the cathedral and thus was built evenly for the most part. The walls also usually enclosed areas which were essentially suburban and also represent actual population. Only in the Low Countries just before the plague did city planners outdo themselves and provide their cities with walls which were not reached for centuries. For many cities an estimate for the fourteenth century city area may be made from modern city maps—the medieval area stands out with its crooked streets and wide avenues preserving traces of former walls against the relatively straight boulevards of the 16th-19th centuries. Sometimes the outline of earlier walls can be seen, as well. The evenness of the settlement and the assurance that areas within walls are actually occupied by buildings produces a better base for guesses than with modern cities.

The average population density of cities was about 100-120 persons to the hectare. The densely populated city might run past 200 to the hectare but this was rare. Thus to suppose that imperial Constantinople, with an inhabited area of little more than a thousand hectares inside a total area of 1200 hectares, had a population of more than 200,000 is venturesome, particularly since these thousand hectares included broad avenues, large public buildings and even the Hippodrome. In Islamic countries the Friday Mosque was supposed to hold all male worshippers of the faith: its size is thus a check upon an estimate based upon the extent of the city as defined by its walls.

In all of this the housing customs are important. If people piled up in the apartments of the cities, the total

1. See examples in R. E. Dickinson, *The West European City: a Geographical Interpretation* (London, 1951).

to the hectare goes up. Both literary and archaeological evidence (such as that upon deserted villages) are helpful here. Even pictures sometimes help: here the more prosaic and less imaginative artists are more helpful.

The total amount of evidence for size of population is considerable. Its value, as has been seen, varies widely and estimates often assume only a rough approximation. The evidence produces patterns and samples of considerable importance which may be used for constructing informed guesses about many areas. In many cases projections based on several types of approach agree and lend more validity to the estimate. In any case such estimates are better than guesses based upon intuition and reduce the limits of conjecture: as mentioned above the likelihood of attributing a million or even half a million people to Constantinople should be out of the question!

The movement of population, it has been asserted, causes changes in economic conditions which give clues to demographic variations. These changes are in wages, rents and prices, particularly of land. The increase of persons should have an adverse effect on wages: the great losses of the initial epidemic of the fourteenth century plague certainly sent wages up after 1350. Increase of population should raise rents and prices of land: both were doing this in the rise of population in thirteenth century England. Despite the apparent value of such indications, not much use has yet been made of them. All of them involve the *ceteribus paribus* assumption during the period in which the changes occurred: an assumption historically unjustified. Eventually, however, more accurate use of such indications of these alterations of wages, rents and prices may be achieved.

PATTERNS OF SETTLEMENT

Even a most casual glance at a map of medieval Europe shows that the larger cities form a pattern of some regularity. They appear along the great Roman highways and on the sea coast at fairly consistent intervals. Recent study of geographical distribution of cities and villages by population shows definite patterns of settlement. The regularity of distribution based upon agriculture and normal economic life is occasionally disturbed by cities depending upon mines or other unusual commercial or industrial activities. This was likewise true of the Middle Ages. If anything, irregularly situated sources of settlement were less frequent, less important then, although the same two influences operated. The regular spacing conforms to requirements of time and distance in the activities of people in satisfying their needs, modified by special opportunities.

The distribution largely followed Zipf's theory of the economy of time and movement.[2] The factors involved were not simple at times and often in conflict. On the village level, for instance, need for protection and the pleasure of close association pointed to a nucleated village whereas the distance from fields and pastures would argue for a hamlet structure. On a higher level the cost of staying more than one day's journey away from home was measured against greater opportunities for sale. Then there was the high cost of transportation by road or even upstream, limiting distant sales of low cost heavy commodities.

The distribution on the village level varied considerably. The Celts and the Slavs seem to have lived for the most part in small hamlets rather than in larger villages: these hamlets were usually not far apart. German groups preferred larger villages at wider intervals. Conditions of long time warfare in Iberia also seem to have led to larger villages, many of them walled. Not for nothing was the meseta called Castilla—land of castles. Within a country, villages varied widely in size but they usually conformed to a statistical pattern with respect to their populations to the bell shaped pattern like the curve of chance. Each culture tended to have a favourite size of village: the Celtic and Slavic at 5-50 persons, the English at 50-150, the Germanic and Spanish at 150-300. These are rough estimates, of course, near the smaller size in the early and the larger during the later pre-plague period.

2. G. K. Zipf, *Human Behaviour and the Principle of the Least Effort* (Cambridge, 1949).

Obviously the small Celtic or Slav hamlet offered a distinct advantage in lesser distances to work. Larger villages usually saw a pattern based on an economy of time: woods and pastures which demanded less time and attention were more distant from the normal compact village than the tilled fields, while gardens and stables were usually close to the house. Of course, at villages in the mountains and highlands, devoted to pastoral or forest economy, special conditions prevailed.

As an example of pattern of settlement the Domesday arrangement of villages of Leicestershire (1086) is given in map 1. The central city, Leicester, had a population of about 1300 persons, and was one of the smaller county seats. Cities of similar size lay in several directions about 25-35 miles away. A series of market towns of several hundred inhabitants were about twelve miles out from Leicester in six directions. The smaller towns showed less uniformities of pattern: they were evenly divided between the 50-100 and 100-200 sized places. Even to the general pattern there were exceptions: the sizeable forest of Charnwood left a gap to the northwest of Leicester. Three unexpectedly large villages about five miles out of Leicester to the south and southwest prove to have been the seats of feudal lords: Oadby of the Countess Judith, Wigston Magna of Hugh de Grandmesil and Aylestone a more complicated settlement held jointly by the Earl of Mellent, Countess Alveva and two vassals of the Earl.

These larger towns illustrate well the basic-nonbasic theory of the development of towns and cities. The basic factor is the one which brings to the community income from the outside. The castles or manor houses of the nobility were supported by manors often miles away from them: the lord and retinue of the lord constituted the basic factor. About an equal number of persons in the community supported this group and are the nonbasic element. In larger cities, monasteries, cathedral chapters, courts, markets and industrial groups consitute basic groups and are responsible for the establishment of the concentration of population at the site.

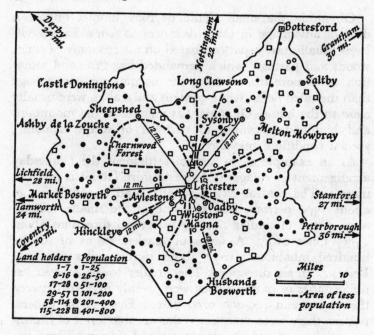

MAP I *Leicestershire Domesday villages*

For more than simple market functions small cities, such as Leicester, usually occur at about a day's journey (20-40 miles) apart. This distance places them at a convenient distance for overland commerce, providing inns or monastic hostels for travellers at the end of the day's travel. For the countryside they offer more diversified market facilities than the simple market towns for people living up to half a day's journey from the city: the weekly or seasonal fairs often attracted large patronage. The size of these small cities was apt to be from two to ten thousand persons, increasing with the general population expansion from 950 to 1300.

Above these small cities was often a regional metropolis with a number of satellite cities (usually about six) radiating about it, although peculiar geographical conditions often modified this pattern. These cities were apt to have a fairly definite demographic relationship to each other. If the metropolis is rated as 100 the satellite cities tend to show a statistical relationship to it of about 57, 39, 30, 24 etc. Since these numbers are averages the variation from it within a particular region is marked. A good example is that of the region of which Barcelona was the metropolis in the fourteenth century (map 2). Its satellite cities were Valencia,

MAP 2 *Region of Barcelona about 1359-1361*

Saragossa, Palma de Mallorca, Perpignan and perhaps Pamplona. A sixth city should have been located in the Tarragona, Tortosa, Morella, Castellon de la Plana segment: its functions were doubtless distributed among the four.

A problem arises in understanding the demographic relationship of cities which are very close to each other. It would seem that they were essentially one urban centre which somehow exercised the functions of a single larger city. This, of course, is evident in the case of cities across a river from each other, such as Buda and Pest or of nearby cities, such as Southampton and Winchester. The same may be true of Venice and Padua as long as Venice stayed on its islands: Venice was the centre of a maritime empire, while Padua exercised the continental functions of the two, since Venice eschewed the mainland of Italy. A maritime empire is hard to understand as a region but doubtless should be considered so since communication was easier on water than on land in the Middle Ages. Thus demographically, such cities as Genoa, Bruges and some of the larger Hanseatic cities were metropolitan cities of essentially maritime regions.

In the first half of the Middle Ages in prosperous eastern regions the metropolis was apt to be about 50-100,000 population with the satellite cities of from ten to 60,000. Very few cities went beyond the 100,000 mark then. The great city, Constantinople, may have had as many as 300,000 in the time of Justinian—at its capture by the Turks in 1453 it was down to about 35,000. Before A.D. 1000 such Islamic centres as Cairo and Cordoba were in the 50-100,000 class along with perhaps Thessalonica and Antioch of the Byzantine empire. In the Christian west no cities reached the 50,000 line.

But after the tenth century population grew rapidly. Just before the plague struck in 1348 Paris, Venice, Florence and Genoa were near the 100,000 mark while Bologna, Barcelona, Brescia, Cordoba, Siena, Palermo, Milan, London, Ghent and Smolensk probably had more than 50,000. Nineteenth century scholars were shocked at the discovery that Nuremberg and Strasbourg had few more than 20,000. Between that number and 50,000 were cities like Bruges, Seville, Toledo, Rouen, Toulouse, Montpellier and the secondary cities of Italy, the great Hanse cities, and the centres of eastern Europe.

Assuming a normal medieval economy, a regular relation between size of cities and total population should hold. The relation of the larger cities to total population of some regions for which data are available seems reasonably consistent with the metropolis having about 1·5% of the region's population. The satellite cities would thus also share in a definite pattern. Thus they seem to represent conditions which have been called the physics of population and seems fundamental in population structure. The size of cities may then be used to estimate total regional population. Elements of uncertainty—level of economic life, size of region, density of city population—make this approach to total population less accurate than more direct approaches. For areas where distribution of settlements alone is available, it does provide valuable demographic clues. For early medieval Europe, particularly in eastern Europe, it has to be relied upon, if cautiously.

Furthermore, if the metropolitan city bears a consistent relationship to total regional population, changes in large city populations should indicate changes in regional population. London shows its 1·5 relationship to all of England in both 1086 and 1377. Paris grew rapidly as French population increased, although it seems to have been the regional centre of only the northern half of France in the Middle Ages. Some cities changed function. The great increase in the size of Naples and Palermo at the end of the Middle Ages probably resulted from their growing commerce. The increased dominance of Florence is reflected in the decline of neighbouring Lucca and then Pisa. The inclusion of Marseilles in the French kingdom reduced Montpellier to a secondary position at the end of the fifteenth century.

Allowance must be made for varying degrees of economic conditions, of course. A region which has cities much smaller than the expected size shows a low standard of economic structure, as, for instance, most of central Europe before the tenth century. Likewise, the presence of un-expectedly large cities, as in Italy in the later Middle Ages, means that the region enjoys a higher standard than usual of economic development. Sometimes information about the density or apparent density of population supplements other information to add to the data about the condition of a region. Statements by writers about Italy and Spain at the beginning of the Middle Ages adds to the impression of their wasted condition.

The estimate of size of places may in some instances be made from the quantity of graves in medieval cemeteries,

TABLE I: Population estimates (in millions) at specified times, A.D. 500-1450

Area	500	650	1000	1340	1450
Greece and Balkans	5	3	5	6	4·5
Italy	4	2·5	5	10	7·5
Iberia	4	3·5	7	9	7
Total—south	13	9	17	25	19
France–Low Countries	5	3	6	19	12
British Isles	0·5	0·5	2	5	3
Germany–Scandinavia	3·5	2	4	11·5	7·5
Total—west and central	9	5·5	12	35·5	22·5
Slavia	5	3			
Russia			6	8	6
Poland–Lithuania			2	3	2
Hungary	0·5	0·5	1·5	2	1·5
Total—east	5·5	3·5	9·5	13	9·5
Total—all Europe	27·5	18	38·5	73·5	50

Sources: Russell, *Late Ancient and Medieval Population.* p. 148: somewhat revised especially for Italy by K. J. Beloch. *Bevölkerungsgeschichte Italiens*, III, 344-352, and for the Balkans by Russell, *Journal of Economic and Social History of the Orient* III (1960) 269-270.

a test made successfully in Hungary and Moravia. This type of excavation and synthesis will probably be more widely used. To the information available about size of cities, much will probably be added. Thus there is hope of knowing much more about the distribution of settlements by size and location and consequently more about the total population of regions and lands.

TRENDS OF GROSS POPULATION

The figures in Table 1 are presented as a tentative estimate of the population of the European-Mediterranean area in the Middle Ages. They have already been changed somewhat from those which appeared in my *Late Ancient and Medieval Population* and probably will be changed more as students test conclusions for the various parts of the area. The estimates for A.D. 650 and 1450 represent generally what should have occurred to the areas as a result of the long series of epidemics which will be discussed in a later chapter. It is assumed that at those years population was at just about the low point produced by the plagues. Some other figures are selected as indicating the course of population change from what seems a good estimate before or after the time of the estimate. It must be admitted also that there is a certain degree of indefiniteness about the boundaries of the divisions: since such concepts as Russia, Hungary, or even France changed markedly in the course of the Middle Ages. These also will be tightened in the course of further research.

Just before the beginning of the period, 500-1500, the two halves of the Roman Empire seem to have experienced a sharp demographic difference. The west seems to have declined in population and, as is well known, succumbed to the attacks of the German tribes from an area which had increased in population, from central Europe to central Asia. Asia Minor and the Balkans seem to have shared in the same general population increase which, perhaps, resulted from warming of the climate which acted favourably upon the north and unfavourably upon the south. Other factors than the climatic change were responsible for the population decline of the west, but it must have helped. In any case population increase probably aided the Byzantine Empire in its survival.

From about A.D. 500 for a half century all parts of the Europe-Mediterranean complex seem to have experienced a slow rise in population, underlying a most promising attempt to rehabilitate the Empire under Justinian. The conquering tribes of the west constituted only a fraction of the total population, at most less than a million of about sixteen millions of Romance peoples. Moreover, they were divided into many tribes, themselves subdivided into many factions. Furthermore, as they scattered over considerable areas as regional and local leaders, they tended to lose that tribal solidarity and military efficiency which they had exhibited as wandering tribes. The Franks were exceptions: in their northern lands they remained peasant farmers. The Visigoths offset their dispersion by those garrisons based upon lands supporting them, still often called the Gothic Fields.

This advance in population was set back abruptly by the terrible series of epidemics of the plague in the sixth century following A.D. 542, which apparently persisted well into the seventh century. The readjustment of population, to be discussed later in more detail, reduced the power of the Byzantine Empire and probably prevented its restoration of the empire in the west. Indeed, so dissipated was Roman power that Islam took over in the south and southeast while the Germans held on in the west. All European areas saw a fairly sizeable increase from A.D. 650 to 700, perhaps a third. Two empires, the Byzantine and the Carolingian, built their strength, in part, upon this demographic growth.

During the period, 500-800, the gains from the low produced by the plague brought European population back to the pre-plague level, perhaps even beyond it in central and northern areas of the continent. In contrast to this recovery was the gradual decline in the Islamic world to the south. Whatever advantage the plague had given it

was lost in the period, 500-1000. A tentative comparison
of the areas is as follows:

	500	1,000
South Europe	13	17
North and central	9	12
East Europe	5·5	9·5
Asia Minor-Syria-Egypt N. Africa	22·5	12·5

In addition to this the original enthusiasm of Islam declined: the Caliphate lost one emirate after another, beginning with Cordoba in 755. The relative advantage which
Christian Europe enjoyed by A.D. 1000 is also the demographic background for the Crusades.

The continual growth of population in central and
eastern Europe poses a problem. It meant cutting back
the great forests of the area. Perhaps, as has been suggested,
the spread of Christianity weakened the taboo which the
Germans and possibly the Slavs had with respect to the
clearing of the forest. The demographic conditions of the
ninth and the first half of the tenth century are among the
most difficult medieval periods to assess properly. Only in a
few places (Iberia, England, perhaps central Europe) does
population seem to have increased much. The Vikings
threatened the north of Europe and the Hungarians, the
east. The great archaeological campaigns going on now
in much of central and eastern Europe are gradually building up information about this historically dark period.

The most rapid population increase came in the second
half of the Middle Ages, beginning in Italy about 950 and
a little later in central and northern Europe. The situation
in Russia and the east is not so clear: the population increase
there may also have started early, perhaps even earlier than
950. In spite of political fragmentation and the subsequent
invasions and domination of the Mongols, the Slavic world
seems to have increased gradually in population up to the
plague period. Mediterranean Europe seems also to have
grown at about the same pace as the Slavic world did over

the same period, although some areas, such as northern Italy, grew very rapidly. Since the Islamic countries seemed to have experienced a similar growth with an especially rapid development in Egypt, the demographic background was inauspicious to the crusades.

Central and northern Europe, like north Italy, saw a threefold growth in the pre-plague period with its most rapid advance from about 1150-1200 to 1300. In this period, for the first time, cities larger than 20,000 appeared: political and commercial centres like Paris, London, Cologne, Prague, to mention a few, went beyond the 30,000 point. Cities constantly added walls to enclose suburban areas which sprang up about the original nuclei. By the last quarter of the thirteenth century population was slowing down in its rate of increase.

Eastern Europe lagged behind, the Russians notably slow under the domination of the Mongols although even there the population apparently increased. The late twelfth century and the thirteenth saw a speeding up of the economy which must have been based in part upon population increase as well as agricultural and especially mining developments. The area of most rapid advance 'extended from the Czech plateau in the west as far as Transylvania and included in the north Silesia and Little Poland and in the south the areas of the Slovaks in *Upper Hungary*'.[3]

The great increase probably brought European population to about seventy-five million people: some believe that the number was larger. In any case the limits of subsistence were being reached within the economy of the time. The climate seems to have been deteriorating: in 1303 and again in 1306-7 the Baltic Sea was frozen over, even in the south. The Little Ice Age was setting in, an era of general lower temperature which lasted well past 1500. The effects were evident in the north of Europe and in the higher altitudes of areas like Provence. In the first half of the fourteenth century population controls, such as no marriage without a means of support, seem to have either slowed total population to a very slow increase or to have

3. M. Malowist, *Economic History Review*, XIX (1966) 20.

stabilised numbers. In some places there were definite decreases.

If the population was only about seventy-five millions before the plague in as large and generally fertile an area as Europe one should expect little overpopulation. Certain sections of Italy apparently were very thickly settled and in economic straits: parts of England are alleged to have been experiencing very hard times. The problem concerns both the actual population estimates and the question of what constitutes overpopulation. That mortality and grain prices increased together is clear: the question is whether the second (assuming grain shortage) caused the first or bad weather conditions caused both.

The second plague period opened with the great epidemic of 1347-51 and paralleled the earlier plague in many ways. Population loss generally was about 25% (with perhaps 20% net subtracting births from the loss), another 20% by 1385 and a few more per cent before a low was reached somewhere before the middle of the fifteenth century. There was probably not much change from about 1400 to 1460. Again, drier areas seem to have suffered less mortality, in Spain and Asia Minor, laying foundations for the great days of the Spanish Habsburgs and Ottoman Empire in the fifteenth and sixteen centuries. The plague's course is discussed elsewhere: it was erratic at times. Areas in the Low Countries and in central and eastern Europe were hardly touched by the first great epidemic. In the course of subsequent epidemics, however, the figures tended to even out.

LENGTH AND EXPECTATION OF LIFE

Length of life is, of course, a very important aspect of demography. The best male evidence for all ages except infancy comes from data in the English inquisitions post mortem from about 1200 to the end of the Middle Ages. It is very good because an exact age of death is given and an age at inheritance which is quite accurate to about thirty years of age and within a few years of accuracy thereafter. From the two, life tables can be constructed for all except infants since so few persons inherited at a very early age. More widespread evidence comes from archaeological study of medieval cemeteries. Some genealogical evidence illustrates the length of life of nobility in some countries. These other types of evidence offer more information about the important period of life. The expectation of life of those thirty years of age and over is remarkably consistent through both plague and non-plague periods. We start with the cemetery data.

Physical anthropologists base estimates of age upon skeletal evidence, especially of the skulls. In the past classification by age groups has been usually set up for these age divisions: (Table 2)

| | | *Expectation* | |
		M	*F*
Infans I	0–7 years		
Infans II	7–14 years		
Iuvenis	14–20 years	30·1	24·8
Adultus	20–40 years	28·4	23·2
Maturus	40–60 years	14·0	14·0
Senilis	60–	10·0	10·0

However, in recent years great advances have been made in fixing the age of skeletons so that early years of life are estimated in terms of months and later periods in terms of about five years. Thus the data vary greatly from days when excavators merely recorded that graves contained 'nothing but bones', then identified men from women and adults from children, to the present much more accurate identification.

Those estimates of expectation are based upon a preliminary study of data from about a hundred cemeteries of all periods of the Middle Ages and from all but the Mediterranean areas (with some exceptions). The evidence of expectation for the young is not included, pending further study. Until archaeological skills reach the levels achieved by its abler practitioners today, cemetery evidence has distinct limitations. Further study will show in all probability variations of conditions of life in time and geographical range. The table, as it stands, implies that conditions were not too noticeably different over Europe and that there was a general pattern of expectation of life. If we were to include child mortality we should probably find two patterns, one for the plague years, another for the plague-free periods. The expectation estimates would seem to show that conditions improved from the stone age to the medieval period.

TABLE 2: Deaths and Age Structure from Medieval Cemetery Data

Age interval	MALE			FEMALE			Sex ratio
	Number dying in interval*		Years lived in interval	Number dying in interval*		Years lived in interval	
Iuvenis 14-19	144	3	19548**	308	3	16710	114
Adultus 20-39	1107	9	51543**	1365	10	38970	123
Maturus 40-59	1665	10	24930**	951	9	14569	143
Senilis 60-	414	10	4140	305	10	3050	136
Total	3330		100161	2929		73299	138***

*Average number of years lived by those who died within the interval.

**Includes the years lived by both those who died within the interval and those who survived it.

***This is the sex ratio of the cumulative total of years lived in all of the intervals. The sex ratio of those alive at fourteen is given in the first interval.

Source: Russell, 'Effects of Pestilence and Plague, 1315-1385,' *Comparative studies in Society and History* VIII (1966) 467.

The data from the inquisitions post mortem of England have certain limitations. Not many concern women: so few, indeed, that it is difficult to derive life tables from them. Few also involve small children since few inherited at an early age. Another fault may be that they provide essentially a social class analysis, being drawn from landholding classes. Their expectation was markedly better than that of the royal family. Comparison of expectation of that class with that of some groups of serfs in England shows, for the period 1280-1340, no noticeable differences. This might be expected. Conditions in manor houses (often crowded and not very sanitary) were little better than peasant cottages, while the upper class diet (heavily meat and wine) was probably no healthier than that of the peasants (vegetables, beer or cheap wine). Unless one believes in persistent starvation or undernourishment of the peasants, there is little reason to assume shorter lives for them in spite of heavy labour.

The inquisitions post mortem do give, what the cemetery evidence cannot show, the age of persons who were very old. Quite a number can be shown to have passed ninety years of age. Alina de Marechale, said to have been ninety when she inherited land, lived on another seven years. In one inquest a Reginald de Colewyk was said to have lived a century. His son probably lived a long life while his grandson passed the eighty mark, indicating that longevity as well as land was inherited.

Some of the aged held very responsible positions. In the seventh century Theodore of Tarsus came to England, sent by the pope to be archbishop of Canterbury, at about the age of sixty-seven and survived another twenty-one years. Jusuf ibn Tashfin, enemy of Le Cid and mighty emir from Africa, was said to have been 100 when he died in 1106. Enrico Dandalo was a leader in the Fourth Crusade, already more than eighty years old. A Master of Arts by 1189, Robert Grosseteste was elected Bishop of Lincoln in 1235 and continued his theological writing while administering his large diocese until he passed away in 1253. The list could be continued and the evidence shows that medieval man, although his average length of life was short, had a normal span of life (potentiality of life): some lived beyond a century then as today.

Medieval women fared much worse than men, as many types of evidence show. Table 2 indicates that while more men died between the ages of 40 and 60 (*maturus*) than between 20 and 40 (*adultus*), the reverse was true of women.

The combination of childbearing and heavy field work was conducive to poor condition of health, making them easier victims of the prevalent malaria and tuberculosis or terminal diseases of shorter duration. They lived, as daughters of Eve, in an inferior position: women were to men as men were to God. Their lot was perhaps in some cases alleviated by late marriage and by the fact that those who survived their husbands were customarily allowed to choose themselves whether to re-marry or to remain widows. Their position improved markedly in the thirteenth century: the rise of love interest in the romances, respectable seating arrangements for them at tournaments, increased enthusiasm for adoration of the Virgin (a symbol of womanhood) and other marks of higher opinion illustrate this change in attitude which must have affected their morale and perhaps their health.

Infant mortality is relatively difficult to ascertain. In late Roman times memorial stones were seldom raised to tiny children. While Christianity tended to encourage proper burial of children, their graves seem too few in many places. Their bones disappear faster in the earth than do those of adults. On the other hand if excavation proceeds very carefully, the shorter length of graves often identifies them as infants' burials: sometimes the persistence of a toy even identifies the sex of the infant. Identification of children in cemeteries and in other evidence is primarily important in defining average length of life, since that figure is very sensitive to the number of infant deaths. It has much less importance upon the relative size of age groups, since their brief life does not disturb the age groups much. Tentative rates of about 15-20% for mortality in the first year of life and 30% by age twenty seem reasonable. Under the rigorous conditions of central Scandinavia, the first year mortality was about fifty per cent: nearer the sea and farther south it was very much less.[4] It must be borne in mind that until more study of infant mortality has been made, the rates are very tentative.

4. N-G. Gejvall, *Westerhus. Medieval Population and Church in the Light of Skeletal Remains* (Lund, 1960), p. 39.

Conditions varied considerably: as one would expect the plague period was especially bad. In England, however, expectation was declining even before the plague among the landowning class (Table 3). The combination of worsening weather and greater density of population doubtless produced that result.

The total death rate may be obtained by dividing length of life into 100. Thus a length of life of about 33 years gives a death rate of three per cent or, as it is usually expressed today, 30 in a 1000. The modern death rate is about half that of the Middle Ages. This, however, is somewhat a distortion since the death rate was high in part because of the large infant mortality.

The length of expectation did not change much over the first twenty years of life. The reason is that the death rate was so high in those years of infancy and youth that those who survived still had a relatively long expectation. The highest expectation was at about the first birthday since mortality of the initial year was high. In apparently the best medieval conditions (Table 3), in thirteenth century England, expectation was 35 years at birth for men, 39 at one year, 29 at twenty years of age and still 18 at forty, while, as mentioned earlier, some lived on to the century mark. Comparatively speaking, the medieval expectation was excellent. It seems better than the Roman, except for the unexplained north African data, better than for undeveloped countries until a few years ago, and even better than for early modern Europe. This is, of course, for the nonplague periods.

The life table (Table 4) shows an age division typical of preindustrial culture: about one-half under the age of twenty-one and a third under the age of fourteen. From the life table some estimate can be made of two conditions: the first of dependency and the second of potential years of work. One must assume that those who live also work.

Dependency ratio normally assumes as dependants those over age 65 and under fifteen years of age. To make direct use of cemetery evidence a slightly different assumption is made here. It assumes that those over age sixty need not

TABLE 3: Estimates of expectation of life for men
(landholders in medieval England)

Age	Born ca 1200 -76	Born 1276- 1300	Born 1301- 25	Born 1326- 48	Born 1348- 75	Born 1376- 1400	Born 1401- 25	Born 1425- 50
0	35·3	31·3	29·8	27·2	17·3	20·5	23·8	32·8
10	36·3	32·2	31·0	28·1	25·1	24·5	29·7	34·5
20	28·7	25·2	23·8	22·1	23·9	21·4	29·4	27·7
30	22·8	21·8	20·0	21·1	22·0	22·3	25·0	24·1
40	17·8	16·6	15·7	17·7	18·1	19·2	19·3	20·4
60	9·4	8·3	9·3	10·8	10·9	10·0	10·5	13·7
80	5·2	3·8	4·5	6·0	4·7	3·1	4·8	7·9

Number of observations

Total	532	391	420	355	340	343	347	352
To age ten	28	42	67	70	87	60	88	47
To age twenty	123	127	158	171	152	124	135	108

The estimate of mortality to age ten is calculated from life tables based on Indian agricultural data which are almost identical with these tables above the age of ten. Examination of medieval cemetery evidence seems to show that they are reasonable.

be considered: that enough of them took care of others of the age group to eliminate them as a factor. At the other end of life those under age fourteen (called anthropologically *infans I and II*) are to be considered dependent. As a matter of fact fourteen is possibly high for the Middle Ages; age ten would probably be a more realistic age to end dependency. Making allowance for the unusual sex ratio (which we take up later) and using certain assumptions about infant mortality, a typical medieval dependency ratio would be about 100 persons aged 14-59 to 52 persons under age fourteen. This is higher than the 100 to 42·6 for the same age groups in the United States of 1949-51. The plague probably did not change the dependency ratio very much. Since we prolong dependency so much longer today, the actual burden of raising children was probably less in the Middle Ages than now.

The index of potential working life is very different in the Middle Ages from that of the present. For 1949-51 the life table would show that persons aged 14-59 lived 92% of their possible years. The medieval period saw a similar age group live only 57% of their possible years. Plague lowered this ratio to about thirty per cent: the terrible effect of the plague is perhaps best illustrated here. The heavy burden of this loss in both plague and nonplague eras was relieved by starting work at least in the early teens, but it meant that society lost much of its childhood freedom and devoted little time to education.

Not much studied are differentials in expectation and length of life caused by geographical and climatic conditions. In Scandinavia, as mentioned earlier infant and adult deathrate was very high at an inland village. Nearer the ocean the deathrates were less. The ocean mitigated the heat of summer and the chill of winter and offered sea food to supplement the land based diet. The sorting of cemetery evidence ought to throw more light on these variations.

The pattern discernible in the age structure shows that men came into their inheritance from their fathers in their early twenties on the average but this still allowed nearly half of them to inherit under the age of 21. Thus in societies where sons inherited a large percentage of minorities was to be expected. To prevent inheritance of responsible positions by minors some early German tribes restricted their choice of king to adults or at least near adult and competent members of the families. The hereditary succession of the Byzantine Empire was frequently upset by, or forced into partnership with, successful generals. Such periods of imperial weakness as occurred in ninth, eleventh and thirteenth centuries were primarily the result of problems of succession which even an efficient bureaucracy could not prevent. The Merovingian dynasty was plagued by many minorities as well as by equal division among sons since, on the average, two sons survived. The later Carolingians also went down under the weight of equal division among heirs and minors.

The early Carolingians had the same principles of inheritance but were saved by one of the most remarkable instances of the operation of chance in history—for five generations they inherited at about age 25 and lived long enough to be succeeded by only one adult son (either because he was the sole surviving son or because only one wished to rule). By almost any calculation this was one chance in many thousands. The necessity of election prevented division of the (Holy) Roman Empire, while the Capetians, following the example of the last Carolingian, adopted primogeniture to attain the same result. In general primogeniture was the feudal answer. This also may have resulted in part from demographic conditions. An older son inheriting at about twenty was in a position to encourage very strongly a younger son, on the average four or more years younger, to seek a clerical career, or at any rate, not to compete with him. On this assumption customary principles of equal inheritance as a form of succession yielded to force.

Feudalism had another demographic weakness—the average age of the knights. A feudal army, assuming most lords served, must have had about half of the members well above the age of thirty—a relatively advanced age for athletes, especially for those who probably did not keep themselves in too good condition, even if they did hunt and participate occasionally in tournaments. A mercenary army, recruited by a wealthy king, could present an array of hungry, young knights and bachelors, physically younger, stronger and normally better trained than the feudal host consisting of men of all ages and conditions of health even if it had a corps of younger men.

Factors of age were also important in the world of guilds. As mentioned earlier city populations seldom replaced themselves by births so that fathers could not count upon sons to succeed themselves in many cases. Feudal lords, who probably did better than guildsmen, lacked male heirs in about a sixth of their cases in the good conditions of thirteenth century England: in time of plague from a fourth to a third of the men had no sons. Furthermore, many guildsmen apparently sought places for their sons in guilds of greater social prestige than their own while many others saw their sons enter the clerical world. Although doubtless many masters trained more than one son with younger sons marrying heiresses in the same guild, there still remained a demographic gap. To fill this void the system of apprenticeship, a kind of substitute sonship, developed. Thus a master without a son satisfied his paternal instinct and passed on his skills and perhaps even his daughter: at the worst he got a lot of hard work done cheaply. As Professor Thrupp has shown even lesser feudal lords regarded apprenticeship of their sons in London with favour.

The number of apprentices can easily be over-estimated. With an expectation of life of about 21 years upon becoming a master (if about 22 years of age), only one-third of the masters need train apprentices for seven years apiece, even if all the masters were to be succeeded by those who had served apprenticeships. Of course apprentices died or dropped out, but many masters' sons succeeded their fathers without serving any apprenticeship. Indeed, if half of the fathers were followed by sons, only a fifth of the masters would need to train apprentices. Of course, as shops increased their size by adding permanent journeymen, a larger proportion of the fewer masters would have to train apprentices.

DISEASE AS A DEMOGRAPHIC FACTOR

If demography has received relatively little attention from scholars, especially historians, disease has received even less. The medieval medical profession has attracted attention but it has largely been limited to the lives of doctors and the oddity of their prescriptions. The plague with its terrible mortality has been written on at considerable length and malaria at less length. Others, such as small pox and dysentery, are occasionally mentioned. The most serious malady was probably tuberculosis, both in numbers of fatalities over the centuries and in loss to humanity. Children's illnesses must have carried away very many.

The infant mortality of the first year of life was probably less than in early modern times, because cities and villages were not so crowded and possibly not so unhygienic in the Middle Ages.

The epidemics were the most spectacular and best recorded phases of illness. Chroniclers, however, seldom gave very good diagnoses of the diseases themselves and liked lurid accounts: their favourite was that the living were scarcely able to bury the dead. There were exceptions: several chroniclers of both the first and second plague give the symptoms of the plague so accurately that it cannot be mistaken for other diseases: the account of Procopius is very well known. Another complication is that of the occurrence of several diseases at once, so that it is not possible to attribute even the greater part of the deaths to one specific disease.

Recent research has shown that the climate varied considerably in the Middle Ages, affecting, of course, central and eastern Europe north of the Alps more than the Mediterranean area by changes in temperature. The variation in moisture probably affected the southern part more through alterations in temperature.

In temperature the warmest was unquestionably in the first century (500-600) of the millennium, perhaps averaging a degree centigrade or about 1·5 degrees Fahrenheit more than the average of about 1900. This was before the great rise from 1900 to 1940 when perhaps a one degree Fahrenheit rise occurred. This may not seem much but 'the average length of the growing season in England as measured by duration of temperatures above 42°F (about 6°C) increased by 2-3 weeks of the year when the period 1920-50 is compared with 1840-1910.[5]' The two extra weeks would make much difference to crops where the weather did not give ordinarily much more than the weeks necessary for growth and where bad years ruined the crops. The coldest time began in the thirteenth century with the onset of the

5. H. H. Lamb, *The Biological Significance of Climatic Changes in Britain* ed. C. G. Johnson and L. P. Smith (London, Academic Press, for the Institute of Biology 1965), p. 5.

Little Ice Age which, with exceptions of occasional periods of warmth lasted until well into the eighteenth century. The worsening of the climate reduced the area of wheat growing in the north, in Denmark for instance, and on the higher lands of Provence which experienced a notable decline in population in the first half of the fourteenth century. An inquest of 1338 in England reveals loss of tilled lands, mostly on the hills of England.

Between 600 and 1250 the conditions of temperature are not so easy to define. Some think that there was a notably warm spell about the year 1200, indicated by temperature of the ocean as defined in study of deposits from the sea-bottom. The warmness of about 600 may have declined somewhat but it remained very warm for centuries. Olive trees existed in England in the eighth and ninth centuries, and Charlemagne (768-814), in one of his capitularies ordered figs planted in his manors. The evidence of glaciers, of ice on the rivers, and even pollen analysis confirm the continuation of relatively warm weather until at least some decline about the year 1000. In general the topic needs more study to define changes in meteorological conditions.

The beginning of the period was one of high rainfall. The area east of Antioch in Syria, now largely desert, saw the founding of many cities and much farming in the fifth and sixth centuries. Yet within a few centuries the territory became arid again. The years of long continued rain, 1315-1316, produced great distress, famine occurring in 1316 and a pestilence of dysentery accompanying it. The level of the Caspian Sea indicates periods of drought in the area which drained into it and shows also a high level in the early fourteenth century. The area of pasture land in the desert borderlands was closely related to rainfall and these in turn to the conditions of the tribes inhabiting them. Periods of declining rainfall encouraged attacks on the settled areas bordering the desert. One such time probably occurred in the seventh century when Islam broke out of the deserts.

The climate had an effect on disease, notably on the range of the more malignant type of malaria. The warmth of the sixth century seems to have carried it, to judge from statements in the saints' lives, well into France. The northern limit of this type in the nineteenth century was just north of the Mediterranean. It is a very debilitating disease, partly responsible by its widespread character for the decline of Mediterranean countries in modern times and possibly in the medieval period, particularly in southern Italy and Sicily. Because of the severity of its symptoms, it was well known and is thus relatively easy to document. Its pattern of mortality conforms to the normal one of increasingly high death rate with advancing age. It is thus difficult to trace its influence in the figures of a life table. In many cases it merely weakened people making them easy victims of terminal diseases.

Tuberculosis was often not easy to diagnose, especially in its early stages. Furthermore, it has no normal course: the struggle between human body and the tuberculosis germs was a long continued battle which might end in a long stalemate lasting over decades. People often got the disease in early childhood but did not become definitely ill with it until early manhood. This length of time between accepting the germs and the actual course of the disease makes the period of developing an immunity against it a very long one at best. Unlike most diseases the highest death rate of tuberculosis was between age fifteen and thirty-five. Thus any abnormal mortality of those years, for men at least, can be used as indications of the disease. The very high rates for that age group would show that tuberculosis was the chief source of death until very modern times: the 'great white plague'. Its effects were particularly devastating because it destroyed or greatly weakened young men and women just as they entered the most useful stage of their careers.

Two other epidemic diseases can be detected upon the basis of medieval descriptions. Chroniclers described the illness of 1315-1317 as *disenteria*, and from their description it seems to have been amoebic dysentery. Of course under the bad conditions of long continued rain, chill, and famine probably other diseases participated in the bad years. The famine caused thousands to flock into the great cities where they expected to receive food, thus creating ideal conditions for dysentery. Some 3000 died in Bruges and 2000 in Ypres in a few months in 1316: the problem is whether to relate these deaths to the cities alone, or to surrounding areas as well. From England the data would show deaths amounting to only a few per cent. Since that disease is largely a terminal disease for those afflicted with serious illness, it sent people to their deaths a few years earlier than they would have gone anyway. These deaths did little to reduce population. It is perhaps a tribute to the generally good health of medieval Europe between the plagues that such a relatively light epidemic should have made such a tremendous impression.

Small pox (*variola*) was also well known, striking fear into peoples as it does today. It seems, as usual, to have varied considerably in its virulence but, like the dysentery, took off numbers of people. It was apparently a regular visitor throughout the period but has not been studied carefully.

There are doubtless many other diseases which were of importance. If serious they would be called a pestilence, or an illness, but were seldom defined accurately. Nor was much medical advance made, despite the several medical schools. It was learned that red was good for the eyes of those who had measles. However, doctors failed to learn even the very simple rest cure for the chief disease, tuberculosis and one cannot really rate medical ingenuity on a very high level.

The most devastating disease of the Middle Ages was the plague. It puzzled contemporary observers: it did not seem to pass directly from the diseased to those who cared for patients so that the pneumonic form of direct passage was probably not important. The complicated aetiology of the disease still baffles people. Why, for instance, if perhaps 70% of those who take the disease, die of it, did only about 25% of the population die in the first great plague epidemic of 1348-50 (and probably of A.D. 542-4) while much smaller percentages were taken off in later plague epidemics? What prevented the contact of the more than fifty per cent who obviously were not infected with it?

The importance of contact shows up, for instance, in the higher percentages of clergy and of older people who died in the first plague. They normally lived alone or with a companion or two, in contrast to other families' usually two adults and differing numbers of children. Now normally, one rat family had the run of a house or even of an apartment house and, on the average, each rat was apt to carry perhaps three fleas. Even here contact was reduced because fleas dislike some people and others seem unable to carry and pass on the plague bacillus. The flea (normally *X cheopis*) also prefers the rat to people and moves off reluctantly and often only after the death of the rat. In India it was discovered that the wave of human deaths follows that of rats by about two weeks. In times between epidemics the disease remained endemic with remarkably few deaths.

The epidemics coincide with the seasons of the year (temperature 20-25°C, humidity 0·03-0·3) when fleas propagate rapidly and in years when the rats also increase in an explosive fashion, usually about every four years. However, the initial epidemics of 542-4 and 1348-50 apparently depleted the carriers of the plague so badly that the next large epidemics came twelve years later in 556 and 1360-1 followed eight years later by the third, before settling down to the four year cycle. Since the epidemics were later in arriving in parts of Europe the cycle also came later in these areas and apparently never arrived at all in some areas, such as the Netherlands and in Germany until quite late. Furthermore, areas which were very dry experienced a much lighter epidemic than the areas with more congenial environment for the fleas: the desert, of course, Egypt and even parts of Iberia.

The first three years, 1348-1350, saw a mortality of about 25 per cent overall but this was offset by births so that the net loss was about a fifth of the population. The mortality, however, varied widely by city. Subsequent epidemics had lesser mortality but the total population was down forty per cent by 1380 and to near one-half in many places by the end of the century, where it stayed for two generations. The second plague was called the plague of the children: the young who had grown since the last plague provided the greater part of the victims. Later plagues also cut deeply into the young. The sixth-seventh century plague seems to have followed the same pattern, as far as the less informative sources of the period indicate.

An immediate effect of the plague was a kind of shock to life, expressed in part by reactions ranging from an intensification of religious observance to secular dissoluteness. Within months, however, the readjustment of wealth offered many survivors more than they had had before, as the interesting documents from Albi show. The number of *pobres* decreased even percentagewise in Aragon and the decline in numbers of elderly raised energy levels in the peoples. However, as the plague continued it reduced the years of potential activity very greatly: about one half of the active years between fourteen and sixty. The heavy loss of children in later epidemics probably left the dependency ratio about where it had been before the plague.

The inquisitions post mortem show (Table 3) that the expectation of life remained about the same for those thirty years of age and above, plague or no plague. Indeed, the expectation at the higher ages was actually greater after the plague's main epidemics. Presumably, the plague eliminated at earlier ages many who would have died of other diseases in later life.

The sharp decline in population must have caused some readjustment in settlements. In England many of the weaker villages disappeared and this probably occurred elsewhere as a part of the long continuing process whereby hamlets were coalescing with nearby villages. The history of the changing size of settlements has yet to be written. In the earlier plague a very interesting development occurred. Apparently much land upon which taxes could not be paid was returned by the great landowners to the emperor. As population recovered the Byzantine government allotted lands to settlements of free farmers regulated by the Farmer's Law and similar legislation. Protected by emperors in these holdings, these farmer-soldiers remained the mainstay of the Byzantine Empire until the eleventh century. In the Balkans great numbers of Slavs seem to have filled part of the vacuum created by the plague.

As yet is is hard to relate disease to particular ages in the medieval period. It is clear, of course, that tuberculosis took a heavy toll of life from 15 to 35 years of age. Similarly, after the first epidemic of the plague, children suffered severely in later plagues because they had been less or never exposed before. Malaria presumably affected all ages. Children were doubtless affected by special diseases as at present but little is known about them. Sudden or unexplained deaths, particularly those which disturbed the stomach or intestines, were too frequently ascribed to poison. Wounds of many kinds tended to end in death by infection.

SEX RATIO, MARRIAGE AND FERTILITY

Death rates in the Middle Ages, except in time of plague or other epidemics, varied but were about three per cent. Since population remained steady or even increased somewhat, the birthrate must have been as high as three per cent or better. Among preindustrial peoples this was a relatively low rate. In the development of this rate the sex ratio (number of men to 100 women), rate of marriage and fertility are the chief factors. The main difficulty in establishing the rate is that the number of births is not very certain, a difficulty already mentioned. From various sources, despite this handicap, estimates of some validity can be made. Fortunately, some of the better records of population, such as the Polyptyque d'Irminon and individual village returns of the 1377 Poll Tax enable one to estimate the percentage of married persons in the population. Even the percentage of married in lists of households can be very approximately judged by applying to total number of men and women mentioned the sex ratio which seems appropriate. Already in Table 2 an estimate of sex ratio has been given.

The sex ratio based on cemetery evidence would appear to be quite high, most marked between the ages of twenty and forty with the very high death rate of women. At birth the sex ratio was probably the normal 104-105, which increased only slightly to age fourteen. From that age to about forty the combination of hard work, childbearing and tuberculosis brought a great loss of women so that the sex ratio in that age group was up as high as 120-130. After age forty women seemed to have survived as well as men so that the sex ratio did not increase much in later life. This is manifestly different from the vast surplus of elderly women in our population. Given this reduction in the number of women, birth control would seem to have been unnecessary for the control of population, even though sermon and confessional literature warn women against practices which would induce abortion, such as violent exercise, or bring accidental death to babies, such as sleeping with them.

The high sex ratio had exceptions, however. The burials among the Avar horsemen who had many wives produce a sex ratio often around 100. The sex ratio also varied with size of settlements, the larger the city the lower the sex ratio. Such small cities as Carlisle, Colchester and Kingston-on-Hull had sex ratios of 93-95 in the poll tax of 1377. German cities of the fifteenth century had much the same ratio. Even some of the larger excavated settlements of the early Middle Ages saw an equality of men and women in numbers. This low sex ratio was, as might be expected, accompanied by fewer marriages, and smaller number of children.

In a monogamous society a high sex ratio meant, of course, a large amount of involuntary celibacy which would probably have caused stress in so marriage-minded a society as that of today. Medieval society, however, exalted celibacy. A most popular treatise explained why one should not marry or at least why men should not marry.

One might have suggested that celibacy was a rationalisa-
tion of celibacy enforced on a high sex ratio, except that
Classical civilisation which probably had the same high sex
ratio had no corresponding enthusiasm for celibacy. This
enthusiasm was essentially religious and Christian—a denial
of the pleasures of this world for the sake of heavenly
rewards. In the quest for these rewards thousands of men
became regular or secular clergy. They number, it seems in
the thirteenth century, more than one per cent of the total
population or three per cent of adult men (over the age of
thirteen), only partially bridging the gap in numbers between men and women. The general enthusiasm for celibacy and conversely, lack of interest in marriage must
have done much to make the difference unimportant. It
explains why the number of unmarried couples was small
and that of illegitimate children relatively small in spite
of the high sex ratio.

This indifference to marriage is illustrated also by the
medieval concession that widows need not remarry unless
they so desired. As article viii of Magna Carta reads:

No widow shall be compelled to marry as long as she
wishes to live without a husband.

In the east the Orthodox Church was strongly opposed
to second marriages and argued prohibitively against more
than two, even for monarchs and others who felt the need
for male heirs. Thus Leo (VI) the Wise, who married four
times before he secured an heir, ran into serious difficulties
with the Patriarch of Constantinople.

Estimates of percentage of married people in the total
medieval population are not easy to secure. In the early
Middle Ages serf populations show examples of about
28-34%, a quite low percentage. Later medieval cities
show variation: Basel 32·8; Ypres 34·6; Freiburg 38·7;
Dresden (part) 49·3. Some of the highest averages are in
the villages in the plague period: Tyrol 42·9; England in
1377 45-55% while its cities had only about 35-45%. In
general these are maxima since they do not include the
few per cent of clergy and another few who escaped enumer-
ation and inclusion. Late medieval marriage rates were

higher than normal since the plague had trimmed off numbers of single persons and offered more opportunities for the younger ones to hold land or jobs and thus to marry. It is also not fair to compare them with modern rates since people live so much longer today and thus spend proportionately more of their life at a marriageable age.

Marriage in the Middle Ages depended largely on economic conditions: romantic love had so little to do with the matter that it was assumed to exist best outside of marriage. For the nobility marriage was often arranged and occurred early—twelve was permitted by the Church, fourteen might be the limit for custody of heiresses until age of discretion. Of course marriage at an early age might be the means of arranging disposition of property thwarting possibilities of having the heiress fall into the hands of a feudal superior on the father's death. In the guilds marriage of widow or heiress might be arranged to care for families left orphaned by death of the father-master. On the manors the bailiff might make arrangements to assure continuation of farm services. Such a case in a court roll showed a bailiff offering two widows to two boys: both asked to consider until the next manor court three weeks later when one boy accepted and the other asked for a further option for thought. The problem was perhaps the ages of the widows: the boys doubtless preferred widows at least within ten or fifteen years of their own age. A medieval widow of forty-five was obviously quite durable and might be expected to live another twenty years! If the boy inherited, he might prefer a girl who had served as a servant in a nearby city long enough to have collected a dowry of some size. Furthermore, a woman of twenty-five to thirty might be expected to be stronger and to have fewer children than a girl of eighteen. All of these were hard realities of medieval life.

The life table is designed to show the expectation of life and the age structure of a population. The age intervals appear in the first column (x to x+n): year 0 is from birth to the first birthday (anniversary); year 1 from that birthday to the second birthday, and so on. The mortality rate (q_x^a)

is the death rate for the age interval: by subtracting the mortality rate from 100 one gets the probability of surviving the age interval (p_x). The next column (l_x) sets up a certain figure, often 1000, at birth with numbers surviving for later ages secured by multiplying against the probability rate (p_x). Sometimes the actual number of deaths for each age interval is used for column l_x. The number of years lived in each age interval (L_x) is calculated by adding (a) the years of the interval multiplied by the number of persons who lived through it, to (b) the years lived by those who died in the interval (assuming usually an average of half of the interval for those who died in the interval). The years remaining at age x (T_x) are secured by adding column l_x from the bottom up. Dividing figures in column T_x by those in l_x gives the years of expectation of life at the beginning of each age interval. If the population is static and not affected by migration, column L_x gives the proportion of each age group in that population, by dividing the top figure of T_x into the figure for the age interval or intervals whose percentage is desired. The life table is thus a very useful device.

The life table (Table 4) is significant for succession by showing age at death and thus one can estimate in a stable population how many children must be born to replace those alive at any age. It does not indicate the number of children to a family although it can be worked out with a complicated procedure. Normally, given the death rate of women, one married at thirty might expect to have an average of four children, at twenty-five an average of five and at twenty, an average of six. This may seem strange but the reason is that so many died between twenty and forty that female expectation of life did not advance very rapidly from twenty to forty. That is, women of twenty might expect to have only about an average of twelve years of potential childbearing (assuming an average top limit of forty years). Women again on the average had a child about every thirty months. The average was so high because of prolonged lactation, stillbirths, interrupted pregnancies and other handicaps. The sudden increase in

TABLE 4: Generation Life Table of Males
born 1276-1300 in England

Age interval	Mortality rate for interval	Probability of surviving the interval	Number surviving to age x of 1000 born	Number of years lived in age interval	Years of life remaining at age x	Expectation of life at age x
x to ^{a} ÷ n	$q_x{}^a$	px	l_x	L_x	T_x	$c_x{}^a$
0	15.	85.	1,000	899	31,298	31·30
1-4	11·	89·	850	3,449	30,399	35·76
5-9	4·35	95·65	756	3,698	26,950	35·65
10-4	4·65	95·35	723	3,530	23,252	32·16
15-9	5·68	94·32	689	3,348	19,722	28·62
20-4	12·6	87·4	650	3,045	16,374	25·19
25-9	13·66	86·34	568	2,645	13,329	23·47
30-4	11·01	88·99	490	2,315	10,684	21·8
35-9	12·7	87·3	436	2,042	8,369	19·19
40-4	18·44	81·56	381	1,730	6,327	16·61
45-9	16·67	83·33	311	1,425	4,597	14·78
50-4	25·	75·	259	1,132	3,172	12·25
55-9	25·66	74·34	194	845	2,040	10·52
60-4	43·86	56·14	144	562	1,195	8·3
65-9	39·39	60·61	81	325	633	7·81
70·4	45·	55·	49	190	308	6·29
75-9	69·56	30·44	27	88	118	4·37
80-4	71·43	28·57	8	25	30	3·75
85-9	100·	0·	2	5	5	2·5

Source: Russell, *British Medieval Population*, p.181. The mortality rates for ages 0 and 1-4 are interpolated from Indian death rates in which length of life is virtually the same as these for other ages. Data from cemeteries show that they are reasonable.

number of children in the noble and royal families about
A.D. 1000 may have resulted from the use of wet nurses.
Eleanor of Aquitaine and Henry II had eight children in
nine years, a later Eleanor had twelve by Edward I, while
the wives of Louis VIII and Louis IX had eleven and twelve
apiece. The sudden expansion of medieval feudalism in
the *Drang nach Osten*, the *Reconquista* and the Crusades may
have come in part from the high birth rate of feudal
families. But, on the average, medieval peasant women had
between five and six children apiece.

MIGRATION

Despite its reputation for static character the Middle Ages
experienced much migration. The movement of the great
tribes occupy an important position in medieval history
because they were responsible for the breaking up of the
western half of the empire. Of course, the Crusades have
also aroused a great deal of attention despite their lack of
ultimate success. These movements involved no noticeable
increase in population. However, some movements such
as the *Drang nach Osten* and other forms of colonisation did
add to intensely cultivated areas and raised the total
population of great areas. Besides these great developments
there was constant moving from the countryside into the
cities and some reverse motion: likewise from city to city.
Such movements as pilgrimages and commerce belong to
travel rather than to migration.

Quantitative studies of the great tribal movements have
been few, so that the number of invading Germans in
Spain (Visigoths, Suevi) can be estimated as high as two
millions although two ·hundred thousand would be a very
liberal estimate. The one fairly certain figure is eighty
thousand for the Vandals as they crossed over into Africa in
429. Most of the tribes were probably not much larger.[6]
These Germans dealt very generously with the ruling class of
Romans in taking from them only one third (or at most two

6. J. B. Bury, *History of the Later Roman Empire* (New York, Dover
reprint, 1950), I, 104-5.

thirds) of their income. Most conquering groups simply drove out previous ruling classes when they took over a country, as the forces of William the Conqueror expelled the English nobility, perhaps a thousand families.

There was much colonisation in the Middle Ages, some apparently with little attention from above but practically all of it with permission of some lord. The colonisation of lands in the Byzantine Empire depleted by the sixth century plague has been mentioned: free peasant villages were an important factor in Byzantine life. In the tenth century began the great German push eastward at the expense of the Slavs (Wends) called the *Drang nach Osten*. Much of this was directed by such families as the Billungs for their benefit and thus the peasants did not improve their economic position with respect to their lords. The Christian Spanish 'populated' areas from which the Moors had been driven but probably this did not increase population over what had been the population under the Moors before the wars. The Dutch learned to reclaim lands from the ocean and the English drained the Fens, opening up rich lands in the thirteenth century.

Colonisation assumes that official permission had been obtained from the lord and was often directed by him. Saxon groups moved from old Saxony to the new along the upper Elbe River. Dutch colonists aided in the reduction of distant swamp lands. Perhaps the Pied Piper of Hamelin was a recruiter for such a venture into new lands. English lords with lands in Ireland saw these increased in population from England as the surnames of residents show. French lords established new cities, the bourgades.

As mentioned earlier the cities had a lower marriage rate and birth rate than the country villages. Since all together produced at best only a very gradual increase, it is obvious that the cities did not replace their population and thus were dependent on the countryside for the difference between their birth and death rate. Since persons of similar type or similar ideas marry each other more readily than persons of diverse appearance and beliefs, the weeding out of the atypical by this process would tend to

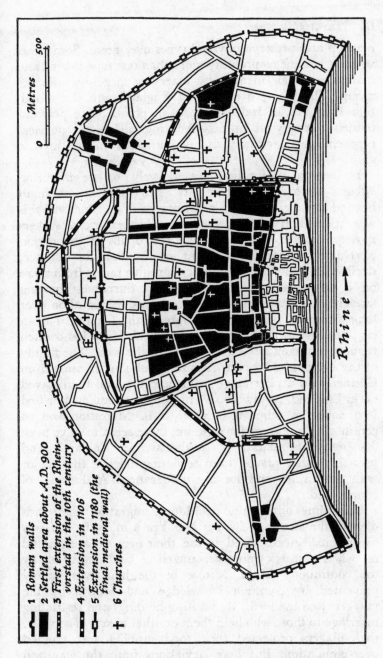

MAP 3 *The historic city of Cologne (from Aubin & Niessen)*

1 *Roman walls*
2 *Settled area about A.D. 900*
3 *First extension of the Rhein-vorstad in the 10th century*
4 *Extension in 1106*
5 *Extension in 1180 (the final medieval wall)*
6 *Churches*

Metres
0 500

Rhine →

develop and preserve physical types over areas. Sometimes within the same community more than one type existed and maintained their identity by marrying largely within the group. The short, dark folk of England and the blond, blue eyed folk of Italy are cases in point. Since peasants tended to marry within neighbouring villages the physical type changed gradually as one moved from one area to another.

In general, migration was largely to neighbouring villages or to the nearest city. Migration seems small beyond the day journey limit because of its expenses: this was especially true of farmers. For guildsmen or city workers moves to other cities or to the metropolis of the region were more common. Movement into London, for instance, declined sharply from beyond twenty-five miles: from there on it was mostly from other cities. Surnames showing foreign provenance indicate a considerable migration over long distances, perhaps even more in the Church than in city business groups. The Franks of the Holy Land often remained in contact with relatives in the west. The family of the London alderman, Arnald Fitzthedmar, came from Germany on a pilgrimage to Canterbury and then stayed on in England. Many who went abroad as students drifted into countries other than their own. Migration was so common that, except for serfdom, there seem to have been few restraints placed by authority. In England, and probably other places, even serfs might leave the manor with permission and for a consideration. And some, of course, fled.

Hard times and famine could force migration: thousands died in the streets of Bruges and Ypres in 1316: this was exceptional. Accustomed to use their eyes, villagers could see when pastures were over-grazed or lands worn out by too continuous tillage. Misuse of the land was largely prevented by common knowledge and control by the villagers and the lords. By limiting holdings and restricting marriage to those who held them or other means of support, the villagers protected their food supplies and avoided over-population. But here deviations from the standard

farm holding were many and are a fertile source of demographic miscalculations. Probably a fifth to a third of
families were actually single persons with few dependants,
often elderly or deficient. Many were hired servants whose
few acres merely supplemented their support as ploughmen,
shepherds, even carpenters, smiths and millers. One need
not see men, wives, many children struggling to live on
inadequate acreage.

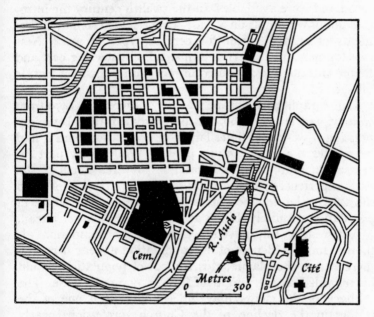

MAP 4 *Carcassonne, showing the old cité and the newer bourgade*

The decrease in the size of holding necessary to support a
family was probably due in part to improvement in farming,
although not in the quality of seed since the returns from
seed seem to have remained about the same at a fourfold
return for wheat, higher for rye. However, the use of a
three field system instead of a two field allowed a sixth more
land to be under cultivation each year, apparently with no
serious depletion. The use of more beans and peas about
the tenth century helped to conserve the soil. The additional

labour required to till under the new system seems to have been supplied by the introduction of the horsehoe, the wheeled plough and better harnessing. The increase of tilled fields or rather of persons dependent upon a certain core of tilled fields raised the question of provision for an equivalent animal quota and its subsistence. Could, for instance, fish from ponds be substituted for certain animal foods if no additional lands for pasture and meadow or woodland were available? In the twelfth century the introduction of windmills on a wide scale released some requirements of animal power for certain types of work. New developments like the rudder instead of a steering oar, and better sails doubtless resulted in more fish in many a seaside village.

Demographically Europe was very different in 1470 from what it had been in 500. At the bottom of the plague depression it was three times larger in population than it had been after the sixth century plague. While every part increased in numbers of inhabitants, the area north of the Alps experienced the greatest growth first, to be followed shortly by the advance in eastern Europe. The centre of population definitely shifted away from the Mediterranean.

Apparently, Europe still controlled its population although some evidences of overpopulation appear here and there before the plague: this control of population should be regarded as a triumph of human common sense. The celibacy of the clergy may indeed have been one of the factors in the decline of the Church: professions nearly always recruit heavily from the sons of their own numbers. The population increase, within limits of subsistence, provided the environment for a more complicated and sophisticated culture, laying the foundations for the great advances of modern times.

BIBLIOGRAPHY

As background for population development, see C. M. Cipolla, *The Economic History of World Population* (Penguin 5th edn. 1969) and M. R. Reinhard, André Armengaud et Jaques Dupagnier *Histoire Generale de la Population Mondiale*, Paris, 1968. William Petersen's *Population* (New York, 1962, Macmillan) has chapters on pre-industrial society which place this period in the general history of population.

Bibliographically, the period A.D. 500-1500 can be approached in my *Late Ancient and Medieval Population* (Philadelphia, 1958, *Transactions of the American Philosophical Society* vol. 43, No. 3) and by a supplementary article, 'Recent Advances in Medieval Demography,' *Speculum* XL (1965) 84-101. Titles of current articles appear in *Annales de démographie historique* (Paris) and in sections A and B of the *Population Index* (Princeton). For information about cemetery evidence, the section 'Vor- und frühgeschichtliche Skelette' in the *Anthropologischer Anzeiger*. I am preparing a study and bibliography of this evidence.

The most detailed study of method is R. J. Mols, S.J. *Introduction à la demographie historique des villes d'Europe du xive au xviiie siècle* (Gembloux, 1954-56, J. Duclot). While it is limited to cities of the later Middle Ages, its treatment is applicable to the whole period. He does not discuss rank-size relationships: for this see my *Medieval Regions and their Cities* (Newton Abbot, 1971, David and Charles).

On the effects of the plagues much has been written. For the early medieval epidemics see my 'That Earlier Plague,' *Demography* V (1968) 174-184. For the later period the literature is immense, but no authoritative work has appeared. On general cemetery data the same situation appears. Some of the finest work is being done in Hungary. As an example, Gy. Acsádi and J. Nemeskévi, *History of Human Life Span and Mortality* (Budapest, 1970, Akadémiai Kiadó), pp. 51-137. Recently J. Szilagyi has revised the statistics of data from Roman tombstones in the same periodical, volumes XIII-XVIII, 1961-1968.

For Italian population history, Julius Beloch's *Bevölkerungsgeschichte Italiens* (Berlin, 1937, 1940, 1961, Walter de Gruyter) is standard. Much has been added by D. Herlihy in his *Medieval and Renaissance Pistoia* (New Haven, 1967, Yale University Press).

For German population see, Erich Keyser, *Bevölkerungsgeschichte Deutschlands* (Leipzig, 1938, S. Hirzel); much information about size of cities in his *Deutsche Städtebuch, Handbuch städtische Geschichte* (Stuttgart, 1939-   ). From France recently E. Baratier, *La démographie provençale du xiiie au xive siècle* (S.E.V.P.E.N. 1961) produces a fine regional study. For an age specific breakdown of a large part of Rouen, P. Desportes, 'La population de Reims de xve siecle d'aprés un dénombrement de 1422,' *Le Moyen Age* LXXII (1966) 463-529.

For England, see my *British Medieval Population* (Albuquerque, 1948, University of New Mexico Press) and my 'The Preplague Population of England,' *Journal of British Studies* VI (1966)–21.

2. The Town as an Agent of Civilisation
1200 – 1500

Jacques Le Goff

The opposition between town and country begins
when barbarism turns to civilisation

KARL MARX. *The German Ideology*

In ancient Greece and above all in Rome the real dicho-
tomy which lay at the heart of the Greek and Roman cultural world was that between town and country. Not
that the evident primacy of the town, the home of civilisation faced with the barbarism of the countryside, went un-
contested. From Varro to Columella, from Cato to Vergil,
from Cicero to Palladius, philosophers, poets and agricul-
turalists were in agreement with the old Latin thinking
which saw virtue only in the virtues of the countryside.
But the antithesis *urbanus—rusticus* was a linguistic legacy
to the men of the middle ages; and Christianity, the child
of the Jewish and Greek colonies and thus of the towns,
reinforced the prejudice against the countryside in making
the countryman (*paganus*) into the pagan, the rebel against
the word of the Christian God.

In spite of appearances this opposition is not found again
in the medieval west, or rather it reappeared only in part,
when the urban renaissance which began in the twelfth
century was accompanied by literary and legal revivals.
The goliardic poets, children of the towns and the culture
of antiquity, mocked at the peasant as some rustic devil.
The *Declinatio rustici*, from thirteenth-century Germany,
had six declensions for the word 'peasant'—villain, rustic,
devil, robber, brigand and looter; and in the plural—
wretches, beggars, liars, rogues, trash and infidels. There is
an echo of this at Venice, 'the most triumphant city' known
to Commynes, in the fifteenth-century anonymous poem

The Villeins' Alphabet, which concludes 'we are the dregs of the world'.

But in the middle ages the fundamental opposition was between the town and the desert. Around the town lay a whole world put in order, inhabited and cultivated; and this included town and countryside. The desert was the uncultivated and the wild; most characteristically it was the forest. In the ecclesiastical and religious field the distinction between the urban and eremitical worlds was equally fundamental. As early as the end of the fourth century, St Martin of Tours, according to Sulpicius Severus, abandoned his urban episcopal see when he felt the need for solitude and wilderness; for him this meant a monastery in the midst of the forest, where he could renew his spiritual energy.

Far from being the provider of communications and services, therefore, the town appeared to a whole line of traditionalists as a den of iniquity. It was the re-creation of Babylon.

For was not the first town the work of Cain (*Genesis* IV 17)? It bore the mark of the first sinner. At Deutz, twin-town of Cologne, early in the twelfth century, the great abbot Rupert contrasted Cain with the patriarchs Abraham, Isaac and Jacob who 'built neither towns nor castles but fled from the towns and lived in hovels, and built the opposite of town and castle, an altar to the honour of God.'

A century later, around 1210, Gervase of Tilbury, an Englishman who was marshal to the emperor Otto IV of Brunswick, recalled in his *Otia Imperialia* the accursed pedigree of the first town, where two things were forced on the population: the economic imposition of the invention of weights and measures, which ended the innocence of pre-urban exchanges, and the military imposition of walls which substituted segregation for familiarity.

No one stigmatised the town as an instrument of perdition more than St Bernard, who in the twelfth century could come to Paris to take students from the city school and lead them to the school of the cloister, where they would find salvation: 'Fly from the midst of Babylon, fly and save your souls.'

In Paris at the same time others dreamt of another urban model at the opposite end of the system of Christian values —Jerusalem. Thus Philip of Harvengt, prior of the Premonstratensian abbey of Bonne-Espérance: 'Driven on by the love of learning you are now at Paris, and you have found the Jerusalem that so many long for. It is the home of David . . . of the wise Solomon.'

The growth of the towns in the twelfth century seemed to exacerbate men's sensibility in their regard. While those who held by the traditional society and culture fulminated away, the towns' seductive force operated ever more strongly. Payen Bolotin, a priest of Chartres, was indignant when he saw even hermits pouring into the towns.

The early middle ages had seen the eclipse of towns; according to Maurice Lombard there was an 'urban anaemia' which accompanied a 'monetary anaemia'. The centres of cultural initiative were no longer towns but monasteries and the royal palace—the latter itinerant, in spite of Charlemagne's attempt to settle it at Aachen.

Yet this period of the early middle ages was not entirely negative, for one urban model still attracted. Towns remained treasure hoards, places where riches of building and ornament piled up. They offered tremendous booty to the greed of the nascent knightly class. *The Song of Roland* crudely expresses the feudal libido:

> By Charlemagne Spain's richness is devoured,
> The castles taken *and the towns deflowered.*

Aimery of Narbonne presents Charlemagne as looking down from a hill upon the town of Narbonne: 'It was well enclosed by walls and pillars, and you never saw a town more solidly laid out . . . You never saw a finer sight. There were twenty towers built of a shining stone. At the centre of the town another tower caught the eye. On top of its main section was erected a fine gold ball from across the seas; they had enclosed within it a ruby which flashed and shone with a splendour like that of the rising sun. On a dark night, and this is no lie, you could see it from four leagues away. On one side was the sea coast, on the other the river Aude, which ran past in a torrent and brought the inhabitants all they could wish for. In the great vessels which tie up there merchants bring to the city so many riches that nothing is lacking that might do a man honour. The king started to contemplate the town, and in his heart he coveted it.'

The whole thinking of men in the early middle ages appears in this passage: the prestige of walls, of stone and of solid buildings, the seduction of vertical lines imposing themselves from afar, the brilliant luxury and colouring of ornament, a prodigality of goods. The urban dream of the western warriors of the early middle ages finally became a reality, with the sack and pillage of Constantinople in 1204.

For all this, urban life was not totally in eclipse in the early middle ages. It was not so much the islands of urban life, above all the episcopal towns, which maintained the continuity of the urban reality and ideal. Lewis Mumford saw clearly that even if for some in the middle ages and later (St Bernard for example) the cloister appeared as an anti-town, a desert environment, in fact the monastery of the early middle ages became a new sort of town. The famous plan of St Gall, from the ninth century, is the plan of a town. Even if the impulse came from elsewhere, from the commercial revival outside, still in several cases a medieval town was born from the development of a monastery—St Riquier, Fulda or Deutz, where Abbot Rupert wrote with precision and an indignant sorrow of the passage from the monastic to the urban state. 'The monastery,' wrote Lewis Mumford, 'was in fact a new kind of *polis*.' For in the cloisters he recognised those facets of organisation and outlook which foreshadowed the town of the later medieval and modern periods: restraint, punctuality, order, a use of each day's time which regulated both work and leisure. There was also its stability: it was 'an island of serenity and peace'.

Again, in fact, it was the revival of commercial exchanges which brought about the birth or re-birth of the town as an area of consecrated peace. As early as the ninth century the council of Meaux-Paris (845–846) considered the *civitas* as an area of peace (*locus pacificus*), for it was an area of active commerce. In the great period of urban organisation the area of the town was a demilitarised zone where only those who preserved order in the name of the public authority were allowed to carry arms. Thus in the privileges granted to the city of Ypres by Count Philip of Flanders between 1168 and 1177: 'He who lives in the outskirts of Ypres may not carry a sword, unless he be a merchant or other person passing through the town on business; if he enters the town with the intention of staying there he must leave his sword outside the town and its suburbs. If he does not do so, his sword will be confiscated and he will pay a fine of 60 sous.'

Thus the medieval town marks an important stage in the evolution of a feeling of security, which Lucien Febvre reckoned an essential chapter in the history of communal feeling.[1] It was a feeling of security that could still be breached by catastrophes, some of them peculiar to the towns, and others that were particularly devastating in an urban setting. Thus fire could consume those towns which, while proud of their stone, remained chiefly built of wood. Thus, after 1348, the plague made rich people especially flee from the towns, where promiscuity multiplied the risks of infection, to the countryside. It became a place of refuge, as in the time of the barbarian invasions. Flight from the plague strengthened the role of the country manors as agents of civilisation at the end of the middle ages; this was above all true of the Italian villas, and one thinks particularly of the villas of the Medici in Tuscany.

From the urban monastic model the medieval town

---

1. It should be noted that in the eleventh and twelfth centuries compared with the insecurity of open country and forest, the castle offered a place of safety of the same kind as the towns. Several of the texts quoted elsewhere associate castle and town: in some respects the castle like the monastery prefigured an urban model.

preserved certain traits which were very often limits, checks to its expansion. Carol Heitz has shown how in the Carolingian period both architecture and liturgy were dominated by the symbolism of the heavenly Jerusalem. Werner Müller, studying the incarnation of the 'Holy City', has found that this heavenly Jerusalem was the perfect model of the medieval town. Urban II, preaching the crusade at Clermont in 1095, exalted Jerusalem, 'the navel of the world, the royal city, placed at the centre of the circle of the earth'. From the beginning of the twelfth century this idea of the town as microcosm 'gained in strength and depth'. From it came those towns set down within a circle of walls and divided into four quarters (*quartiers*) by the four main streets—as in the *Roma quadrata* of antiquity— which represented the four roads and the four parts of the world. The four-part plan, which Werner Müller calls the 'gothic plan' and which he finds most exactly realised at London and Copenhagen, is found also, for example, in a whole series of towns founded within the area of twelfth- century Germany: the markets created by the Zähringer in the south-west of the Empire, Villingen (1119), Freiburg- im-Breisgau (1120), Rottweil (between 1120 and 1150), Fribourg (1157), Nuremberg (1181) and Berne (1191).

But it was the thirteenth century that was the golden age of these quadripartite towns, the incarnation of the new spirit of civic organisation. At the centre of the town, the crossroads of the *quadrivium*, there was usually a square where you would find the law-court and the pillory, the fountain and the market-cross. The judicial and economic functions of the town, essential aspects of its culture, were thus founded upon a sacred tradition. They retained something of the quality of taboo, and this was a check to the liberal and lay progress of urban civilisation.

Further than this, the medieval town retained the self- sufficient economic mentality of the early medieval monas- tery. Everything should be produced if not within the walls at least in the immediate neighbourhood. The outsider should not be admitted, or at very least he should be con- fined to particular buildings, (thus the Venetian *fondacco*,

on the model of the Byzantine *mitaton* and Muslim *funduk*);
if that were not possible, he should be placed in a judicial
environment which made him a foreigner, a minor in the
eyes of the law. Over-production, which forced men to seek
outlets outside the local market, should be avoided. In all
these ways the Benedictine rule seemed to regulate the
urban economy and its mentality. The best illustration of
this is certainly the organisation of the guilds which tended,
as Gunnar Mickwitz has clearly shown, to act as a cartel
and realise the Malthusian ideal. There are numerous
examples of the medieval town's persistent distrust of
strangers, especially foreign merchants, whose access to the
town was curtailed so that it might benefit from the exchanges the merchants made possible while preventing
their becoming dangerous competitors. Although the
Italians enjoyed important privileges in some northern
towns, foreign merchants (even outside the Venetian
fondachi) were fixed both in time and in space. Their stay
was usually limited to forty days—a special type of quaran-
tine—as at Bristol in 1188, and at London early in the
twelfth century for the merchants of Germany, Lorraine,
Denmark and Norway. In 1463 the municipal council of
London ordered all foreign tradesmen to congregate in the
area of Whitechapel near Mark Lane. Almost everywhere foreign merchants were segregated in one corner
of the market and had to get up and go as soon as the
closing bell sounded. An act of 1439 compelled foreign
merchants arriving at an English port to supply the name of
an inn-keeper, who had to receive them during their stay
and send in a report twice a year to the Exchequer. The
towns may have revived from the beginning of the eleventh
century, because of the development of an artisan class
and of trade, but generally speaking right up to the thirteenth century the urban mentality was above all negative
and passive. Against the insecurity of the feudal world it set
the peace of the town; it welcomed goods from outside,
whether from rural manors or from the Byzantine and Muslim east.

In some places from the mid-twelfth century onwards,

and everywhere from the thirteenth, this position was reversed. While the town always remained a centre of exchanges, it now became above all a centre of production: production of goods, of ideas, and of material and cultural models. The towns took the initiative. Between town and country there now started the dialogue between earner and spender which gave its name to the fourteenth-century English allegorical poem *Winner and Waster*, with its morally instructive content.

This driving force of the towns from the thirteenth century onwards, no one at the time perhaps understood better than the heads of the new mendicant orders—Franciscans, Dominicans, Augustinians and Carmelites—which took root right in the midst of the towns.

This was an over-turning of monastic tradition, substituting for a flight into solitude a presence in the most provocative of worlds, that of the towns; and it encountered resistance within those orders that had eremitical traits. But in each of these orders there were authorities to justify the choice of the towns. Thus Humbert of Romans, who was Master General of the Dominicans between 1254 and 1263 and who died in 1277, listed in his *De eruditione praedicatorum* (book II, ch. 72) three reasons why the friars should prefer the towns for their apostolate. (1) Preaching was quantitatively more effective in towns, for there were more people there. This underlines the role of the towns in helping men grasp the idea of quantity, that interest in figures which meant that at the turn of the thirteenth and fourteenth centuries the middle ages entered the statistical era. (2) Preaching was qualitatively more necessary in towns, for morals were worse there (*ibi sunt plura peccata*). This belief in the immorality of the cities is the other side of the coin stamped with their civilising mission. (3) Through the towns you influence the countryside, for the country emulates the town. This is a remarkable expression of the role of the towns as producers of cultural models which they exported to the countryside.

Another famous Dominican of the thirteenth century, Albert the Great, in a sermon preached at Augsburg either in 1257 or 1263 took as his text Matthew 5, 14: 'Non potest civitas abscondi supra montem posita' ('a city placed on a hilltop cannot be hidden'), and commented: 'The doctors of the faith have been called a city; this is because like a city they give security (*munitio*), urbanity (*urbanitas*), unity (*unitas*) and liberty (*libertas*).'

The chief active role of the town in the later middle ages was the attraction which it exercised over the outside world. The force of this attraction, certainly, varied in proportion to the importance of the town. The horizon of the great cities was international, that of the smaller towns regional. But it is interesting to note that the zone of attraction of the great majority of medieval towns was limited to the surrounding countryside. The work of Hektor Ammann on a series of towns in Swabia has shown that most of the immigrants came from the region up to thirty miles away, while a smaller group came from up to sixty miles away. For Metz in the thirteenth century Charles-Edmond Perrin would place the great majority of immigrants within twenty-five miles of the town. Philippe Wolff observed a similar phenomenon at Toulouse between 1360 and 1450. Toulouse, however, exercised an attraction outside its own region (for example, Brittany) and even abroad (especially Spain).

This capacity to attract men had a number of important consequences. It brought a wealth of labour to the urban patriciate and artisans, and enabled their workshops to function. It shackled men to the enterprises of the nascent bourgeoisie, but in return it gave them liberty in a legal sense. The German proverb 'Stadtluft macht frei' ('the town's air makes a man free') is by and large true. It might also be said that town air gave freedom outside its walls: the town could force rural lords to free their serfs, as happened on a large scale in thirteenth-century Italy, at Vercelli in 1243, Bologna in 1256–1257 and Florence in 1289. Here self-interested motives were not necessarily either expressed or even formulated, and the context of all these measures was highly complicated: nonetheless, the traditional opinion that the medieval town patriciate wrenched the peasant from servitude to the land to tie him to servitude in the workshop remains true in its essentials. One result of this capture of the country by the town is that very often the captive forced his customs and patterns of thought upon the town. As has often been said, the medieval town was impregnated with the countryside; the majority of its inhabitants were peasants. Urban folklore was very often simply the imported folklore of the countryside. The area in which this folklore particularly flourished was very often simply a village community within the town. While it had country origins, however, it seems that in the early middle ages the town's folklore became urbanised. The carnivals, in which the town guilds played a predominant part, with their giants and dwarfs, dragons and processional monsters, and savages (for instance the 'green man' and 'wild man' of London), were strictly urban festivals. In his remarkable book on Rabelais, Mikhail Bakhtin has linked the carnival comedy of the middle ages with the town's public square. Between 1150 and 1300, the monsters and animals which would become the protective badges of their towns began to appear as weathervanes, especially on the public buildings of the towns of northern France and Belgium. In the majority of cases this symbolic animal was a dragon: it was so at Tournai, Ypres, Bethune, Brussels and at Ghent, whose reconstituted *Drak*, 11 ft. high and weighing 875 lbs., is still preserved in the belfry. Most often this dragon perched upon the tower of the building which contained the commune's treasure and its archives. Without a doubt this is the old dragon which guarded treasure. The town had taken it over.

Two festivals which come from the urban folklore of the later middle ages may be taken as examples of this sociological phenomenon. At Tarascon there was the festival of the Tarasque, recognised by Louis Dumont as 'the eponymous beast, the protector of the community . . . associated with the great local parade of the traders' guilds'. At London there was the famous Lord Mayor's Show, where the guilds took their carnival figures in procession; as early as 1417 a document could refer to this as ancient custom.

The towns drained from the countryside not only men

but also produce. Although we cannot say what caused it, we notice a great rural expansion which from the tenth and above all the eleventh century added to the cultivated area and increased its yields. The urban revival, while it may not have prompted this growth, nonetheless gave it an irresistible impetus. The dissymmetric plough, an improved harness, the use of horses for ploughing and three-course rotation, all spread to the rhythm of urban growth. The medieval town ate the grain of the countryside and also bought its wine and the plants it needed for industry, especially dyestuffs. In the thirteenth century, for example, Amiens covered Picardy with fields of woad, and in the following century Toulouse did the same for the Lauragais and the Albigeois. Roger Dion has shown how the Paris wine-trade grew up along with the expansion of the city. A striking text of 1330 shows Montpellier in the midst of a sea of vines, expanding in waves which forced the corn farther and farther away, so that it had to import grain in increasing quantities. Antonio Petino has shown how saffron (crocus) took the hills of Tuscany by storm, at San Gimignano, Volterra, around Lucca, and then in the fourteenth and fifteenth centuries conquered the Marches, Abruzzi, Lombardy, Aragon, Catalonia and the Albigeois. Two sectors of the economy received a spectacular impetus from urban demand: the cloth trade and the building trade.

As centres of consumption and as markets for the distribution of goods, the towns recovered the great monetary role that had been theirs in antiquity. Money became, perhaps once more, the symbol of urban prosperity. The French monarchy for its own profit took control of the issue of the two town currencies which prospered in the twelfth century—those of Tours (the *tournois*) and Paris (the *parisis*).

When gold coins were struck again—the genois (1252), the Florentine florin (1252) and the Venetian ducat (1284) —they were an expression of what Roberto Lopez has called 'municipal pride'. On the florin appeared the lily and the patron saint of the town, St John the Baptist, in whose honour the baptistry ('il bel San Giovanni' of Dante) was built. On the ducat were St Mark with Doge Dandolo at the feet of the patron-evangelist. Commercial prosperity supported the urban ideology.

As well as being centres of attraction, medieval towns were centres of diffusion also.

Manufactured goods no less than money showed a town's strength and self-reliance. Here again cloth provides a particularly good example. Each major town had its own measurements for a bale of cloth, and its seal on exported cloths was both a guarantee of quality and an expression of the urban personality. Thus the town took from the economic sphere a new form of security—control. The town's guarantee was what really assured the success of its products. Any merchant who attempted to act independently rapidly lost all credit. In the second half of the fourteenth century Paolo di Messer Pace di Certaldo of Florence, in his *Libro di buoni costumi* (*Book of Good Usages*), put this very well: 'Never engage in any trade forbidden by your commune, for if ill-fortune strikes, you will have nowhere to turn . . . cherish the honour, the good and the prosperity of your town and its head, pledge yourself and your goods to this cause, do not join any party against your commune. "Your commune" and "your town" you must take to be the place where you live with your family and where your possessions and your relatives are.'

This extract also brings out very well the human social bases of town life. A house first of all: only princes and the great feudal lords could move from one residence to another, and the fortified house (the castle) was the model for the merchant house; but the feudal world still remained far more tied to persons than to houses, while the urban world confined society within the walls of its houses and its towns. The town created a new type of outcast, the man with 'neither hearth nor home'. The communal statutes of the Lombard rural communes of the fourteenth century, imitating those of the urban communes, tended to exclude 'the indigent and the vagabond, and not the stranger as such'. After the house and along with the house, what was important for the townsman was his family. The lineal family group, abundantly supplied with children if that were possible, replaced the concept of kith and kin, the group of 'friends by blood' (*amis charnels*). Alongside the urban community, then, we have here the second base of security—family solidarity. Alongside that, still within the same town, there was a third protective circle—a man's goods and relatives. This new type of family created new forms of sensibility; we have proof of this, at least for the towns of medieval Italy. Combining demographic and literary sources, David Herlihy has shown how at Florence after 1350 there was the growth of a happy family circle and an affectionate interest in children. Giovanni Morelli declared: 'Welcome joy and happiness within your family, and in their company seek a good and healthy life.' And Giovanni Dominici in his *Regola del governo e cura familiare* presents a picture of fathers playing ball with their children, of mothers spending long periods combing and bleaching the hair of their little girls, and of children learning to dance for the delight of their parents and friends.

The town was a centre of attraction and diffusion, but above all it was a centre of production. The town was a crossroads and a terminus: through contacts, meetings and exchanges it could play a major creative role.

The urban workshop, being a result of the division of labour, was first of all a place for exchanges and the creation of new techniques. From the monastic workshop, a centre of Roman techniques—witness the *De diversis artibus* of the monk Theophilus early in the twelfth century —the impetus turned towards the urban workshop, the melting-pot of the material and spiritual sides of Gothic civilisation. The change from seigneurially-controlled to urban weaving was a technical as well as an economic and social event, for the purely manual vertical loom gave way to a horizontal pedal-operated one. A mid-thirteenth century miniature from a manuscript at Trinity College, Cambridge, gives us one of the first pictures of this new machine. The crane which unloaded trading ships in the town ports became so familiar a feature of the urban landscape that in paintings from Ghent, Lüneburg and Danzig it serves as a symbol of the fifteenth century town.

It was in culture and the world of ideas above all that the medieval town was a crossroads—a workshop of cultural models, a meeting-place of experiences. The twelfth century saw the beginning of the great movement which took the dispensaries of knowledge from the monasteries into the towns. There was a renaissance of the episcopal schools, encouraged by the decrees of the Third and Fourth Lateran Councils (1179 and 1215). There was a development of the urban monastic schools, one of the most famous of them being that of St Victor at Paris, on the slopes of the Mont Sainte-Geneviève. There was a growth in the number of masters teaching more or less independently; some of them were supported by a religious community, others taught in private premises. The most famous of these new urban masters was Abelard. At last we have the beginning of an institutional development which in some towns would lead to the formation of centres of higher education which influenced the whole Christian world. The *licentia ubique docendi* conferred the right to teach anywhere, whether the privilege was obtained by law (by a papal bull) or simply by reputation. These institutions were formed on the pattern of the other guilds of town workers. In some places, as at Paris, this guild was dominated by the masters; in others, for instance Bologna, by the students. The guild had its own statutes, privileges and seal, and (though this was acquired with difficulty) the right to strike. Some of these masters lived off the fees their students gave them, and were accused by traditionalists of being 'sellers of words' and of sacrilege, for 'knowledge, the gift of God, cannot be sold'. Others lived off ecclesiastical benefices, while in some trading centres salaries were provided by the public authorities. Bologna, Naples, Vercelli, Salamanca, Angers and Toulouse were the chief university centres founded, with varying fortunes, in the first half of the thirteenth century. There appeared a new power figure—the graduate. To set against the nobility of birth and of blood, this was the second of the aristocracies created by the medieval town. After (and almost along with) the town patriciate founded on wealth in the first instance, there was the intellectual élite created by success in examination—the university mandarins.

The success of the new urban model was such that gradually even the most foreign groups, and those most hostile to the town, were gathered within it. For the brightest of their novices the Cistercians founded a college in 1245 adjacent to the university of Paris, the *Collège des Bernardins*. While teaching was still largely by word of mouth, the new guild multiplied the books which were its tools, and were also objects of trade. Processes were invented which made possible relatively speedy copying (the *pecia*); from being a sacred object the book became a working tool; and there was an increase in the number of booksellers (*stationarii*) attached to the universities. Yet books remained expensive. This was a bottle-neck in the diffusion of university and urban culture.

But the true cultural influence of the town was at a more elementary level than this. For we must not forget that under the universities were the schools—what we would call primary and secondary schools, although very often the universities took the place of the latter. There a child might learn to read, write and add up without being as before committed to becoming a clerk. Henri Pirenne, in a famous article, pointed out that as early as 1179 the burgesses of Ghent obtained recognition from the count of the schools they had founded; and in 1191 they had from Countess Matilda a guarantee 'that if any suitable and capable person wished to open a school in the town of Ghent, no one might stop him'.

After Pirenne, Armando Sapori, Fritz Rörig, Amintore Fanfani and Yves Renouard, to mention only those who have produced the most striking work, have illuminated and appraised the merchant culture. It was a practical culture above all, founded upon writing and arithmetic. According to Giovanni Villani, at Florence in 1338 there were 8,000 to 10,000 boys and girls learning to read, and six mathematical schools where 1,000 to 1,200 pupils were learning commercial usage before going on to a practical stage with a merchant.

According to Rörig what assured the hegemony of the Hanseatic merchants of northern Europe was their 'intellectual superiority'. Another manifestation of this was in Italy, with the perfecting of commercial techniques: bills of exchange, double-entry book-keeping, and the use of manuals specially written for merchants (the *pratiche della mercatura*). The instruction provided by the medieval town was one of the preconditions of economic growth, and of the industrial revolution of modern times.

Alongside this practical instruction the urban bourgeoisie at times tried to impose its own culture, ethic and political outlook; the inspiration was drawn from the works of Greco-Roman antiquity but it was founded chiefly on urban patriotism and formed by the city's environment. According to Hans Baron this was true of one section of the bourgeoisie of Florence at the turn of the fourteenth and fifteenth centuries. This aspect and phase of pre-humanism he calls 'civic humanism'. Humanism appears as an urban phenomenon at the end of the middle ages. This is true at every level, even though the humanists felt that the countryside must complement the town, as did the villa the palace, and the park the market square. Printing, the vehicle of humanism, was a technique connected with the town. When in 1470 Guillaume Fichet congratulated the prior of the Sorbonne on having printed the letters of Gasparino of Bergamo, the first book printed at Paris, he said; 'These makers of books whom you have brought into this city from your own country of Germany produce extremely accurate books which follow the text they have been given . . . You merit the same praise as Quintilius [*sic*] . . . for having restored to Gasparino his sweet eloquence and having inspired the great majority of the noble minds of this city with a loathing of barbarity, allowing them to taste and drink every day at the source of an eloquence that is sweeter than honey.'

Perhaps the most important way the urban bourgeoisie spread its culture was the revolution it effected in the mental categories of medieval man.

The most spectacular of these revolutions, without a

doubt, was the one that concerned the concept and measurement of time.

Time in the early middle ages was tied to the church clock. It was liturgical, following the natural world and based on the natural fixed points of the day, the rising and setting of the sun; it was both religious and rural.

The need to schedule working time led the towns first of all to demand special bells for the lay townsfolk, and then led to the construction of machines and instruments which divided time into fixed and equal portions—clocks and watches based upon the hours.

At Tournai, for example, as early as 1188, the burgesses proudly recorded amongst the privileges granted them by King Philip Augustus of France, the right to have a bell 'in the town at an appropriate place', which was to sound 'at the townsmen's good pleasure for the town's own affairs'.

As to mechanical clocks, according to Carlo Cipolla, they first appeared at Milan (St Eustorgio) in 1309, at Beauvais cathedral before 1324, at Milan again (St Gothard) in 1335—a clock which struck the twenty-four hours of the day—at Padua in 1344, Bologna in 1356 and Ferrara in 1362. In 1370 Charles V of France installed a clock that struck the hours on one of the towers of the royal palace, so that every Parisian might know the time 'whether the sun shone or not'. This rationalising and laicising of time marked the transfer from nature to culture, and was an essential contribution to town life. It so struck contemporaries that the famous chronicler Froissart wrote this poem on the clock of Charles V, the king who read Aristotle:

> The clock is, to regard the matter well,
> A most important, beautiful device,
> And useful and ingenious besides.
> It lets us see the time both day and night,
> Which its great cunning makes it know aright
> Even when the sun completely hides his rays;
> For this the clock is worthy of much praise.

Charles V certainly had something to live up to, for his grandfather Philip the Fair, who died in 1314, had his own watch. Up to the sixteenth century mechanical public clocks, and above all domestic clocks, remained rarities. There were very few specialist clock-makers. In 1368 we find Edward III of England giving a safe conduct to three Dutchmen from Delft, 'clock-makers who have come to the kingdom to practise their craft'.

On a larger scale the urban way of life developed a sensitivity to measurement and numbering, a mentality which thought in quantitative terms. Within the towns in the fourteenth century, the medieval west entered the statistical age. The best example of this is the famous work of Giovanni Villani which set the city of Florence out in tables—here it matters little whether or not these were correct.

At the same time the medieval townsman became aware of the organisation of space. Thus if he were in a 'new town', it would very often have been founded upon a fixed quadrilateral or concentric plan. The organisation of town space was also shown in the creation of various set pieces, above all in the squares which had either a communal purpose (as in the *palais communal* or the area of the general assembly), or an economic function (the market-place), or a religious function of a new sort (as with the friars of the mendicant orders, preaching in the open air in front of their churches).

This planning of space in the town was not necessarily 'regular', for it might have to follow the contours of the land. Here the great triumph of medieval town planning was undoubtedly Siena, both in its main square, which was the shape of a shell, and in its general lay-out. Finally medieval towns responded to aesthetic needs, which could not be reduced to any single pattern. That the urban environment was expected to radiate beauty can be seen not only in looking at the towns but also in some of the texts. In 1290, for example, the commune of Siena required the Dominicans to take down a wall which hid their church and prevented its being seen from a distance, giving as their reason that the church contributed to the beauty of the town landscape.

It was undoubtedly the towns also—those of Italy in the second half of the thirteenth century—that gave birth to a new kind of vision, perspective. The streets, drawn up in ranks as it were, and the squares, presenting the question of the best disposition of space, taught the eye to look through this new perceptual grid of perspective by which they themselves were regulated.

The urbanism that developed to a great extent in the thirteenth century and even more in the fourteenth mingled ideas that we have now come to distinguish: beauty, propriety, rationality.

The streets of Paris were paved on Philip Augustus's orders in 1184 but those of London only under Edward I at the end of the thirteenth century; in the fourteenth century paving became general. The monumental fountains which were both necessary for hygiene, and aesthetically satisfying, show well the many-sided nature of medieval urbanism.

Streets became narrower and narrower. Corbelled houses rose higher and higher and at ground level there appeared lean-to sheds and the entrances to cellars, so that the streets lessened their width both at rooftop and ground levels. Severe measures were taken against this, for example at Douai (in 1245) and at Ratisbon. Avignon in 1243 ordered that streets and bridges should be at least two *cannes* wide—around 12 feet 6 inches. At the same time men were often required to align the fronts of their houses and at Prague in 1331 all building needed the prior authorisation of the town council.

It must not be assumed, however, that the medieval town was a model of rationality and order and a centre of regularisation.

Philip Jones has forcefully reminded us that until the eighteenth century the towns of Italy and the city states of the middle ages juxtaposed 'a mass of incoherences'. The benevolent influence of the medieval town was limited and counter-balanced by injustices due to egotism and ignorance, by the laissez-faire attitude of the groups in control, in particular the town patriciate. The medieval town gave birth to the twin curses of town life, which reached their culmination in the West in the nineteenth century—poverty and theft. Not only was urban poverty more ingrained and more spectacular than rural poverty; it had its own special character, from overcrowded hovels to the special cultural forms which foreshadow what Oscar Lewis has called 'the culture of poverty'.

In the later middle ages the 'city mob' was much in evidence. This world of delinquency and crime had its own organisation and jargon, (we have Villon as witness to the latter), its ugliness and sometimes its charm. Bronislaw Geremek has shown the battle fought by the French royal and municipal authorities against vagabonds, the 'caymans and caymandes' of Paris and other cities, in the fourteenth and fifteenth centuries. A Paris edict against 'rascals and ragamuffins' from the first half of the fifteenth century, beggars who pretended to be crippled and infirm, conjures up exactly the world of 'The Beggar's Opera'.

There was at least one area where the injustice and inequality that reigned in urban society prevented its government from imposing order, and that was finance. The town oligarchy levied unequal taxes, and illegal taxes that had not been granted by the proper institutions; it misused public money and put justice up for sale. In thirteenth century France the chicanery of city finances led to repeated interventions from the monarchy, which little by little imposed its authority on the towns and whittled away their privileges. At the end of this century Philip de Beaumanoir stigmatised the exploitation of the small townsfolk by the great men in his famous *Coutumes du Beauvaisis*. At Douai Georges Espinas contends that during the 'revolutionary period' from 1296 to 1311, the 'democratic revolution' was simply 'a revolt against fiscal tyranny'. A. B. Hibbert has shown that in England at the turn of the thirteenth and fourteenth centuries there was similar discontent in most towns, for example, London, Leicester, Lincoln, Oxford, King's Lynn, Norwich and Ipswich. The medieval town also produced riots.

We must also ask the question considered by Roberto Lopez, whether town patronage, the luxury and waste of its buildings, did not to some degree ruin the towns; whether the cathedrals and town halls did not prevent urban fortunes from being more profitably invested, so that they took up not only the town's prosperity but the whole of its economic development. Was the truth not the opposite of Victor Hugo's picture, that it was the cathedral that killed the economy? The question is undoubtedly badly put. The economic model of the medieval town of the thirteenth century, and this includes the inhabitants' mental attitudes, left no possibility of alternative investment. Besides, extravagance in building was not tied solely to the socio-economic structure, and to the necessity for compensating by aesthetic illusion (though this of itself produced real values) for the reality of underdevelopment. Town patronage was an instrument of patrician power, for it turned the discontented to satisfaction, or at least distraction, in the aesthetic field; this was an essential aspect of patriotism, of an urban pride which cut across social boundaries. Lastly it must not be forgotten that if in some ways the medieval town attacked the feudal world, by certain aspects of its social equality (itself limited to certain areas), by its spirit of economic enterprise and by an atmosphere of calculation, nonetheless the medieval town lived in a feudal world. It had to adapt itself to the feudal system, and one of the ways it did so was to act as a feudal lord itself. The *signorie* which grew up in Italy from the fourteenth century onwards may appear to be the product of specific Italian conditions but, whatever may be said, they represented a normal development within the medieval feudal system.

This fundamental point brings us back to the relationship between town and countryside in the later middle ages.

Everyone is familiar with the celebrated phrases in which Marx in his *German Ideology* and with Engels in the *Communist Manifesto* spoke of the urban bourgeoisie as having enslaved the countryside. In this matter his dialectic was doubly satisfied, for this was a positive evolution in that for him the countryside represented barbarism, while the selfishness thus shown by the urban bourgeoisie revealed for the first time its moral depravity and filthy appetites. 'The bourgeoisie,' said the *Communist Manifesto*, 'has enslaved the countryside to the town. It has created huge cities; it has prodigiously increased the population of the towns by comparison with that of the country; and in this way it has taken the great majority of the population from the brutalising narrowness of country life. As the countryside has submitted to the town, the barbarian or semi-barbarian countries to the civilised, so it has subordinated the peasant races to the bourgeois, the East to the West.'

Certainly the traditional opinion of historians of the towns, above all in Italy, is that the commune did conquer the *contado* and enslave it. The peasants went from servitude to lords to servitude to townsmen. The thesis is not confined to Italy. Jean Schneider has admirably shown how Metz in the thirteenth and fourteenth centuries came to dominate its countryside, economically, socially and politically. But Plesner studying rural immigration into Florence, and later Fiumi who reconsidered the problem as a whole, thought that this picture of the town-country relationship should be corrected and to some degree reversed. The countryside, at least in medieval Italy, profited as much as it suffered from the dominance of the towns; while strictly speaking, as we have suggested, it was the *contado* that conquered the town, from the inside, by immigration. If this is to some extent playing with words and does not really come to grips with the traditional thesis, the idea nonetheless has some truth in it. The amount of opposition between town and country in the middle ages was often trifling. In spite of the enclosure and the town's entrenchment behind its walls, its gates permitted plenty of traffic in both directions for free exchanges with the countryside.

There is no better illustration of this fact than the witness of medieval painting. A single masterpiece, the frescoes of Good and Bad Government painted by Ambrogio Lorenzetti in the city hall of Siena between 1337 and 1339, has claimed the attention both of historians of the town in

medieval art like Pierre Lavedan and of historians of the
Italian rural landscape like Emilio Sereni. While Lavedan
sees in this 'a revelation of beauty and of town life', Sereni
finds, 'a model picture of the sub-urban countryside of the
Italy of the communes: the general security entices the
inhabitants out of the narrow area of the fortified city
and they disperse among the occasionally isolated farms:
meanwhile, a whole army of country police defend the
fields against the ravages of livestock and theft: alongside
the tree plantations, there develops a whole network of
country roads, and pathways run between the fields.'
Looking beyond the outskirts of the town, Sereni discovers
in the life and landscape of the countryside around 'the
civilising and organising influence of the town'.

Is the debate therefore to be settled in favour of the town,
the active and more beneficial of the two? This would be
to simplify the reality.

The reality is rather that the pair formed a single whole.
In different regions and above all in different periods, the
direction and value of exchanges complicated and sometimes
reversed their relationship. The civilising influence of the
towns brought about a true marriage.

Until around 1280 in the greater part of the Christian
world the wave of urban prosperity overflowed into the
countryside, bringing technical and economic progress,
freeing men and urbanising the rural areas. From 1280,
even more from about 1330, and then desperately with the
plague of 1348, urban civilisation was in crisis. There was a
hardening of the arteries as its values became rigid; the
measurement of time became an instrument for dominating
the labouring classes; it rejected manual work from the
sphere of values and with Dante lamented the past:

> Florence, within the ancient circle walled
> From where her summons rang to terce and none,
> At peace and in a temperate modesty dwelt.
> (*Paradiso* XV, 97–99)

The city imposed her will on the countryside, for does not

the fresco of Lorenzetti express an ideal rather than the reality? At the same time, less sure of herself and less able to sustain the pressure from the countryside, to some extent she became ruralised: the reaction against 'the Giottesque' in painting shows this at Florence, according to Antal. And to some extent the countryside escaped from domination; the efforts of the mendicant orders to implant themselves there met with no success and rural industry (the 'new drapery' in particular) in part set itself up against urban industry.

Then in the course of the fifteenth century the town re-captured direction of the whole: but this with two important changes. The new and active element was not the great city but the 'small town', as a network of these set up a kind of fine weft under the stretched and loosened warp of a population decimated by the plague and thinly scattered because of deserted villages (*Wüstungen*). And this 'small town' is from another point of view a large village. Town or country? The other novelty was that the town became integrated into the territorial states, either becoming absorbed in them or (as in Italy) expanding to the dimensions of the city-state. To all appearances this was the zenith of urban civilisation and influence. It was the golden age of the guilds, the period of the great merchants, from the Medici to the Fugger. But the state had taken over the baton from the towns, with the task of disseminating their models.

It is certainly true that the mental attitudes of the medieval town were indispensable to the growth of capitalism and to the industrial revolution. Beyond the urban measurement of time can be seen the outline of time-and-motion studies, such as Frederick Winslow Taylor's, beyond communal town-planning the modern organisation of space, beyond the town schools the education and scientific progress of our day; beyond their spirit of initiative lay the spirit of enterprise of the modern world. But all this would have had nothing to build on without the primary factor of the accumulation of capital, which gave economic and social evolution its essential driving force. For, as R. H.

Hilton justly points out, the economy and mental attitudes of the towns contributed little to this process. The profits of trade and urban industry were chiefly invested in town property, and this property was not a source of capital formation. It was the surpluses and the profits of the rural economy that gave birth to capital. The medieval town was already the town of the Ancien Régime, as described by Fernand Braudel: 'an example of profound disequilibrium, of unbalanced growth, of investment that was irrational and unproductive to the nation.' But would it not be fairer of us to take our leave of the medieval town with the impression the medieval citizens had of themselves, that they owed to urban organisation a communal sense that was one of the great acquisitions of civilisation? Here it is perhaps inexact to oppose town and nation. Brygida Kurbis maintains that in medieval Poland 'the national language formed much more quickly in the urban centres, and this just as much in the residence of a feudal lord as in an artisan's workshop or in the market-place. Side by side with the language, the national consciousness grew ever stronger.' In a famous sermon preached in the church of Santa Maria Novella of Florence in 1304, the Dominican Fra Giordano da Rivolto said of the city: 'Città (*civitas*) tanto suona come amore (*caritas*), perocchè si dilettano le gente di stare insieme.' 'City and charity—that is to say city and love—sound so much alike because men love to live there together.'

BIBLIOGRAPHY

Out of a huge literature concerning the town, this guide contains only those studies most particularly used, or those which seemed to provide the best introduction to the problems and aspects of the urban phenomenon that have been touched on here.

It must not be forgotten that in this area more than in any other, the historian must make use of the other disciplines which concern themselves with towns: geography, sociology, town-planning. Comparisons, over time and between areas, are particularly illuminating.

To be forewarned of the dangers of an urban view of history, particularly insidious for the middle ages whose civilisation was essentially rural, read W. Diamond, 'On the dangers of an urban interpretation of history', in E. Goldman (ed.), *Historiography and Urbanisation* (1941), pp. 67–108.

General perspectives concerning method and historiography will be found in three collective works: *Urban Research Methods*, ed. J. P. Gibbs (Princeton, 1961); *The Study of Urban History*, ed. H. J. Dyos (1968); *The Historian and the City*, ed. O. Handlin and J. Burchard (M.I.T. and Harvard, 1963). The last of these contains a brilliant article by R. S. Lopez, 'The Crossroads within the Wall', taking up the image and idea of A. H. Allcroft, *The Circle and the Cross* (1927): a town is a crossroads inside a circle, a convergence of ways protected by a wall.

We should remember the impulse given to sociology and urban history by a famous article of Louis Wirth, 'Urbanism as a Way of Life', *American Journal of Sociology*, xliv (1938), reprinted in *On Cities and Social Life* (Chicago, 1964). Beyond this pessimistic analysis of urban life—the town is a centre of social desegregation, where primary kinship groups decline and the individual is left prey to isolation—it is possible to grasp, without making value judgements, the following features of medieval town life: the destruction of the large family community; a ground favourable to individualism, whether it was unhappy or free, destructive or creative.

The views of Max Weber on the town, which made a great contribution to history and to the study of *the* medieval town (but was there only *one* kind?), are worked out in *The City* (New York, 1958), which contains an introduction by Don Martindale on 'The Theory of the City'.

On the history of towns two works are particularly suggestive: G. Sjoberg, *The Preindustrial City* (Glencoe, 1960), and L. Mumford, who followed his *The Culture of Cities* (New York, 1938) with *The City in History* (New York, 1961). With the latter read the review articles of Sylvia Thrupp, *Comparative Studies in Sociology and History*, iv (1961–2), pp. 53–64, and Asa Briggs, *History and Theory*, ii (1962), pp. 296–301.

The two volumes on *La Ville* in the *Recueils de la Société Jean Bodin*, vi (Brussels, 1955–6) are useful, though the perspective is predominantly legal and institutional.

The collected works of Henri Pirenne on medieval towns, *Les villes et les institutions urbaines*, 2 vols (Paris-Brussels, 1939) remain classic and fundamental, though the point of view is predominantly economic on the one hand and institutional on the other. The same is true of *The Medieval Town* (Princeton, 1958) a small paperback, containing documents chosen and introduced by J. H. Mundy and P. Riesenberg. There is an excellent historiographical sketch in F. Vercauteren, 'Conceptions et méthodes de l'histoire des villes mediévales au cours du dernier demi-siècle', in *12th International Congress of Historical Sciences* (Vienna, 1965), v. 649–666.

On the triad town-country-forest, large comparative views are opened up by work on philology and the history of religions: G. Dumezil, particularly in *Mythe et Epopée*, with the opposition Mithras-town-palace-prosperity-peace on the one hand, and Varuna-cosmos-forest-war on the other (pp. 147–9, 156), and E. Benveniste, in *Le vocabulaire des institutions indo-européennes* (Paris, 1969), see (for example) the remarks on gateway (*porte*), which physically and mentally was essential to the medieval town, giving access, welcoming and sending away.

There is an excellent study of vocabulary in P. Michaud-

98   *The Middle Ages*

Quantin, *Universitas. Expressions du mouvement communautaire dans le Moyen-Age latin* (Paris, 1970), ch. 4—'La cité, ses subdivisions et ses environs'. Notable here is the suggestion that in the middle ages the term *civitas* could stand for an area either smaller or greater than a town. Sometimes it meant only the ancient town centre (here 'city' was opposed to 'town', as it was in fact, judically and socially, in many towns); sometimes it extended to the immediate neighbourhood. Monald of Capo D'Istria, writing in the early fourteenth century, says that the word *city* includes along with the town the land up to a thousand paces from the ramparts.

On the relations between town and countryside the papers and discussion in the colloquium *Villes et campagnes. Civilisation urbaine et civilisation rurale en France* (ed. G. Friedmann, Paris, 1951) while not specially concerned with the middle ages, are suggestive. O. Dobiache-Rojdesvensky, *Les poésies des Goliards* (Paris. 1931) contains a Latin text and French translation of the *Declinatio rustici* on p. 166. *L'alfabeto dei villani* (in Venetian dialect of the fifteenth century) is edited in C. Muscetta and D. Ponchiroli, *Poesia del Quattrocento e del Cinquecento* (Parnaso Italiano, IV; Einaudi, Turin, 1959), p. 365.

On the antagonism between peasants and citizens in Italy at the end of the middle ages, P. S. Leicht, *Operai, artigiani, agricoltori in Italia dal secolo VI al XVI* (Milan, 1946), pp. 183 ff.

The traditional views of the enslaving of the country by the town were contested by J. Plesner, *L'émigration de la campagnie à la ville libre de Florence au XIIIe siècle* (Copenhagen, 1934), which should be supplemented by G. Luzzatto's review article in *Studi di storia e diritto in onore di E. Besta* (Milan, 1939), ii. 185–203, and by E. Fiumi, 'Sui rapporti tra città e contado nell, età comunale', *Archivio Storico Italiano*, cxiv (1956), pp. 18–68. See also G. Volpe *Studi sulle instituzioni comunali a Pisa: città e contado* . . . new edn. (Florence, 1970).

On the role of the town in freeing peasants, the following classical works are now rather dated: W. Silberschmidt,

'Die Bedeutung der Gilde, inbesondere der Handelsgilde, für die Entstehung der italienischen Städtefreiheit', *Zeitschrift der Savignystiftung für Rechtsgeschichte* (Germ. Abt., 51, 1931), whose perspective is chiefly urban, and P. Vaccari, *Le affrancazioni collettive dei servi della gleba* (Milan, 1939). On this whole problem, from a largely judicial standpoint, there is an important publication of the Spa colloquium, *Les libertés urbaines et rurales du XIe au XIVe siècle* (1968). R. Fossier judiciously takes up the idea of the 'triumph of the town' in his remarkable *Histoire Sociale de l'Occident médiéval* (Paris, 1970), pp. 317 ff.

On the formation of the urban area, in addition to the classic work of G. von Below, *Territorium und Stadt* (2nd edn., Munich-Berlin, 1922), there are interesting specialist works: for Bruges, A. Verhulst, 'Die Binnenkolonisation und die Anfänge der Langemeinde in Seeflandern', *Vorträge und Forschungen*, vii/viii (ed. T. Mayer, Constance, 1964); for Lübeck, G. Fink, 'Lübecks Stadtgebiet (Geschichte und Rechtsverhältnisse im Überblick)', in *Städtewesen und Bürgertum als geschichtliche Kräfte. Gedächtnisschrift für Fritz Rörig*, ed. A. Von Brandt and W. Koppe, (Lübeck, 1953), pp. 243–296; and above all, for Metz, J. Schneider, *La Ville de Metz aux XIIIe et XIVe siècle* (Nancy, 1950), an exemplary study.

In his fine work, *Histoire de la vigne et du vin en France des origines aux XIX siècle* (Paris, 1959), R. Dion has made a special study of the creation of vineyards because of urban demand, especially the Paris vineyards (pp. 219 ff.), as a fact of economic and human civilisation ('alimentary civilisation').

The evolution of towns in the early middle ages has been tackled in a brilliant and original article by M. Lombard, 'L'évolution urbaine pendant le Haut Moyen Age', *Annales, E.S.C.* (1957), pp. 7–28, and studied as a whole in *La Citta nell'alto Medioevo* (VI Settimana di studi del Centro Italiano di Studi sull'Alto Medioevo, Spoleto, 1950), which shows very well the civilising role of the town in the early middle ages.

For the urban models of the early period see: Mumford,

City in History, ch. 9, for the monastery-town; C. Heitz, *Recherches sur les rapports entre architecture et liturgie à l'époque carolingienne* (Paris, 1963), for the image of the heavenly Jerusalem, which is taken up and followed in detail in the idea and plan of the 'gothic town' by W. Müller, *Die heilige Stadt. Roma quadrata, himmlisches Jerusalem und die Mythe vom Weltnabel* (Stuttgart, 1961).

The 'Malthusian' character of the economy of the town guilds has been shown by G. Mickwitz, *Die Kartellfunktionen der Zünfte und ihre Bedeutung bei der Entstehung des Zunftwesens* (Helsinki, 1936).

The old reflex of distrusting strangers, shown by the western towns of the middle ages in their dealings with foreign merchants, has been underlined by A. B. Hibbert, 'The Economic Policies of Towns', in *The Cambridge Economic History of Europe*, iii (1963), pp. 157–229. In the same volume E. Miller shows that in the fifteenth century 'urban xenophobia was broadening into economic nationalism' (pp. 328 ff.). These judgements, which rest chiefly on English examples, apply *grosso modo* over the whole of Christian Europe.

The cycle of seven sermons delivered by Albert the Great as a commentary on Matthew 5, 14 ('non potest civitas abscondi super montem posita') has been published by J. B. Schneyer, 'Alberts des Grossen Augsburger Predigtyzklus über den hl. Augustinus', *Recherches de Théologie ancienne et médiévale*, xxxvi (1969), 100–147. They exalt the town, especially glorified by its beauty and the joy it gives its inhabitants and visitors, and they compare the doctors of the church to it.

On zones of attraction and immigration into the towns there are generally similar pictures in: for Metz, C. E. Perrin, 'Le droit de bourgeoisie et l'immigration rurale à Metz au XIIIe siècle', *Annuaire de la Société d'histoire et d'archéologie de la Lorraine*, xxx (1921). 513–639, and xxxiii (1924), 148–152; for Toulouse, P. Wolff, *Commerces et marchands de Toulouse, vers 1350–vers 1450* (Paris, 1954), pp. 79 ff., and maps A. B. C.; and for the towns of Swabia H. Ammann, 'Vom Lebensraum der mittelalterlichen

Stadt. Eine Untersuchung an Schwäbischen Beispielen',
Berichte zur deutschen Landeskunde, 31 (1963), pp. 284–316
(with maps).

On urban folklore see: M. Bakhtin, *Rabelais and His
World* (Cambridge, Mass., 1968); A. van Gennep, *Le
folklore de la Flandre et du Hainaut, département du Nord* (Paris,
1935), which has on pp. 154–177 a complete list of all the
human and animal giants of northern France, Belgium
and Holland, with a map of their distribution and a table
showing the dates of their appearance; G. Unwin, *The
Gilds and Companies of London* (1908), ch. XVI—'The Lord
Mayor's Show'; L. Dumont, *La Tarasque. Essai de description
d'un fait local d'un point de vue ethnographique* (Paris, 1951);
on the carnival as the 'town games', with particular
reference to fifteenth-century Nuremberg, J. Lefebvre, *Les
fols et la folie. Etude sur les genres du comique et la création
littéraire en Allemagne pendant la Renaissance* (Paris, 1969);
P. Saintyves, 'Le tour de la ville et la chute de Jéricho',
in *Essais de folklore biblique* (Paris, 1923), pp. 177–204.

On the Christian vision of the town there is an interesting
and disconcerting book, J. Comblin, *Théologie de la ville*
(Paris, 1968).

There is an English translation of the text of Messer
Pace da Certaldo in R. S. Lopez and I. W. Raymond,
Medieval Trade in the Mediterranean World (New York, 1955),
p. 424. See also D. Herlihy, 'Family Solidarity in Medieval
Italian History', *Explorations in Economic History,* 7 (1969–70),
173–184.

The communal statutes of the Italian towns show us an
urban microcosm, which took an urban style of life into
the very heart of the countryside: P. Toubert, 'Les statuts
communaux et l'histoire des campagnes lombardes au
XIVe siècle', *Melanges d'Archéologie et d'Histoire.* 1960,
pp. 397–508.

On the towns as teaching centres: P. Delhaye, 'L'
organisation scolaire au XIIe siècle', *Traditio,* v (1947),
211–268; J. Le Goff, *Les intellectuels au moyen âge* (1957),
links the universities with the towns and the teaching trade
with the other urban trades—a point made, from a legal

LINCOLN CHRISTIAN COLLEGE

and institutional point of view, by G. Post, 'Parisian Masters as a Corporation, 1200–1246', *Speculum*, 9 (1934), pp. 421–445. For the opposition to the sale of knowledge as though it were merchandise, G. Post, K. Giocarini, R. Kay, 'The Medieval Heritage of a Humanistic Ideal: *scientia donum Dei est, unde vendi non potest*', *Traditio* (1955). On the importance for a town of its having a university, J. Paquet, 'Bourgeois et universitaires à la fin du Moyen Age. A propos du cas de Louvain', *Le Moyen Age* (1961), pp. 325–340. On the culture of the medieval town merchant: H. Pirenne, 'L'instruction des marchands au Moyen Age', *Annales*, i (1929), 13–28; F. Rörig, 'Les raisons d'une supérmatie intellectuelle: la Hanse', *Ibid.* ii (1930), 481–494; A. Sapori, 'La cultura del mercante medievale italiano', *Rivista di Storia Economica*, ii (1937–8), 89–125; Y. Renouard, *Les hommes d'affaires italiens du Moyen Age*, new edn. (Paris, 1968).

Among many works dealing with the spread of the cultural influence of medieval towns, note: J. Lestocquoy, *Les villes de Flandre et d'Italie sous le gouvernement des patriciens* (Paris, 1952); P. Dollingér, *The German Hansa* (1970); Y. Renouard, *Les villes d'Italie de la fin du Xe siècle au début du XIVe siècle*, new edn. (Paris, 1969); and a book of more general implications, F. Rörig, *Die europäische Stadt und die Kultur des Bürgertums im Mittelalter*, 3rd edn. (Göttingen, 1964).

Then there are works on particular aspects of this culture. The 'puy', a cultural association fostered by the patriciate at Arras, is placed in a much broader social context by M. Ungureanu, *Société et littérature bourgeoise d'Arras aux XIIe et XIIIe siècles* (Arras, 1955). The role of the Italian town notary in the writing of town chronicles and the formation of city culture and patriotism is brought out by G. Arnaldi, 'Il notaio-chronista e le cronache cittadine in Italia', in *La storia del diritto nel quadro delle scienze storiche* (Florence, 1966). On these chronicles as literary, political and mental models see H. Schmidt, *Die deutschen Städtechroniken als Spiegel des bürgerlichen Selbstverständnisses im Spätmittelalter* (1958); J. B. Menke, 'Geschichtsschreibung und Politik in deutschen Städten des Spätmittelalters (Die

Entstehung deutscher Geschichtsprosa in Köln, Braun-
schweig, Lübeck, Mainz und Magdeburg)', *Jahrbuch des
Kölnischen Geschichtsvereins*, 33 and 34/35 (1958–60); C.
Dericum, *Das Bild der Städte in der burgundischen Geschichtsschreibung des 15 Jahrhunderts* (Heidelberg, 1961); N. Rubinstein, 'The Beginnings of Political Thought in Florence',
Journal of the Warburg and Courtauld Institutes, 5 (1942),
pp. 198–225.

Hans Baron's great work, *The Crisis of the Early Italian
Renaissance, Civic Humanism and Republican Liberty in an age
of Classicism and Tyranny*, new edn. (Princeton, 1966), has
been criticised by J. E. Seigel, ' "Civic Humanism" or
Ciceronian Rhetoric?', *Past and Present*, 34 (1966), pp. 3–48:
the humanism of Bruni, not much different to that of
Petrarch, was predominantly literary and had little contact
with the social situation of the bourgeoisie of Florence
around 1400.

The personality and patronage of the medieval town,
and the elaboration of aesthetic models within the towns,
are touched on in numerous works, most of them dealing
with Italy. On urban literature note two stimulating works:
P. Francastel, 'Imagination et réalité dans l'architecture
civile du Quattrocento', in *Eventail de l'Histoire vivante*
(Paris, 1953), ii. 195–206, and W. Braunfels, *Mittelalterliche
Stadtbaukunst in der Toskana* (Berlin, 1953). For a sociological
explanation of painting, F. Antal, *Florentine Painting and
its Social Background* (1947). On the relationship between art
and politics within the towns, H. Wieruszowski, 'Art and
the Commune in the Time of Dante', *Speculum*, xix (1944),
14–33, and N. Rubinstein, 'Political Ideas in Sienese Art',
Journal of the Warburg and Courtauld Institutes, xxi (1958),
179–207. On paintings of towns, and the idea of the town
that these were meant to convey, see: P. Lavedan, *Repré-
sentation des villes dans l'art du Moyen Age* (Paris, 1954);
G. Volpe, L. Volpicelli and others, *La città medioevale
italiana nella miniatura* (Rome, 1960); and, essential for
showing the urbanisation of the countryside, E. Sereni,
Histoire du Paysage rural Italien (trans. from Italian, Paris,
1964).

The views of R. S. Lopez on the misdeeds of towns in their artistic policies during the thirteenth century (*Annales, E.S.C.*, 1952, pp. 433–438) have started a recent debate in *Explorations in Economic History*, 1967–8.

On the black side of the picture (1). Urban poverty: M. Mollat, 'La notion de la pauvretè au Moyen Age: position de problèmes', *Revue d'Histoire de l'Eglise de France*, 1966, pp. 5–23; F. Graus, 'Au bas Moyen Age: pauvres de villes et pauvres de campagnes', *Annales, E.S.C.*, 1961; B. Tierney, *Medieval Poor Law: a Sketch of Canonical Theory and its Application to England* (Berkeley, 1959). (2) Vagabondage and crime within the towns: B. Geremek, 'La lutte contre le vagabondage à Paris aux XIVe et XVe siècles', in *Ricerche Storiche ed Economiche in Memoria di Corrado Barbagallo* (Naples, 1970), II. 213–236. (3) On injustice and financial chicanery: G. Espinas, *Les finances de la commune de Douai des origines au XVe siècle* (Paris, 1902); *Finances et comptabilité urbaines du XIIIe au XIVe siècle* (international symposium at Blankenberg, 1962; Brussels, 1964).

It must be remembered that the Jews also lived in the towns, and that this had effects on culture, on men's attitudes and on the economy. One example, out of an enormous literature, is a study of an urban Jewish community, showing the spread of a town's financial operations and peasant indebtedness: R. W. Emery, *The Jews of Perpignan in the Thirteenth Century* (New York, 1959).

On towns as centres of heresy, J. Le Goff (ed), *Hérésies et sociétés dans l'Europe préindustrielle (11e–18e siècle)*, (Paris, 1968), notably the articles by C. Violante ('Hérésies urbaines et hérésies rurales en Italie du 11e au 13e siècle', pp. 171–198), P. Wolff ('Villes et campagnes dans l'hérésie cathare', pp. 203–207) and J. Macek ('Villes et campagnes dans le hussitisme', pp. 243–258).

For the image which the towns wished to give of themselves—their beauty, their wealth, their influence—see the chronicle of Benzo d'Alessandria (early fourteenth century), edited and introduced by J. R. Berrigan, 'Benzo d'Alessandria and the cities of northern Italy', in *Studies in Medieval and Renaissance History*, ed. W. M. Bowski (Lincoln, Neb., 1967), pp. 127–192.

Of the numerous monographs on medieval towns which bring out the cultural side very well—art, literature, town-planning—note one old study, F. Schevill, *Siena. The History of a Medieval Commune* (1909), and two recent studies, one of a southern and one of a northern city, M. B. Becker, *Florence in Transition*, ii (Baltimore, 1968), G. Williams, *Medieval London: From Commune to Capital* (1963).

On the transition from town to city-state: J. Lejeune, *Liège. Naissance d'une nation* (1948); P. J. Jones, 'Communes and Despots: the City-State in Late-Medieval Italy', *Trans. Royal Historical Society*, 5th ser., 15 (1965), pp. 71–96; A. Tenenti, *Florence à l'époque des Medicis. De la cité à l'état* (Paris, 1969).

For the creation of a new secular environment in the towns of the later middle ages: C. Cipolla, *Clocks and Culture. 1300–1700* (London, 1967; reprinted in paperback as part of *European Culture and Overseas Expansion*, 1970); J. Le Goff, 'Au moyen âge: temps de l'Eglise et temps du marchand', *Annales E.S.C.*, 1960, and 'Le temps du travail dans la "crise" du XIVe siècle: du temps médiéval au temps modern', *Le Moyen Age*, 1963; P. Wolff, 'Le temps et sa mesure au Moyen Age', *Annales, E.S.C.*, 1962.

On the role of the towns in technical and scientific progress see the various histories of science and technology, e.g. B. Gille in *Les origines de la civilisation technique*, Vol. I of the *Histoire Générale des Techniques*, ed. M. Daumas (Paris, 1962), and G. Beaujouan, in *La science antique et médiévale*, Vol. I of the *Histoire générale des sciences*, ed. R. Taton (Paris, 1957).

The cultural and national role of Polish towns in the middle ages has been shown by B. Kurbis, 'Le problème de la culture intellectuelle dans les villes polonaises du Xe au XIIe siècle', in *L'artisanat et la vie urbaine en Pologne médiévale* (Warsaw, 1962).

The pattern in the network of small towns in the later middle ages has been brought out by H. Stoob, 'Minder-städte. Formen der Stadtentstehung im Spätmittelalter',

Vierteljahrschrift für Sozial-und Wirtschaftsgeschichte (1959), pp. 1–28, and noted by J. Le Goff as part of an enquiry studying a religious apostolate which had an urban base, that of the Friars between the thirteenth and fifteenth centuries: 'Ordres mendients et urbanisation dans la France médiévale, *Annales, E.S.C.*, 1970, pp. 924 ff. The same phenomenon is found, for example, in Hungary: G. Szekely, 'Le développement des bourgs hongrois à l'époque du féodalisme florissant et tardif', *Annales Universitatis Scientiarum Budapestensis*, Sectio Historica, v (1963), 53–87, and J. Szucs, *Das Stadtwesen in Ungarn im 15–17 Jh.*, 53, pp. 97–165.

The fundamental study of the paradox of the medieval town, growing from and fighting against feudalism at one and the same time, is the work of J. L. Romero, *La revolucion burguesa en el mundo feudal* (Buenos Aires, 1967).

The weak part played by the medieval town in the primary accumulation of capital is underlined by R. H. Hilton, 'Rent and Capital Formation in Feudal Society', *Second International Conference of Economic History* (Paris-The Hague, 1965), pp. 33–68.

Enormous horizons on the role of the town are opened up by F. Braudel, *Civilisation Matérielle et Capitalisme, XVe–XVIIIe siècles* (Paris, 1967), ch. 8—'Les villes'.

In order to compare the civilisation of the medieval towns of the west with those of the Muslim west and those of the east: L. Torres Balbas, 'Les villes musulmanes d'Espagne et leur urbanisation', *Annales de l'Institut d'Etudes Orientales*, Algiers, 1942–7, and M. Tikhomirov, *The Towns of Ancient Rus* (Moscow, 1959), ch. 7—'Urban Culture'.

3. Patterns and Structure of Demand 1000-1500*
Richard Roehl

Our understanding of the economic history of medieval
Europe has been greatly enhanced during the past fifty
years or so. Of course, this achievement is not the product
exclusively of the last half-century. Much was accomplished
in the nineteenth as well as in the twentieth century, particularly in terms of making source materials available, and
interpreting and synthesising them. Yet one might reasonably maintain that it is with Bloch, Dopsch and Pirenne
that interpretation and synthesis really come into their own;
their names seem to mark a transition in economic history
from description and narration to a new technique and
medium of inquiry and explanation.

Many individual scholars have contributed to the construction of the picture which we now possess of western
Europe's economy in the medieval period. It is not necessary
here to review the details of these many components. What
I would like to call attention to is a characteristic which I
think is common to most of them, i.e. the fact that their
orientation is almost invariably towards the *supply* side of
economic relationships. Thus, for example, agrarian studies
normally deal with the production or output of agricultural
commodities. Activities of merchants are examined to
determine (a) the origins of members of this class (that is,
the supply of a certain type of skilled labour and of entrepreneurship), (b) the goods in which these agents dealt, or
(c) the supply channels of transportation and distribution.
Urban historians focus upon the goods and services supplied
by town-dwellers, and the organisation of production as
influenced by judicial customs and by the growth and
development of guilds.

* The author wishes to acknowledge his indebtedness and gratitude
to the Institute of International Studies, for financial support; to
Edward F. Lucas, for research assistance; and above all to Carlo M.
Cipolla, for guidance and inspiration at every step.

Obviously, there do exist exceptions to my generalisation. Indeed, many items in the literature would not be described by the economist as exhibiting either a supply or a demand approach to analysis. However, I suggest that of those works which can be so classified, the overwhelming majority is supply-side oriented.

There are, I think, basically two reasons why this is the case. First, to the extent that writers have been informed by the theories of economics, a bias was introduced and reinforced from this quarter. Classical economic theory is itself supply oriented. Adam Smith, for example, was really concerned with the production of 'the wealth of nations'; Malthus's worry was the supply response of population to the relationships of aggregate food supply. Marx was mainly interested in the forces and relationships of production, though he did recognise more clearly than others the critical role which demand could play. Classical and neo-classical theory, then, essentially ignored the question of the determination of the level and composition of demand; the assumption always was that the economy automatically operated at the full employment level and therefore the interesting problems were those of how economic agents and factors responded to this equilibrium value of demand.

The 'Keynesian Revolution' changed this situation. By demonstrating that the economy might achieve equilibrium at a level of aggregate demand lower than that required for the full employment of resources, Keynes directed the attention of theorists away from the former exclusive pre-occupation with the economics of supply. Economic historians too have begun to appreciate the critical importance that demand can have in the economy.

Keynes's theoretical insights did correct for one bias; but they also revealed another. The work of testing and applying Keynesian theory made increasingly clear the relative scarcity of the kinds of data necessary in discussions of demand, as compared with many other types of economic information. It is simply the case that historical statistics dealing with categories such as output, production, exports, etc., are often recorded and preserved, whereas those con-

cerning the various components of consumption and investment demand are much more rarely encountered. Moreover, even when they do occur the latter data are almost
always reported on the micro level, for a single household
or firm. Thus these statistics are much less readily useful
than those in the former category, which frequently occur
in aggregate form. It is these peculiarities of the data,
coupled with the inclinations of classical economic theory,
that have, I believe, resulted in the predominance of a
supply orientation in the literature of economic history.

The present essay intends to review briefly but explicitly
the components of demand in the economy of medieval
Europe. The data problems have not been, and are unlikely ever to be, overcome; and their deficiencies, noted
above, apply *a fortiori* to the chronically data-poor Middle
Ages. There is no possibility of conducting a rigorous
quantitative analysis. I do not propose to compute any
elasticities of demand either specific or aggregate, nor to
calculate propensities to consume, average or marginal.
These procedures are challenging enough for students of
the contemporary era, with its vastly more adequate
statistical sources. But there are some figures and estimates
for the medieval period, and they can suggest certain
orders of magnitude, certain dimensions for the variables
in which we are interested. They must be used with great
caution; but I do believe that more can be done on the
basis of the extant materials than has been done so far.

There are some conceptual matters which should be mentioned at the outset. Economic theory defines aggregate
demand as composed of three basic elements: consumption;
investment; and government (plus, for completeness, a
foreign sector). For present purposes, however, it is both
more realistic and more practical to regard aggregate
demand as comprising only consumption and investment,
each of which may then be separated into two components,
'private' and 'public.' The entity of government as it has
developed within the framework of modern nation-states
obviously is not comparable with the feudal and dynastic

régimes which formed the apex of the medieval polity. The categories of modern economic theory were developed for and refer to an integrated national economy; quite clearly, the concepts of national income accounting and modern institutional law make little sense in the medieval context, especially for the earlier period. Yet the aristocracy, the Church and urban organisations did, in certain of their functions, have the capacity of public or quasi-governmental agencies, and some of their offices and activities did partake of a 'public' nature. It is not always an easy or simple matter to distinguish in which of the two roles, public or private, a given functionary is performing, and to some extent the judgments and classifications must be *ad hoc* and arbitrary. In the Middle Ages, government was far more personalised, and the fact of the matter is that the distinction between private and public was blurred in the consciousness of medieval people, though it gradually became more clarified as time passed. Nevertheless, I feel that the taxonomy adopted here is useful for the analysis that follows.

It should be clearly understood that the attribution of a significant role to demand in the operation of an economy rests upon the presupposition that the economy has already achieved a certain threshold of development or maturity. Demand exists and is met, of course, even in an economy in which all individual agents are completely self-sufficient; but its role becomes of greater strategic importance the higher the degree of monetisation and the frequency of resort to markets. The degrees of monetisation and market activity are not entirely unrelated, for, while it is possible to observe fairly widespread employment of barter and direct exchange markets without a large volume of money transactions, the reverse does not hold; that is, a high degree of monetisation implies a market economy.

The distinction between 'Naturalwirtschaft' and 'Geldwirtschaft' as applied to the medieval economy has by now been established as misleading. The *per capita* volume of money circulating in the medieval economy certainly varied considerably through the period, and the variations were neither continuous nor general. The basic fact, however, is that the economy was to some extent monetised even in the so-called dark ages, and was becoming progressively more so after the tenth century.

In discussing patterns of demand in medieval. Europe it is evident that numerous exceptions will always be found to any generalisation. In the first place, there was no homogeneous 'European economy' in this period; variety and diversity are the most striking characteristics of the whole. The major dimensions along which the medieval economy was differentiated were (1) from region to region, (2) according to the sequence and chronology of economic development, and (3) by socio-economic class. On the regional level, for example, the debate concerning economic trends during the Renaissance has at least established that it was possible for the economy in one area of western Europe to be relatively depressed while elsewhere economic life enjoyed fairly vigorous health. Nor would anyone suggest that all parts of Europe passed through precisely the same stages, or developed at the same rate through time; southern France in the twelfth century, for instance, was at a very different state of development than was, say, Saxony.

Despite the undisputed importance of such regional and chronological disparities, the sharpest degree of differentiation with respect to patterns of demand was probably due to class affiliation. Of course, class composition was no more uniform over the period or within Europe than the other features just mentioned. The percentage of small holders in the British population would be different in 1300 from what it was either three hundred years earlier or later; and the relative number of town inhabitants in 1200 would be much greater in northern Italy or the Low Countries than, for instance, in Spain. But the broad categories of classes are generally applicable to Europe as a whole in this period; and in this context discussion on a general level may be offered.

Although medieval Europe was not a subsistence economy

in the strict sense of the term, there were nonetheless those within it who lived at or close to a subsistence level. Many of these were members of the lower ranks of the peasantry, landless or nearly landless wage labourers and cottagers; others would be classed as the urban poor. We can get an impression of what this level of existence was like from information concerning the provisioning of prisoners in Perugia, in 1312, who were to be supplied with twenty ounces of bread per day. If one accepts a conversion rate of 3,200 calories per kilogram — and caution must be exercised in extrapolating from caloric equivalents derived from modern commodities — this implies a daily intake of less than 1,800 calories.[1] Although the prisoners' diet may have been occasionally supplemented with such items as vegetable soup or the less enticing parts of fish, this must be considered as the barest minimum for survival. It should also be noted that this threshold level was only practical because of two particular features of the prisoners' circumstances: the climate of this area was relatively mild; and they were physically idle virtually all of the time. (Medieval people, it may also be noted, were of somewhat smaller physical stature than their present-day descendants.)

Peasants who were engaged in working the land, of course, would have required a somewhat larger caloric intake. A variety of sources suggests that an average of 2,000 to 2,200 calories daily might have been sufficient to keep a man alive and able to perform his work, if not at the peak of health; women consumed somewhat less. The diet constructed by Abel for a seventeenth- or eighteenth-century peasant family proposes a figure close to 3,000 calories per day.[2] This is probably not an unreasonable figure for our period as well, though we must observe that this example apparently has to do with a family substantially above the lowest rank of the peasantry, for Abel endows it with a holding of 35·5 hectares, almost 90 acres. The quarter- or the semi-virgate were more typical units for

1. This is the rate of conversion employed by W. Abel, *Geschichte der deutschen Landwirtschaft* (Stuttgart, 1962), p. 100.
2. *Loc. cit.*

the small holder, who constituted a sizeable segment of the peasantry. A quarter-virgate was normally in the range of six to ten acres, and probably more often towards the lower than the upper end of that span. For a family of four or five, this implies an average of one and one-half or two acres *per capita*, as compared to almost fifteen for Abel's hypothetical family of six. Average peasant holdings in Germany during our period were larger than in many other parts of Europe, but still Abel's description must be taken as referring to a moderately comfortable peasant family.[3]

A picture thus may be drawn of an average daily ration somewhat greater than 2,000 calories for peasants and others near the lower end of the social spectrum, a level of something like 3,000 for middling peasants, and reaching perhaps 4,000 calories or better for those who were relatively well off. The requirements, as suggested, would vary directly with the rigour of the climate, from region to region; and the nature and strenuousness of the labour performed would also have an effect. Lane, for instance, has reported that Venetian seamen whom he describes as 'reasonably well fed' received an average daily ration of almost 4,000 calories in 1310.[4] A collection of data summarised by Spooner is in general agreement with these conclusions.[5]

Account must also be taken, however, of the problem of distribution through time. The day-to-day variance about these mean figures could be substantial, in both directions. Occasional feasts and celebrations raised the consumption level above the average, while the attrition of stores during the winter and as harvest times approached could drastically

3. Cf. A. Grotjahn, 'Ueber Wandlungen in der Volksernährung', *Staats- und socialwissenschaftliche Forschungen*, XX (1902), p. 4.

4. F. C. Lane, 'Salaires et régime alimentaires des marins au debut du XIVe siècle', *Annales: Économies, Sociétés, Civilisations*, XVIII (1963); this has been translated and appears in the collection of his essays, *Venice and History* (Baltimore, 1966).

5. In the *Annales: Économies, Sociétés, Civilisations*, XVI (1961). See also the figures in C. Clark, *The Economics of Subsistence Agriculture* (London and New York, 1967), especially Chapter 8; and the appendix in J. C. Drummond and A. Wilbraham, *The Englishman's Food* (London, 1939).

lower it. This precarious situation, with the average level of consumption so close to the pure subsistence minimum, accounts for the tragic frequency with which starvation was a reality in medieval society.

There are calories and there are calories, and so it is of interest to inquire as to the form in which the medieval peasant secured his. We have no budgets for peasant households from the Middle Ages, so conclusions regarding the specific kinds of food consumed must be derived indirectly and speculatively.[6] The materials upon which to draw in studying patterns of consumption are very scattered and of a highly discontinuous nature; much basic research remains to be done before the information can be worked up sufficiently to support a general synthesis. But within the constraints of the present state of the data, some comments may be offered.

Cereals were the foundation of the lower class diet; and they were consumed for their calorific value. Although bread was not the only food item consumed, it was firmly established as the staple. This bread of the lower classes was usually baked from barley or rye, sometimes from oats or mixed grains, rarely from wheat. Almost as common on the tables of the poor were the various meal-based porridges and gruels. Finally, the most frequently consumed beverage was ale, which was fermented from grain, normally barley (though wine and, to a much lesser extent, mead would be substituted in some regions).

Barley, rye and even oats thus constituted the most important basic elements in the diet of the lower classes. Most peasants produced themselves the greater portion of the grains they consumed. Consequently, in normal times the items basic to peasant subsistence produced only a weak expression in terms of effective market demand, though

6. J. Z. Titow, *English Rural Society 1200–1350* (London, 1969), pp. 80 f. There is a summary of some of the English data in E. A. Kosminsky. *Studies in the Agrarian History of England in the Thirteenth Century* (Oxford, 1956), pp. 230 f. See also the discussion by G. Duby, *L'Économie Rurale et Vie des Campagnes dans l'Occident médiéval* (Paris, 1962), pp. 139 f.; and the comments in R. H. Hilton's fine regional study, *A Medieval Society* (New York, 1966), pp. 110 f. and Chapter 4, *passim*.

aggregate (market plus non-market) demand from peasants for grain was of course very large. Light bread baked from wheat was a rarity and a luxury for peasants, and virtually all of the wheat produced was consumed by members of the wealthier classes. Yet many peasants produced at least some wheat, and a transfer was effected either through the medium of payment of taxes, tithes and other peasant dues, or through sale on the market. Wheat was thus, for the peasant, almost exclusively a cash crop, or one required to discharge his obligations. This situation accounts for the fact that the relatively abundant price statistics which we sometimes have for the grain trade in medieval Europe refer primarily to wheat.

The peasant did not subsist solely on dark bread and ale, though their primary importance is testified to by the fact that it was precisely these — and only these — two consumption commodities which were regulated by an assize. He did, however, supplement his diet, to a greater or lesser extent, with a number of items. Probably the most important among these were legumes — the various peas and beans available in most parts of Europe. (It is interesting to note that legumes are often referred to as 'the poor man's meat.') Additionally, he might consume small quantities of dairy products; but these would not appear too frequently on his menu. Fruits and vegetables, often in dried form, were occasionally available, depending upon the climate of the region and the seasons. Though the use of sugar gradually became more important, especially for the upper classes, for the peasant honey was the major sweetening agent, and was extensively used. Fish was an important item in the diet of peasants and of the other classes as well; this is a topic very much in need and deserving of further research. Peasants ate meat only seldom, perhaps on average half a pound per week. It was predominantly lamb and pork; in England, for example, more often the former, while in Germany the latter was favoured. Beef, fowl and venison were not commonly consumed by members of the lower classes. The *per capita* consumption of meat varied greatly within Europe, being in general at a relatively much lower level in southern and Mediterranean Europe than farther to the north where population densities had not yet forced the inhabitants so far back upon a starch diet.[7]

The basic dietary pattern among the lower classes, then, was quite simple; it was one in which a few staples, mainly carbohydrates, constituted the bulk of the fare. Socio-economic differences were reflected, as has been indicated, in the level of average caloric intake, and by the distribution of supplementary items in the diet. An improvement in real income would be reflected in a shift towards the so-called protective food items which are higher in vitamins, proteins and other nutrients, and a movement away from those foods eaten mainly for their content in calories.[8] Those who could afford to do so would consume a smaller proportion of their calories in the form of bread, porridge and ale (though we should note that ale was not consumed solely for its nutritional qualities, but also because it was enjoyed). Given this framework, certain aspects of the mass psychology become clearer. In societies in which large numbers of small-scale, primary producers pass their lives in uncomfortably close proximity to hunger, socio-economic status is naturally judged by the amount of food consumed: the wealthy man is the one who eats to the point of satiety. In the medieval world, where many individuals were of slight physique and often undernourished simply because food was in relatively scarce supply, to be robust and hefty symbolised well-being and security. The most fitting manner in which to celebrate was to feast. In their depiction of men, women and children

7. See W. Abel, 'Wandlungen des Fleischverbrauchs und der Fleischversorgung in Deutschland seit dem ausgehenden Mittelalter', *Berichte über Landwirtschaft*, XXII (1937); and K. Hintze, *Geographie und Geschichte der Ernährung* (Leipzig, 1934), pp. 90 f. As always, certain progressive areas were able to overcome the constraints of the traditional relationships. For example, the 'marcite' system employed in Lombardy during the fifteenth century successfully integrated grass cultivation and stall feeding of livestock. I am indebted to Carlo Cipolla for this information.

8. For some interesting comments in this connection, see H. Ilzhöfer, 'Die Deckung des Vitaminbedarfes in früheren Jahrhunderten', *Archiv für Hygiene*, CXXVII (1941).

gorging themselves on food and drink, the paintings of the elder Brueghel, though referring to a slightly later point in time, capture the real spirit of a medieval revel.

The implications from this picture of the peasant diet for the structure of demand are fairly straightforward. Much of what the peasant consumed he produced himself. Thus, only a minor portion of the total volume of demand passed through the markets. The average producer would have only a small marketable surplus, the revenue from which went mainly to acquit the various obligations under which he operated. Bad harvests could mean severe privation, but good harvests were welcomed for they meant more to eat and more to sell; it is really only in the modern economy that abundant harvests have come to imply distress for the average agricultural producer. Finally, we may comment that changes in demand for the basic foodstuffs would be dependent mainly upon demographic movements, while that for other foods would display greater elasticity with respect to both price and income.

The nature of peasant demand for commodities other than food can be largely inferred from the preceding discussion of the diet. Any class with such a precarious grasp on physical sustenance will exhibit a marginal propensity to consume food close to one hundred per cent. The average propensity to consume foods will also be very high, though probably lower than the marginal value. That is, the peasant household will devote a high proportion (i.e. 80–90 per cent) of its real income to the provision of food; and any improvements in the real income position will be translated almost exclusively into quantitative and qualitative improvements in diet. That small portion of income not devoted to food consumption will mainly go towards providing the other basic necessities of life — clothing, shelter and heating.

The medieval peasant's clothing was functional, if little else.[9] It was intended to keep his body protected against the elements, to which he was often exposed. Rough blouses,

9. Information on and illustrations of clothing can be found in V.

smocks, jerkins and leggings are typical, though in many cases these would merely be euphemisms for swatches of cloth or hides wrapped about the peasant's trunk and limbs. Items of clothing would seldom be replaced with new pieces; instead, the original garments would be indefinitely repaired, mended and patched. The cloth required, if not the home-woven, unbleached linen, would be purchased from the most inexpensive and coarsest output of the weaver. Peasant demand for textiles and clothing, then, was quite weak, i.e. at a low level and very elastic in both price and income terms — purchases could always be postponed.

The peasant might provide for his own housing; but often this would be the lord's responsibility as a provision of the tenurial agreement, as many peasants simply would have been unable to do it on their own. In general peasant dwellings were hardly more than crude huts, barely meriting the description of 'furnished.' The inventories that survive from this period indicate the most common household possessions — a chest or rough box, a few stools, perhaps a table or bench, one or two sleeping pallets, some cooking utensils of copper or pewter.[10] Heating the interior was no minor problem, particularly in the more northernly regions. One arrangement commonly resorted to was to bring livestock within the home, in order to benefit from the body heat they radiated.[11] Typically, the house would be in one of two basic styles: two bays on one level, or two stories with one bay each. The livestock would then be kept in either the adjoining or the lower room.[12] Later in our period there

Husa, *et al.*, *Traditional Crafts and Skills* (London, 1967), pp. 26–27 and *passim*.

10. See H. S. Bennett, *Life on the English Manor* (Cambridge, Eng., 1960, first published 1937), pp. 233 f.; Duby, *L'Économie Rurale, op. cit.*, pp. 529–530, 607; J. G. Hurst, 'The Medieval Peasant House,' in A. Small, ed., *The Fourth Viking Congress; York, 1961* (Edinburgh, 1965); and M. W. Labarge, *A Baronial Household of the Thirteenth Century* (New York, 1965), pp. 34 f.

11. M. W. Barley, *The English Farmhouse and Cottage* (London, 1961), p. 10.

12. R. K. Field, 'Worcestershire Peasant Buildings, Household

appears to have been a trend in favour of the latter design. Fires, too, would be needed, for cooking as well as for heating. Fuel was normally gathered from the ground-wood of the common and the wastes and also, with the lord's permission, from the forests and woods. In addition, peat was used as a fuel.

Reflection on the peasant's style of life suggests how very mild were the expressions of market demand arising from this quarter. Certainly the aggregate demand generated in feeding, clothing and housing this class was substantial, for this was the largest single group in the society, accounting for 80 to 90 per cent of the population. But much of what was consumed he produced for himself, while some was provided by his lord by terms of the leasing agreement. Only for a small portion of his total needs did he resort to the market. This is an important feature of the medieval economy, one which it shares with others that have not experienced modern economic growth.

When we turn our attention away from the peasants and towards other classes in the society we immediately encounter severe problems of terminology and of nomenclature. The traditional division of medieval society into those who hunted and fought, those who worked and those who prayed is really a drastic simplification; and this is most true with respect to the first category. In the Middle Ages nobility was essentially a function of birth, and so there was no necessary correlation between social station and economic position. Thus it could well be the case that some of the most prosperous peasants, though inferior socially to those we may term the lesser gentry, were nonetheless economically superior. Land was the principal source of wealth in this economy, and noble birth was usually associated with hereditary lordship over some lands. Yet there were always younger sons, whose best recourse might be the accession to some ecclesiastical office — the term 'lords of the Church' was a very meaningful designation. And, of course, wealth could be dissipated, and title to lands lost for a variety of reasons. Some nobles whose lordships were of only modest extent might be economically indistinguishable from the most well-to-do peasants, even though the legal distinctions would remain. The range of economic status within the aristocracy was thus tremendous, and the differences in standards of living between the lower gentry and members of the royal or superior religious courts were immense. It thus can become quite meaningless to speak of 'the lords' or 'the nobles,' and this great diversity needs always to be kept firmly in mind. However, one must somehow deal with the members of these groups even though distortion and some violence to the reality are inevitable. The following discussion will have reference to the wealthy members of medieval society, comprised of a very few of the most prosperous peasants, the nobles and others whose lordships were of substantial amounts of lands or of revenues, the various administrative officials, particularly those of the manors, and the economically successful artisans, craftsmen, merchants and landlords in the towns and cities.

These members of the middle and upper classes, though numerically a tiny minority in the total population, could generate important levels and concentrations of demand. It is clear, for instance, that their food consumption was on average greater than was that of the peasants. They ate the light bread made from the wheat which the peasants grew but did not consume. Beyond this, greater abundance and variety of foods were the distinguishing features of their diets.[13] There was, in fact, a rather strong tendency towards conspicuous consumption which, as always, was a social phenomenon. Social rank, dignity and prestige, particularly among the courtly households, found one expression in the number of and style in which retainers were supported.[14] In a society in which many often go hungry,

13. See, e.g., Labarge, *Baronial Household*, ch. 4; W. E. Mead, *The English Medieval Feast* (London, 1931).

14. Duby, *L'Économie Rurale, op. cit.*, pp. 221 f.; W. O. Hassall, *How*

dining acquires great social import: if the peasant's ideal of a proper celebration was to feast, the wealthy individual displayed his superiority by frequent feasting.

Provisioning of the middle and upper class households must therefore have had an impact upon the structure of demand. The nature of this impact was in part a function of the specific relationships. Insofar as the wealthy had dependent peasants who discharged their obligations in the form of labour services on the lord's demesne and/or as payments in kind, to a greater or lesser extent the lord's food consumption did not involve recourse to markets.[15] On the other hand, when revenues took the form of money payments, the wealthy would have to purchase their food. In general, the trend over this period — though far from unilinear — was towards the commutation of peasant dues to a monetary basis: the percentage of tenurial contracts acquitted by money payments was much larger in 1500 than it had been five or six hundred years earlier. This was of great importance, for even if the peasant marketed some of his production solely in order to be able to pay his rents and other dues, he nevertheless became more and more familiar with the processes of buying and selling in the market. And the wealthy, for their part, became accustomed to relying on the market for the satisfaction of their needs and wants. The significance of these developments should not be ignored.

The wealthy constituted an important source of demand not only for the basic commodities available locally, such as grains, fish, meat and dairy products, but also, as their diets were more varied, for many amenities of more specialised incidence and production. For example, the

---

They Lived (Oxford 1962), pp. 130, 149–152; and Labarge, *Baronial Household*, *op. cit.*, pp. 53 f. Also see the interesting comments of Sir John Hicks, *A Theory of Economic History* (Oxford, 1969), pp. 22–23.

15. See, for example, the commodities which certain Swiss peasants were to deliver as payments in kind; document No. 79, in G. Franz, ed., *Quellen zur Geschichte der deutschen Bauernstandes im Mittelalter* (Darmstadt 1967).

Gascon and Bordeaux wines which crossed the Channel were intended for their cups, not for those of the English peasant.[16] The special products from the lands bordering the Mediterranean were enjoyed far to the north of their natural provinces. And the most obvious category of all is spices. Tastes, of course, varied from one region to another; but the difficulties of preservation and the limitations of the contemporary transportation technology were responsible for reinforcing differences in taste and probably did more to maintain them than any other factor.

The middle and upper classes also accounted for an important segment of the demand for cloths, fabrics and other furnishings. This was before the day of mass markets for inexpensive, coarser textiles, and the spinners and weavers catered much more to the desires of the wealthy: 'finery' is not for the common folk. Just as we noted in the case of diets, so the consumption of clothing had and has a social function. Fine cloths and refined apparel were reserved for those of 'quality.' Where the price mechanism was inadequate to the enforcement of social prerogatives, legislation was available. Sumptuary acts, regulating dress and clothing in detail, kept the rural and urban poor — and even the middle classes — in their places. The association of such legislation with periods of secularly rising wage rates bears articulate witness to the sensitivity of the authorities to any sartorial excesses on the part of their 'inferiors.'[17]

These wealthier groups were also consumers on a large scale of the various timber products. Much wood was required for warming the large, damp and draughty rooms of their residences; and there was the additional need to

16. See M. K. James, 'The Fluctuations of the Anglo-Gascon Wine Trade during the Fourteenth Century', *Economic History Review*, ser. 2, IV (1951); and Y. Renouard, 'Le grand commerce des vins de Gascogne au Moyen Age', *Revue Historique*, CCXXI (1959). Also see the discussion by Labarge, *Baronial Household, op cit.*, Chapter 6.

17. See, e.g., F. E. Baldwin, *Sumptuary Legislation and Personal Regulation in England* (Baltimore, 1926); Franz, *Quellen, op. cit.*, documents No. 82 and 122; Hassall, *How They Lived, op. cit.*, p. 196.

furnish them. Timber was also used in construction, though in the houses of the well-to-do it was gradually displaced by stone and other masonry. This transition was substantially accomplished during the thirteenth century in the northern parts of Europe and somewhat earlier to the south, where stands of timber became much more scarce at an earlier date.[18]

The preceding discussion has dealt with members of the middle and upper classes of medieval society in general, applying as well to those who resided in the countryside as to those resident in the towns and cities. For many purposes this is the most convenient framework in which to analyse patterns of consumption. However, we want also to note certain features peculiar to the urban sector of the economy. The most obvious point is that the inhabitants of towns and cities had to rely to a very great extent upon markets to satisfy their needs. This applies above all to the problem of food supply. It is true that some residents of towns, particularly the smaller ones, might receive produce from lands which they held in the surrounding region; as landlords, they were entitled to a share of the crop or to rents which could be paid in kind. But on balance this met only a small fraction of the total demand; and it is certainly clear that towns and cities represented a strong source of demand to large and small agricultural producers alike.

It is also clear that the material standard of living of someone in the lower strata of urban society was broadly similar to that of his rural counterpart, and that such an individual was required to devote virtually all of his budget to securing the most basic necessities of life. His diet was probably even more heavily dependent upon grains than was the peasant's, for the latter possessed opportunities for gardening, the keeping of a few animals, hunting and foraging which the urban poor did not. In aggregate, the total market demand generated by urban inhabitants must

18. See G. P. Jones, 'Building in Stone in Medieval Western Europe,' Chapter 8 of Volume II in the *Cambridge Economic History of Europe* (Cambridge, Eng., 1952), especially section 1.

have been of quite substantial magnitude; moreover, it grew significantly, in both relative and absolute terms, over this period.

Housing, too, was a problem for the town dweller. An excess of demand over supply for urban housing is a phenomenon neither confined nor original to the modern era; such a state of affairs was probably the normal one in towns and cities of medieval Europe. The consequences were the same then as they are today; the poor were wretchedly, yet not inexpensively, housed — if anything, they were even worse off than many peasants. For their part, the middle and upper classes had to spend a large chunk of their incomes in obtaining somewhat more comfortable accommodations. At any rate, what this means is that a considerable volume of housing units was being supplied, which in turn implies a sizeable demand for the construction materials, for the transportation services required to move these materials, and for labour services at the construction sites.

Having said this, it is important to avoid placing too much emphasis upon the urban sector of the medieval economy. Urban life is, after all, present in every peasant economy. Medieval Europe was an agrarian society which was, even by the end of our period, only very moderately urbanised. Towns do, I believe, play a strategic role in the economic history of the Middle Ages, particularly in terms of producing or inducing change. But on the level of aggregate demand it is likely that influences of a more common order outweigh those of an exclusively urban character.

We now turn to another important distinct class in medieval society, i.e. the churchmen, and the impact of the medieval Church upon the patterns and structure of demand. It is true of the Church, as of few other things, that it was common to virtually all of western Europe during the Middle Ages. An institution with a centralised administration and an official language, it easily embraced local and regional diversity, linguistic and otherwise. Heir to a sophisticated organisational structure, it permeated and integrated the society, touching the life of every citizen.

There were many significant economic implications from this situation. For example, as has recently been written, 'the only regular taxation with which the population was burdened at the time was that imposed for the benefit of the Church — tithe.'[19] On a somewhat different level, we may note that the demand for fish, already mentioned several times as an important element in the diet, was at least partially a derivative of theological dictates. The consumption of wine had also a connection with religious theory and practice. We may note incidentally that the extension of vineyards, and particularly of those producing the better quality wines, usually occurred around the towns and cities which were the residences of the higher clergy and the location of courts.[20]

Any institution operating on such a scale as did the medieval Church must have left a firm imprint upon the society if for no other reason than sheer numbers. It would be an interesting enterprise to attempt to calculate the ratio of those in holy orders to the total population of medieval Europe at various points in time.[21] To start with, there were the members of the ecclesiastical hierarchy, from lowly parish priest to the papal curia. In addition, there were the regular clergy, the canons, monks, and so on. The former category probably bore some rough but more or less consistent relationship to the size of the overall population, expanding and contracting in mild correlation with the general demographic trends. The relative significance of the latter group, however, probably grew over this period. Cathedrals and monasteries proliferated as the older orders expanded and new ones were established at intervals. Of particular interest in this context are the mendicants, whose sphere of action was the town. The appearance and growing

19. Titow, *English Rural Society, op. cit.,* p. 55.
20. See Duby, *L'Économie Rurale, op. cit.,* p. 237.
21. Some studies in this direction have of course been made; e.g., J. C. Russell, 'The Clerical Population of Medieval England,' *Traditio,* II (1944).

importance of the mendicant orders are indicative of the gradual urbanisation of medieval society.

For the purposes of the present subject, however, separate treatment of the clergy is not really necessary, particularly when discussing patterns of consumption. The fact of the matter is that, in many respects, clerics were economically indistinguishable from other members of their respective social classes. The typical village priest existed on about the same material level as did his flock, and his diet, clothing and housing were broadly analogous to those of his peasant neighbours. At the other end of the spectrum, the consumption patterns of those who resided at court were quite similar whether that court were an ecclesiastical or a secular one. The parallels hold throughout the socio-economic range.

This class homogeneity is of considerable value to the historian of the Middle Ages, for members of the clergy were, on average, more likely to be literate than were most laymen. It is for this reason that so much of medieval history is written in terms of the Church. It was Churchmen who were very often the chroniclers, the recorders of documents, the letter-writers. Were it not for the Church we would know far less of the economic, and other, history of the Middle Ages than we do.

It is appropriate to give one example of the useful information we can derive from this source. Thus far, little has been said specifically about the consumption habits of those in the middle class. As a proxy for this intermediate level of living we may consider the accounts which we have from the household of two chantry priests of fifteenth-century England.[22] They were supported on a modest level by an endowment of rental income. Even though they did produce some of their own food, still from one-half to three-fourths of their budget was devoted to purchases of food, which was

22. K. L. Wood-Legh, *A Small Household of the XVth Century* (Manchester, n.d.). Non-ecclesiastical sources do, of course, exist; compare, for example, 'A Household Expense Roll, 1328,' presented by G. H. Fowler in the *English Historical Review*, LV (1940); and J. Heers, *Le Livre de Comptes de Giovanni Piccamiglio, hommes d'affaires Génois* (Paris, 1959).

mostly bread, meat and ale – wine appears to have been reserved primarily for entertaining the occasional visitors. They consumed beef, mutton and pork which they purchased throughout the year, presumably fresh. They had fish every week. Their diet was enhanced by a variety of semi-luxuries — butter, eggs, milk, figs, raisins, chicken, etc. The provision of fuel accounted for something like one-twentieth of the annual income. The house itself, provided as part of the 'living,' seems to have been comfortable enough.[23] Little is reported concerning the consumption of other items, e.g. textiles.

This description provides a general impression of the standard of living enjoyed by the middle classes, though of course specific details would vary from region to region. In the more southern areas, for example, wine would have replaced ale as the basic beverage consumed.

There are two other topics more or less peculiar to the Church to which some attention should be given. Both involve what was earlier termed 'public consumption.' The first concerns ecclesiastical construction beyond the simple though ubiquitous edifices of village church and chantry, i.e. the larger churches, monasteries and cathedrals. Treating religious construction under the rubric of consumption rather than that of investment is to some extent an arbitrary distinction. Yet it is clear that the construction of cathedrals and monasteries, and worship in them, did constitute consumption for the Church authorities and for the worshippers. There are a variety of activities, such as this type of building and also some of the martial operations characteristic of medieval society, which are very difficult to categorise, often appearing to resemble some kind of 'public service' more than anything else. It has been suggested, regarding this period, that 'significant portions of the total product went into (1) Ecclesiastical or Religious Consumption, (2) Political Consumption, (3) Conspicuous Consump-

23. On the general subject of housing, an excellent study is A. H. Thompson's 'The English House,' reprinted in the superb collection of essays edited by G. Barraclough, *Social Life in Early England* (London, 1960).

tion'.[24] Presuming that certain military activities would be subsumed under the second title, I think that this system of classification is quite relevant, and I will treat this kind of ecclesiastical construction as consumption.

Historians of architecture regrettably have yet to show much interest in the economic implications of their subject. Such topics as the comparison of construction costs for building in various architectural styles, the effects of changes in fashion on the demand for construction materials, and the economic impact of developments in engineering knowledge have hardly been investigated. Similarly, there have been few attempts to assess the economic implications specifically of religious construction. A notable exception is the recent article by Johnson, which concludes that, though felt essentially on the local level, the effects there could well have been substantial.[25] The scattered evidence from other sources inclines one to agree with Johnson's conclusions.

The other aspect of 'public consumption' concerns the welfare functions performed by the Church. In a very real sense, the Church was the welfare state of the Middle Ages; no other institution possessed the wealth, organisation, ubiquity and propensity necessary for this role. The Church offered hospitality for pilgrims and other travellers, primarily in the form of monasteries; hospitals were for these persons, as well as for the aged, the infirm and the ailing. Arrangements were also frequently made for the care of widows and orphans. Doles of bread and other items were often established on a regular basis by the various religious communities.[26] And, as one of the few bodies capable of retaining a surplus from one harvest to the next, in times of distress the Church was often the dispenser of the emergency

24. F. C. Lane, 'Consumption and Economic Change', *Journal of Economic History*, XV (1955).

25. H. T. Johnson, 'Cathedral Building and the Medieval Economy', *Explorations in Entrepreneurial History*, n.s., IV (1967); see also the literature cited there and in the exchange which followed in subsequent numbers of that journal.

26. A typical example occurs in the *Chronica Monasterii de Melsa*, E. A. Bond, ed., Volume II (London, 1943), pp. 64–65.

rations that stood between the disadvantaged and outright starvation.

In some areas, of course, such welfare services were performed also or instead by other agencies — the greater secular lords or, more usually, the town patriciates and urban communal authorities. The activities of these bodies were important and ought not be overlooked. But, in the last resort, it was always to the Church that one turned. The point to be made here is that the volume of goods and services thus consumed must have been large. The 'public' segment was not insignificant in total consumption.

There are a few commodities which deserve particular attention due simply to the sheer magnitude of their total consumption; while individual demand for these items may not have been of tremendous volume, in aggregate their consumption assumes considerable importance. Grain, of course, was the fundamental consumption good of the period; but I have in mind here certain other items that may have enjoyed mass markets. One such commodity, for example, was salt, which was in great demand as the basic — that is to say, virtually the only — preservative for many foodstuffs, e.g. meats, fish, butter.[27]

Wood is another important item of this type. As has already been mentioned, wood, together with peat, was widely used for domestic heating and cooking. It was also the major fuel consumed in those production processes that required combustion at some stage, and demand from this quarter was growing. The rights to gather windfall kindling — not to mention the right to fell fresh timber — were jealously guarded and protected. Records from the period often reflect the valuable nature of such rights in forest or woodland by the prices attached to their transfer.

The history and significance of forests and woodlands in the medieval economy has yet to be written. A separate volume would be needed to do justice to the subject.[28] In

27. Cf. Duby, *L'Économie Rurale, op. cit.*, p. 252.
28. See the comments of Titow, *English Rural Society, op. cit.*, p. 51.

the present context only brief mention can be made of the various elements of demand which were related to this source.

Timber remained throughout this period the single most important construction material. It constituted the basic structural support for much of the housing, particularly the more modest residences. Construction in urban as well as rural areas relied heavily upon wood. Houses, shops, tools and equipment in the towns, and agricultural buildings and implements in the country, absorbed large quantities of timber of different qualities and characteristics. Moreover, shipbuilding relied exclusively upon wood construction and, given the contemporary technology, replacement alone would have generated a substantial level of demand; this, together with the general expansion of water transportation during this period, had the result that the demand for timber for ship construction was strong and sustained most of the time.[29]

Timber, of course, is not a homogeneous category. For many purposes, as for example interior finishing or for certain types of furniture, some types of woods are preferable to others. For these reasons one of the major items in the regional trade of medieval Europe was higher quality timber of specific characteristics.

Timber was not the only product of value which the woods afforded. Many items of medicinal or dietary nature could be gathered there, for the consumption of the peasants or their lords. Wild and domestic pigs foraged for acorns and roots. Branches were always sought for constructing the fences to confine or exclude livestock to or from certain fields and areas, as their seasonal usage rotated. It is really not to be wondered at that so much of the litigation and other less civilised disputes revolved around questions concerning the use of forests and woodlands: they constituted a valuable resource.

Another instance of very broad and generalised demand might be the case of candles. It is perhaps difficult for us, in this age, to appreciate what it means to operate in a

29. See Duby, *L'Économie Rurale, op. cit.*, pp. 244 f.

world which is largely governed by the passage of the sun. Yet for medieval man, the open hearth or the use of candles (supplemented somewhat by the burning of bulrushes, oil or tallow) were the only alternatives to darkness when the sun was hidden.[30] Although it is true that candles made from wax remained a semi-luxury for the poor throughout the Middle Ages, it is clear that the demand for them arising from the other classes could be quite strong; and it is not without reason that the candlestick maker appears so regularly in scenes from the life of the period. When in addition to the practical matter of illumination one considers the demand resulting from the religious use of candles, the level of consumption of this commodity can be presumed to have been substantial.

Finally, mention might be made of the demand for services. The subjects of transportation services and those services which were mainly of a commercial nature, particularly banking and insurance, are very adequately treated in the literature.[31] However, many other more common services seem to me to have been unduly neglected, e.g. those of the local brewer, miller, baker, blacksmith, carpenter, barber (who was also the surgeon and bloodletter), etc. Furthermore, there were numerous domestics, such as nurses, laundresses, and so on, who served the urban and rural wealthy.[32] Mols cites figures for the proportion of servants in town populations of the fifteenth century, for example, which range from 9 to 18 per cent.[33] It is generally the case in pre-industrial societies that the volume of consumption of these and other services is quite high as a proportion of total consumption; and I suspect that this

30. See the comments of E. E. Power, *Medieval People* (London, 1924), p. 23; and Labarge, *Baronial Household, op. cit.*, pp. 36, 99 f., and 120.

31. See, *inter alia*, R. S. Lopez, 'The Evolution of Land Transport in the Middle Ages', *Past and Present*, 9 (1956); this was originally published in *Bollettino Civico dell' Instituto Colombiano* (1953), which was not available to this author.

32. See, e.g., Labarge, *Baronial Household, op. cit.*, Chapter 3.

33. R. Mols, *Introduction à la Demographie Historique*, Volume II (Louvain, 1955), p. 181.

description applies as well to the medieval economy. A detailed investigation of this subject would certainly be a valuable contribution to our knowledge of medieval economic history; and a comparison of the relative importance of the secondary and tertiary sectors might produce some provocative conclusions.

It is appropriate now to turn directly to some consideration of the subject of investment demand. Unfortunately, questions of the investment component of demand in the medieval economy are even less well studied and murkier than those of consumption. Until quite recently, few scholars had addressed themselves to this problem. What follows here, then, must of necessity be even more brief, general and tentative than the preceding discussion of consumption.

The largest sector in the economy, agriculture, suggests itself as an obvious point of departure. Some observations concerning investment are implicit in the earlier discussion of consumption patterns and levels. It is intuitively clear, for instance, that peasants simply had little or no capacity for investment out of their own resources.[34] In the normal course of things it was a struggle just to secure the basic necessities of life. The few pieces of capital equipment which a peasant might have to work with — primarily agricultural implements — were crude affairs either provided by his lord as part of the tenure agreement or made by himself. (The incapacity of the average peasant cultivator is reflected in the evidence from share-cropping areas where the peasant cultivator was unable to supply from his own resources even the seed for planting.) Insofar as these were durable goods, they would be passed along from one generation to the next.[35]

In addition to the severe limitations on the peasant's ability to invest, there were also certain institutional relationships of an adverse nature. The conditions of tenure

34. See the comments of S. Pollard and D. W. Crossley, *The Wealth of Britain* (London, 1968), pp. 35 f., and Chapters 1–2, *passim*.

35. See R. K. Field, *op. cit.* in *Medieval Archaeology*.

often meant that the peasant had claim to only a small portion of any increase he might achieve in production. Moreover, the communal regulations under which so much agricultural production was carried out could make it difficult or impossible to introduce innovations raising productivity. The combination of these institutional disincentives with the severely limited means of the average producer largely account for the very low rate of investment in agriculture; although the marginal productivity of capital in this sector could frequently be quite high, it was not possible for him to translate this into effective demand for investment.

The investment in agriculture which did occur, therefore, must be viewed as resulting largely from the activities of the landlords and others who cultivated and produced on a greater scale. These were the parties likely to have the ability as well as incentive to invest. The scattered and imperfect indications and figures suggest an average of 4 to 5 per cent of revenues devoted to investment as a reasonable estimate for this class. It must be emphasised, however, that the figures refer to gross investment and thus include a sizeable component for the replacement of depreciated capital stock, mainly buildings. Net capital formation would rarely have constituted as much as half of the gross investment ratio; a level of 1 or 2 per cent for net investment is probably quite representative.[36] Much of this investment by landlords, moreover, would have taken the form of land improvement or irrigation, reclamation of waste, and so on. This is not to disparage such forms of capitalisation; indeed, in some of the more progressive agricultural regions such capital formation was of great importance. The irrigation canals of the Low Countries and the Po Valley are one example of the potential value of this type of investment. The point to be emphasised, however, is that much of the

36. A few examples can be found in F. G. Davenport, *The Economic Development of a Norfolk Manor, 1086–1565* (London, 1906), pp. 37 f.; E. Robo, *Mediaeval Farnham* (Farnham, 1935), pp. 6–7; and document No. 19 ('The Cost of a New Barn') in Titow, *English Rural Society, op. cit.*

net investment in agriculture represented capital widening (i.e. the extension of given and constant technologies to new lands) more often than capital deepening.

The question of capital investment in land must be treated carefully. With a given technology, the exchange or purchase of arable (i.e. land under cultivation) normally does not constitute productive investment but merely a transfer of ownership. However, if the purpose or at least the result of acquisition is consolidation, then it is possible that some capital formation takes place. Conversely, the dispersion, partition and fragmentation of land holdings must be regarded as disinvestment; and we know that these processes reached significant proportions at various times and places in medieval Europe. In general, this type of disinvestment is correlated with increasing population densities on the land, although this is not invariably the case and some major exceptions do occur (e.g. in northern and central Italy, from the eleventh century onwards, increasing population densities might be prevented by legislation from inducing increased disintegration of holdings).

One of the most important embodiments of capital in medieval agriculture was livestock.[37] Animals were, in relative terms, expensive to acquire and costly to maintain. In the absence of specialised fodder crops and stall feeding, animal husbandry requires extensive land utilisation; and, as compared with arable devoted to grain production, it is inefficient as a supplier of foods — and especially of calories — for human consumption. It is not difficult to understand, then, why the average agricultural producer was normally unable to keep livestock in optimal proportions with other factors of production, i.e. to supplement human labour and to supply fertiliser for the land. Beyond a certain point, animals begin to compete with humans for the use of the land; and, in general, the densities of the two populations vary inversely (though plagues among either

37. Though this importance is generally recognised, as yet little work has been done in this area. See, however, the important study by M. M. Postan, 'Village Livestock in the Thirteenth Century,' *Economic History Review*, ser. 2, XV (1962).

humans or animals could disturb these trends). As pointed out earlier, this can have a deleterious effect on patterns of consumption: generally, in the more thickly settled areas of medieval Europe the average level of *per capita* consumption of animal products was significantly lower than in the less populated areas.[38]

Shifting the focus away from agriculture, the problems of capital formation become even more complex. We have come to regard economically underdeveloped societies as often being 'dual economies,' with a 'traditional' primary sector on the one hand and a 'capitalistic' secondary sector on the other. But this was not the situation in the Middle Ages. Industry was predominantly at the handicraft stage, employing very little fixed capital equipment; and, as J. R. Hicks has recently commented, 'handicraft industry . . . is barely distinguishable from trade.'[39] Human capital in the form of skilled and experienced craftsmen was probably at least as important as physical capital.

The few instances of capital-intensive production that existed in medieval Europe were those associated with the mining and metallurgical trades, and with the shipbuilding and shipping industries. The mining of various ores and certain phases in the production of metal products could require substantial capital investment; and mines and forges constituted a major component of the total fixed capital in the economy. Mills were another major category in fixed capital stock. Mills powered by animate energy, by water and, later in the period, by wind were to be found in every region of Europe. Most were for the grinding of grains for bread and beer, and also for the pressing of oils; but growing numbers were constructed for use in the metallurgical trades and even for the fulling of cloth in the textile industry. The facilities of shipyards, and ships themselves, also represent large chunks of fixed capital.

Fixed capital, however, was not the only requirement. Pollard has argued convincingly that, for the early phases of the industrial revolution in Britain, working capital was

38. See the references cited note 7, above.
39. *A Theory of Economic History, op. cit.*, p. 141.

of considerably greater importance than fixed.[40] I believe
that this applied *a fortiori* to the medieval economy. Much
research still needs to be done in this area; but one has only
to reflect upon the sizeable amounts of capital that must
have been tied up in stores of raw materials, inventories of
finished goods, and stocks of goods in transit, to appreciate
how great was the demand for working capital. Again,
shipping is a typical example of a trade in which capital
investment in the form of working capital was of significant
proportions. It is important to note that this relationship
between fixed and working capital results in the fact that
the aggregate capital/output ratio for the economy was considerably higher than is often assumed. Due basically to the
state of communications and transportation technology, the
demand for working capital was very substantial; but the
increases in productivity which result from this kind of
investment usually are quite minor. Commercial capital
was of much greater importance than industrial capital.
The returns to investment thus accrued largely to merchants
rather than to producers. Indicative of this is the fact that
the precocious development of credit instruments during
the latter part of this period is almost exclusively associated
with the needs of the commercial sector.[41]

The structure and patterns of investment demand have
some implications for the operation of capital markets. Such
markets were, of course, much less efficacious and sophisticated than those which have developed with the modern
economy, but they did exist and they were able to provide
some mobility to capital assets. The capital market, however, was of quite uneven incidence among the several
sectors of the economy. In agriculture, as has been seen,
most of the investment was undertaken by the larger,
wealthy producers; and their financing was usually internal,
from their own resources. It was not uncommon for
members of the middle and upper classes to borrow — and

40. S. Pollard, 'Fixed Capital in the Industrial Revolution in Britain,'
Journal of Economic History, XXIV (1964).

41. See R. S. Lopez and I. W. Raymond, eds., *Medieval Trade in the
Mediterranean World* (New York, 1955), especially Part 3.

frequently to over-extend themselves — for the purpose of undertaking some construction or the purchase of land; and the debts so incurred could often become burdensome and troublesome. The interest charges on such loans might be fairly high, but this reflected a risk premium against default rather than any expected real rate of return on the investment. The point here is that such credit extensions seldom represented investment in productive capital formation.

It was, of course, unlikely that the average peasant producer would dispose over a surplus sufficient to permit self-financing of productive investment. As argued earlier, his opportunities for new capital formation were few; and this situation, together with the large element of risk which was intrinsic to agricultural production at this stage, meant that it was extremely difficult for the smaller cultivator to secure a loan for purposes of productive investment. Among peasants, by far the most common from of debt was the consumption loan.[42] This should not be surprising, for it has been seen that many were living on the true margin of subsistence. Loans of this type were normally short-term, often extending from the planting season to harvest time, and were usually payable in kind. Interest rates charged on consumption loans might easily reach 100 per cent or more, and were almost purely exploitative. Again, these did not represent debt contraction with the object or result of productive investment.

It was in the secondary sector that capital markets were most applicable; and, as the description of the relative roles of fixed *versus* working capital suggests, the most active market was that involved with the creation of commercial credit. The rates of interest obtainable on credit extension for production or commercial ventures were substantially inflated by discounts for risk and uncertainty.[43] They are

42. See Duby, *L'Économie Rurale, op. cit.*, pp. 492 f.

43. For an analytical discussion of the importance of the risk and uncertainty margins, see D. C. North, 'Innovation and the Diffusion of Technology: A Theoretical Framework,' forthcoming in the *Proceedings of the Fourth International Conference of Economic History; Bloomington, 1968*.

thus very unreliable as measures of expected gains from productivity increases, and the recorded interest rates from the period must be interpreted with great care. Moreover, the credit instruments do not always make clear the kind of loan which is involved; and the statements often disguise the real terms, or report only the amount to be repaid, so that it is impossible to calculate the true rate of interest. It was obviously in the urban setting that capital markets were of the greatest importance. Yet in general we are still quite ill-informed on this subject for the medieval period. The list of Bernau burghers, for example, who, in 1461, were indebted to the Jewish money-lenders there, raises far more questions than it answers.[44] One can only speculate as to the terms of the loans, the purposes for which they were contracted, and so on. This is a topic that would certainly reward scholarly attention.

As a final category, we may note the contribution of a small volume of 'public investment.' This could take many forms. Certain individuals and agencies might assume the responsibility for the construction and upkeep of such facilities as roads, bridges, harbours and waterways.[45] In the cities, in addition, there might be the maintenance of the town walls, the supply of some very rudimentary sanitation, and the provision of such facilities as water supplies, public baths, hospitals, etc. Where the town authorities or other officials concerned met the costs of such investments by means of a general levy, then this taxation began to assume (or resume) a truly public character.

Most of this public investment had to do with the formation of what is termed social overhead capital. Such investment may well be highly desirable and even a necessary condition for further economic growth; but the immediate and direct rates of return on this type of capital formation normally are not very large. One of the striking differences in the composition of demand in the medieval as opposed

44. Presented by G. Sello in *Forschungen zur Brandenburgischen und Preussischen Geschichte*, IV (1891).

45. Concerning bridges, for example, see Labarge, *Baronial Household*, *op. cit.*, p. 155.

to a modern economy is precisely the minor component of productive public investment in the former.

This essay began by affirming the advances achieved in the state of our knowledge concerning the medieval economy. The intervening pages have hopefully served at least to indicate that much still remains to be done. A number of the points that have been touched upon in this discussion of the patterns and structure of demand are clearly in need of further investigation and elaboration. The agenda for future research is imposing.

BIBLIOGRAPHY

Very little literature exists that is addressed directly to the subject of the patterns and structure of demand in the medieval economy. The following references make no pretension to comprehensiveness, but merely indicate a few suggestions for introduction to the various topics.

On the broader conceptual or theoretical level the obvious starting point is J. M. Keynes, *The General Theory of Employment Interest and Money* (New York, 1936). Keynes's appreciation of the important role of demand was anticipated, in a limited sense, by E. W. Gilboy, 'Demand as a Factor in the Industrial Revolution,' which first appeared in the Festschrift for E. F. Gay, *Facts and Factors in Economic History* (Cambridge, Mass., 1932), and has now been reprinted in R. M. Hartwell, ed., *The Causes of the Industrial Revolution in England* (London, 1967). The much later essay by Gilboy, *A Primer on the Economics of Consumption* (New York, 1968), is also worth consulting.

For a general historical introduction, the most competent and complete treatment is G. Duby, *L'Économie Rurale et la Vie des Campagnes dans l'Occident Médiéval* (Paris, 1962), which is also available in English. Also useful are B. H. Slicher van Bath, *The Agrarian History of Western Europe A.D. 500–1850* (O. Ordish, trans., London, 1963); and C. T. Smith, *Historical Geography of Western Europe Before 1800* (London, 1967). For a discussion of a special sub-period of major economic change, see H. A. Miskimin, *The Economy of Early Renaissance Europe 1300–1460* (Englewood Cliffs, 1969).

Information on consumption in the medieval economy is quite varied. There are, first of all, those sources which may be termed antiquarian studies. These are very numerous and can be quite valuable to the historian. A couple of typical examples might be: H. T. Turner, ed., *Manners and Household Expenses of the Thirteenth and Fifteenth Centuries* (Roxburghe Club, 1841); and U. T. Holmes, Jr., *Daily Living in the Twelfth Century* (Madison, 1962).

There is also much material contained in the various

bulletins in the 'Enquêtes ouvertes' series on 'Vie matérielle et comportements biologiques' beginning in 1961, in the *Annales: Économies, Sociétés, Civilisations.*

For a very brief and general introduction to the topic there is the interesting essay by A. E. Levett, *The Consumer in History* (London, 1929).

The work of W. Sombart is important for its early recognition of the significance of consumption patterns. The two standard works are his *Der moderne Kapitalismus* (Leipzig, 1902) and *Luxus und Kapitalismus* (2nd ed., Munich, 1922), the latter available in English translation.

Finally, there is a vast number of specific treatments and monographs. Representatives from this large group could include the fine study of E. Fiumi, 'Economia e vita privata dei fiorentini nelle rivelazioni statistiche di Giovanni Villani,' *Archivio Storica Italiano*, III (1953); and G. Luzzatoo, 'Il costa della vita a Venezia nel Trecento', in his *Studi di Storia Economica Venezia* (Padua, 1954). The second edition of W. Abel's *Agrarkrisen und Agrarkonjunktur* (Hamburg and Berlin, 1966) is a competent and useful synthesis and interpretation of information from the field of price history. The study by D. Knoop and G. P. Jones, *The Medieval Mason* (3rd ed., Manchester, 1967), contains a wealth of material, particularly on the matter of wage rates; similar works dealing with other trades are very much to be desired. A. R. Bridbury's *England and the Salt Trade in the Later Middle Ages* (Oxford, 1955) is a model which could profitably be followed for the study of other items which entered into the trade of medieval Europe. Imitation would also be welcome of the fine article by Y. Renouard: 'La consommation des grands vins de Bourbonnais et de Bourgogne à la cour pontificale d'Avignon,' *Annales de Bourgogne*, XXIV (1952), reprinted in Renouard's *Etudes D'Histoire Medievale*; or that of E. Baratier, 'Production et exportation du vin du terroir de Marseille du XIIIᵉ au XVIᵉ siecle', *Bulletin Philogique et Historique* (1959).

On the topic of investment in the medieval economy the state of the literature reaches its nadir. Only in the past few years has really serious work begun. We now have invaluable surveys from two of Britain's foremost medieval economic historians: R. H. Hilton's 'Rent and Capital Formation in Feudal Society,' *Proceedings of the Second International Conference of Economic History; Aix-en-Provence, 1962* (Paris, 1965); and M. M. Postan's 'Investment in Medieval Agriculture,' *Journal of Economic History*, XXVII (1967). The titles notwithstanding, however, both of these articles refer almost exclusively to England.

The nearest thing that we have to a general discussion of the existence and functioning of a capital market is by a scholar who is not a professional historian, i.e. Part 2 of S. Homer's *A History of Interest Rates* (New Brunswick, 1963).

Additional references may be found in the footnotes to the text. The standard reference remains the *Cambridge Economic History of Europe*, Vols. I–III, which is particularly strong on topics relating to towns.

4. The Expansion of Technology 500-1500

Lynn White Jr

The growth of technology is the least developed and most rapidly shifting part of economic history. Historians prefer to work with ample documents such as have been left to us by merchants, bankers and landowners—those who manipulate goods. Unfortunately the peasants, craftsmen and engineers who produce the goods have generally provided sparse words. The state of records and the tastes of historians have thus combined to distort past activities. Today our view is being somewhat rectified by a surge of interest in studying, with what evidence is available, improved methods of production and transportation, the emergence of new types of goods, and changing ways of living and thinking which altered the market for goods and the kinds of investment.

This essay attempts to codify what we now know about the development of the more important branches of technology in Europe during the millennium before Columbus, Vasco da Gama and Magellan broke Ocean's barrier and opened the first global epoch in human history: the four hundred and fifty years of European imperialism.

The millennial span of the Middle Ages has inherent fascination simply as a phenomenon, but to us who stand at the end of the European Age it has the additional interest of being the period during which Europe built up the self-confidence and the technical competence which, after 1500, enabled it to invade the rest of the world, conquering, looting, trading and colonising. Romans were as predatory as were early modern Europeans, but the Romans were not equipped to spread their dominance far beyond the basin of the Mediterranean. They lacked (1) the agricultural productivity, (2) the industrial skills, (3) the superiority in weapons, and, (4) the nautical arts available in Europe by 1500. The implementation which made possible Europe's overseas expansion was largely medieval.

We know little about the psychic elements influencing the degree of technological dynamism in a society. Necessity explains nothing until the need is felt, and we cannot yet tell why some groups respond to needs—or desires—which in other groups remain unformulated and unfilled. Presumably the attitude of a culture towards technological improvement is related to what most of its participants think about man's relation to nature, about the degree of reverence which one should show towards tradition, about the amount of autonomy which the individual possesses in relation to the established order, both human and natural, and about the respectability of manual labour. Several sophisticated cultures, notably that of India, have shown relatively little interest in technological change. Others, like China from the Han dynasty until the Ming, have been vastly creative in this area.

This essay will record, but will not try to explain, the observable fact that from about the sixth century Europe began to show innovations in technology more significant than those found in the more elaborate, neighbouring, and kindred cultures of Byzantium and Islam. By the middle of the fourteenth century, after the invention of the mechanical clock had increased the number of artisans skilled in making intricate metal machines, Europe surpassed China and seized global leadership in technology. Some innovations were borrowed, notably from China; others were internally generated. The end result of medieval developments was the physical equipment of the early modern capitalist world.

Because practically all the written records and famous monuments of Antiquity were produced in cities, we generally think of ancient societies as having been essentially urban. They were, in fact, agricultural to a degree which we can scarcely grasp. It is a conservative guess that even in fairly prosperous regions over ten people were needed on the land to enable a single person to live away from the land. Cities were atolls of civilisation (etymologically 'citification') on an ocean of rural primitivism. They were supported by a terrifyingly slender margin of surplus agricultural production which could be destroyed swiftly by drought, flood, plague, social disorder or warfare. Since the peasants were closest to the sources of food, in time of hunger they secreted what they could and prevented supplies from reaching the cities. This reduced city populations both directly by starvation and indirectly by destroying the country market for goods made in the cities.

Urban life, and the higher realms of culture of which the ancient cities were creators and custodians, were fragile because ancient agriculture had a low level of productivity per peasant. Despite their ruthlessness and their talent for law, the Romans were at last defeated politically by this fundamental technological weakness. The great plague of the late second century and the anarchy of the third century crumbled a society that was inherently friable.

Agriculture had been invented in the Near East in a form suited to that region's light soils and arid climate. The basic tool was the scratch plough drawn by a pair of oxen. Half the arable was planted each autumn; the other half lay fallow to renew its strength. The plough did not turn a furrow but merely disturbed the soil; cross-ploughing was needed to pulverise the earth in order to prevent evaporation of the scanty moisture and to bring subsoil nutrients to the surface by capillary attraction.

Slowly, over millennia, the Near East had built up a dense, although impoverished, rural population capable of sustaining the semi-circle of large cities which lay around the Eastern Mediterranean from Alexandria to Thessalonica. While this region was badly injured by the plague and by the chaos of the third century, it had resources to provide fairly rapid reconstruction. The Byzantines of the sixth century, the Muslims of the seventh and eighth, were quite unaware that they had declined and fallen. But in the north-western provinces, which in any case were the most recently civilised and the most thinly populated of the Roman Empire, there was indeed a catastrophic and long continued disintegration of urban culture which the myopia of Western historians has seen wrongly as the general human condition during the early Middle Ages.

The essential reason for this collapse in the Occident was that the part of the Empire north of the Western Mediterranean and the Ebro, and especially north of the Alps and the Loire, was agriculturally the weakest in the Roman world. The methods of cultivation invented in the Near East and early introduced to Europe were not operable there except in well drained sandy or chalky soils of low fertility. In the Near East the problem had been to preserve water; in the North the problem was how to drain the fields. The best soils of the North were alluvial; many were sticky clays which the originally southern scratch plough could scarcely handle.

The Romans were not stupid. We have evidence that in Gaul, Britain, Germany and the Po Valley they attempted new agricultural methods. For example, Pliny tells us of an eight-ox wheeled plough used in the Alpine region. But we know from Vergil that this wheeled plough had a curved pole; therefore it was not the stout and efficient medieval wheeled plough which had a quadrangular frame. Despite their experiments, the Romans never managed to adapt the imported pattern of Near Eastern agriculture to the radically different soils and climate of their north-western region. This failure does much to explain the lack of resilience in the West, as compared with the East, from the third to the eighth centuries.

The prime event in Europe's history during the early Middle Ages was the development, between the sixth and the late eighth centuries, of a novel system of agriculture appropriate to the northern lands. As its elements emerged, consolidated into a new pattern of cultivation and spread, it proved to be the most productive agrarian method, in relation to man-power, that the world had seen. By Charlemagne's time its impact was sufficient to shift the centre of European culture away from the shores of the Mediterranean to the great northern plains where it has remained ever since. The ravages of Vikings in the ninth century, and of Magyars in the early tenth, delayed further beneficent effects until the later tenth century. But somewhat before the year 1000 we begin to observe a steady and rapid increase of population, urbanism and commerce over much of the West which is unintelligible apart from increased quantities of food and an improved peasant productivity which allowed a larger proportion of the population to leave tillage for other pursuits.

The agricultural revolution of the early Middle Ages began, obscurely, in the sixth century with the appearance, among the Slavs, of the heavy wheeled plough. Since in *Lex Salica* of the early sixth century the Rhineland Germans were still using the word *carruca* to mean a two-wheeled cart, they had not yet received it; but in *Lex Alemannorum* of the 720's *carruca* had come to mean the new wheeled plough. It had moved into the Po Valley a bit earlier: there it is mentioned in 643. In the present state of the evidence, it did not reach Britain until the Norse invasions of the ninth century.

There were variant forms of the heavy plough, and the diffusion and applications of these are in much debate. Nevertheless, its general effect is clear.

Its first great advantage was that it could handle heavy soils which produced larger crops than the light soils normally cultivated with the scratch plough. Second, human labour was spared by the fact that the heavy plough's mould-board turned the furrow, thus making cross-ploughing unnecessary. Third, the drainage of fields was helped by a new pattern of ploughing in long strips: the mould-board normally turned the furrow towards the right, thus gradually mounding the dirt towards the centre of the strip and providing a drainage furrow between strips. Clearly, the northern peasant had at last found a plough suited to his ecology.

To adopt it, however, was no simple matter. The vertical coulter (a knife to cut the sod in the line of the furrow), the horizontal plough-share, and the angled mould-board to tear loose and overturn the sliced earth, combined to offer far more friction with the soil than the old plough. While the scratch plough was habitually pulled by a yoke of two oxen, the new plough often demanded eight. But few peasants would own eight oxen. The solution was a pooling of the oxen of several peasants in a joint plough team, and division of ploughed strips according to what each put into the pool. Such a pooling, however, would be difficult in meagrely populated areas, or in settlements so small that the death or theft of a couple of oxen would destroy the pool. Thus while the new plough eventually increased population by increasing food production, it could not be adopted without a certain initial density of settlement.

Yet, paradoxically, the existence of a fairly dense peasantry was itself an obstacle to its adoption. Since the scratch plough demanded cross-ploughing, it generally produced squarish fields. The laying out of the long strips which were the most efficient field-shape for the heavy plough would destroy all existing field-marks and individual property rights. Psychologically this would be so difficult that we may safely assume that the new plough spread primarily through the reclamation of land hitherto un-cultivated or long abandoned. Fearful plagues struck once more in the sixth century, which probably marks the nadir of population in Europe after the long decline of the Late Roman Empire. Thereafter there are scattered, but increasing, evidence of land clearance and new settlement. Presumably the heavy plough dominated many of the freshly reclaimed areas in Northern Europe.

The psychological shock involved in making the social adjustments necessary to use the heavy plough may help us to understand the openness of the later medieval mentality towards technological change or towards change in general. The novel shaping of fields into strips involved radically new patterns of peasant co-operation even broader than the organisation of joint plough teams. Squarish fields could efficiently be fenced, but it would have been folly to fence fields laid out in strips. The new plough demanded that all the cultivated land of a village be split into two large 'open' fields, one for the autumn planting, the other to be left fallow for a year to regain its fertility. Each of these two big fields was normally fenced or hedged against animals, but there were no barriers between the privately owned strips within each field. This meant that all cultivation had to be carried out under the strict control of a village council: the times of ploughing, sowing, harrowing and harvesting were regulated for each community not simply according to tradition but in relation to variations of weather and other factors. The heavy plough of Northern Europe reduced individualism but built among the peasants a strong system of self-government for their own affairs. When the increase of agricultural surplus enabled more peasants to move to cities, they carried with them a habit of communal autonomy far more vivid than anything known under the Roman Empire. As soon as cities started to grow in Europe once more, they began struggling, often with success, to turn themselves into burgher communes free of all but nominal allegiance to a higher authority.

The open-field method had some significant by-products. Under Romans, Germans, and Celts the cultivation of cereals was not, as a rule, closely related to animal husbandry, although naturally every scratch plough needed its pair of oxen. In the earlier period the cattle and sheep of a village generally foraged in the forest or on wild pasture. As a result, their manure was lost. Under the two-field system, animals often browsed on the fallow field or on the stubble of the sown field after the harvest. Thus their droppings on the open fields fattened the next harvest.

The scythe is the symbol of an extension of this fusion of the Germanic herding economy with the cereal agriculture of the Mediterranean. While Roman scythes exist, they are so rare that their dating was long doubted. They are the typical tool for haying, and under the Franks scythes, haying and stall-feeding of cattle became so common that Charlemagne tried to change the name of July to 'Haying Month.' The manure from barns was carefully saved for spreading on the fields. Thus by the eighth century the northern peasantry had worked out an agrarian pattern which produced more meat, dairy products, hides and wool than ever before, but at the same time improved the harvest of grain.

In the late eighth century another notable advance appears on the fertile plains between the Seine and the Rhine. There is some evidence that in the Baltic region peasants had long planted their crops in the spring rather than in the autumn as was the Mediterranean habit. In Charlemagne's reign we find some peasants dividing their lands not into two fields but into three: a fallow, an autumn field sown chiefly in wheat, rye and barley, and a spring field planted largely with oats and plants of the bean family. Since this new three-field system put greater strain on the soil than had the older two-field rotation, it could be applied only to lands of great inherent fertility, despite the fact that the extensive use of plants of the bean family in the spring planting, by putting nitrogen into the earth, reinforced its productivity.

The advantages of the three-field pattern over the two-field were considerable. Two plantings at different seasons added insurance against crop failure and resulting famine. With three fields rather than two, the labour of ploughing could be spread more evenly throughout the year. For intricate reasons internal to the system, a shift from a two-field to a three-field economy enabled a peasant community to increase its production per peasant by about fifty per cent, provided that enough new land could be cleared. The result was a vast new wave of reclamation.

Not all northern villages could find new land to take full advantage of the improved technology. Not all soils were rich enough to sustain it. Yet everywhere, in the regions where summer rains made a spring planting feasible, the peasants hastened to get what benefits they could from the new form of agriculture. Where no third field could be found, where the soil was stingy, or where vested interests prevented re-division of the existing two fields into three, they usually divided the planted field into two (often unequal) parts, sowing one in the autumn and the other in the spring. The peasants knew their business, and they were not conservative when they saw better ways of doing things. The stupid yokel is a myth invented by city-dwellers who have forgotten their rural ancestors.

The increase in cultivation of peas, beans, lentils and chickpeas in the spring planting of the triennial rotation raised the consumption of proteins by the common people, presumably with good effect on their energy. But the oat crop which was also typical of the spring planting was perhaps even more important in enabling the European North to exploit horse-power for the first time in agriculture, transport and industry.

From its earliest domestication, the horse had been an adjunct of war. The first harness, the yoke, had been developed for oxen, for whose anatomy it is appropriate. But yokes are amazingly inefficient on horses: they strangle the neck and prevent adequate breathing and circulation of blood to the head, with the result that a pair of yoked horses can pull scarcely more than 500 pounds total weight: a light chariot or cart with two men, but not more for any long haul.

Efficient methods of harnessing horses developed either in China or Central Asia and spread westwards. The earlier form, a breast strap attached to lateral shafts, first appears in Europe in an Irish bas relief credited to the eighth century. The commoner form of modern horse harness, a rigid collar attached to the load by shafts or traces, is first found in a Carolingian miniature of about the year 800. With the new harness, which was not notably more expensive than the old type, horses could pull between four and five times the load which they could draw with the yoke. Now, for the first time, horses were available for heavy field labour and for hauling. Moreover, since horses move much faster than oxen, and do about twice as much work in a day as oxen do, the saving of human labour by substituting the horse for the ox was great.

But again, there were obstacles. Oxen require little grain fodder to work well; horses need much grain. The best grain for horses is oats. The necessary surplus of oats was produced by the spring planting of the three-field rotation. By the latter part of the Middle Ages there is a definite geographic correlation between the triennial rotation and the use of the horse in agriculture and transport. Except for limited areas in Northern Spain, Provence and Northern Italy, summer rains were insufficient south of the Loire and the Alps to permit substitution of the three-field for the two-field system. The result was that, with regional exceptions, the Mediterranean peasant lacked the quantity of oats which would enable him to abandon the slow ox for the swifter, but more costly, horse as a farm animal. This is a major reason for the relatively more rapid expansion of Northern European culture during the later Middle Ages.

Another obstacle to the economic use of the horse is the fragility of its hoofs, especially in moist climates like that of Northern Europe. A century ago Roman, and even Celtic, nailed horseshoes were common in European museums. The failure of any ancient text to mention them, or of any ancient monument to show them, led to renewed scrutiny of the archaeological evidence. At present only the English are able to find Roman nailed horseshoes. Why this very useful invention should have required some seven centuries to cross the Channel is unexplained. In Eurasia the horseshoe appeared almost simultaneously about the year 900 in Central Siberia, in Byzantium and in Germany. The fact that our first evidence of horses ploughing habitually comes from Norway in the late ninth century may be related to this development.

The swiftness of the horse made it particularly time-saving in harrowing to cover the seed, break the clods, and smooth the fields to facilitate the harvest. A new form of spiked harrow was invented, and the first evidence of horse-harrowing comes from Southern Germany about 1050.

Because the horse is a fast and impetuous creature, the modern harness had to be supplemented before horses could be used for heavy hauling. If the load is attached directly to the traces, a left turn puts all the strain on the right trace, and *vice versa*, with resultant risk of breaking the harness and overturning the wagon. Probably a horse could plough or harrow with traces directly attached, because furrows tend to go in straight lines. But roads do not. The solution was the whipple tree, a rod hinged at its middle to the centre of the load and attached at each tip to the end of one of the traces. Its function is to equalise the tension on both traces. It first appears in the Bayeux Tapestry not later than 1077. The whipple tree made possible the building of large wagons for farmers and merchants, and these appear in the early twelfth century as *longae carretae* holding much goods or many people.

The heavy plough, open fields, the new integration of agriculture and herding, three-field rotation, modern horse-harness, nailed horseshoes and the whipple tree had combined into a total system of agrarian exploitation by the year 1100 to provide a zone of peasant prosperity stretching across Northern Europe from the Atlantic to the Dnieper. A curious Latin poem, *Ruodlieb*, written in Southern Germany about 1050, gives us incidental glimpses of a rough but immensely vigorous and productive peasant society for which there is no precedent in earlier history. That society was the product of the agricultural revolution which had occurred during the previous five hundred years.

During the next centuries there were no comparable improvements in agrarian technology, at least in the North. Refinements of cultivation, such as additional ploughings of the fallow, increased production but perhaps at a cost in labour which made them doubtful economically. As population grew in response to the new supplies of food, marginal land was reclaimed which was soon worn out and abandoned. By the late thirteenth century the agriculture of the North was showing strains. The catastrophes of the fourteenth century produced new problems to which there was little technological response, and the condition of the northern peasantry in many regions seems steadily to have worsened.

The history of Mediterranean agricultural technology is less well known than that of the North. For climatic reasons the South could not widely adopt the triennial rotation and thus, as we have seen, it could not convert from ox to horse in its farming operations. Nevertheless it begins to appear that in the eleventh century, when Northern Europe was ceasing to innovate in agriculture, Northern Italy was starting to make notable improvements which help us to understand the vigour of that region in later generations.

For a thousand years the Po Valley has been the economic heart of Italy. Today a film of water flows over it from Alps and Apennines, directed by an astonishing web of canals, great and small. The result is an intensive and vastly productive agriculture. The Romans had practised irrigation, but in no such sophisticated way. One suspects, but cannot yet prove, Islamic influence conveying out of India methods first developed for such Indic crops as rice, cotton and sugar cane which require, or flourish best with, such irrigation. The beginnings of this network are at least as early as the eleventh century, In 1177 and 1229 Milan built, primarily for irrigation, the Naviglio Grande and the Muzza which remain today the largest canals in the region. Less ambitious projects were undertaken elsewhere, particularly in Tuscany.

Italy was also the door by which many crops and, even animals, were introduced from Asia to Europe. The water buffalo, a sturdy creature under the yoke and a source of rich milk, arrived from India about the year 600 but did not spread widely outside Italy. Sorghum came from sub-Saharan Africa in the ninth century. In the late tenth century mulberries and silk worms, ultimately from China, were grown near Brescia. At an unknown date somewhat later durum wheat, so rich in protein, arrived from Islam, and by the early fourteenth century (perhaps under Chinese influence) pasta made of durum flour was common in many forms. In the later fifteenth century the cultivation of rice was introduced, first to the lower Arno and then to the Po Valley. With intensive irrigation and gardening, the Italians took particular interest in new fruits and vegetables: cantaloups (from Armenia), asparagus, artichokes, apricots and the like. As these spread northward, the diet of Europe was much improved.

During the early Middle Ages in the North, and during the later Middle Ages in Northern Italy, new food-producing technologies were developed which effected so large and relatively constant a surplus that urban culture ceased to be precarious as it had been in Antiquity. Moreover, the efficiency of the individual peasant became such that a higher proportion of the population—exactly how much higher we do not know—could move to the cities. Even the grisly demographic decline of the fourteenth and fifteenth centuries did not affect the new ratio of rural to urban populations: the roots of the modern trend towards increasing urbanisation lie in the technological originality of medieval rustics.

Throughout the Middle Ages water-mills were much more common than churches. They were also more distinctive, since every society has had shrines but few have had power machines. Water-mills appeared almost simultaneously in China, Denmark and Northern Anatolia in the first century before Christ, but in Europe they did not spread rapidly until the early Middle Ages. By 1086, William the Conqueror's *Domesday Book* records that the 3,000 settlements in England—most of them very small—averaged nearly two mills apiece. While we have no comparable statistics from a large area of the Continent, there is every reason to believe that the same general pattern prevailed there. By the eleventh century everyone in Europe, North and South, was living daily in the presence of powered labour-saving engines. Every sizeable community had millwrights to make and repair them.

For more than nine centuries after its first appearance we have no firm evidence that anyone in Europe used water-power for any process other than grinding grain. Then, perhaps in 822 but certainly in 861—both instances are in Picardy—the mill for making mash for beer appears. This is the more important because there is some reason to believe that a new machine was involved: a series of vertical stamps activated by cams on the axle of the water-wheel. Probably by 990 in the Dauphiné, but certainly by 1040 both at Grenoble and Lérins, such stamp-mills were used for processing hemp and fulling cloth. By 1087 the fulling mill had reached the borders of Normandy, and thereafter it spread all over France, continuing to England and Germany by the late twelfth century. Fulling was laborious, and the new process revolutionised the textile industry to the point where its focus in England shifted during the thirteenth century from the south-east towards the north-west where mill sites were more easily available.

Next to textiles, the chief industry was metallurgy. In late Frankish times the production and use of iron increased, replacing bronze for most purposes. For example, the ornamental elaboration of iron hinges and braces on doors has not been traced earlier than the tenth century. Peasants were using more iron tools: we have mentioned the scythe. As we shall see, armour was becoming heavier. But iron is a difficult metal to work, requiring great force and high temperatures. The appearance in Southern Germany, before 1028, of the place-name Schmidmühlen suggests that blacksmiths were already using water-wheels to power the hammers or bellows of their forges. Yet definitive evidence of water-power in the metal industries is long delayed: in 1135 there is a powered ore-stamp in Styria; a knife-grinding mill appears in Normandy in 1204; by 1224 in Southern Sweden a mill is mentioned 'where iron is worked.' The thirteenth century provides evidence of the mechanisation of forges from Calabria in the south to Britain and Silesia in the north. By 1269 in Moravia there is clear indication of hydraulic bellows in smelting operations, and by 1384 cast iron was being produced at Liège. In Augsburg wire was being drawn by water-power in 1351, while the metal-cutting mill appears near Nevers in 1443. Once invented, each new device spread widely.

During the later Middle Ages there was a passion for the mechanisation of industry such as no other culture had known. There were tanbark mills near Paris in 1135; the first sawmill dates from 1204 in Normandy; in the Forez by 1251 there was even a mill to grind mustard and in Artois, by 1348, one for preparing pigments; in 1433

Dauphiné had a water-driven lathe. By the later fifteenth century any large industrial city like Milan or Augsburg can be pictured much as a mid-sixteenth-century traveller described Bologna: a sluice from the river Reno provided water 'to turn various machines . . . to grind grain, to make copper pots and weapons of war, to pound herbs as well as oakgalls [for dyeing], to spin silk, polish arms, sharpen various instruments, saw planks.' The Europe which rose to global dominance about 1500 had an industrial capacity and skill vastly greater than that of any of the cultures of Asia—not to mention Africa or America—which it challenged.

The forward surge of European machine technology from the eleventh century onwards must be understood not as an accumulation of isolated items but as a single phenomenon of prime historical importance. Areas so flat that the fall of streams was too sluggish for mills felt deprived; so in 1044 we find the first tidal mills operating in the Venetian lagoons. Vertical-axle windmills were first invented in the tenth century in Eastern Persia, but there is no firm evidence that they ever spread to other parts of Islam. The horizontal-axle windmill appeared in Yorkshire in 1185 as an independent invention; within seven years German Crusaders took it to Syria; within ten years the papacy was trying to tax it. By the early fourteenth century an English chronicler lamented that the search for long beams for the vanes of windmills was a major cause of deforestation.

Along with the quest for new sources and applications of power went a notable development of machine design.

The basic means of linking reciprocating with continuous rotary motion is the crank. It was known in China under the Han dynasty but does not appear in the West until about the year 830, near Rheims. Since the crank is a mechanical element which can spread only as part of a larger device, and since it appears in Europe first on the rotary grindstone and then on the hurdy-gurdy neither of which was used in China, it was probably reinvented in the West. By the early twelfth century cranks were in common use in Europe. The compound crank turns up in 1335 as part of machine sketches of dubious practicality made by an Italian physician in the service of the Queen of France. The idea did not enter the general consciousness until the 1420's when an unknown Flemish carpenter or shipwright invented the bit and brace. Now that it was in the hands of artisans, the idea spread quickly: by about 1440 compound cranks and connecting rods were appearing in machines in Germany and Italy.

The natural motions of the body being reciprocating, the conscious thrust of late medieval machine design was towards exploring and amplifying the novelty of continuous rotary motion. By 1122-23 the book of a German Benedictine monk, Theophilus, describes the earliest flywheels to equalise such rotation. It is curious that the pendulum, which serves the same function for reciprocating motion, was unknown until Leonardo da Vinci and was not widely applied to machine design until the work of Jacques Besson, first completely published in 1578: enthusiasm for the new led to prolonged neglect of the implications of the old.

The cam occurs twice in Hero of Alexandria's toy machines, but its first practical use was probably in the Carolingian beer mills mentioned above. It was basic to the whole later development of automation. For example, the first automatic machine having more than a single motion was a sawmill sketched about 1235 by the Picard engineer Villard de Honnecourt: the cutting stroke of the saw is effected by cams on the axle of a water-wheel; the return stroke depends on a sapling spring (a thirteenth-century novelty); while a spiked wheel on the axle serves as a feed to keep the log pressed against the saw.

The greatest triumph of late medieval machine design was the weight-driven clock. Its invention must be understood in the context of its time. By about 1260 the English Franciscan, Friar Roger Bacon, was foreseeing a world of automobiles, submarines and airplanes. About 1267 a surgeon who was also an Italian bishop remarked that 'every day a new instrument and a new method is invented' for extraction of arrows. In a sermon preached in Santa Maria

Novella in Florence in 1306, the speaker, while providing us with the best evidence for the Tuscan discovery of eye-glasses in the 1280's, is in essence singing the praises of the current technological movement. Not all the arts, he says, have yet been found: 'There are many which have not yet been discovered. Every day you could find one, and there would still be new ones to find . . . It is not twenty years since there was discovered the art of making spectacles which help one to see well, an art which is one of the best and most necessary in the world. And that is such a short time ago that a new art which never before existed was discovered. I myself saw the man who found and practised it, and I spoke with him.'

Here was a mood without historical precedent: it marks the invention of invention as a total project. It was the mood of Europe's technicians from the later thirteenth century onwards.

Thanks to massive translations of Greek and Arabic treatises during the twelfth and thirteenth centuries, astrology experienced a great revival. By the later thirteenth century a good physician was also an astrologer because the casting of nativities was essential to diagnosis and cure of disease. Professional medical skill depended in part on ability to make exact observations of astronomical transits. But water-clocks were unsatisfactory, especially in the chilly North where at night they tended to freeze. Some new time-measuring device was needed.

Sand-glasses were unsatisfactory not merely because the sand quickly enlarged the orifice through which it flowed: the prime difficulty was that, unlike a liquid, sand does not lie level to permit exact calibration. It was not until the early fourteenth century that the sand-glass's problem of abrasion was solved by developing the standard 'sand' therafter used in it: finely powdered eggshell. Even then it was chiefly useful on shipboard for measuring watches of equal length.

In 1269 a Picard military engineer, Peter of Maricourt, suggests that a sphere of magnetic iron, mounted without friction parallel to the axis of Earth, would rotate once daily in sympathy with the celestial spheres and thus would make the perfect clock. Unfortunately no one could mount it without friction and test the theory, In 1271 Robert the Englishman talks about plans for a weight-driven clock but admits that the problem of the escapement has not quite been worked out. At almost the same time, at the court of Alfonso the Wise of Castile, Rabbi Isaac ben Sid of Toledo discusses not only new kinds of water-clocks which, he asserts, are far superior to anything known in the past: he also describes, with a diagram, a weight-driven clock equipped with a brake consisting of an internally compartmented drum containing mercury flowing through small holes from section to section. Clearly, many men of high intelligence were working on the clock problem from the 1260's onward. Apparently it was not until the 1330's that the definitive solution was found in two forms: the verge and the wheel escapements.

Then, almost explosively, mechanical clocks spread over Europe. The most intricate of them was completed in 1364 by Giovanni de' Dondi who was professor of medicine and astrology successively at the Universities of Pavia and Padua. Its gearing and the perfect co-ordination of hundreds of moving metal parts—for it was a planetarium and a perpetual calendar as well as a clock—mark it as one of the great achievements of mankind.

The diffusion of clocks created an increasing corps of craftsmen to make and repair them, and able to carry their skills into related fields. From the middle of the fourteenth century—a dismal age in most ways—the velocity of European technical growth increases markedly.

New products and new markets helped the process onward in ways which we are only beginning to understand. The printed book may illustrate the point.

The spinning-wheel—which, incidentally, offers the first example in Europe of the cord drive—was known in eleventh-century China and appears in the West at Speyer about 1280. The appearance of the heddle-treadle loom in the 1190's (perhaps also ultimately from China) had so speeded up the production of common cloth that one weaver could keep several spinners busy providing yarn, and thus spinning had become a relatively more costly part of making textiles. The new spinning-wheel, although it still lacked the flyer (which appears in the 1480's) and the treadle (which is of the 1520's), increased yarn production and thus cheapened the common grades of cloth. The fourteenth century therefore saw a vast increase in the consumption of linen in particular: shirts, underclothes, sheets, towels, handkerchiefs, napkins and the like. This meant that there was a growing quantity of linen rags, the European raw material for paper.

Paper was a Chinese invention, diffused to Islam in the eighth century. There is no firm evidence that paper-making in Islam was ever mechanised. It is typical of the distinctive medieval European style of technology that the first two instances of paper manufacture in Latin Christendom—at Fabriano in 1276 and Xátiva in 1280—both involved water-powered preparation of the pulp. This lowered the price of paper, and the supply of rags during the next century presumably lowered it further. Parchment and vellum continued to be costly, and the parchment for a large Bible is estimated to have taken the hides of between 200 and 300 sheep. While Gutenberg printed occasionally on vellum, it would not have been economically feasible to invest in the elaborate apparatus needed for printing if the proportion of the cost of a book going into the material of the pages had remained so high. Not merely paper but cheap paper was a presupposition of the invention of printing.

The increase of urban life, commerce and general communication put a premium on literacy and thus increased the market for books. But that market was also much enlarged by the invention of eyeglasses, as noted earlier, in late thirteenth-century Tuscany. Lenses had been in use among scientists like Roger Bacon for two or three decades before eyeglasses developed, but it would seem that spectacles were far less a practical application of optics than an empirical outgrowth of the recent Italian invention of a perfectly clear glass and new methods of cutting gems, crystal and glass. A preacher at Santa Maria Novella in 1306 implies that many of his audience are using them, and towards the middle of the century Petrarch boasts that he has never found them necessary, leading one to believe that by then they were normal for men of his age. In earlier generations educated men had spent their youth reading and their presbyopic decades talking. From the end of the thirteenth century one could read for a lifetime, and the market for books obviously waxed.

Yet, before printing, books remained fearfully costly because, despite the cheapening of paper, vast labour of a literate copyist went into each volume, and rising demand kept the price high. It has been estimated that in the 1440's, while Gutenberg in Mainz was perfecting printing with cast movable type, the annual salary of an average professor in the University of Pavia, if entirely spent on books, would purchase less than two volumes of law (which were bulky) and ten in medicine. Gutenberg, by saving expensive labour, brought the cost of books within the reach of a huge potential market, with the result that in the second half of the fifteenth century printing became a major European industry. But Gutenberg's achievement, and the nature of the market it served, must be understood in the context of items like the spinning wheel, optical glass and water-powered mills for pulping rags. The dynamism of late medieval industry involved stimuli of many sorts: innovation bred more innovation. The Europe which, after 1500 enveloped the globe, was equipped to do so by an ever accelerating quest for natural power, labour-saving mechanisms and new productive skills which had started about the year 1000 and which continues at the end of the twentieth century.

Medieval Europe likewise showed unprecedented talent in developing the arts of slaughter. Mankind has always made war, but most war has been inefficient. Beginning in the eighth century, Europe led the world in improving military technology.

The most significant invention in the history of warfare

prior to gunpowder was the stirrup. So long as a mounted warrior had to cling to his horse with his knees, his actions could not involve much direct assault: archery and javelins were the favoured weapons; sword-play was limited; and the lance was generally wielded at the end of the arm. A two-handed lance was attempted, but since this could not be used in conjuction with a shield it was satisfactory only when cavalry fought footmen.

In conjunction with a saddle having a high pommel and cantle, stirrups welded horse and rider into a single organism. The long lance could now be held 'at rest' under the right armpit; the fighter's hand merely guided the blow, which was delivered by the impetus of a charging warhorse. The increase in violence was immense.

The germinal idea of the stirrup appeared in the late second century B.C. in India as a loose surcingle under the belly of a horse to support the rider's feet. Soon small rings were added into which the big toes were stuck. The idea spread to China, where, because the climate demanded shoes, the stirrup was enlarged by the fifth century to fit the whole foot. In the late seventh century the stirrup swept westward from China, reaching the Muslim armies in Iran in 694 and arriving in the Frankish kingdom about 730.

The Franks were thus among the last of the horse-riding peoples to get the stirrup, but they were the first to realise its radical implications. Charles Martel, or his military advisers, decided that the new method of mounted shock combat was by far the most effective available and that the Frankish army, which had been composed almost entirely of infantry, must be swiftly reoriented towards cavalry equipped and trained in the new style. In 732 he began confiscating church lands and distributing them to vassals on condition that they stand ready to fight in the improved way. When he met and defeated Muslim invaders from Spain at Poitiers in 733, his army—like theirs—was still overwhelmingly on foot, but exasperation at lack of mobility which prevented him from exploiting victory adequately led him to push on swiftly with his military reforms. More lands were confiscated, the Church was compensated at the expense of the common people by the establishment of tithes, and a new class of warriors was created, endowed and obligated to do battle in the latest fashion.

Mounted shock combat, of which the stirrup is the technical presupposition, is the key not only to the essential feudal institution of knight's service, but also to understanding the knight's self-image and most aspects of chivalric ('horsy') culture. The new mode of fighting was so difficult that to practise it one had to start as a youth with other young men who developed a corporate sense of their unique function. The most admired sport was the joust which stylised mounted shock combat with maximum magnificence. The pennon, originally a cloth nailed on a spear shaft behind the blade to prevent such deep penetration of the victim that retraction of the weapon would be difficult, became ornamented with personal insignia. As the mounting violence of warfare required always heavier armour masking the wearer, these symbols spread over shield and surcoat for identification, soon becoming the 'arms' of aristocracy. Even when the feudal warriors developed into a governing as well as a military *élite*, they thought of themselves as ruling because of their ability to fight rather than as fighting because of their right to rule: if they ceased to fight at the call of the liege lord, their endowment was, in theory, forfeited.

The violence of shock combat profoundly affected the metal industries because of the constant quest for stronger armour. Down to the later thirteenth century, except for helmets which were made of riveted plates, armour consisted of mail, or of plates or rings sewn on quilted garments. In the thirteenth century the application of water-power to forging led to the gradual replacement of such coverings by plate armour. By the end of the fifteenth century a good suit of armour was both a work of art and a superb technological achievement involving close articulation of scores of shaped steel plates.

By that time, however, armour was nearly obsolete for military purposes, although, like the tournament, it was valued as a status symbol. Europe was developing missiles to the point where no metal carapace was an effective defence.

The process began with the emergence, towards the end of the eleventh century, of a powerful crossbow which both Byzantines and Arabs regarded as a Frankish novelty, and which they quickly adopted as they did most Western military innovations. But the next change was not in hand weapons but rather to a new form of artillery.

In 1004 the Chinese were using a huge stone-thrower consisting of a beam pivoted on a frame and activated by men pulling in unison on ropes at the end of the beam away from the sling. It appears in Europe in 1147 in the hands of French soldiers besieging the Muslim city of Lisbon. During the assault on Lisbon this engine was operated by shifts of 100 men. To save labour, by the end of the century a caisson of earth or rocks had been placed at the short end of the pivoted beam; this could be raised slowly by capstan and pulley, and then the shot released by a trigger. In addition to reducing manpower costs, this trebuchet, as it was called, made possible an accuracy of aim impossible in the gang-operated form in which the speed and force of the pull would vary. With the same weight of both caisson and missile, and the same length of sling and beam, one could hit the same spot on a fortress wall repeatedly and gradually shatter the masonry. Quickly it was realised that friction of the air with the bullet also made a difference. By 1244 round trebuchet stones were being produced in England exactly calibrated to engineer's specifications: the cannon-ball before the cannon. The trebuchet proved so useful that the torsion and tension artillery inherited from the ancient world fell out of use.

The fact that in 1248 saltpetre was being called 'Chinese snow' in Egypt probably indicates that gunpowder reached Europe through Islam from China. In 1258 rockets were used at Cologne, and a year or so later Roger Bacon knew them. The question of whether the cannon (i.e., a metal tube from which expanding gases expel a missile) was first invented in China or Europe is not yet clear. Cannons appear in the West in the 1320's, and with certainty in

China only in 1332. Islam got the cannon from the West, as did Japan in the sixteenth century. Contact between Europe and China in the early fourteenth century was so vivid that the borrowing may have been in either direction.

The impact of gunpowder artillery on Europe was slow to develop, and hand guns did not become serious weapons until the second half of the fifteenth century. Nevertheless, by 1500 Europeans had by far the best equipment in the world for military purposes, and they had built up a large chemical industry to supply gunpowder as well as heavy metallurgy to provide cannons. They had built an arsenal adequate for global conquest.

To reach the trans-Oceanic parts of the world, Europe needed ships and nautical methods appropriate to long voyages on the brine.

Advance beyond the Roman level began in the sixth century. As early as the first century B.C., fore-and-aft rigs, permitting tacking against the wind, were sometimes used on small boats running about a Mediterranean harbour or among the Greek islands. No such rig, however, was applied in Roman times to a big merchant ship, presumably because the design of keels did not keep up with that of sails. Tacking without a keel biting deep into the water involves considerable sideward drift. On short trips, always within sight of land, allowance can be made for such drift. Large ships, however, sailing for days beyond sight of land (as the Romans often did), would have found accurate navigation impossible in such circumstances and would therefore have preferred square sails and a general avoidance of tacking, although this could be managed, painfully, even with a square sail. Towards the middle of the sixth century, in the harbour of Marseilles, we find three large merchant ships called *latenae*, i.e., equipped with lateen sails. Evidently the keels of such vessels were getting deep enough to permit efficient tacking with its considerable advantages.

Some time in the Middle Ages a change in the procedure

for building ships occurred which must have revolutionised the economics of maritime commerce. Today we take it for granted that in constructing a ship one first lays a keel, then builds the skeleton of ribs, and finally nails the skin of the hull to that skeleton. Recent evidence shows that, as late as the Emperor Heraclius (610-641), Mediterranean shipwrights (like those of the Indian Ocean and the Vikings) went about their business 'backward': first they built up the shell of the hull, laboriously joining each plank to the one beneath by mortices, tenons and dowels; when the shell was finished they sculptured and inserted into the hull whatever ribs and braces were necessary. This method built a strong ship, but one very costly of labour even in a slave society. The medieval invention of the skeleton-first sequence notably reduced the investment necessary to build a ship, and thus increased the profit on capital. We have at present no sure evidence of the new method in the Mediterranean before the eleventh century, but one is tempted to guess that the change was related to the new burst of seaborne commerce during the tenth century in such Italian ports as Amalfi, Venice and Pisa. The date may some day be provided by underwater archaeology.

Another great advance both in safety and in profit was caused by the arrival of the magnetic compass in Europe from China in the last decade of the twelfth century; within a few years it was widely employed. By the late thirteenth century the compass, and the amazingly detailed sea charts which were developed on the basis of it in the Mediterranean, enabled a ship from a western city like Venice or Genoa which formerly had made only a single voyage to the Levant during the year to make two such trips. Obviously the return on capital would be much improved, sailors would be better employed, and the tempo of trade would grow more lively.

In the North during the early thirteenth century another essential step towards modern navigation was taken. All early rudders were lateral oars. Practically all modern rudders are hinged firmly to the sternpost of the ship. The lateral oar is much more vulnerable to breakage in ocean storms than is the modern rudder. The fitter form, which is first shown on a baptismal font in Winchester Cathedral and on the seals of North Sea and Baltic cities, was adopted in the Mediterranean during the fourteenth century.

By the end of the thirteenth century some adventurous Europeans felt ready for global voyaging. In 1291 two Genoese ships equipped by the Vivaldi family sailed through the Strait of Gibraltar to reach the treasures of India. The expedition was not heard of again. During the next two centuries Portuguese, Spaniards, Italians, Flemings and Normans probed deep westwards and southwards into the Atlantic, finding and colonising new islands, perfecting their rigging and hulls to cope with oceanic conditions, and enlarging their repertory of navigational methods. In the last decade of the fifteenth century, sailing sturdy vessels armoured with invincible cannons, Europeans seized the rule of both the Indies.

By 1500 the technological dynamism of the Middle Ages had provided Europe with a steady supply of food, a mechanical and industrial competence, an advantage in arms, and a skill in venturing upon the sea which enabled Westerners of that age to weld the hitherto separate histories of peoples into a single experience of all mankind. This was an epochal act: it could happen only once.

But the creativity of the Middle Ages is better viewed by us who approach the year 2000 than by the men of 1500. Much that was done by medieval technicians lay dormant for centuries: its implications did not emerge until much later.

One set of illustrations may demonstrate the point. The later Middle Ages were much interested in the uses of air. About 1010 an Anglo-Saxon Benedictine monk named Eilmer built a glider, took off from the tower of Malmesbury Abbey, and flew six hundred feet. He crashed and broke his legs because, according to his own diagnosis, he forgot to put a tail on the rear end—'caudam in posteriore parte.' In the later twelfth century, as we have seen, the horizontal-axle windmill appeared in the North Sea region. Perhaps by the middle of the thirteenth century and certainly in the fourteenth, the resistance of air was being used in fan escapements to decelerate the fall of the weight in striking trains, first of water-clocks and then of mechanical clocks. By 1425 the blowgun had reached Europe bringing its Malay name with it (Malay *sumpitan*; Arabic *zabatāna*; Italian *cerbottana*; English *sarbacand*), and this led to experiments with air-guns and air pressures. In 1474 a Nuremberg picture shows a winehandler using a specialised form of bellows to force wine through a tube from one cask to another. The notebook of a Sienese engineer of the 1430's shows the earliest of several fifteenth-century pictures of a whirligig top for children which was perhaps borrowed from China and which, at the end of the century, inspired Leonardo's helicopter design. This same Sienese manuscript also shows the first suction pump, which uses air pressure to raise water. Finally no later than the early 1480's an anonymous Italian engineer in the Sienese tradition invented the ideas of the parachute. Within a very few years Leonardo sketched another.

Among all these devices only the windmill and the suction pump spread and developed with any speed. Eilmer of Malmesbury was never forgotten—for example John Milton mentions him—and his feat was known to the pioneers of aviation in the nineteenth century. Nevertheless, there was little point in gliding until men saw some prospect of an engine to propel the glider. The helicopter suffered the same handicap: until a very light but powerful motor was available, it was a technological dead-end street. The air-gun and suction pump were the chief empirical bases for continuing scientific studies of vacua and pressures, but contributed to no further important technological developments until the harnessing of steam in the eighteenth century. Compressed air for transporting materials—first massively applied to the handling of grain in the late 1800's—could not be widely developed until powerful blowing machines were developed with more flexibility of location than is possible for a water-wheel. As for the parachute, which first reached publication in 1615 in a famous book of machines by Fausto Veranzio, a Dalmatian bishop, it had no function until the emergence of ballooning in the late eighteenth century. But when, after three hundred years in which the idea of the parachute lay dormant, a use for it developed, it was available in the Western consciousness. Today the parachute is basic to the retrieval of space capsules, not to mention its massive military applications. No small part of the modern world's debt to the technicians of the Middle Ages arises out of their purely speculative adventurousness. They originated many ideas which were not immediately, or soon, applicable but which, like recessive conceptual genes, lay idle in the repertory of engineers until new needs and new circumstances made them feasible.

Technological creativity was consonant with the spirit of Western medieval culture. The monks, for centuries the most learned group in the society, were dedicated to work as a form of worship. In the twelfth century the contemporary biographer of St. Bernard describes with pride the series of water-wheels in his Abbey of Clairvaux which operated several industrial processes. In 1248, when installing a group of Premonstratensian canons in a decayed monastery, the Archbishop of Mainz praises them as engineers: 'I have found men after my own heart . . . Not only do they give witness of unblemished religion and a holy life, but also they are very active and skilled in building roads, in raising aqueducts, in draining swamps —such as have greatly weakened the monastery in that area—and generally in the mechanic arts.' A century earlier, for the first time in the Western tradition, the canon Hugh of St. Victor had given the mechanic arts a recognised intellectual place in the scheme of human activity. In the middle of the fifteenth century, while the first wave of European world conquerors was growing up, artists suddenly and incongruously clothed the allegorical representation of Temperance, then generally considered the greatest of the seven Virtues, with a panoply of the new technology: on her head she wore that triumph of machine design the mechanical clock; in her right hand she held eyeglasses, the chief new boon to the mature literate man; she stood on a tower windmill, the most recent form (it appears in the 1390's) of the most recent power machine. The late Middle Ages considered its advancing technology profoundly virtuous, a manifestation of obedience to God's command that mankind should rule the Earth. Despite rising doubts, and the secularisation of attitudes once religious, the beneficence of technology remains an axiom of the West.

BIBLIOGRAPHY

The most comprehensive survey of medieval European technology is that by Bertrand Gille in *Histoire générale des techniques*, ed. Maurice Daumas, Vol. I (Paris 1962), 429-598, and Vol. II (1965), 2-139. See also Lynn White, jr., *Medieval Technology and Social Change* (Oxford 1962). *A History of Technology*, ed. Charles Singer, etc., Vols. II (Oxford 1956) and III (1957), is a mine of information but irregular in accuracy. No student of European technology before 1800 can neglect Joseph Needham, *Science and Civilization in China*, 4 vols. in 5, to date (Cambridge, Eng. 1961-65) for European relations with China. Franz M. Feldhaus, *Die Technik der Vorzeit, der geschichtlichen Zeit und der Naturvölker* (Leipzig 1914) is useful over a surprising range of topics, as is Umberto Forti, *Storia della tecnica dal Medioevo al Rinascimento* (Florence 1957).

For northern agricultural technology see the chapter rewritten by Charles Parain in *The Cambridge Economic History of Europe*, Vol. I: *The Agrarian Life of the Middle Ages*, ed. M. M. Postan, 2nd edn. (Cambridge, Eng. 1966), 125-175, and for Italian agriculture the entirely new chapter by Philip Jones, *ibid.*, 352-383; also, primarily for the North, B. H. Slicher van Bath, *The Agrarian History of Western Europe, A.D. 500-1850* (New York 1963). Georges Duby, *L'économie rurale et la vie des campagnes dans l'Occident médiéval*, 2 vols. (Paris 1962) is excellent for the later period but neglects the crucial developments prior to the ninth century.

As regards the exploitation of natural power, Marc Bloch's classic 'The Advent and Triumph of the Watermill,' may now be found in a volume of his selected papers, *Land and Work in Medieval Europe*, tr. J. E. Anderson (Berkeley and Los Angeles 1967), 136-168. A. M. Bautier, 'Les plus anciennes mentions de moulins hydrauliques industriels et de moulins à vent,' *Bulletin philologique et historique* (1960), 567-626, is basic for the region of France, while E. M. Carus-Wilson, 'An Industrial Revolution of the Thirteenth Century,' *Economic History Review*, XI (1941), 39-60, is a model discussion of the fulling mill in England.

The only documented study of waterpower in Europe as a whole is Bradford B. Blaine, *The Application of Waterpower to Industry during the Middle Ages*, doctoral dissertation, University of Calfornia, Los Angeles, 1966.

For the development of machine design, Theodor Beck, *Beiträge zur Geschichte des Maschinenbaues* (Berlin 1899), has not been displaced, but see Bertrand Gille, *Engineers of the Renaissance* (Cambridge, Mass. 1966), and White, *op. cit.*, 103-129; also Carlo M. Cipolla, *Clocks and Culture, 1300-1700* (London 1967).

The stirrup and its implications are discussed by White, *op. cit.*, 1-38, who bases his work on the insights of Richard Lefebvre des Noëttes, *L'attelage, le cheval de selle à travers les âges*, 2 vols., (Paris 1931). For the development of chemical artillery J. R. Partington, *History of Greek Fire and Gunpowder* (Cambridge, Eng. 1960), is basic, although obscure. The relation of both military and nautical technology to the new imperialism is discussed by Carlo M. Cipolla, *Guns and Sails in the Early Phase of European Expansion, 1400-1700* (London 1966).

There is no adequate discussion of the early developments of the fore-and-aft rig. The medieval reversal of the sequence in which a ship was built is established by Lionel Casson. 'Ancient Shipbuilding: New Light on an Old Source,' *Transactions and Proceedings of the American Philological Association*, XCIV (1963), 28-33. The essential study of the sternpost rudder remains Richard Lefebvre des Noëttes, *De la marine antique à la marine moderne* (Paris 1935). On the compass see Frederick C. Lane, 'The Economic Meaning of the Invention of the Compass,' *American Historical Review*, LXVIII (1963), 605-617.

For changing attitudes towards technology, and the development of a unified and speculative attitude towards invention, see Peter Sternagel, *Die artes mechanicae im Mittelalter. Begriffs-und Bedeutungsgeschichte bis zum Ende des 13 Jahrhunderts* (Regensburg 1966), Lynn White, jr., 'The Invention of the Parachute,' *Technology and Culture*, IX (1968), 462-467, and *idem*, 'The Iconography of Temperance and the Virtuousness of Technology,' in *Action and*

Conviction in Early Modern Europe: Essays in Memory of E. Harris Harbison, ed. J. E. Seigel and T. K. Rabb (Princeton 1969), 197-219.

5. Medieval Agriculture 900-1500

Georges Duby

INTRODUCTION

At the start of the tenth century, the unity of European civilisation was an incontestable fact. It was expressed in the notion of Latin Christendom—one faith and one people under Pope and Emperor. It fed on a common cultural inheritance, the bequest of ancient Rome. And—particularly important for our present purpose—it was grounded in a sameness in the way of life: the nations of this part of the world all led very similar lives, they ate more or less the same things, and were all, directly or indirectly, tied to the land and its cultivation. Fundamentally, then, a peasant civilisation rooted in regions tilled by stay-at-home farmers, who alone accounted for almost the total population; the rulers, the priests, the soldiers, the men of affairs, the town craftsmen, all were countrymen for an essential part of their lives. This unity makes it possible to consider our subject in the round. However, in our attempts to get an overall view of the problems, we have to bear in mind that this land was then still extremely diverse. Because the peasant communities kept to their own provinces, their own cantons, their native heaths, extremely isolated in a world of primitive communications, mistrustful of strangers and strangeness, and because each village and seigneurie had its own history and customs, we are constantly forced, when undertaking detailed research, to make adjustments to our generalisations to fit each locality. Any attempt at synthesis is further hampered by three broad groups of differentiating factors:

1. In the first place, we have to consider the diversity of the physical conditions. Agriculture is a war between men and nature: soil, weeds and climate are three wild forces that have still completely to be tamed. But in the Middle Ages the extreme ineffectiveness of farm imple-

ments gave nature an overwhelming superiority over peasant labour. Western Europe is incontestably one of the most varied regions in the world in its local agricultural conditions. Hence, any serious study of rural economy in the Europe of our period requires an intimate knowledge of regional natural geography. In no other field of historical research is the collaboration of the geographer so necessary. In particular, the historian has to appreciate fundamental contrasts from region to region due to differences in climate, the three main types of which are: (a) the mountain regions and the Atlantic seaboard, too wet for good results with the vine and cereal crops, hence fostering grazing and forestry; (b) the Mediterranean regions, suitable for certain plantation crops, but subject to arid summers, violent erosion, and rapid soil exhaustion, necessitating severe measures of drainage and irrigation; (c) the intermediate zone, where the irregular rainfall causes considerable yearly variations in the corn harvests.

2. Further diversity results from conditions that are more strictly historical: the unequal stages of development reached by the different regions of Europe. By 900, some of them, in the north and east, were barely emerging from pre-history; as tribes gradually came to settle down in them, a recognisable landscape began to take shape. On the other hand, in the Mediterranean regions and Gaul, where rural development was much more advanced, many vestiges of a very ancient organisation still existed: the network of markets, the structure of the great demesnes, the use of written contracts. In many French provinces—Périgord or Mâconnais, for example—the rural landscape was little different at the start of the tenth century from what it is now, or had already been seven centuries earlier at the end of the Roman colonisation. These differences in regional development are behind certain permanent time-lags in the evolution of the medieval economy and they explain why the most vigorous and persistent spurts of progress occurred in the very regions that got off to a late start. It seems clear, for instance, that development in the Carolingian period was much more far-reaching in Ger-

many than in the regions of Northern Gaul. Later on, in the twelfth century, the changes brought about by improvements in agricultural techniques were far more revolutionary in the Slav regions east of the Elbe than in Normandy.

3. Finally, other causes of diversity are due to the conditions of historical research itself; they are a further considerable impediment to observing the economic phenomena in the round. The written sources available for a given country in a given period are far from having equal weight. For example, if we consider the end of the eleventh century, we have a great deal to go on in Campania or Catalonia, nothing at all in Poland, and precious little in Scandinavia. Quite apart from this uneven distribution, the texts are vastly different in nature and informativeness. Hence the documents from Italy, for the most part land leases, and the documents from Northern France, mostly deeds of gift to churches or agreements between rival landlords, present the historian with very dissimilar aspects of rural life. This original diversity in the sources due to differences in levels of culture and legal traditions is made even more acute for the historian by an unequal conservation of the documents (in England, for instance, the archives are in a much better state than in France), and by the fact that historical research, which has never been quite the same in the different nations of Europe, has taken a different direction in each. The nature of the sources and the scientific traditions have combined to favour, in Scandinavia and the East European countries, archaeological exploration of the rural home and peasant implements; in Germany and France, the study of the landscape and the legal framework; in Italy, the study of relations between town and country. The richness of English archives, an earlier abundance of numerical data in the written sources, and the historians' practice of applying the techniques of the economist to the interpretation of these data have advanced agrarian economic history in England distinctly beyond that of its neighbours. Divergences such as these are further reasons for making constant adjustments if we are to avoid distorting the perspective in our *tableau d'ensemble*.

SOURCES

The source material available to the historian of country
life is complex. He can learn much from observing the
present landscape: research based on cartography (maps,
land registers, aerial photographs), agrology (analyses of
the soil and surface vegetation), toponymy (the names of
hamlets, even the fields themselves), and archaeology (excavations on the sites of abandoned settlements) can un-
earth traces of ancient peasant tilling. But with these
methods it is always difficult to date the traces precisely.
To be exact, the results have to be corrected by reference
to the texts. So most of what we can discover about medieval
rural economy inevitably depends upon these rare and
frequently thorny written sources. As for the distribution
of these source documents, we can distinguish—with all due
allowance made for the regional discrepancies mentioned
above—between three broad periods:

1. While the written sources for the ninth century and
the part of Europe governed by the Carolingians are
relatively plentiful, the documentation for the period that
followed is distinctly less rich. For the effort employed by
Charlemagne and his successors to impose the keeping of
written records on the royal and ecclesiastical demesnes
flagged swiftly as the Empire declined. What did persist
for a time, however, was the custom of drawing up a
periodical inventory of landholdings and bondages. Hence,
in those regions that bore the impress of Carolingian
domination, there was some continuity between the ninth
century *polyptyques* and the twelfth century *censiers* or
coutumiers. However, after 900, and for more than two
centuries, throughout rural Europe, the conveyance of
land and labour and dealings between lords and peasants
ceased, practically, to give rise to the drawing up of documents and to refer to texts. They came to be based on
public ceremonies, ritual utterances and gestures before
witnesses, and on the collective memory, that depository
of the subtle fluid corpus of rules called custom. The heads
of the great religious establishments, who constituted the

élite of the educated classes, themselves gave up the use of accounts in the administration of their estates. They did, however, hold on to their archives, which they kept in good order, and from which they composed cartularies, collected transcriptions of the parchments listing the rights of these houses over their lands and serfs. For this reason, some texts have come down to us. Since they are not administrative documents, but title deeds, these records contain little in the way of numerical data, and the information they provide about the management and internal economy of the estate is slender. But they do bring out the great increase in charitable gifts, which conveyed land from lay hands to the Church, and the resistance that arose thereto. Finally, and above all, they throw a certain amount of light on the legal framework behind the estate economy, notably on the workings of bondage and tenancy. The deficiencies in the sources impose singular restrictions on our knowledge; in particular, they prevent us from appreciating what links, if any, existed between the growth mechanisms perceptible from the Carolingian sources and the great expansion apparent in the thirteenth century. Yet we should note two exceptions: (a) the decline in the keeping of accounts was less pronounced in Italy; and (b) a political event in 1086 suddenly jolted rural England out of its centuries of darkness: the new king, William the Conqueror, caused to be drawn up, by Norman clerks, a general inventory of all lordly possessions throughout his newly won kingdom. Though not easy to interpret, Domesday Book, the account of this survey, provides us with the first, incomparable element of statistics for a history of rural economy in Europe.

2. Between 1150 and 1180, cultural progress in the more advanced countries of Western Europe resulted in a return to the use of accounts in day-to-day business. As literacy increased, people had more faith in the legal value of written documents than in spoken promises, ritual gestures, and uncertain testimony. Two obvious signs of the restoration of account-keeping were the renaissance of notaryship in the Mediterranean countries, starting with the Italian

city states, and the need felt by both landlords and peasants to fix the points of custom establishing their respective rights on parchments called, in the lands of the Empire, *Weistümer* ('records of custom'), and in France, 'franchise' charters or 'liberty' charters—for stabilising the purview of lordly exploitation by putting it in writing seemed a regular liberation to the landlords' subjects. Henceforth, many landlords, led by some of the richest of them, the great monastic establishments, again took the management of their estates in hand. They employed increasingly competent assistants whose administration was based on inventories and accounts. Most of the increased numbers of documents resulting from the new administrative practices have disappeared. They are, however, numerous still in archives in England where, from the thirteenth century onwards, it is possible to study the workings of the manorial economy with precision. Also in England at this time there emerged an 'agronomic' literature dealing with the proper management of estates.

3. When we come to the fourteenth and fifteenth centuries, the source material is quite different. In the first place, there is too much of it, with the result that we have to modify our methods of research and resort to sampling procedures. In the second place, changes in the content open up completely new vistas on to the rural past. In particular, the public administration documents, especially those relating to the state fiscal system, provide us with less disappointing demographic data. The remains of the accounts of religious establishments, the royal courts, and —in Southern Europe—a few men of affairs provide us also with the first usable evidence concerning the consumption of agricultural products. Further, the innumerable notarial registers that were kept in the Mediterranean towns and larger villages furnish a few elements suitable for a quantitative evaluation of economic phenomena. With all this at our disposal, it is no longer altogether impossible to use statistical method. In addition, the history of technique becomes less uncertain: agrarian practice is described in more detail in the farming leases; painters and sculptors

turned their hands to depicting reality, and their work provides us with a precious iconography of farm implements and the rural landscape; and, lastly, most of the medieval utensils unearthed by the archaeologists date from these two centuries. The source material dating from the end of the Middle Ages enables us therefore: (1) to get a much less discontinuous view of rural phenomena; (2) to give figures; and (3) to break away from the one-sided, purely aristocratic, viewpoint afforded by earlier sources.

THE CONDITIONS OF AGRICULTURAL PRODUCTION

POPULATION NUMBERS

As we have just suggested in our discussion of the sources, the numerical data for a demographic study of medieval rural life are late in date, fragmentary, and difficult to interpret. The earliest after Domesday Book are again concerned with England: the manorial accounts make it possible to study the population on certain demesnes such as the dependencies of the Bishopric of Winchester. But as far as Europe as a whole is concerned, we have to wait until the years around 1300, when improvements in fiscal technique brought an increase in the numbers of tax lists. In fact, these lists never enable us to know the numbers of inhabitants in a given region, even in a given locality, with certainty. What they do provide, however, is some idea of the general population trends, and this is perhaps more useful than anything else.

These trends are examined in detail below; for the moment, therefore, we shall merely give an outline of the main aspects. The broad movement of growth that seems to have begun as early as the tenth century, if not earlier, continued at rates that varied considerably from one village to another. (This naturally precludes generalising from local observations to a kingdom or province.) The intensity of the progression depended largely on inheritance customs, which could act as a brake on the marriage and birth rates and encourage the young to emigrate. Population growth was therefore the cause of migration (it is clear from any close study of these questions that the medieval peasantry was extremely mobile), which permitted the settlement and reclamation of zones that were deserted and uncultivated, and the growth of the towns.

However, whatever the amplitude of these outpourings of inhabitants, the growth within was so powerful that the density of the population of every parish had become excessive by the end of the thirteenth century, even in the zones that had been recently colonised. This over-population and the concomitant phenomenon of malnutrition were the prime factors behind the reversal in population trends apparent in the first statistical data.

The start of the regression is all the more difficult to date since it did not occur everywhere at the same moment. In Provence, it was before 1320; in England, it seems to have coincided with the series of bad harvests from 1317 to 1319. In the majority of European provinces, the initially slow decline gave way to a catastrophic drop after the epidemic of 1348-1350. To the depredations of the plague we must add the depredations of warfare, which ravaged certain regions for more than half a century.

However, the drop in rural populations was not everywhere of the same proportions. The regression seems to have doubly affected those regions, villages, and hamlets that were the least favoured agriculturally. Although the losses of human life were probably no greater there than in the good agricultural regions, the possibility of moving from the bad to the good—temporarily undercultivated as a result of mortality—deprived the unproductive lands of large numbers of their survivors. Hence, in the second half of the fifteenth century, when a new increase in population began to make itself felt throughout Europe, a striking contrast existed among the various regions. As a whole, they were less populated than at the end of the thirteenth century. But the fertile zones, where the population had never dropped for long and was still abundant, stood out from zones that had become almost deserted owing to the harshness of the climate or the poverty of the soil.

WORK COMMUNITIES

1. *The Family.* The basic unit of agrarian economy was the family, the work-team, consisting of the parental group, its servants, and its draught animals. This social unit lived on an enclosed piece of land that was often designated by the patronymic borne by the family group. This *mansus, croft, masure, cour, toft,* or *Hof*—to give it a few of the names by which it was known in the various dialects—served as a basis for all the fiscal requirements of the landlord and, later on, the State. As a result, when we catch a glimpse of the medieval peasant family, the viewpoint taken in the documents is almost always that of the men who exploited it—which is to say that we see it very imperfectly. A great deal of work remains to be done on this aspect of medieval history; solutions to many of the unanswered questions concerning it could render signal services to our knowledge of the main aspects of rural economy in our period. It is possible, moreover, from the thirteenth century onwards, in certain regions, to study the history of the family in depth, using wills and notarial archives, and this field of research can be considered one of the most fruitful still to be explored.

(a) The structures of peasant *kinship* do not appear to have undergone any appreciable modifications during the Middle Ages. The family was of the conjugal type that we find described at the beginning of the ninth century in certain Carolingian inventories; hence the group was limited to the representatives of two, or at the most three, generations. The cohesion of this group was directly dependent on the customs governing the devolution of family possessions at the moment of a succession, and it seems that, for this reason, the cohesion varied somewhat during our period. Although there had always been, even at the lowest levels of rural society, land-holdings (the 'allods') exempt from subjection to a lord, most families worked lands belonging to a master. Hence, the structure of peasant families was influenced by the legal regime of tenure. Until the twelfth century, so long as population numbers remained very low, the landlords took good care lest their concessions be deprived of labour and lose their unity: the grant of land was therefore hereditary, but successional partitions, sales, and any kind of parcelling out were forbidden. Consequently, children either had to stay at home, working the land in common during the indefinite period of joint heirship, or seek their fortunes elsewhere, joining in clearing operations and founding homes of their own on new land. In the thirteenth century, when the rural population was much higher, the circulation of wealth increasing, and labour plentiful, we find increases in the number of leases, on the one hand, and, on the other, peasants obtaining the right to divide and parcel out inheritances in exchange for the payment of taxes on conveyances and successions. These facilities favoured the fluidity of the peasant patrimony, the relaxation of family ties, the development of individual enterprise, the rise of some and the ruin of others. This phase of expansion, which coincided with the continued climb in the rural population, was followed towards the middle of the fourteenth century by an inverse movement: while the demographic catastrophes and the concomitant migrations were leading to disintegration of the family framework (in one Languedoc village in the fifteenth century, 13 per cent of tax-paying peasants disappear from the lists every ten years without leaving a tax-paying male heir), it seems that the bonds of kinship grew tighter in the face of need. The large family units subject to the strict control of the eldest male again came into being, and the *affrèrements*, fraternal joint-ownership associations frequently grouping together men from different families, increased in number. These compact groups were the only effective defence against the difficulties resulting from depopulation.

(b) Study of the *servants* is difficult in all but the richest rural households. It is at least certain that the landlords were far from being the only people to, keep full-time

servants; a good number of peasants also employed
auxiliary workers, who formed part of their families. In
the eleventh century, the condition of domestics in most
European provinces still came under the legal heading of
slavery. Men and women kept as servants were possessions
of the family group by birth and they obeyed this collective
master to whom they owed everything yet who owed them
nothing. This servile forced labour was still widespread in
the *mansi indominicati*, the aristocratic family enclosures and
the great religious houses. Most of the slaves did lead
family lives of their own, however, on land granted in
tenure from which they drew their subsistence: in this
position of relative economic independence they remained
part-time servitors in person and owed certain days of
service to their master, putting at his disposal labour that
was both unpaid and of unlimited application. Their
owner also recruited full-time servants for his household
from the fittest of their children. This total alienation of a
class of men doomed by their birth to a lifetime in the
unpaid service of others persisted in certain regions for a
long time, notably in England where, at the height of the
thirteenth century, the great monastic farms were fed with
labour by the villein system. However, almost everywhere,
the general trend was towards a slow relaxation of the bonds
of servitude. In the thirteenth century, most household
servitors were henceforth signed on and paid: the notarial
registers from Southern Europe have preserved the contracts stipulating the conditions of service. Certain late
thirteenth century inventories and account rolls give us our
first glimpses of the condition of the wage-earning employees.
It appears that this labour force was very mobile (on one
big demesne in Artois, for instance, nine in fifteen jobs
changed hands between 1325 and 1328), but well paid:
domestics got yearly grain rations and a cash allowance
(varying according to responsibility) for clothing and the
companagium, food to go with the bread. It can be established
that the servitors working in the rural houses of the Hos-
pitallers in Provence in 1338 were much better off than
peasants working small independent holdings; above all,

they were much more secure, for their income was un-affected by weather hazards and crop variations. After the middle of the fourteenth century it would seem that de-population and the consequent reabsorption of the rural proletariat resulted in increases in wages, shortage of labour, and an overall reduction in the numbers of do-mestics. In England, however, the *servientes* or domestic workers inventoried for the 1377 Poll Tax were still numerous.

(c) From the documents dating from the concluding three centuries of our period that are suscepfible of statistical analysis, it is clear that individual farming units belonging to the same village or dependent on the same lord differed considerably as regards both man-power (20 to 30 em-ployees on the great aristocratic demesnes) and acreage worked. The disparities were even greater, and had even more important repercussions on the running of the farm, as regards *working stock*. In medieval Europe, oxen were bred first and foremost for their strength at the plough. Around 1200, in the north and east of the Paris basin and in Flanders, oxen were replaced by horses. The use of these much faster moving animals increased the rate of ploughing and hence the number of tillings possible in the year, with consequent improvements in land fertility. How-ever, the thirteenth century English agronomic treatises advised the use of oxen rather than horses because oxen were cheaper to keep, and in fact teams of oxen continued to be used throughout Europe. There is reason to believe that the quality of working stock went up between the tenth and thirteenth centuries, and that the progress here was one of the deciding factors in the agricultural expansion of the period. It is certain, at any rate, that the heavy livestock essential for use of the most effective tilling imple-ments was still too rare, and that the main weaknesses in the medieval agrarian system were due to this deficiency. The prime concern in those days was the feeding of the peasant population, a population constantly on the verge of famine as a result of fluctuations in demographic trends. For this reason, the space allotted to forage crops was

severely limited and the reserves of hay for wintering heavy
livestock were far too low. Hence, throughout the Middle
Ages, even the wealthiest agricultural holdings had insufficient stabled cattle to meet the needs of the fields;
draught stock was very expensive; the portion of capital
that it represented for each family was perhaps greater—
and definitely less secure—than the portion represented by
landholdings, and quite out of proportion to its relative
importance. Many details attest this value of plough teams:
the chief servant was everywhere called the *bovarius*,
because he was in charge of the oxen. Seizing the heavy
stock was a landlord's surest means of putting pressure on
his dependants, and the first thing peasants would do
when warned of marauding troops was to put their draught
cattle out of harm's way. A large number of rural households lacked sufficient means to acquire ploughing stock.
Some contracted for their use with a capitalist, who would
lend them an animal or its cost in exchange for advantages
that were all the more substantial as the loan was necessary.
For all that, many peasants had no working stock at all:
on certain manors in the bishopric of Winchester in the
thirteenth century, this was the case for 40 per cent of the
personal dependants. This unfavoured class of men seemed
so clearly beneath the rest that the fundamental social
distinction apparent in rural France as early as the tenth
century finally split the peasantry into two distinct groups:
those that had to work the land by hand, and, vastly
superior to them, the *laboratores*, those rich enough to possess
a plough team.

(d) The labour potential represented by the domestic
work team was never completely adapted to the needs of
the farm, which varied considerably from season to season.
During off-peak periods, when there was insufficient work
for all the family, it was preferable to evacuate part of the
labour force by selling the spare livestock—which created a
need for seasonal cattle-markets—and by sending some
members of the family out in search of temporary work
elsewhere. Sometimes the entire household moved in this
way: tax inspectors visiting a Provençal mountain village

in the winter of 1340 found a third of the houses barred and shuttered—their inhabitants had gone down into the valley in search of a wage. During the winter months, in the fourteenth century, the towns were full of out-of-work peasants offering their labour to the artisans. Inversely, certain work on the land—ploughing, vine-dressing, hay-making, harvesting, etc.—required considerable reinforcements of labour for periods that were short yet closely circumscribed by climatic conditions. Observing customs left over from the early Middle Ages, the seigneurial farms of the tenth and eleventh centuries procured this indispensable aid by means of obligatory, unpaid labour services or *corvées*, exacted from their dependent families. The best defined forms of work service—those that were economically the most advantageous and hence the longest in disappearing—were all grouped around the peak periods in the farming calendar. The *corvée* system was still in force, reinvigorated, in the great monastic lordships of thirteenth century England, and nowhere did it disappear altogether. However, as soon as money became a more supple instrument for rural purposes—in France by the end of the eleventh century—the great landlords dropped their custom of requisitioning these large forced-labour gangs, which they rightly believed to be unproductive in the first place and very costly in the second, since it was necessary to provide them with decent meals. They recruited paid journeymen instead, drawing on the peasant households with little land that were only too glad to sell their spare time. Such households grew continually in number, along with the rise in population, until the great mortalities of the fourteenth century. So temporary labour played a considerable role in the rural economy, particularly during the thirteenth and early fourteenth centuries. It has been calculated that at least a third of the English peasant population then worked for a wage. In this way, great quantities of money regularly found their way from the richest landowners to the poorest. The drop in population later caused a considerable decrease in work available, and imposed the need for a better adaptation of the acreage worked to the labour potential of the family group. This adaptation was achieved (1) by reducing the acreage worked, or (2) by reinforcing the family group through increased cohesion or the creation of *affrèrements*, the numbers of which grew considerably after 1350.

2. *The Village.* Peasant households that were too poor to employ journeymen got their seasonal reinforcements of labour from arrangements for mutal aid with neighbours. For, in fact, the basic family unit generally belonged to a broader community, comprising the various groups that worked the same *terroir*. Widely dispersed forms of habitation, in which the family enclosures were utterly isolated from one another, did exist; but normally the land was worked within the framework of a village, the population and concentration of which depended on whether the lie of the cultivable land permitted the working of wide open spaces or made it necessary to farm small scattered lots. The perfect type of village community stood at the centre of an open field landscape: all the different family enclosures were grouped together into a single coherent mass, itself often protected by an outer hedge. Around this compact nucleus of houses and gardens, within which each family was its own master and landlord, lay the broad ring of arable—an enormously intricate pattern of parcels of land without any permanent fences at all, for except when grain was growing in the fields individual ownership was a secondary consideration, and the total arable became an expanse of collective pastureland. Around the periphery lay the wastes and woods, the use of which was almost entirely communal. This agrarian system was widespread in tenth and eleventh century Europe, and throughout our period we can observe a gradual reinforcement of village solidarity as the result of certain external factors.

In some regions, however, this trend towards the concentration of settlement resulted from internal developments in agriculture itself. In North-West Germany, for instance, the cultivation of cereals gradually progressed during the twelfth and thirteenth centuries at the expense of a primitive agrarian system based on pig-breeding and the depredatory exploitation of forest resources. The dwellings, which had formerly been widely dispersed among the oak thickets, gradually drew closer together as what amounted to regular cereal farms came to be created. The progressive hardening in the parish framework —which had been in place almost everywhere since the tenth century, but which gradually became more rigid, especially during the war against heresy in the thirteenth century—also favoured concentration. It was in the interests of the village community to present a united front before the landlords, particularly those who wielded disciplinary and fiscal authority over whole parishes. Their solidarity expressed itself in the drawing up of *Weistümer*, in negotiations for franchise charters with landlords, in the collection and sharing out of taxes, and—at the close of the Middle Ages, when the danger of marauding troops became universal—in the collective organisation of defence. A final incentive to village cohesion came once the advance in clearing operations and seigneurial interdictions had progressively reduced the area of the common pastureland to such an extent that it became necessary to exercise stricter control over the working of the cultivated clearings. Probably as the result of demographic pressure and land hunger at the end of the thirteenth and beginning of the fourteenth centuries, collective controls became more severe in some regions, leading to restrictions in the use of the commons, extensions in grazing rights in the fallow, and the imposition of obligatory crop rotation.

Yet neighbourly ties tended to slacken as a result of rising differences in economic conditions within peasant society— these led to further differences between the best interests of poor and rich and to internal conflict, particularly as regards grazing rights—and as a result of a gradual evolution that was taking place in the agrarian system. Growing interest in forest products, grass, viticulture, and plantation-crops led in the thirteenth century to greater and greater tracts of land being permanently fenced and closed to collective grazing, and resulted in the development of forms of working and dwelling that were alien to the village. First, certain landlords, especially the new communities of Cistercian monks or canons regular, then townspeople or rich peasants who had broken away from the village community, created large isolated farms in the uncultivated regions between the agricultural clearings. This separatism, completely alien to the *terroir* spirit of solidarity, seems to have spread after the first quarter of the thirteenth century. Then new techniques of estate management on the great seigneurial demesnes, with the introduction of *fermes*, *métairies*, and *podere*, in certain recently colonised regions hastened the dispersal of the peasant families themselves. It was probably then that the open-field system began to give way to the *bocage* system, in which the land was divided up by hedges—evidence of a new agrarian individualism. The *bocage* system nonetheless adapted the landscape better to new production methods that favoured stock-raising.

THE SYSTEM OF HUSBANDRY

The organisation of agricultural production was—and is—determined by the living standards and dietary habits of the population. In the tenth century, the system of husbandry that prevailed in the whole of Europe was still similar to the system described in such Carolingian sources as the rules of management drawn up for the great monastic estates: the prime aim was to grow the subsistence staple, i.e. grain. The traditional diet of cereals—and, to a lesser extent, peas and vetches—consumed as bread, porridge, or thick soup-like ale, was thus behind the ubiquitous cultivated fields. This peasant civilisation, a slave to its eating habits, persisted in growing grain even where the climate was unsuitable: along the Atlantic seaboard, for instance, it was often too wet. The first result of the general expansion that was beginning to move through Europe in the tenth century was an increase in the proportionate importance of cereals in the systems of husbandry practised along the North Sea and the Baltic littorals, in the Western Isles, in Scandinavia, Saxony, and the Slav countries. Everywhere the expansion led to the production of better species: in the most primitive areas, for example, millet went out of cultivation altogether, and wheat gradually superseded barley and rye in such highly evolved regions as Languedoc. Progress brought appreciable changes in the face of the countryside: wastes and forests, the former homes of flocks and herds and itinerant slash-and-burn cultivators, became permanent ploughland. Stock-raising was increasingly subordinated to agriculture. Inasmuch as cattle and sheep played a fundamental role in the renewal of field fertility— the first by helping to till the soil, the second by manuring it—animal husbandry and agriculture drew closer together. But the breeding of livestock always remained marginal and distinctly insufficient. Close calculations have shown that, even in supposedly pastoral regions such as England, the total numbers of livestock were far below modern estimates of the minimum numbers required for a well-balanced farming of the arable.

However, in the most advanced countries, this grain-centred system of husbandry began to be unsettled by the requirement of the gradual rise in aristocratic and urban living standards. The demand for high-quality wine grew continually during our period; urban expansion, house-building, boat-building, metal-working, tanning, weaving, all required ever-increasing amounts of timber and fire-wood, leather, wool, yarn (linen and hemp), and dye-stuffs such as *gaide* or saffron. And then the rich, soon followed by the less rich—for a widespread popularisation of aristocratic usage reached even the peasant world by the four-teenth century—grew accustomed to adding complementary foods, meat in particular, to their basic diet of bread. As soon as the available sources start shedding a little light on daily life, around the end of the thirteenth century, we discover the dietary importance of the *companagium* (bacon, salt herrings, cheese) at every level of society, even among serfs and alms men. There are many reasons for thinking that the consumption of animal products underwent a further general increase in the fifteenth century, when every town had its butchers (who were at the same time entrepreneurs, cattle merchants, meat merchants, and leather merchants), all of them prosperous: the new men of the pastoral economy, and its absolute masters.

As a result, the systems of husbandry diversified. New products were brought in that (1) enlarged the domain of gardening at the expense of farming proper (e.g. the vine); (2) involved a more rational exploitation of forest and meadow; (3) extended the use of permanent fences; (4) burdened the farming calendar with additional labour requirements; and (5) tended to increase the numbers of sheep bred for their wool, and to modify the economic functions of cattle-breeding as new outlets for beef and milk were added to the traditional function, the supply of labour. The widening consumer market behind these changes in the system of production was not, for the most part, rural. The changes were therefore symptomatic of the opening of the country economy to exchanges, and went hand in hand with the gradual penetration of money and credit. They stimulated the growth of a host of small market towns inhabited by dealers in wine, grain, and cattle, and moneylenders. And, lastly, these changes went deepest in regions close to towns and to lines of communication, where transport of surplus produce was relatively easy. The thirteenth century saw the appearance of new landscapes, almost wholly without ploughland, given up to viticulture or stock-raising. In France, every town had its surrounding belt of vineyards, while more important—sometimes monocultural—wine regions exported their produce along the Seine, the Loire, and the Atlantic coast; in 1245 a Franciscan traveller was astonished to find the inhabitants of Auxerre living off the proceeds of their shipments of wine sent up to Paris by river, and growing no grain at all. Forms of stock-raising that broke completely away from the cereal economy developed (1) in England, along the edges of the forests and marshes; (2) in the mountain regions of the continent (the entire output of the *Schwaighöfe* in the German Alps came from their herds of milch cows); and (3) in the Mediterranean regions, Southern France and, to a far greater extent, the Iberian and Italian peninsulas. Here, sheep-breeding grew to such proportions that by the twelfth century it became necessary to regulate the long flock movements to and from the mountain pastures (in fifteenth century Apulia alone, such migration affected half a million head of cattle); the grain-growing communities waged a bitter struggle against the cattle entrepreneurs, whose herds swept across their land and invaded their common pastures; but they usually had to give in to this speculative economy, backed as it was by money and influence. In Southern Italy, agriculture was thus pushed gradually into the background by an extensive, all-conquering pastoral economy that despoiled the land.

We may wonder whether the extension of urban demand for forest products, cattle products, and wine in the second half of the thirteenth century, and the contraction of cereal production to which it gave rise, was not behind the food shortages that occurred in the most advanced regions in the decades around 1300. In the most densely urbanised regions (Flanders and Lombardy), one definite result of these grain crises was the introduction of the new departures in husbandry—animal husbandry especially—within the existing, mainly agricultural, system. This led to an intensification in agricultural practice: by the thirteenth century forage plants were being cultivated on the fallow around Flemish towns, while in the Po plain, the highly productive association of meadow and heavily manured ploughland achieved a happy balance between the production of cheese, leather and meat and the production of grain.

TECHNIQUES AND ACREAGE WORKED

Despite these gradual improvements, popular belief remained anchored in the production of grain—the god-given *panem quotidianum*, the fundamental foodstuff of mankind. Work on the land was considered to lie first and foremost in tilling, sowing, harvesting, and ploughing, the practices upon which whole regions did in fact depend for their livelihood, and which undeniably played a central role in the rural economy of the Middle Ages on account of the numbers of men required to perform them. In view of the economic importance of this cereal-cropping, the historian has to tackle the thorny question of agricultural techniques.

1. In order to give anything like a satisfactory explanation of practically any of the perceptible economic phenomena—demographic trends, the evolution of the demesnes, the commercialisation of land produce—we would need to be quite clear about yield/seed ratios and their fluctuations in our period. Strictly speaking, this is impossible. No data at all are available until the mid-twelfth century, and no continuity occurs in them until the English manorial account rolls in the thirteenth century. To be valid, interpretation has to be based on many continuous series of such data, for the yields were extremely variable, depending on the quality of the soil (the wheat yields of two quite close Cluniac estates were in the ratio 6:1 and 2:1 respectively, to judge from a mid-twelfth century inventory), and on the climate, especially rainfall (in one village in Burgundy, the yield gave 10:1 in 1380, and 3:3 in 1381; on a small estate belonging to a Florentine financier, the yield fell from a yearly average of 4:1 or 5:1 to 1.6:1 in 1348). The thirteenth and fourteenth century sources sometimes record high productivity levels: for example, on lands belonging to the Abbey of St. Denis near Paris, the average wheat yield was in the ratio 8:1; on a demesne in Artois it had risen to 15:1 in 1335. Taking all this into account, however, we can make a fair guess that most European peasants were satisfied with a grain yield of between three and four times what they had sown. These ratios seem unbelievably low; what makes them appear even lower, when compared with modern ratios for equivalent acreages, is that seed was sown much thinner then

than it is nowadays. It is evident, then, that the land was unkind, at a time when civilisation as a whole depended on farming for its progress. After about 1150, when detailed research becomes possible, the returns seem to have been somewhat higher than they had been in Carolingian days. In the ninth century, the average yield could rarely have been much above 2:1. In Poland, even in Normandy around Neufbourg, this very low level of yield still obtained in the thirteenth century. Yet there is reason to believe that a general rise in productivity occurred between the ninth and twelfth centuries—a period for which the relevant source material is unfortunately meagre. The rise was significant: a yield of 3:1 as against the former 2:1 represented a profit increase of 100 per cent, which made it possible to cut down the acreage of arable land needed to feed a family, hence the portion of the demesne reserved for the landlord, to make reductions in the labour force, and to alleviate the *corvées*. This rise in productivity was probably bound up with improvements in fertilising techniques.

2. There was apparently no progress at all in manuring: outside Flanders and Lombardy, as has already been pointed out, the development of stock-raising took place independently, and to the detriment, of agriculture. Stabled cattle were rare, so manure was rare; it was often kept for the garden and the vines, the spread of which meant that the grain fields had to do without. The rarity of manure is clear from a number of thirteenth century texts, which mention it as being hard to get and expensive; some farm leases in the Paris basin stipulate that manure had to be spread on the land at least once every 10 years; some forbid the farmer to sell the manure to others. As regards the organisation of crop rotation, here again there were no changes likely to help raise productivity. On the contrary, it seems that demographic pressure and hopes of raising cereal production led, in the twelfth and thirteenth centuries, to the extension of three-year rotation—which forced the land to produce for two consecutive years and rested it for only one year—at the expense of less intensive

systems. In regions where the soil was not so rich as in North-West France, this restriction in the period of fallow (unadvisable, according to the prudent author of the English *Fleta*) usually brought a definite drop in productivity: over a six-year period the land yielded four crops instead of three, but the four were poorer than the three. In regions like Alsace, where the spread of viticulture restricted manuring, a return was made to two-year rotation. The sole apparent improvement in fertilising techniques was concerned with ploughing. This practice served two different purposes in different regions: in the Mediterranean countries, it was intended to do no more than air and break up the topsoil, and to counter the proliferation of weeds; ploughing here had to be light in order to safeguard the thin layer of fertile topsoil. In the wet regions of Europe, however, the land has to be turned over to a good depth for it to benefit from the reconstituting effects of the buried surface vegetation. So it would seem that progress, in North and West Europe, took the form of a more powerful ploughing implement drawn by stronger teams and fitted with an asymmetrical share and an effective mould board. The developments in rural iron-working in the eleventh and twelfth centuries, the spreading of the village smithies, the demesne administrators' concern with improving the ploughing instrument, and the privileged household status of the ploughmen are all indications of this improvement in technique, which moved down through rural society from its beginnings among the wealthy. But it never caught on in the thin-soiled countries of the south, and never did it reach the whole mass of the peasantry. In the most advanced regions, the poor could not stand the additional heavy expense needed for the use of the *charrue* and its plough team; they carried on working the land by hand with the hoe, or using the old wooden *araire*. At any rate, this improvement confirmed the social superiority of the *laboureurs* over the *manouvriers*, and the agronomic superiority of the broad regions in which it became widespread, Northern France and the Germano-Slav plain in particular.

3. Despite this progress, the series of precise numerical data provided by the English manor rolls showed that in the course of the thirteenth century, on the best managed, best manured, and best manned seigneurial lands, agricultural yields tended to fall off. Everything leads us to suppose that the food needs of the ever-increasing population had necessitated an abusive exploitation of the land, and that the land was nearing exhaustion. The continual exhausting of undermanured, overworked, and under-rested arable land seems to have been an inherent feature of the agrarian system of medieval Europe. It involved the periodical abandoning of the fields that had become barren and were no longer worth sowing, and replacing them with fresh ploughland broken out of free lying land whose nutritional reserves were intact. Agriculture in those days seems to have required a very slow rotation, so to speak, of the infield, within a vast expanse of virgin outfield. The practice of assart (grubbing up forest land) was then a permanent task of restoration that compensated for the constant deterioration of long overworked land. From agronomical necessities alone, the medieval peasant was first and foremost a coloniser.

However, between the tenth and thirteenth centuries, clearance operations intensified. In many regions of Europe, clearing became more than mere compensation; it turned into a regular conquest. This advance of ploughland at the expense of pasture, marsh, or forests, more often than not took the form of a progressive broadening of agricultural clearing around the village. The phenomenon has usually left no written trace: we know of it merely from the present landscape, the layout of the fields and cart-tracks, the existing vegetation, and the placenames that commemorate the primitive surface cover. The progress made was considerable: in one Lombardy village, the wasteland that took up nearly half the territory in 1240 had dwindled by two-thirds 80 years later. But the attack sometimes went forward away from the established rural settlements; lands that had been abandoned in harder times were brought back into cultivation, and former agricultural units came back to life; encouraged by the landlords, who saw profit for themselves in populating their wastes, settlers created new isolated villages that can sometimes still be recognised from their names (*Neuville*, *Villanova*, Germanic placenames ending with *-rode*, *-reuth*, etc.), or from their shapes (the Lorraine *villages-rues*, the Germanic *Waldhufendörfer*). The written population charters organising the creation of some of these new villages have sometimes come down to us. It is difficult, however, to put a precise date on this progress. In certain regions, such as the Mâconnais, in France, all the usable land was already occupied by 1000. The marshes of the Flanders seaboard, which had been silting up naturally and attracting settlers since the middle of the eleventh century, began to be diked systematically in the second quarter of the twelfth, as did those of the lower Loire valley at the end of the twelfth century, when large-scale clearances for settlement were being hacked out of the English forests. In the Ile-de-France, the movement was at its height around 1200; at the same time, the pioneering movement east of the Elbe was getting fully under way. This considerable extension of the arable, which kept Europe clear of serious food shortages for two-and-a-half centuries, was stimulated by demographic pressures, technical progress (the *charrue* made it possible to exploit fertile land that had been too heavy for the implements formerly available), and capital grants made to the settlers by the landlords themselves, by monied religious establishments that went into partnership with the landlords, or by entrepreneurs (former stewards or townsmen). The great clearance movement, which backed up the soaring increases in the population, is at all events the most spectacular and the most decisive economic event in the whole of our period.

4. Almost everywhere, however, the extension came to an end around the middle of the thirteenth century. It seems that all the lands susceptible of being profitably worked with the renewed techniques had by then been brought into production. The clearances had perhaps gone too far and reduced the woods excessively, when their

value was rising all the time, and cut down the area of available pastureland that was indispensable for stock-raising and manuring. It seems that the settlers had attempted to reclaim too much marginal land, which after a few years of mediocre crops failed to come up to their expectations, and had to be left to grow wild again. In the sources after 1250, we come across increasing references to abortive clearance ventures, and the first traces of the *Wüstungen*, ploughland overrun by a return of the scrub, and deserted villages. Yet this halt, these failures, and these early slumps did nothing to slow down the rate of demographic growth. Overcrowding was inevitable: during the second half of the thirteenth century and the beginning of the fourteenth, the land shortage in the villages got more acute with every generation—and a generation in those days was very short. Arable land prices went up continually, the numbers of wholly landless peasant families increased and, in many areas, households impoverished to the extent of farming less than eight acres became the majority. Light stock-raising, the skilled crafts, and wage-earning on a wealthy demesne did indeed provide this proletariat with supplementary resources. But the development of these complementary activities did nothing to hold back the increase in malnutrition due to over-population. The precariousness of the implements available and the lowness of the average corn yield made this over-population even more disastrous than it may appear from a cursory examination of the statistics. This situation led to the first famines, the successive epidemics, and the post-1350 demographic slump.

Regions in which land improvement and economic and demographic expansion managed to continue together in the last two centuries of the Middle Ages were few and far between. The most conspicuous example of one that did is Northern Italy. While urban capital financed the construction of vast amphitheatres and terraces for growing corn, trees, and vines around the cities and *castelli* in the hills, in the Po plain the tenacious collective struggle to dike and canalise the streams for irrigation purposes, a struggle formerly undertaken by the great communes, was continued by the despots who had seized the great *signoria*. But in almost all the other regions of Europe, the first land regressions, after a false start in the thirteenth century, set to in earnest a century later, this time under the effects of depopulation. All along the pioneering fringe-areas, in all the agronomically marginal regions incapable of attracting immigrants to fill the gaps left by the excess of deaths over births, the fields and villages showed a distinct setback. Analysis of the pollens conserved in the peateries of central Germany shows that the proportion of grain in the vegetation of these regions dropped considerably between 1350 and 1450 in favour of, first, fast-growing trees, then tall beech forests; in England, 2000 rural settlements abandoned at the end of the fifteenth and the beginning of the sixteenth centuries have been traced. And in those zones that remained under cultivation, the demographic slump generally made it possible to group several farms into a single larger unit, economically more viable: in the fifteenth century, the proportion of middling landowners in one Languedoc village moved up from 26 to 40 per cent, the proportion of smallholders moving down correlatively.

THE MAIN PHASES

The few precise chronological landmarks that can be observed in the gradual evolution in rural production in Europe from 900 to 1500, the general appearance of the population curve, the main stages in land settlement, and, perhaps most of all, the changes that can be observed in the distribution and content of the documentary material, all give reason for picking out three main phases in the history of the medieval rural economy. It is hard to put an exact date on the shift from one phase to the next, particularly since it occurred at different times in different regions. But what we *can* do, in the present state of our knowledge, is situate the zones of transition between the phases, the first in the last two decades of the twelfth century, and the second in the first quarter of the fourteenth century. We shall now take a look at these phases one after the other, attempting to link our preceding remarks on the mechanisms of production to considerations of social environment, political relationships, and the economy as a whole.

For, in fact, movements in agrarian economy are not determined solely by population numbers, the state of technical development, and the system of husbandry. They also depend on three other general factors.

1. *Power.* The social structure left over from the early Middle Ages was notably hierarchical; the distribution of wealth and landownership (which included the men who worked the land) was then very unequal. Throughout Europe in our period small independent peasant properties did exist, but were few and far between, virtually defenceless, and threatened on all sides. A small number of men in power—the heads of the Church and the great religious houses, the secular princes, the war lords, the members of the military aristocracy whose privileges and solidarity grew continually—soon joined by a few less important men of affairs, who had made their fortunes in the towns, held almost all the land. The prerogatives that they owed to the survival of degraded forms of the ancient institution of slavery, together with their monopoly of political power, also gave them the right to command and exploit the working mass. Consequently, the rural economy was under the complete control of that vague and ill-defined institution, the *seigneurie*; we should add that most of the sources are concerned directly with the seigneurie and only incidentally with the peasantry.

2. Another factor was the increasing pressure of the exchange economy. In 900, towns had almost entirely disappeared from the European landscape and business activity was virtually nil. But by the eleventh century trade was starting up again, monetary circulation was quickening, towns were once more taking shape, and a movement

of expansion was beginning to make headway in the country, teaching the peasants to count, exchange, and save, and awakening their sense of profit.

3. A final factor was a progressive improvement in fiscal techniques and the strengthening of the state. Gradually, sometimes as early as the twelfth century, the royal tax collectors became more insistent and exacting. So heavily was the rural economy oppressed by taxation that much of its history can be explained in terms of this alone; the phenomena of stagnation, capital shortage, and the ever-widening economic gap between the country and the towns, which were always much less heavily taxed.

900-1180

The first phase is one of historical uncertainty on account of the lack of documents and, above all, numerical data. The framework of observation is invariably the *seigneurie*, notably the Church.

1. The widespread gifting of land to the Church continued in the tenth and eleventh centuries; together with the practice of dividing up inheritances, it gradually ate away the fortunes of the lay aristocracy. In point of fact, transfers in the other direction did come in to compensate for the impoverishment of the noble families, who contrived to obtain from the clergy virtually gratuitous concessions of demesnes or to retain by force the property alienated by their inconsiderately charitable forebears. In addition, a defence reaction took place in the closing years of the eleventh century; legal rulings were gradually adopted to slow down the dividing-up of the patrimony among the heirs and family control over the gifts of joint heirs limited their prodigality towards the religious institutions. It seems that this brought some stability into the distribution of land fortunes in the twelfth century: the extension of the clearings and the creation of new villages—often jointly organised by two great lords, one of them a layman who opened up the forest to colonisation, the other an ecclesiastic who provided the capital and recruited the labour—en-

abled the aristocracy of large landowners to absorb with impunity the new religious communities, the Cistercians in particular, which duly increased and prospered.

2. The monastic cartularies inform us about the economic attitudes of the great landlords, who were incapable of eating the produce of their demesnes *in situ*, even by keeping constantly on the move. Their first concern was to pass the buck of management; they farmed out each demesne in return for a pension payable every so often and calculated to bring a regular and superabundant supply of victuals into the lordly 'hall'. This manner of indirect management, which was practised on the estates of the great English abbeys in the twelfth century, was certainly very widespread. It literally 'made' the motley class of what the texts from Germany and North-Eastern France call *ministeriales*, whose status varied considerably from region to region, as did the terms of the contracts binding them to the landlords, but who took a harsh hold over the bondmen and were the first to profit from the agrarian expansion and the increments in production.

3. As in Carolingian days, each large land unit was divided up into two parts: the 'demesne' worked for the landlord's direct profit, and the 'tenements' conceded to peasant families. Neither the extent nor the economic role of the demesne seems to have diminished significantly in this period. The swelling numbers of Cistercian abbeys and other new-style religious communities, which imposed manual labour on their monks and refused to exploit the toil of others, were perhaps behind the spread of direct exploitation of large-scale farming in certain regions. The land reserved for the landlord was worked by a permanent team of bondmen, the *familia*, a system favoured by the continued existence of some forms of slavery. The slave trade along the Mediterranean seaboard, on the frontiers with Islam, never ceased entirely; but the last traces of it in the Channel ports appear at the beginning of the eleventh century, and elsewhere, throughout civilised Europe, it had already disappeared. However, the labour force kept in the seigneurial households was easily restocked by forcibly

recruiting young domestics from the tenant families still bound in servitude.

4. During this period of demographic expansion and agricultural conquest, the numbers of landleases went up considerably: those that already existed, which the rise in productivity had caused to be too large for the needs of a single family, were split up; the assarts created innumerable new ones. The growth of exchanges began to have repercussions on most country regions in the eleventh century and money gradually got less scarce. In the second half of this century, in Northern Italy, commerce in land produce became centred on the urban markets and there emerged a new class of men, the *negociantes* of the market towns, the agents of trade between town and country. At the same moment, the French peasants were beginning to be aware of the different kinds of money in circulation, to take an interest in the fairs, and to solicit exemptions from tolls. However, there is no clear evidence that the lords and tenants ever wished to convert the payments in kind into money. The most definite change that affected the dues of tenure was the lightening of the *corvées*, made possible by improvements in plough teams and implements on the large demesnes and by a greater facility in recruiting paid labour. In southern Europe, where they always seem to have been light, the *corvées* either went out altogether or dwindled to a few days' ploughing and carting service in the year. In the former Carolingian region, the unfree tenants' obligation to work three days a week for nothing and the liveries of produce prepared in the dependants' families went out around the turn of the tenth century. Here the *corvées* still had a definite economic value; they provided the reinforcements of men and (especially) ploughs that were indispensable for working the demesnes at peak periods in the farming calendar; but they were infinitely less onerous than those described in the ninth century inventories. It was then that the economic bond between tenure and the working of the demesnes was severed. Liveries in money redeemed work service. Taxes levied on sales or divisions of tenures became less exceptional from the end of the eleventh

century onwards. After 1150, fixed money-rents replaced
the crop-sharing payments (called in France *champarts* or
tasques) that had formerly been levied in the clearance
zones. Together with these two new sources of revenue, the
corvée dues fed the seigneurial 'halls' with money, but little
of it.

5. The elements of the *seigneurie* that earned the most
were, according to the first estimates possible from the
documents after the middle of the twelfth century: (a) the
demesnes (it brought in four times as much as the tenures
on the lands of the Abbey of Cluny); (b) the installations
that the lord placed at the disposal of his tenants' families
and their neighbours: church, mill, bakehouse, smithy, and
inn; (c) the tithes levied on all the crops in the parish
territory that were supposed to go to the bishop, the priest,
and the poor, but in fact went to the lord, be he layman or
churchman. The profits coming from these last two
sources rose constantly in this period under the effect of the
increasing population, the progress in land settlement, and
a certain rise in the peasants' standard of living (people
ate more bread, used more cloth and metal, so resorted
more often to the mill and bakehouse, flail and forge). The
general rise in seigneurial income explains the increasing
affluence that appears to have been the lot of the whole
aristocracy at that time.

6. One of the major facts in the economic history of this
period was the bringing in of new methods of exploiting
the men that worked the land and of transferring the surpluses of rural production to the 'halls' of the wealthy.
The dissolution of public authority, which led to what we
call feudalism, resulted in the appearance of a whole body
of taxes levied by the castle occupant in return for his protection. These 'customs' or 'aids', together with the fines
he imposed to punish breaches of the peace, were levied on
all the peasant families living within the area covered by
the protection and jurisdiction of the fortress. They were
fixed at the lords' whim, especially as regards what was
called *taille* or *tolte* (both meaning 'grasp') in France, and
Bede ('requisition') in Germany: these were levies on the

savings of the protected households, raised every time the lord needed money. These exactions were onerous, much more so than the dues of tenure, to such an extent that they cancelled out all the economic differences that should have existed between tenants and small independent landowners and between the free and the unfree. Grouped together for mutual defence, the village communities, especially those in France, sometimes obtained a written stipulation of what taxes were due and when. But these 'customs' charters, even the so-called 'liberty' charters, never abolished this levy altogether: they merely gave it a definition, and frequently the dependants paid for this limitation on their lord's whim with increased contributions. In France, these 'customs' began to be collected in money in the twelfth century. The conversion is one of the surest signs for the dating of the penetration of the monetary medium into peasant society; thanks to it, most of the wage money earned by the rural population was taken away from them. It was not the landlord class as a whole that benefited from this levy, but merely a small number of them, those that had inherited the right to command and punish over a given territory; their economic superiority imposed itself within the aristocracy.

1180-1320

Since thirteenth century rural history has the benefit of far less meagre source material, many trends revealed there for the first time may have begun previously without leaving any trace in the sources available to us: hence, the innovations of this period are perhaps fewer than they seem. It is certain, however, that the influence of the urban economy became much keener than before. The towns got bigger; the greater part of their population was made up of men who were all but peasants and drew their own and their neighbours' food from their personal lands, grazed sheep, and grew vines; the towns also became the centres of many *seigneuries*, and produce from the surrounding countryside came in direct without going through the exchanges. Hence only a limited proportion of the urban consumption of foodstuffs and raw materials was bought from the countrymen. Nevertheless, increasing demand for these products quickened the growth of the rural economy, and intensified the role played by the merchants, fairs, money, and credit. Regular streams of trade supplied the most densely urbanised zones, in Flanders and along the Mediterranean littoral, with grain, and there was a distinct rise in cattle traffic on the roads and in wood and wine shipments on the waterways (at the start of the fourteenth century, Bordeaux exported a yearly average of 700,000 hectolitres of wine to England). Money was less scarce in the peasants' purses: we know, for instance that, in the thirteenth century villagers in the Paris region offered enormous sums to their landlords in return for 'liberty' charters that did away with the last vestiges of servitude: those at Orly offered 4,000 *livres*. It is doubtful whether they paid all this cash down; they borrowed, but their creditors trusted them because they knew that their financial situation was secure and that they were able to make regular, substantial earnings at the markets. At this time, every farm down to the smallest of all, whose possessors had nothing to sell but their labour, opened up to trade in a big way.

1. The first consequence was a falling-off in economic solidarity within rural society. Handling money, haggling prices with the grain merchant or wine dealer, joining a gang of journeymen, or going off for a few months to try one's luck in town were individual acts inspired by a personal sense of enterprise, which inevitably tested the cohesion of the family group. Personal fortunes became more fluid, and it is not entirely due to the better source material if we can count a marked increase in property conveyances, buying, selling, and dividing inheritances, which testifies to an expanding mobility in this domain. Within the villages, it was at this time that the relative economic uniformity obtaining among the majority of the husbandmen, a uniformity due to the landlords' onerous 'customs' and 'exactions', disappeared. In the first place,

the henceforth predominant role played by individual enterprise, together with the continuance of the demographic expansion and the growing scarcity of land fit for settlement resulted in the emergence of small groups of wealthy villagers wanting to govern the communities or quit them in order to avoid the constraints of productivity and to get better profits from their capital. On the other hand, a fair proportion of the peasantry got poorer and poorer. In these areas, despite the daily rise in population, trade, and (it would seem) prosperity, poverty progressed, swelling the ranks of the proletariat left at the mercy of the exploiting landlords and wealthy peasants. Many peasant families that had not sought their safety in the towns were unable to earn their living without working for wages or turning their hand to skilled crafts. The irregularity of the crops—hence of the price of food and the work available at harvesting time—aggravated the precarious situation of this hard-pressed class, ravaged by deaths at every famine, and often unable to marry off its young. (These considerations were probably the underlying causes behind the reversal in demographic trends at the end of the thirteenth century.) In their hardship, the poor became the prey of the money-lenders then thriving: wealthy farmers whose loans within the village were repaid by so many days' work; Jews from the towns in southern France and Spain, who bought standing crops cheaply at times of major difficulties: and 'Lombards', whose booths began to become a regular feature of French market towns at the end of the thirteenth century. Land-hunger and just plain hunger favoured the resurgence of servitude; to get themselves set up on a holding, young men had to bind themselves and their heirs to the landlords, who would otherwise refuse the concessions. In some provinces, this led to the redevelopment of a form of bondage that was specifically economic in its origins and nature. At the same time, hardships among the *enfants* (labourers, journeymen, and young men living in forced celibacy) or the *pâtres* (landless peasants living off small-scale stock-raising) caused scattered incidents that sometimes burst out into revolt, pillage, and marauding.

2. The new conjecture in the rural economy also brought a change in the attitudes of the landlords: it gave them a sense of profit. In some regions at least (England for instance, as if shown by the great success and the tone of the treatises counselling pinch-and-save property management) the aristocracy itself fell in with the preoccupation with gain, despite the fact that its code condemned the love of money and the avarice of the bourgeois. However, the concern with profit developed mainly within the group of the entrepreneurs, stewards and merchants, the intermediaries between the peasants and the big landowners on the one hand, and the masters of urban trade on the other. This class of men played a predominant role in the initiation of economic trends at this time.

3. It seems that so far as the distribution of land-ownership is concerned this movement in the economy affected the aristocracy less than the peasantry. A few men did slip through into the ranks of the landlords; but, except in North Italy, and perhaps Spain, they were not 'men of affairs' but mostly members of princely households or, lower down the scale, descendants of *ministeriales*. The mass of *seigneuries* stayed in the hands of the Church and the military aristocracy.

4. Many members of this wealthy class moved away from their demesnes. Though the greater part of the lesser nobility carried on living among the peasants, and the Benedictine communities, overwhelmed with debts and beset with difficulties, put an end to the *fermes* and came back to direct management, numbers of landlords elected to live in town for at least part of the year, as their peers in Italy, Spain and Southern France had long since been doing. Their money requirements got more acute, partly on account of this change of residence, but mostly because convention obliged them to live in luxury and dissipation. The growth of the states, furthermore, placed increasingly onerous burdens upon them, while withholding a major part of their resources by abrogating the superior powers of justice and peace to the sovereign. Dogged by necessity, they became more attentive to what could be gained from their lands.

5. Economic conditions were all in favour of the big farms. Demographic pressure kept the prices of agricultural produce high and sent the wage level down and down; the quality of their equipment, their situation within the parishes, their power even, put the great demesnes in the best possible position for the production and disposal of land produce; their masters negotiated, not without profit to themselves, the sale of surpluses from neighbouring peasant farms. Their control over the organisation of the farming calendar, the rotation of crops, and the management of the commons, the work they provided, the wages and assistance they distributed, all put the great demesnes in a commanding position over the village economy as a whole. But it was increasingly common for them not to be managed directly by their owners. From the end of the twelfth century, first the great families, the bishops and cathedral chapters, then lesser lords, got accustomed to leasing the 'demesne' to a *fermier*. At first the leases ran for the farmer's lifetime, then the period was limited. This made possible periodical readjustments to the rent, paid in money or in kind, to bring it into line with increases in productivity, while all precautions were taken to see that the farmer did nothing to depreciate the capital. For such landlords, this was a safe way of passing the buck of management; for the small group of entrepreneurs it was a means of setting themselves up in the economic position of the greatest landlords themselves, of dominating the village, and of getting rich quicker.

6. Different methods of indirect management were preferred for viticulture and stock-raising. Leases were used, but they were often for very short periods and related to much lower capital amounts; the man who provided his labour and the man who provided the land or capital entered into a partnership to share the risks and profits. These extremely varied forms of share-cropping enabled a much broader section of the peasantry to participate in the management of seigneurial capital. The keenest and earliest success they seem to have met with at this time was in Italy, where town and country were much closer knit, and

where the system of *coltura promiscua* was developing a more intimate combination of agriculture with grazing and wine-growing activities.

1320-1440

In the first half of the fourteenth century there is a shift of emphasis in the source material, which is no longer concerned exclusively with the *seigneurie*: in particular, the mass of seigneurial accounts disappear as the result of the abandonment of direct management. It is perhaps an illusion nourished by this change in the sources but it would seem indeed that, at this time when agrarian history was dominated by the drop in the population and by the consequent reabsorption of the rural proletariat, the *seigneurie* lost its hold over the country economy—in the West at any rate, for in East Europe depopulation gave opposite results: a consolidation in the aristocratic demesnes and an aggravation in the regime of *corvées* and bondage. In Western Europe, the evolution may be summarised under the following four headings:

1. The big estates were very prosperous around 1300, but their profit margins were extremely narrow. The reduction in the numbers of poor workers in the villages, who having no lands of their own were forced to buy part of their food and to stand in line for work, caused a drop in grain prices and a rise in labour prices, which cut the landlords' profits down to almost nothing or ruled out profit altogether. Those landlords that still managed their demesnes themselves preferred to stop doing so, and *fermage* made great progress during the fourteenth century. But it became difficult—except in the few privileged regions, such as Lombardy, that escaped the depression—to find *fermiers* for large cereal farms needing a lot of paid labour. The farming leases henceforth bore upon much smaller amounts of land, as the share-cropping leases had done previously, and the great demesnes were split up into moderate-sized concessions suited to the capabilities of a single peasant family, whose numbers were strengthened

by the consolidation of family ties and by a more frequent use of joint ownership.

2. The troubles of these times, the ravages of war and pestilence, forced the landlords to be less exacting towards their tenants and bondmen, even though they themselves were affected by the calamities and perhaps more in need of money than ever before. Their problem was to persuade the peasants to stay on their lands, to repopulate them when they were deserted, and to put them back in order when passing troops or long disuse had deteriorated them. Some landlords attempted to tighten the bonds of servitude and tie the workers closer to the soil; they failed: it was too easy to abscond; and this emigration contributed towards the total disappearance of bondage in most of Western Europe (in the East it was on the increase). The only way to keep or attract tenants, *fermiers*, or *metayers* was to give in to their demands and lighten their dues. Peasant families were much less numerous; they handed over an ever decreasing share of their working profits: hence the period saw a considerable fall in seigneurial income. This fall was perceptible as early as 1320 in a few English shires; it quickened in the second half of the fourteenth century. Between 1430 and 1456, the income of the Teutonic Knights on their manor at Coblenz fell by 40 per cent; the tenants of a *seigneurie* in Normandy paid 152 *livres* in 1397, 112 in 1428, 52 in 1437, and 10 *livres* in 1444.

3. This decline of the seigneurial estates was undeniably to the profit of the peasant economy, which suffered, however, from the restriction of urban consumption (the demographic crises were sometimes more acute in the towns than they were in the country) as is attested in particular by the continual fall in cereal prices. The peasant economy also underwent levies of a different kind. From the fourteenth century onwards the documents show clearly to what an extent the peasantry was exploited by the entrepreneurs and princely tax collectors. The plentiful information that can be gleaned from the notarial registers of Southern Europe gives a vivid picture of activities of the ubiquitous grainbrokers, woolbrokers, dyestuff brokers from the market

towns, who arrived at the farms when money was at its scarcest, the cattle speculators, and the moneylenders. All of them took advantage of the monetary famine from which the countryside, used as it had become to trade, was then suffering even more than were the towns. In point of fact, we are perhaps tempted to give too much weight to these activities, simply because we see more of them in the sources. Things are quite different as regards the pressure of taxation, which, there can be no doubt, weighed much heavier on the country from the fourteenth century onwards. There can be no doubt either that this was one of the main economic changes of this period. That the importance of the change was clearly understood is proved by the peasant insurrections of that time: the French Jacquerie in 1358 and England's Peasants' Revolt in 1381 were led by men who were angrier with the avidity of the soldiery and tax collectors than with the sequels of lordly exploitation. It may be thought that these ruthless State levies prevented the peasant economy from closing down completely to external trade—the demands of the princes had to be met somehow, and the peasants had to sell to get the money. But without a doubt they did more than anything else to slow down the rise of rural living standards.

4. There is a reason to believe, however, that the standard of living did not go down, but even rose slightly, during this period, which must consequently not be judged too pessimistically so far as the country economy is concerned. Since they were far fewer in number, the peasants at the close of the fourteenth century found themselves in an economic milieu in which capital had not depreciated to any great extent and the hold of the *seigneurie* had already slackened considerably and was slackening still further; in fact, they were probably less needy than their forebears had been a hundred years earlier. Their lands were certainly more extensive or of better quality; the space available for grazing had greatly expanded; what is more, the skilled crafts were developing in the villages: the movement of expansion in the textile crafts in the country reached its culmination at this time. Archaeological, textual, and

iconographical research into the daily life of the period is barely under way. Will it confirm the impression that the peasants at the end of the Middle Ages were better fed, better clothed, and better housed than they were in the over-population and the landlord-profiting prosperity of the thirteenth century? It would seem, at any rate, that the survivors of the great demographic depression had built up considerable reserves of vitality.

Around 1440, the first scattered signs of recovery became apparent in all the regions that had undergone depopulation. A new wave of expansion set in, but was very slow in getting fully under way. The population numbers began to go up, and the land recently fallen into waste began to tempt colonisers once again. But the regions where the expansion made any marked headway before 1550 were few and far between. This expansion, based as it was on the land fortunes of the aristocracy and on peasant labour, was set in motion by the same small group of grasping entrepreneurs that we saw at work in the climate of expansion of the thirteenth century. But if it started from a much higher level than the expansion that had begun before 1000, this new forward trend never managed, before the agricultural improvement of the eighteenth century, to push the production and disposal of land produce and the density of agrarian settlement to the level reached before 1300, in the great rush of rural conquest that sustained the flowering of medieval civilisation.

BIBLIOGRAPHY

GENERAL The most useful general surveys and the fullest bibliographical information are to be found in the works of Duby and Postan cited below.

Abel, W., *Agrarkrisen unde Agrarkonjonctur. Eine Geschichte der Land-und Ernährungswirtschaft Mittleuropas set dem hohen Mittelalter*, 2nd ed., Hamburg/Berlin, 1966.
   Geschichte der deutschen Landwirtschaft vom frühen Mittelalter bis zum XIX. Jahrhundert, Vol. II of *Deutsche Agrargeschichte* (ed. G. Franz), Stuttgart, 1962.

Bloch, M., *French Rural History; An Essay on its original characteristics*, Trans. J. Sondheimer, London, 1966.
   Les caractères originaux de l'histoire rurale française, 2nd ed., Vol. II, Paris, 1956.

Cipolla, C. M., *Storia dell' economia italiana*, vol. I, Turin, 1959.
   Deuxième conférence internationale d'histoire économique. Aix-en-Provence, 1962, Paris, 1965.

Duby, G., *Rural Economy and Country Life in the Medieval West*, Trans. Lady Cynthia Postan, London, 1968.

Franz, G., *Geschichte des Bauernstandes*, Vol. VI of *Deutsche Agrargeschichte*, Stuttgart, 1963.

Hilton, R. H., 'The Content and Sources of English Agrarian History before 1500', *Agricultural History Review*, 1955.

Jones, P. J., 'Per la storia agraria italiana nel medio evo; lineamenti e problemi', *Rivista storica italiana*, 1964.

Lütge, F., *Geschichte der deutschen Agrarverfassung vom frühen Mittelalter bis zum XIX*, Vol. III of *Deutsche Agrargeschichte* (ed. G. Franz) Stuttgart, 1963.

Luzzato, G., *Storia economica d'Italia. I l'Antichità e il Medio Evo*, Rome, 1949.

Postan, M. M., ed., *The Cambridge Economic History of Europe*, Vol. I, *The Agrarian Life of the Middle Ages*, 2nd ed., Cambridge, 1966.

Slicher van Bath, B. H., *The Agrarian History of Western Europe*, 500-1850, London, 1963.

Vicens Vives, J., *Manual de Historia economica de España*, 3rd ed., Barcelona, 1964.

Violante, C., 'Storia ed economia dell' Italia medievale', *Rivista storica italiana*, 1961.

DEMOGRAPHY For a thorough study the reader is referred to Vol. 1 Chapter 1 of the *Fontana Economic History of Europe* (also published separately in pamphlet form: J. C. Russell *Population in Europe 500-1500*).

Abel, W., *Die Wüstungen des ausgehenden Mittelalters. Ein Beitrag zur Siedlungs—und Agrargeschichte Deutschlands*, Jena, 1943.

Baratier, E., *La démographie provençale du XIIIè au XVIè siècle avec chiffres de comparaison pour le XVIIIè siècle*, Paris, 1961.

Hallam, H. E., 'Some Thirteenth Century Censuses', *Economic History Review*, 1958.

Russell, J. C., *Late Ancient and Medieval Population*, Philadelphia, 1958.

Titow, J. Z., 'Some evidences of the Thirteenth Century Population Increase', *Economic History Review*, 1961.

   'Some Differences between Manors and their Effects on the Condition of the Peasant in the Thirteenth Century', *Agricultural History Review*, 1962.

   Villages désertés et histoire économique, XI-XVIIIè siècles, Paris, 1965.

NATURAL CONDITIONS AND HUSBANDRY The works cited below describe the main problems. For regional studies reference should be made to the works of the geographers.

Beresford, M. W., and Saint Joseph, J. K. S., *Medieval England. An Aerial Survey*, Cambridge, 1958.

Darby, H., ed. *An Historical Geography of England*, Cambridge, 1936.

Dion, R., *Histoire de la vigne et du vin en France, des origines au XIXè siècle*, Paris, 1959.

   Géographie et Histoire agraire, Nancy, 1959.

Higounet, C., *La grange de Vaulerent. Structure et exploitation d'un terroir cistercien de la plaine de France, XIIè-XVè siècles*, Paris, 1965.

Postan, M. M., 'Village Livestock in the Thirteenth Century', *Economic History Review*, 1962.

Sereni, E., *Storia del paesaggio agrario italiano*, Bari, 1961.

Verhulst, A., *Histoire du paysage rural en Flandre de l'époque romaine au XVIIIè siècle*, Brussels, 1966.

SOCIAL STRUCTURE The studies of Finberg, Hilton and Miller are models of historical method.

Bader, K., *Dorfgenossenschaft und Dorfgemeinde*. Vol. I. *Das Mittelalterliche Dorf als Friedens und Rechtsbereich*, Vol. II. *Studien zur Rechtsgeschichte des mittelalterlichen Dorfes*, Weimar, 1957, 1962.

Duboulay, F. R. H., *The Lordship of Canterbury. An essay on medieval Society*, London, 1966.

Finberg, H. P. R., *Tavistock Abbey. A Study in the social and economic History of Devon*, Cambridge, 1951.

Genicot, L., *L'Economie rurale namuroise au bas Moyen Age* (1199-1429), Vol. I, *La Seigneurie foncière*, Namur, 1943; Vol. II. *Les hommes: la noblesse*, Louvain, 1960.

Herlihy, D., 'Population, Plague and social Change in rural Pistoia 1201-1430', *Economic History Review*, 1965.

Hilton, R. H., *Social structures of rural Warwickshire in the Middle Ages*, Oxford, 1950.

Leicht, P. S., *Operai, artigiani, agricoltori in Italia del secolo VI al XVI*, Milan, 1946.

Miller, E., *The Abbey and Bishopric of Ely. The social History of an Ecclesiastical Estate from the Xth century to the early XIVth century*, Cambridge, 1951.

Platelle, H., *Le temporel de l'abbaye de Saint-Amand, des origines à 1340*, Paris, 1962.

Raftis, J. A., *The Estates of Ramsey Abbey. A study in Economic Growth and organisation*, Toronto, 1957.

Steinback, F., *Ursprung und Wesen der Landgemeinde nach rheinischen Quellen*, Cologne, 1960.

Verhulst. A. E., *De Sint-Baafsaddij te Gent en haar Grondbezit*, Brussels, 1958.

10TH-12TH CENTURIES As an introduction to the subject the books of Duby and Lennard will be found particularly valuable.

Deléage, A., *La vie rurale en Bourgogne jusqu'au début du XI siècle*, Mâcon, 1941.

Duby, G., *La société aux XIè et XIIè siècles dans la région mâconnaise*, Paris, 1953.

Galbraith, V. H., *The Making of Domesday Book*, Oxford, 1961.

Lennard, R., *Rural England, 1068-1135. A Study of Social and Agrarian Conditions*, Oxford, 1959.

Perrin, C. E., *Recherches sur la seigneurie rurale en Lorraine d'après les plus anciens censieurs (Xè-XIIè siècles)*, Strasbourg, 1935.

Postan, M. M., *The 'Famulus', the estate Labourer in the XIIth and XIIIth centuries*, Cambridge, 1954.

Van de Kieft, C., *Etude sur le chartrier et la seigneurie du prieuré de la Chapelle-Aude (XIè-XIIIè siècles)*, Amsterdam, 1960.

13TH CENTURY Hilton's regional monograph can be recommended as the best book on the subject in the context of this period.

Conti, E., *La formazione della structura agraria moderna vel contado fioreltino, I: le campagne neln'età precomunale*, Rome, 1965.

Hilton, R. H., *A medieval society. The West Midlands at the End of the Thirteenth century*, London, 1966.

Kosminsky, E. A., *Studies in the Agrarian History of England in the XIIIth century*, Oxford, 1958.

Plesner, J., *L'émigration de la campagne à la ville libre de Florence au XIIIè siècle*, Copenhagen, 1934.

Postan, M. M., 'The Rise of a Money Economy', *Economic History Review*, 1944.

Renouard, Y., 'Le grand commerce des vins de Gascogne ua Moyen-Age', *Revue Historique*, 1959.

14TH-15TH CENTURIES There are a great many detailed studies. Those listed below give the reader an immediate grasp of the central issues.

Duby, G., 'La seigneurie et l'économie paysannes. Alpes du Sud, 1338', *Etudes rurales*, 1969.

Bean, J. M. W., *The Estates of the Percy Family, 1416-1537*, Oxford, 1958.

Boutruche, R., *La crise d'une société. Seigneurs et paysans du Bordelais pendant la guerre de Cent Ans*, Strasburg, 1947.

Cipolla C. M., 'Revisions on Economic History: the Trends in Italian Economic History in the later Middle Ages', *Economic History Review*, 1949.

'L'économia milanese. I movimenti economici generali, 1350-1500', *Storia di Milano*, Milan, 1957.

Craeybeckx, J., *Un grand commerce d'importation. Les vins de France aux anciens Pays-Bas (XIIIè-XVIè siècles)*, Paris, 1958.

Fourquin, G., 'Les débuts du fermage: l'exemple de Saint-Denis', *Etudes rurales*, 1966.

Fourquin, G., *Les campagnes de la région parisienne à la fin du moyen âge (du milieu du XIIè siècle au début du XVIè)*, Paris, 1964.

Haenens, A. D., *L'abbaye de Saint Martin de Tournai de 1290 à 1350. Origines, évolution et dénouement d'une crise*, Louvain, 1961.

Hilton, R. H. and Fagan, H., *The English Rising of 1381*, London, 1954.

Holmes, G. A., *The Estates of the Higher Nobility in XIVth century England*, Cambridge, 1957.

Le Roy Ladurie, E., *Les paysans du Languedoc*, Paris, 1966.

Plaisse, A., *La baronnie du Neufbourg. Essai d'histoire agraire, économique et sociale*, Paris, 1957.

Postan, M. M., 'The Fifteenth Century', *Economic History Review*, 1938-1939.

Verhulst, A., 'L'économie rurale de la Flandre et la dépression économique du bas moyen-âge', *Etudes rurales*, 1963.

6. Medieval Industry 1000-1500

Sylvia L. Thrupp

MEDIEVAL INDUSTRY IN EVOLUTIONARY PERSPECTIVE

The industrial litter that people leave behind them forms the earliest record of human society that we possess. In Europe the litter that has been examined so far suggests that industrial activity of one sort or another has been going on there continuously, at a conservative estimate, for some forty thousand years. From the point of view of how such activity was fitted into the general organisation of societies, however, this immense span of time is commonly viewed as falling into just three ages. The age of the primitive hunting-band covers some three-quarters of the span. Almost all of the remaining time has been passed in a series of primarily agrarian civilisations which it is currently fashionable to lump together under the somewhat negative label of 'pre-industrial'. The infinitely more complex organisation of modern industrialism, dated from Britain's pioneering advances in the late eighteenth century A.D., has been dominant for barely half of one per cent of the total stretch of time. To look briefly at the central contrasts between these ages will help to bring medieval problems and achievements into perspective.

THE THREE AGES OF INDUSTRIAL EVOLUTION

In the first age, men's attitude to the natural environment was almost wholly predatory. Towards each other, it was co-operative within the small hunting-band that roved a given territory. In such a life, any possessions beyond a portable kit of tools and weapons, and such clothing as may be considered functional, are a nuisance. It follows that people are not acquisitive, nor are they dependent on specialists: every child has to learn to make and repair

what is essential. Since we think of a man who has all that
he wants as affluent, an American anthropologist has lately
styled the aboriginal world the first age of affluence. This
description would perhaps hold true only as the first crude
hunting kits were improved by sharper cutting edges and
stronger projectiles, and the affluence would have been
stable only while population remained so sparse as not to
reduce the requisite quotas of edible wild life and vegetation. Any continuous upsetting of this balance would sooner
or later oblige people to look at their environment differently, with an eye to controlling at least some auxiliary
food supply through herding and sowing. Ultimately, as
population grew through intermittent immigration from
Asia, these had to become the main sources of food, with
hunting an auxiliary source.

South-eastern Europe took the lead in the definitive
transition to farmstead life, apparently through direct introduction of agrarian techniques from the more advanced
Middle East. Wherever the new life was adopted, it generated a new set of wants and the skill to satisfy them by more
solid housing, more comfortable clothing, and better processing of food and drink. Archaeological evidence is accumulating to suggest also that household groups need not have
been limited to consuming only what their own members
produced, but were open, if only as a means to maintaining
friendly relations within a district, to exchange of goods.
This could and did lead on to purposeful production for
exchange. A whole community, if it had exceptionally fine
raw materials at hand, might engage in this. A well-known
example dating from early in the second millennium B.C.
—it is by no means necessarily the oldest—was located at
rich flint deposits in Norfolk. The flint was mined with
horn and bone picks and worked up on the spot. There is
no means of telling, from skeletal remains, whether or not
the families of these mining craftsmen were wholly divorced
from farming, but the men clearly worked at their craft for
a large part of the year. Fully professional craftsmanship
that could be combined with farming or divorced from it
spread through advances in technique that called for a keen

intelligence, as was the case with kiln-fired pottery and still more so with metallurgy. Smiths rearmed military chieftains and with diffusion of the use of iron began the retooling of construction work and of agriculture. Under military chieftains, however, the new techniques achieved little but support of a warrior nobility. Industry first became a means to wider prosperity only as governmental power came to be organised from urban centres fostering a market economy and attracting a heterogeneous population. Here, with merchants to supply them with materials and expand their market by export, craftsmen could develop higher skill and experiment more freely with division of labour.

But the expansive power of urban industry was severely limited by pre-industrial Europe's inefficiency in feeding herself. Most of the working population had always to live dispersed about the countrysides in small settlements, growing grain on underfertilised soil and herding underfed animals, overworked in the harvest season but with time free in the winter to carry on the traditional rural industries. These tended, as population growth reduced the size of peasant holdings, to pass into the hands of the families with the least land. The fundamental problem, that of low grain yields and poor animal fodder, might have been resolved more quickly if rich landowners had regularly set aside a part of the land and labour at their disposal for experimentation, as they ultimately did on a large scale in eighteenth-century England. Industry might also have increased the output of its limited full-time labour force by regularly diverting some of it to the improvement of mechanical equipment. There was progress on both these fronts, but it was at best fitful and dawdling, and over large areas for long periods there was none at all.

Some historians have described any ancient or medieval city where the majority of the working population lived by industries with more than a local market—ancient Athens' port suburb and medieval Florence are examples—as examples of industrialisation. It seems a little absurd to insist on the prefix 'pre-industrial', but until a better terminology is generally accepted one has to do so. For industrialisation is commonly understood as meaning entry into the third age, our own, in which large-scale production has been continuously transforming the conditions of working life.

Seen in the perspective of the late twentieth century the hallmark of successful industrialisation is the attainment, through organisation channelling investment to that end, of self-sustaining economic growth. At this point a country can normally expect each year's total production to exceed that of the previous year by some small percentage that will exceed the percentage increase in its population over the same period. In short, statistical measures will show regular increases in output per head even of a steadily growing national population. The produce of the land is included in the measure of total output, but industry will dominate the picture.

MEDIEVAL INDUSTRY'S CONTRIBUTION TO ECONOMIC GROWTH: PROBLEMS OF MEASUREMENT AND SOURCES OF EVIDENCE

The centuries between the years 1000 and 1500 A.D. stand out as the first to see town-building in all parts of Europe save the fringes of tribal culture in the far north. The larger towns, nodal points of a commercial network that in the south-east stretched out to mesh with Islamic trade, set the members of the various moneyed groups they drew together competing socially in habits of display, their craftsmen catering to these habits by cultivating artistic skill. The smaller towns did their best to stir up trade and new demand for better products in the villages. The age stands out also as the first to make any substantial use of automation in industrial processes that otherwise absorbed a great deal of labour in heavy drudgery.

These movements give the age a place of fundamental importance in Europe's industrial evolution. However, if we had medieval statistics comparable with those by which rates of economic growth are measured today, for any of the territories covered by modern governments, industry's showing would be dismally unimpressive. It is usually assumed that a country dominated by rentier landlords not seriously interested in economic development will devote barely five per cent of its total annual economic effort to new improvement of productive equipment including transport facilities, a proportion which can make for no more than a one per cent increase in total annual production. Nor can this increase be steadily cumulative, since so backward a country is peculiarly vulnerable to crop failure, famine and epidemic disease which may temporarily disrupt all economic effort. Phyllis Deane estimates that England was attaining a fairly steady one per cent rate of growth in the mid-eighteenth century, by which time grain yields were from two to four times those on medieval estates, credit organisation was vastly better, and industrial entrepreneurship was on the rise. Actually we have no really valid aggregate statistics from any country so backward, for their collection in poor countries is haphazard and cannot possibly include the value of garden crops that peasants consume as they grow, nor the output of do-it-yourself industry for home use; nor can one accurately gauge the value of part-time industry for local exchange. In a medieval village these items were substantial. But such comparisons as are feasible do at least suggest that in all other forms of production taken together, including the high proportion of field crops not marketed but consumed by the peasant producers or going directly to the kitchens of their lords, over the whole of any territory covered by a modern European government the best medieval rates of general economic growth, if they could be averaged by decades to balance the effects of good and bad harvests, would have been perhaps half of one per cent.

The more urbanised and commercialised areas must have done better than this, for sleepy outlying regions would always have pulled down the average. Rates of growth of production in and around the rapidly expanding manufacturing towns of north-eastern France and in Flanders and in the Po valley, in the twelfth and thirteenth centuries may have been several times the average over France as a whole or Italy as a whole. These 'boom' conditions subsided as general population growth towards the close of the thirteenth century slowed down. The expansion of town size had ground to a halt well before the catastrophe of the Black Death cut population over the western half of Europe by about a third, and thereafter an erratic series of local epidemics of various kinds prevented any widespread resumption of population growth until near the close of the fifteenth century. It is agreed that the net result of all these miseries was to encourage more efficient agriculture, by relieving the pressure to sow grain on poor land, and to raise levels of food consumption both in villages and in towns. The industrial response cannot be summed up so simply. Production per head seems to have gone up in some regions in some decades, but in others it went down and in still others stayed about the same. A great deal more quantitative research is needed, with mapping of the results against findings in local demographic research, before we can come to any sound conclusions for Europe as a whole.

Written sources relating to industry are quite rich in the western countries from the thirteenth century on, but the further back one goes in time, the more they thin out. The oldest are brief descriptions of goods traded and records of juridical and fiscal arrangements fitting industrial activity into seigneurial administrative structures. These sources are succeeded by gild records which though discontinuous become fuller and allow of occasional spot-checks on productive capacity. Tax records become fuller, and are often a guide to the income classes in which smaller and larger producers belonged. Building costs, and production for military purposes come to be better documented. Operating problems come into view in contracts and litigation over them and in prosecutions for deviating from price and wage regulations or from standards of quality. The wills of craftsmen and of merchants, inventories of their stock, and merchants' accounts, yield detail as to investment, credit relationships, and relations with apprentices and servants. Hardly any letters or accounts written by craftsmen survive. Yet each occupational group made an impression on contemporaries that is reflected in literary sources, and every town industry was a subject of civic pride. The concern of late medieval governments with preserving and developing industry gave rise also to a kind of 'policy' literature. Full of special pleading, exaggerations and prejudice, it is nevertheless of some help in distinguishing industries that were in a condition to meet new competition from those that were not. Most of the written sources are heavily weighted by evidence from towns, but medieval village archaeology is helping to balance the picture.

INDUSTRY OUTSIDE THE TOWNS UP TO 1300 A.D.

CONTINUITIES

The ancient part-time industrial activity of the countrysides dies only as agriculture is reorganised along modern lines and under the competition of modern mass-production factory methods. In Europe it survived the urbanisation of the ancient world and was in the long run strengthened by medieval urbanisation.

In the ex-Roman world one of the questions at issue is the degree of continuity in the planning of industrial production on landed estates by the lord and with his capital. Interest in the question stems from excavation of late Roman villas and from the earliest documents that we have, which date from the late eighth century and from the ninth century, on the management of the larger manors of that time. Roman villas were originally built simply as country houses where their owners could spend the hot summer months more pleasantly than in the cities. When the real exodus from the late imperial cities to the country began, it is likely that there was not much change in customary villa management save an effort, in order to conserve reduced incomes for outlay on luxuries, to get the labour staff to meet as many of the everyday wants of the household as possible. It had always been stock advice to a Roman landowner to keep slaves fully occupied all the year round. A few of the fourth-century villas that have been excavated in Britain had enough cloth-fulling troughs to show that they were centres of commercial manufacture, but most of them show little or no sign of industry beyond a small forge. All appear to have been destroyed in the invasions of the fifth century.

Over the next three centuries almost the only evidence that is relevant is in information about inter-regional trade, and in the growing number of grants by which lay and ecclesiastical lords obtained the right to tax and police local trade by channelling it into supervised market places, where their deputies could collect tolls and adjudicate disputes. Although evidence from the ninth century on shows the bulk of the business so channelled to have been in agricultural produce and in raw materials for industry, it was customary to let stalls also to craftsmen, and in Roman times craftsmen had used local markets as an outlet for everything from metal wares to ready-made clothing. That ready-made clothing was on sale in the eighth century is known from the high reputation of the woollen cloaks known as Frisian because they were sold by Frisian merchants. Some of the cloaks sold on the continent were of English origin. The earliest record of a complaint about the quality of English exports is a letter from Charlemagne to King Offa of Mercia in 796 mentioning that these garments had lately been unsatisfactory. English cloth entered also into Viking trade.

Meanwhile, faced with changes in methods of cultivation and in crops, landed proprietors were constantly changing their management policies and continued to do so. In general, a shift to serf labour reduced the industrial needs of an estate. To the extent that they settled for a small permanent staff to cultivate the land of a home farm (demesne) with the help of corvée labour from tenants who looked after their own households, the lords needed only to keep up the stock of tools for the demesne, such storage barns and processing apparatus as the demesne harvest and rents paid in kind by tenants required, and housing for the permanent staff.

Ninth-century sources show manors drawing on craft services both from tenants and from their landless servile staff. Much of the ideal planning of the operation of Carolingian royal estates, as it is envisaged in the celebrated document *De Villis*, is concerned with assuring the means for suitable entertainment at royal hunting parties. Grapes are not to be pressed with dirty feet but in wine-presses. The main house is to be kept comfortably furnished, so that there be no scurrying about at the last moment to buy or borrow bedding, tablecloths, dishes, kitchen ware and repair tools. In practice, to judge from an actual inventory of the fourteen-room manorial 'palace' at Annapes, in the Low Countries, this is probably what happened, the total furnishing being limited to one set of bedding, one tablecloth, one lamp, two drinking cups, a firedog and two washbasins. There is no mention of the *gynaecea* prescribed in the ideal plan, where women would 'in season' weave and sew cloth from the manor's own wool and flax. On the other hand, the dairy and smokehouse servants had accumulated large stocks of cheese, sausages and bacon, there were four brew-houses, and five sets of apparatus for grinding grain.

In the ideal plan, the official in charge of a group of royal manors, the seneschal, would see that there were craftsmen of all kinds in his district. Militarily, it would have been dangerous for any district to be short of smiths, carpenters, wheelwrights or workers in leather. These skills were of course essential also to the peace-time needs of the villagers of any farming district, but royal manorial officials may have long helped to keep craftsmen well dispersed by letting it be known that small holdings were available in return for competent craft services rather than field labour dues. One of the seneschal's duties, as described in the *De Villis*, when he received orders to ship manorial produce for army provisions, was to get flour packed into waterproof leather containers, and to arm the driver of each cartload with an iron-tipped lance, a shield, a bow and arrows. Although he may sometimes have had to improvise workshops to produce these things, it is likely that he would have some supply on hand from the rental deliveries of men with forges and worksheds attached to their houses in the villages. These men would live partly from the food they could raise on a small holding and partly by making tools, arms, cartwheels and miscellaneous leather articles for sale or by charges for working up customers' materials. There was a constant demand for arms, since free men liable to military service were supposed to furnish their own standard equipment, and also for wheels. Anyone possessing a cart was liable to have it requisitioned for army supply transport, in which case he might never see it again.

Except for food processing, then, centralised manorial workshops would ordinarily have been necessary only where labour and materials were scarce in relation to special needs, as might be the case at points of military danger and at newly founded or isolated monasteries. The Bavarian monastery of Staffelsee had two dozen serf women at work in a *gynaeceum* in the early ninth century. A sketch plan of the monastery of St. Gall and the outbuildings grouped around it at this time shows a handicraft house with workrooms and sleeping quarters for tanners, shoemakers and saddlers, goldsmiths, blacksmiths, swordsmiths and shieldmakers, woodworkers, and fullers. Adjoining the brewery was a larger woodworking shop with a special space for turning out barrels. With cloth being woven for them by women in their serfs' homes, the monks of St. Gall, if the plan was materialised, were meeting all their industrial needs by imposing a rational and disciplined division of labour on their work force. But west of the Rhine the investment that this required was unusual except in the art industry that great monasteries fostered and in the large bakeries and breweries essential for their daily meals and for alms and hospitality. The monks of Ferrières in this century were buying their robes—and their sandals—ready-made, and this, or the purchase of cloth to be tailored by lay brothers who worked for nothing but their keep, or by other servants, became the normal monastic practice. It is known that many Cistercian houses revived the older industrial planning, but no one has made a complete survey of their workshop operations. It is known also that some German religious houses continued to exact weaving services from serf women as late as the fourteenth century; again, there is no complete German survey of the dates when these were terminated.

The spread of religious houses, and growth in their size, stimulated marketing in other ways. The migrant builders who constructed them had money to spend on drink and clothing. Quarries had to be opened. There was work for sawyers. Pilgrims came. A rag-taggle of market-men making shoes and tapers and selling drink and provisions would settle around monastery gates, and at stopping points on popular pilgrimage routes. In the eleventh century the extraordinary popularity of the cult of St. James of Compostella set scores of villages along the roads through Castile and Leon to Compostella thriving and growing.

Exchange within villages and between the villages and hamlets of a district grew also with population density and money supply. Archaeologists now opening deserted village sites are beginning to establish roughly dated correlations between these two variables and types of local industry and of articles that may have been brought in from other places. Excavations in central Europe, Russia, England and in the south of France are accumulating evidence of the versatility of village smiths in making little household articles, and of the skills and activity of potters. The popular notion that peasants bought only iron farm tools and salt, relying on their wives to make everything else they wanted, is for this and other reasons no longer tenable. One of the earliest documents illustrating the circulation of goods in a northern French countryside that has been printed so far describes trade in the 1080's in and out of the manor of Méron, whose lords, the monks of St. Aubin in Angers, decided then to institute, or perhaps only to revise, tariffs on it. The industrial items, carried on a man's back or on a donkey's, were modest. One paid a penny or a halfpenny on feathers, a load of wool, a table, a bedroll, and on skins of cats, lambs and other animals if they were being taken to market on someone else's behalf; wedding outfits, which probably included the woman's ring, were tariffed at 4d. Other possessions—knives, harness, bows and arrows and shields—mentioned as small things the theft of which does not entail prosecution for larceny—had no doubt been circulating in Anjou by gift, sale and theft ever since they were invented, in Neolithic times. The Méron tariffs sound discouragingly high, but their fixing by written regulation meant that the rates would automatically fall as quality and prices rose over the next two centuries.

Other seigneurial taxation that could be levied arbitrarily at the lord's will tended to damp village enterprise by draining off the savings of the unfree. It encouraged the tendency for production to concentrate on festival drink, and for such savings as could be concealed to be dispersed unproductively in small money-lending to neighbours who found the taxes genuinely oppressive, in the acquisition of scraps of land already under cultivation to be rented out without further improvement, and in perpetual litigation. At the same time the lords played some part in innovative movements that had more positive economic effects.

INNOVATIVE MOVEMENTS

The first of these was the improvement of powered flour-mills, and their wider diffusion. The ancient Mediterranean world had developed several types of watermill, a primitive one suitable only for shallow streams, others adaptable to rivers, and another requiring a controlled fall of water. It is believed that the simplest kind had been diffused northward to the Baltic very early in the Christian era. Since it is known to have had a horizontal wheel, A. P. Usher suggested that it was probably identical in principle with the so-called Greek or Norse mill widely used in peasant areas in the nineteenth century. With wheel and stones on the same shaft, and only a small iron fitting, this was popular because any carpenter could make one in a week. Besides, it could be housed in a shed, and though the grinding was slow there was no necessity to pay a miller to watch it.

The other types of watermill in use among the Romans, having vertical wheels geared to a separate shaft for the stones to regulate their speed, represented much more of an investment. They either had undershot wheels and could be moored floating in a river or built into the banks, or had overshot wheels turned by water from an aqueduct whose fall served a series of mills ranging down a slope. A double row of eight of these, iron-axled, built near Arles in the fourth century presumably for army supply, would have far surpassed the output of a one-wheeled undershot mill near Naples, the energy of which is estimated as about three horse power, enabling it to grind as much flour as forty slaves could with manual apparatus.

When the overshot type of mill died out after the smashing of the aqueducts at Rome, there were still enough good Italian engineering carpenters and smiths to moor geared mills in the Tiber. The question of the continuity of fixed or floating mills on other Italian rivers has not been well enough studied. The Lombard code and other Germanic codes of law define mills in a way that suggests, as Usher pointed out, that the type envisaged was the simple gearless type. Under the Germanic laws a mill was private property of a unique kind under special protection against wilful damage because the owner had to allow anyone paying for its use free access to the premises even in his absence. The picture this evokes is of members of a peasant group who used a little mill walking in, as was customary in nineteenth-century Norse mills, to pour their own grain into the hopper above the stones when they found it empty. This casual kind of milling may well have come to be more widely diffused in the early medieval centuries. Where it was not suitable there may in the north have been no means of grinding but by mortar and pestle, handmills, or unfortunate animals hitched to a bar attached to grindstones and forced to push it round and round. In parts of the lower Rhineland late ninth-century records show tenants obliged to grind set quantities of grain for their lord by hand with their own apparatus.

Handmills ground on, daily, in the soggier low-lying country and on dry plateaus, until well into the twelfth century, when northern windpower was at last harnessed. By that time geared watermills of varying size had been spreading in the northern river valleys for at least three hundred years. The technical skill for construction was developed out of the experience of village smiths and carpenters with the primitive Norse mill; iron fittings were kept to a minimum, carpenters learning to cut even the gear teeth from wood. The importance of the geared mill lay in the fact that it could be adapted to a variety of industrial purposes.

The labour that powered flourmilling saved was mostly women's time, making this potentially available for more intensive garden cultivation of vegetables, flax and hemp and, if there was a market for cloth, for more textile work in the winter. In a community well served by milling and subsisting mainly on bread, the net addition to the reservoir of free time may, for every five adults, have been in the order of about one person's full time for one day a week. When the cost was negligible, as had been the case at the cheap little mills that did not require the services of a professional miller, the extra free time was worth having. In the Domesday survey of England in 1086 a great many of the over five thousand mills for which the annual value to the lord is given were bringing in only a few shillings, some of them less than a shilling. It is very likely that these were of the old-fashioned type, and there may have been others on small freemen's lands, not listed. But where absence of these gave a lord's new and larger mill a natural monopoly on a manor, the cost went up, becoming fixed by custom, for manor tenants, at a sixteenth of any grain brought to the mill. In short, to give his wife more free time a peasant had to surrender $6\frac{2}{3}$ per cent of the grain he was counting on to feed his family.

Some peasants, considering this absurd, continued manual grinding at home. How far lords' legal rights to forbid the practice were enforced is not really clear. As is well known, the right was a part of the monopolistic system of *banalités* that in the twelfth century became clearly defined and was fairly general but not universal in England, France and Germany. Every writer on medieval rural life cites instances of harsh lords ordering the confiscation and destruction of handmills. Yet since both watermills and wind-mills frequently broke down and might occasionally stay unrepaired, from scarcity of mechanically skilled carpenters or on a badly administered manor from sheer carelessness, for months on end, it was essential for villagers to have access to handmills. Bouts of destruction would simply, by raising their price, have encouraged craftsmen to make more of them, for covert sale.

In districts well watered by manageable streams, country carpenters more or less specialising as millwrights developed a professional pride in improving a mill's grinding speed and capacity by better gearing and, where it was possible to divert a stream of water and control the flow through damming, by constructing an overshot wheel. These improvements, and a measure of competition for business as mills came to be bought and sold and leased, made for a slight lowering of costs to the user.

Population growth inevitably brought about progressive subdivision of all peasant holdings not obstinately kept intact by a strong tradition of permitting only one son to inherit the land. But all peasant families, both those that restricted inheritance and those that by subdividing or sharing among heirs were reduced to five acres or less to support a household, had to throw out surplus sons, and daughters who could not be placed as servants or married locally, to make their own way as best they could. For as long as was feasible, these young people followed the age-old pattern of clearing woods and breaking in waste land near to their old homes, forming new hamlets and villages to reproduce the only kind of life they knew. In country with easily opened mineral veins, some could become miners with little more capital than a pick and shovel, and in wooded mining country could make their own charcoal for their own small smithy. Others sought work in the growing industrial and commercial towns. But many preferred the less drastic break of moving to a rural market centre where they might combine intensive work on a small plot of land with a trade.

In the twelfth and thirteenth centuries this last movement

was considerable. Landed proprietors and princes encouraged it by planned foundation of new centres both on frontiers of settlement and on any sites where soil or trading opportunities had not yet been energetically exploited. Settlers were offered small plots of land at a fixed money rent, and timber for building. The new community might be directly adjacent to an existing manor, or the whole of an existing community might be promoted to a higher status through various privileges.

The majority of these experiments failed to generate any more manufacturing activity than was becoming common in the general run of ordinary villages. The more prosperous peasants were getting their best clothes tailored for them and buying more household things, and there was enough wage-earning for the landless to be able to buy bread and a few other necessities. Among the minority of district market centres that actually grew by industry, some were perhaps at first just displacing it from nearby villages. Most of the people holding burgage plots in Stratford-on-Avon in 1252, two generations after it had been founded as a privileged market centre, appear to have come from places within a radius of sixteen miles and to have been practising the trades of that countryside. However, there was a little more specialisation, some of it, since the lord had installed a fulling mill and three dye pans, perhaps in finishing cloth from village looms. There was a scattering of little towns like this all through the continent. Up to a population size of about 1,500, or perhaps twice that size in Mediterranean areas, they were still very rural. Successful craftsmen and traders still cultivated gardens or vineyards, the less successful merging into the peasantry; yards were noisy with pigs and geese and the streets at sundown filled with cattle strolling home from the fields.

If the slow rise in peasant purchasing was the most widespread stimulus to rural industry in this period, there were other influences stemming more directly from the larger towns. Their commerce called for continual construction and repair of the means of transport. Some of this work was done in villages along trade routes and in little fishing ports.

Genoa had several satellite ports of the kind where ship-building went on. The sacks and baling canvas in which grain and wool were shipped to town merchants, and the string and rope for making the loads fast could be made most economically from locally grown hemp or from bark in the villages where shipments originated. The extractive industries, too, creating demand for rough woollen and leather clothing for miners, fishermen and salt workers, kept local villagers well occupied.

A final influence that will be discussed in the section on late medieval developments was a drift of industry from the towns to the countryside on account of lower costs. This was already marked in England in the thirteenth century.

These innovative movements came later in eastern Europe than in the west, powered milling apparently not reaching Poland in any form before the twelfth century. Princely power running ahead of productive power, an experiment in forcing the latter was tried in the mid-tenth century, that of drafting serfs into specialised industrial villages where they had both to raise their own food and turn out some particular product for the use of the large body of ducal officials and military retainers. At the time these did not have estates but lived together in forts. Over four hundred of these villages have been identified as named after the product they were bound to deliver. They supplied flour, simple military accoutrements, boats and sledges, blankets and even goldsmiths' work. The list is reminiscent of the Carolingian *De Villis* in including hunting services. Supplemented by a system of ducal monopolies over the few industries practised at periodic fairs frequented by western merchants and over exchange of their money, the service villages were part of a plan to conserve money revenues for the purchase of foreign luxuries and arms. In the eleventh century, as increased money supply enabled rural markets to be set up, the forced deliveries gave way to voluntary production for sale. This was developing already in towns, and small-scale production by free enterprise was stimulated further by the eastward drive of German colonisation.

EXTRACTIVE INDUSTRIES AND METALLURGY

Popular association of medieval Europe with iron-clad knights, church bells and ploughshares makes it hard to realise how metal-poor the whole age was. All metals were precious. Total production of all of them taken together probably never amounted to more than a few pounds by weight per head of Europe's population in any given year. Smiths' supplies were rounded out by sedulously collected scrap of all kinds. Battlefields were cleared of all the dented armour of the dead, to be repaired.

In the worst period of metal poverty, the first few post-Roman centuries, people were not conscious of it as a handicap. Most of the mines the Romans had been working were abandoned from sheer indifference. Among those abandoned were deep mines the Romans had sunk in Spain with shafts zigzagging in a fashion that simplified problems of ventilation and pump-drainage. The north Italians continued to hack some iron and silver ores out of the Alps, there was some shallow digging in the Rhineland, Brabant, Normandy and other scattered areas; the Swedes fished lumps of rich iron ore out of their lakes. All of these techniques were prehistoric.

Christianisation stretched supplies a little by putting a stop to the Germanic pagan practice of burying a dead man's most valuable possessions with his body. But by the ninth century resources for coinage, arms and tools were being strained to the point of creating a mild expansion of mining. Gold mines in the Austrian Alps deserted since the fifth century and other abandoned works were re-opened. By the twelfth century there was active prospecting, resulting in a series of rushes to new discoveries of silver, copper, iron, tin, lead and gold that went on through the thirteenth century. The bulk of these were mountain finds in the eastern Alps, the Carpathians, the Harz region in Saxony, and in the Pyrenees, with Devon and Cornwall remaining among the best sources of tin and lead. Some of the increases in production were spectacular. The output of Eng-

lish tin, for example, one of the few items for which we have
any figures, in the latter part of the thirteenth century grew
about fivefold.

Just as town air made free, in the German saying, so did
mine dust. Territorial overlords permitted anyone to stake
and register a claim, in return taking up to ten per cent
of the product by virtue of fresh elaboration of the legal
tradition of regalian right. In the mountains and on waste
moors there was no one else to deal with, but on other sites
the miners, who usually put up the forges and did their
own smelting on the spot, had also to recompense a local
lord for use of his timber and his streams. They co-operated
in small groups in the heavy work of getting the ore out of
the ground and of breaking it up into smaller pieces by
sledge-hammer. They showed great ingenuity in adapting
the watermill for further crushing and in some places for
powering a forced draught to develop more heat in a furnace.
They always retained formal independence in controlling
their own working customs and in dealing with administrative authorities. Yet if they got into debt to the merchants who bought their metal it must always have been
very hard to extricate themselves; rising costs made this
still more difficult. Alongside the independent miner-
metallurgists, then, were men who worked for them for
wages or at piece rates for contractors financed by merchants.

Mining costs inevitably went up as soon as diggings were
deep enough to run into water. Mill-pumping was tried
but at rising expense and until the sixteenth century with
little success. By the end of the thirteenth century the deeper
silver and copper diggings in Saxony were unworkable
muddy pools. Smelting costs rose, too, because of competition for fuel and timber from other industries, and from
forest-owners' preference for planned cutting as against the
havoc that unrestricted use created. Surface coal seams
were being pecked at, for miscellaneous heating purposes.
But in the iron industry, the heaviest user of fuel, the only
solution to reduced supply was to cut back production of
the metal. Smiths in the older French and German iron-

working districts began forming agreements to share cut-backs fairly. Licences to operate in the ancient iron-working areas of the Forest of Dean came to be limited.

Salt was mined in a few central inland regions but was for the most part extracted from seawater by solar evaporation or by slow boiling with peat fuel. The evaporation pans, leased to part-time peasant salters who did the upkeep work, represented little or no investment on the part of the landlord.

TOWN INDUSTRY IN THE 12th AND 13th CENTURIES

Industrially, the function of medieval towns was to foster and satisfy demand for things of better quality than village work could supply. In the Mediterranean world there had been no break in reliance on the market for this purpose, and current re-examination of the background of urban industrial revival in north-eastern France and Flanders is discovering more and more scraps of evidence pointing to some degree of continuity in urban production for sale and export throughout the early medieval centuries. Wherever merchants wintered there were craftsmen. In Kiev and Novgorod and other Russian trading towns they were making copper icons and crosses for domestic export at least as early as the tenth century. By the eleventh century Cologne and London had a high reputation for fine gold-smiths' work, and Liège and Milan for arms. By the twelfth century, demand for town-made goods was clearly rising, and continued to rise more or less steadily for nearly two hundred years. The largest bulk sales at fairs were of cloth. Any stuff that was warm, and more regular in weave or more smoothly finished than country cloth could find a market.

Town industries in this age of expansion will be examined here from three points of view. What were the sources and role of capital? How far was the division of labour carried? Is there any evidence as to the degree of intensity of work?

FIXED CAPITAL

The logical starting-point is the provision of capital for
building the towns themselves. The walled area covered by
Ghent grew in this period more than eightfold and that of
a number of Italian towns tenfold, with suburban building
still continuing, and houses becoming taller. Quite apart
from the housing problem, the construction of parish
churches, cathedrals, and fortifications represented a huge
investment. The cost of the non-industrial parts of these
prolonged building programmes fell mainly on the lay
population. New fortifications, bridges, and city government offices and halls were paid for by tolls and beverage
taxes that affected everyone. Merchants had voluntarily
paid for building the first churches beside town market-
places, and probably bore much of the cost of the multipli-
cation of parish churches as a town grew. Merchant families
were also among the pious founders and benefactors of new
monastic houses and of the houses and churches built for
the mendicant orders. They contributed substantially to
cathedral funds as well. Roberto Lopez some years ago
played with the idea that construction of some of the
grander cathedrals may have drawn so heavily on merchant
savings as seriously to curtail local investment in trade and
industry.

On the other hand, ecclesiastical bodies had large holdings of town land and invested a good deal in covering
them with houses and shops. Since most medieval shops
were primarily workshops with a dwelling-room or two
above or at the rear where a man's wife might be carrying
on some craft, investment of this kind made a certain
amount of fixed capital, as it were, available for rent. To
some extent this was true of the tenement housing where
poorer working families and single unskilled people, in the
larger towns, crowded together. Most of the workers in the
textile town of Arras paid their rent to one or other of a few
wealthy religious houses. Noble holders of land in the path of
a town's growth were more likely to be content with long

leases at a fixed ground rent, leaving the enterprise of speculative building to merchants or craftsmen who had been leasing the land as pasture for cattle and horses. Except for the danger of fire, such enterprise was virtually risk-free. On a smaller scale, similar opportunities occurred in the minority of little towns founded by a lord that became a success: the heirs to the original burgage plots filled their garden spaces with workshops and dwellings for sale or rent.

The more spectacular building projects financed by royal and ecclesiastical funds were unique in assembling hundreds of workers under the direction of a single workmaster and entirely on the basis of money wages. The bigger mines had hundreds of men at work but in separately organised groups. The swarm of unskilled labourers needed to prepare the foundations for any great stone building, the masons and carpenters, the smiths kept on hand to repair their tools, the men who mixed the mortar and the crews on the hoisting cranes were recruited in part by impressment. The masons were migratory workers paid according to their varying degrees of skill. The proliferation of great building plans in thirteenth-century Paris enabled an unusual number of masons to settle there: at the close of the century about four hundred were taxpayers.

Most of the flour mills serving northern towns before 1300 had been put up by lay or ecclesiastical lords who were willing, under pressure from craftsmen, to add other types of mill. Bishop Barthélemy of Beauvais in the third quarter of the twelfth century added over thirty fulling mills and another, with the help of a loan from a group of tanners, for grinding the oak bark that was the source of the industry's tannic acid.

In the south an ingenious system of corporate financing of watermills by groups of citizens was evolving. At Toulouse. in the twelfth century millers themselves and other craftsmen were taking the initiative in this. The mills here were the undershot type that could be set up most cheaply by attaching them to boats moored to the river bank, but enough capital was raised to increase their power by placing them in palisaded earthbanked canals through which the already swift current of the Garonne would shoot at higher speed. Enough mills were constructed not only to supply the whole city with flour but to full its cloth, crush woad and tanners' bark and grind the cutler's knives. Customers at the flour mills paid by surrendering a sixteenth of their grain, the shareholders preferring this to a money payment because it protected them personally against the sharp rise in grain prices that followed poor harvests.

Somewhat similar forms of corporate enterprise in milling existed in other cities of southern France, but there is no comprehensive study of their success, nor of the effectiveness of Italian use of floating mills. A thirteenth-century code detailing the duties of flour-millers in Piacenza and its country territory refers to their obligation to help each other move their mills from sites where the flow of water was poor to better ones. There were apparently many small mills, some just tied to a stake in a drainage canal; the city's religious houses each had their own. But there were also large ones: an entry in the register of contracts kept by the notary Manuellus de Orlandis records the sale in 1292 of half rights in a covered mill with three wheels on one side and two on the other. For every watercourse there was an official known as the archmiller, who was supposed to make an inspection patrol of it twice a year. A further sign of the importance attached to watermills was a rule that no trees were to be cut anywhere in the territory without formal permission from all of the archmillers.

An inventory of fixed industrial equipment inside the towns in this period would probably show the most valuable to have been the furnaces and moulds of bell-founders and other metalworkers, bakehouse ovens and brewers' malting kilns and vats rating next in order of their size. Other equipment consisted of looms, storage bins, and the moveable paraphernalia of heating, soaking and cleansing processes. Standing in the cramped workshops and cluttered yards attached to living quarters, these bits of capital were for the most part the property of individual masters, or of partners. Along with hand tools they were assembled by careful strategies of family saving and investment and with the help of loans from merchants.

The most valuable concentrations of industrial 'plant' were usually on the edge of a town or in a waterside suburb or satellite settlement. Here were the shipyards, the mills, and the larger tanneries and dyeworks, and it was here that some corporate financing of industry was to be found. In addition to the syndicate ownership seen in the Toulouse milling business there was some pooling of capital by members of gilds to lease a suitable site and install facilities on it for their common use at the lowest possible fee. The best known example is that of the riverside dyeworks managed by the Florentine woollen manufacturers' gild. There was much less corporate effort of the kind in northern Europe, almost the only cases on record being of small bark-crushing mills run by tanners' gilds. The enterprise that was most 'modern' in character was that of building the larger ships in yards around the big seaport towns. These yards were destined to grow in size as new types of ship were developed. However, there was no mass production of small boats.

WORKING CAPITAL

The working capital that was needed to operate town industry was in the aggregate probably far greater than the value of its equipment. Any craftsman who aspired to live as an independent producer for the market had to be able to buy his own materials and to cover all the costs he would incur before receiving payment for his finished product. In the sleepy little towns of the early Middle Ages the need had been smaller because many customers supplied their own materials, even taking their own dough to the baker. These practices did not die out, but they receded into unimportance as craftsmen put more and more ready-made goods on the market and developed the productive capacity for export. How did they find the working capital to do so?

To document the answer by facts and figures from the

eleventh or early twelfth centuries, when the movement
was first gathering force, is virtually impossible, because so
little detailed information has survived from any one place
or group. Yet the general outlines of the situation are clear
enough. In the first place, one can dismiss as a legend any
idea that penniless country boys could succeed as town
masters simply by learning a craft as apprentices and then
saving out of their wages for a few years as servants. Wages
were too low to have allowed even the most strong-willed
young man to have saved enough. Demonstrating a capacity
to save may well have helped many young servants to
marry the master's daughter or widow, and in this way to
get both the fixed capital of a workshop and some stock of
materials. But individual success stories of this kind do not
account for growth in productive capacity. Nor do they
account for growth in the ability to produce for export,
which called for the means to buy the best possible materials,
to organise contact with markets at a distance and to wait
long periods for payment.

By themselves, craftsmen could not possibly have built
up export industries. They had to rely on the services of
merchants, who were gradually drawn into supplying them
with working capital through credit on supplies and advance payment on sales. Ultimately, as is well documented
for the textile industries, the merchants organised the whole
process of production. The craftsmen lost their worries over
working capital, but they also lost their independence. The
merchants were able to assume this position of dominance,
as the chapters in this volume that deal with trade and the
structure of demand explain more fully, because their
profits on general wholesale trade, including the growing
trade in foodstuffs, made them the wealthiest group in the
towns.

Mercantile profit was also a large part of the answer to
the independent craftsman's need of working capital, the
need of the men who were content to produce for the local
market. One tends to assume that a man identified as a
baker, a butcher, or a carpenter did nothing but make
bread, cut and sell meat, or work with hammer and saw.

But in fact the more successful men in these and all of the other handicraft occupations also traded in materials related to their craft. As soon as one has records of local trade, bakers and butchers are found dealing in hay and other animal feed, and carpenters in wood. Nor did they stop at these seemingly appropriate lines of trade. Any type of craftsman was alert to stray opportunities for profit in buying odd lots of grain or wine or second-hand goods of any kind for quick resale. In Genoa miscellaneous groups of craftsmen formed partnerships for little ventures in export trade. One can only conclude that alertness to chances of mercantile profit was essential to a craftsman's success.

The élite among the craftsmen also frequently owned bits of vineyard or other productive land, and relied on investment of this kind and in house property for auxiliary income. Ten of the first twenty-five London laymen who happened to have their wills regarding property registered in the city's Husting court between 1259 and 1261 were craftsmen, eight of whom owned one or more houses, rented out, besides the one they lived in. One was a smith from Normandy who had kept his house in Rouen. One was a wimple-maker who had lands in Cambridgeshire. One can draw two reasonable conclusions from this kind of evidence. First, it seems that the more prosperous small landowners and working peasantry made a substantial contribution to the capital needs of town industry, through sharing inheritances with family members who settled in the towns. Second, it is clear that town craftsmen found more security in putting savings into house property for rent, which they could probably keep in repair by their own labour, than by expanding the size of their workshops and staff. Very few men producing for the local market kept a regular staff of more than five men and boys.

The problem of working capital was eased also by credit arrangements similar to those traditional among rural craftsmen and traders but influenced also by the more sophisticated practices among merchants. In both cases the cost of credit was brought well below moneylenders' rates on loans to consumers in distress, by reducing the risk of default. In the countryside neighbours and relatives stood as pledges for honest repayment of each other's debts. The town master craftsman's wider world came to be equally tightly knit through the spread of parish and occupational fraternities, or gilds. The latter accumulated administrative functions and privileges, in most medieval towns becoming the basis of political organisation. Their function in binding men of the same craft together as 'brothers' willing to support each other's credit was, however, a lasting one. The brother supported had, of course, to be of good reputation and the more property he had as independent security for loans the better.

To the man who owned nothing but his tools and could barely pay rent in a back street, the only material advantage of buying his way into a gild was the right that this gave him to get small boys and youths to work in his household without pay, as apprentices. If they were too unhappy to work well, he could sell the remaining years of their term to another master. But thoroughly unhappy boys were apt to run away before a sale could be arranged. The small gild master without working capital led a hand-to-mouth existence, always liable to be reduced to seeking wage-work by standing in the hiring-place of his trade. Every large town had a number of these customary standing-places, usually beside a church.

A compromise solution, less demeaning, that left such a man free to work at home, was offered by the putting-out system. The majority of gild masters of middling status avoided long contracts with more than one or two servants and kept only one or two apprentices. When they had a rush of orders to fill they might hire extra men by the day or the week, but it might be more convenient to put the orders out along with the material they wished to be used, to the poorer gild masters or to outsiders, paying piece-rates. Random use of a variant form of the system by merchants who knew of special sales opportunities in miscellaneous small wares also occurred. David Herlihy has printed contracts giving Pisan cappers large orders for hats of a French style at set figures covering the price of the

wool used, which at the time, the 1260s, came to more than
the cappers could charge for the labour alone. In Paris,
merchants could oblige small craftsmen to work up material
for them whether they wanted to or not. Paris citizens also
took craftsmen into their houses to make things for their
household use.

Pisan tanners were responsible for a remarkable cost-
cutting innovation in the late thirteenth century. Previously
their outlay on skins and hides was regularly tied up for
six months, the customary period for soaking them in a
cold tanning solution. A new technique using different sub-
stances and hot water now did the tanning in ten days. The
results were good enough, as Herlihy shows in his account
of the innovation, for the bigger shields, bound with two
cowhides or two horsehides each, that military commanders
were ordering for their troops, and with a little further
treatment proved adaptable to changing uses of leather in
new styles of clothing that were coming in. The Pisan
tanners' short-cut method of production came to be generalised in Italy.

Industrial growth through the making of better cloth,
however, was in Flanders and adjacent regions of north-
eastern France, in the Po valley and in Florence as also in
a number of Spanish towns, due entirely to merchant
capital. Merchants took over all supply and marketing
functions through the putting-out system, paying for work
done, at piece rates. Production was dispersed in hundreds
of workshops, the more skilled work being done under
qualified masters, the less skilled in the workers' own tenement rooms or in peasant homes in nearby villages. The
skilled masters equipped their own shops at their own expense, and paid their own staff out of the merchant-
employers' payment for the week's output of the shop. Our
knowledge of the system is derived, for the north, from
regulative codes drawn up in the thirteenth century, more
than a century after manufacturing for export had got under
way there. In being based on import of the best wool
obtainable, English wool, the industry had not changed,
but the element of collective control over it may have been

tightening. In the Flemish towns the surviving codes tie wages to the cost of food; they also subject the skilled masters to supervision by a board of inspectors with the status of town officials who had the power to confiscate any cloth not up to the technical specifications laid down, to inflict fines, and to send angry men before the town magistrates for further punishment. It has been estimated that in Douai around the middle of the thirteenth century there were a hundred and fifty merchant drapers each keeping about a hundred people employed. But there is no record of profits or costs, or of how earnings were affected by the strikes that were intermittent from 1245 on.

The northern drapers counted on getting their best profit from very heavy cloth, highly finished, that only the rich could afford. The Florentines and Genoese outdid them by bringing this northern cloth down to the south to be even more highly finished, and better dyed. But the north Italians more typically employed their capital in organising the production of lighter cloth that needed no lengthy finishing. They were doing this by the twelfth century, by importing cotton and having it mixed with local wool or linen.

DIVISION OF LABOUR

Adam Smith's famous discourse on the division of labour, in the opening chapter of *The Wealth of Nations*, although its stress on self-interest would have shocked medieval clergy says nothing that would have been new or surprising to the laymen carrying on medieval town industries. None of them were making very much use of the kind of division of labour within workshops on whose advantages Smith dwells, yet all could have tried to defend their practices in terms of his own emphasis on the character and extent of the market.

The small men who had no assets but manual skill were none of them attempting to make things like pins from lumps of metal, an enterprise which in the hands of one man, as Smith observes, somewhat labouring the point, would result in minuscule output. One-man or man-and-wife workshops typically specialised in one or more of the odds and ends of semi-luxury articles that women in particular shopped for in towns—buckles and belts, little carved images, silk hairnets and so on. Paris abounded in such trades, the number at any time far exceeding the long list for which the city's provost in the late thirteenth century was codifying gild regulations. Demand in these trades as a whole had then long been expanding but could never have been very great for any single item, and in fact its growth depended on the craftsman's response to customers' desire for individuality within fashion trends that throve on innovation. The principle of the Paris gild regulations, to protect the customer against fraud by restricting craftsmen to the use of one particular type of metal or leather, was only partially enforceable.

The larger independent workshops specialised in things for which demand was less volatile, and in orders that came with particular specifications, as was the case with arms in time of war or commissions for great church bells. The brass-founders making the little bells traditionally tinkling on horses' harness in Milan each had 'many' assistants, a friar writing in 1288 informs us; he adds that there were thirty of these foundries in the city, and over a hundred armourers' workshops. From an order limiting London cordwainers, in the 1270s, to eight servants apiece one may infer that some of them, who were buying Spanish skins in large quantities, were exceeding that number. Two partners among them, deciding to give their whole time to trade, set a manager over their workshop at a salary of 13s. 4d. a year.

The Flemish textile regulations aimed at separation of each of the many processes through which the wool had to go. Sorting it into different grades was done by women at the warehouse. Beating the larger pieces of dirt out of it was done by men. It was then put out to women working alone or with their children in town rooms or in the villages nearby for washing, combing, spinning (without spinning wheels) and for sizing of the yarn with melted lard or butter. The rest of the work was performed mostly by pairs of partners making mechanical movements. The looms for the heavy cloth took two men alternately throwing the shuttle and pressing the pedals and bars that locked the thread in place. A master weaver was limited to three looms, for which he would need five assistants and the help of women who went from shop to shop to lend a hand in attaching the warp. From the loom a cloth went to the fulling trough to be scoured and thickened with alkaline earth in hot water and urine and then washed. Instead of investing in mills for this purpose, which could beat the cloth with wooden mallets, the northern drapers clung to the ancient method of having it 'walked', trampled by men's bare feet. A master fuller was restricted to four or five troughs. The men were so frequently forbidden to work naked that one can only suppose they did. Dyers, who handled the cloth next, were allowed up to eighteen vats, which if in continuous use would keep twenty men busy. Three more finishing processes followed; stretching on tenter-racks with pulleys, teazling (rubbing with a species of thistle to raise the nap), and trimming with broad-bladed shears on a sloping table. It is likely that these last finishing processes were in practice carried on side by side, and that the whole organisation of the work was more casual than it looks in the regulations.

Medieval division of labour was carried as far as the size of a work group permitted, the size being limited by the equipment that a single master could afford, could understand and could oversee. The expansion of textile markets altered the situation only in imposing a loose organisational control over the poor domestic workers, whose productivity per head was abysmally low. The supply of these people was so abundant, however, that there was no incentive to try to group them or to encourage experiment in mechanising their work. The overhead cost of employing them was kept down to the wages of an office clerk tallying their fetching and returning of material, a few pounds at a time. In big building projects, there had to be managers capable of organising large numbers of men effectively and of assessing differentials in the value of their labour in wage scales as complex as those of a modern factory. In castle-building these managers were military engineers with long experience of organisational problems. In church-building the managers were architects who had help in these matters from clerics with long experience of authoritarian bureaucracy.

WORK INTENSITY

The problem of the intensity of medieval industrial labour besides being of psychological interest, is of central economic importance. Attempts to calculate physical productivity per head in any particular industry have to consider the length of a working day and the kinds of interruption that might punctuate it, and the number and duration of work stoppages during the year.

At first sight, medieval work habits appear appallingly strenuous. Like the farm day, the workshop day began at dawn, but whereas labour in the fields necessarily ended at sundown, numerous gild rules either prohibiting or permitting work by candle-light, and occasional squabbles over disturbance of neighbours' sleep by the clatter of tools, show that a good many craftsmen were under an extreme compulsion to continue at their benches far into the night. The evidence is from latitudes where the sunlight day in summer runs up to seventeen hours.

The reasons for deciding to tolerate or to ban self-sweating beyond these limits become clear on close reading of the gild rules of any related set of trades. The sections of the late thirteenth-century regulative code for Paris that relate to twelve of the principal leather crafts will serve as a good enough illustration. Nine of these twelve sets of rules raise the question of candle-light work, dealing with it as follows: four ban it outright, two permit it freely, one bans it in summer as 'trop penable' but implicitly allows it in winter, two permit it for rush work and in making things for the worker's own use. Looking at the other rules for these crafts, one can see that night work was a characteristic of occupations in which men lived from hand to mouth, peddling in the mornings what they had made in the afternoon and night before. The newly codified rules were trying to ban peddling by gildsmen since it associated them with professional hawkers, a group despised for their poverty and suspected of thievery. The makers of belts ornamented with metal studs, for example, although still permitted night work in emergencies, were to stop the practice of hawking their wares in the city streets and in the countryside around. This group contained men already too poor to care properly for the one apprentice they were allowed: the gild officers are ordered to take charge of boys whose masters become impoverished. The rules, if they were actually enforced, could not have eliminated the nightworker-peddler; they would merely have forced this miserable class out of the gild. The makers of horse-collars managed to retain both night work and peddling within their gild by agreeing to have peddlers' packs inspected for bad stuffing. Neither night work nor peddling was a problem among men preparing soft leather, nor among those making the leather parts of saddles to be assembled in the saddlers' shops and decorated for sale to nobles. So long as demand for things like these was brisk, the workers who made them could use the whole of the sunlight day productively. The poor man finishing cheap small wares could not.

No matter whether trade was brisk or slow, everybody's working time was curtailed by the Church's designation of more than a quarter of the year as sacred time. Looked at from this angle, medieval work habits appear, if not leisurely, at least punctuated with plenty of rest periods. In the first place, there were weekends. To knock off work at noon on Saturday, in order to prepare for Sunday, was in the thinking of the clergy a religious duty. They conceded, however, that a servant must obey his master's orders in the matter; consequently, the break is believed in most trades to have been nearer three or four p.m. The same norm applied to the vigil of each saint's festival, that is, to the day preceding it. The actual practice in this regard is less clear, and the number of saints' days observed varied from one locality to another and from one trade to another. The four major Marian festivals, the days sacred to the apostles and the evangelists, Christmas week and Easter week (the last theoretically a fortnight), were the core holiday periods. Addition of a few local saints' festivals, and a day in each trade sacred to its patron saint, reduced the working year, allowing for weekends and for festivals coinciding with these, very considerably. At Narbonne the town mills ran 265 days in the year, at Toulouse 281 days; church-building work in Paris in 1320 went on for 275 days.

In the north, winter weather took further toll of production. When a chronicler mentions that there was 'a great frost' one may picture mills immobilised by ice and many unheated workshops, too, by icy hands. Storms were a perpetual hazard to windmills. Rain in all seasons slowed the finishing of cloth, which called for open-air drying after the several washings involved. Summer heat slowed down all business in the larger towns, because rich customers moved to the country. Some Paris workers, and many in the Low Countries, took August off to join harvesting gangs in the country. In Pisa the main summer activity was swatting mosquitoes or sweating out malarial fever. Yet this wretched season was the only time in which the Pisan smiths, who spent the winter mining and smelting iron on the island of Elba and in coastal areas still more heavily mosquito-infested, could bring it to the city to work it into tools and arms.

Metallurgical workers probably utilised a longer working year than anyone else, for they sometimes made the excuse, against prohibition of work on festivals, that they could not let furnace fires go out. Besides, the more remote mountain mines were not at first provided with chapels. Some service industries maintained very heavy work schedules. Bakers' servants commonly were obliged to work through the night and had only Sundays off. On the other hand, dry summers idled many watermills, forcing a return to manual grinding of grain, and throwing water-powered furnace bellows and other automated apparatus out of action.

Relying entirely on manual labour, the northern textile entrepreneurs did not have this particular problem. The towns where they operated have a most businesslike sound, with the bells of a particular church, or of the town hall, serving like a factory whistle to mark the start and the finish of the working day. Yet whether the hours were standardised at a summer length and a winter length or were lengthened and shortened as the light changed with the gradual alteration of the seasons is not always clear. Taking the longer and the shorter days together, E. Perroy estimates that they averaged about 250 to a year. The one thing that was really standardised seems to have been the measurements of a cloth in each quality that was made. The finest were about 44 yards long after final shrinking, and over a yard wide, or were made in halves of that length with the same width. Two weavers could turn out a whole cloth in a winter week, perhaps 45 or so in a year. The finishing processes were quicker, but included so much washing and drying that their co-ordination in wet weather must have been peculiarly difficult. Perroy stresses the very slow pace of production, the weaving and finishing of one full-length cloth taking three to four weeks without counting the time taken in preparing the yarn. In a mid-nineteenth-century factory still using some child labour to roll the cleaned wool before spinning, but with all other operations more or less mechanised, the same piece of cloth could have been produced in about eighty hours, that is, in less than one medieval summer week. Yet the medieval work was intense, and the handling of the wet cloth most arduous: the industry obliged men to *be* machines.

INDUSTRIAL TRENDS c. 1300–1500 A.D.

SETBACKS VERSUS ADVANCES

War financed by heavier taxation, contractions of long-distance trade, the inroads of plague, inter-town competition for markets that were for long periods more or less static, deliberate holding down of production by privileged gilds, and continued shortages of money supply cloud the late medieval scene until the 1470s. The industries dispensing cheer did best of all in the towns: brewers and taverners multiplied. But there were always rational efforts to deal with the difficulties. These will be illustrated here from some regional examples of changing fortunes.

Grumbling about industrial problems in the early years of the fourteenth century is along familiar lines. All that is new is an accentuation of trouble in Flanders through difficulty in getting enough wool for the looms. There is no general deepening of trouble. Indeed, by the 1340s there is a general livening of activity in two areas: in Bohemia through new mining for gold, silver and zinc, and in south Germany through following the Italian example of commercialising rural and small-town skill in making linen and other cheap cloth of mixed weave. The tenants of the old monastery of St. Gall, who once made cloth only for themselves and for their lords, have expanded the village by the monastery into one of the leading linen towns. A cheap German rain-cloak made like a Mexican poncho is coming on the market. These modest but solid advances stand in sharp contrast to the ruin of the aristocratic cloth industry in southern Flanders. To the north, the cities of Bruges, Ghent and Ypres are in a state of fluctuating decline. The Flemish luxury cloth industry has in effect been transferred to the wool-growing countrysides of England and to the towns of Aragon and their environs.

The Bohemian gold veins were soon exhausted, and the silver miners were scattered by the Hussite wars. The only mining areas to sustain continued advance were those bearing the rich iron and copper ores of Sweden, the latter being developed by the capital of Hanseatic Germans. German, Norman and Italian ironmasters ever since fuel costs had risen had economised on labour by using water-powered hammers on the forged iron and by the fourteenth century were experimenting with powered bellows. Yet iron prices continued to rise until the fifteenth century. Machines were not necessarily efficient. In 1410 an inexperienced staff at a forge belonging to the Bishop of

Durham after equipping it with a pair of powered bellows had to keep one of the men's wives at work perpetually adjusting the things. In free intervals this sturdy creature saved the bishop the cost of a mechanical hammer by breaking up the forged iron herself, all for a penny a day and three sips of beer in the year.

Central and east European mining went ahead again after the Hussite wars subsided. Directed by German engineers, manned largely by German miners and financed by the capital of such famous merchant families as the Fuggers of Augsburg, who had a finger in every profitable pie in Europe, mines were brought under central management and integrated on a larger scale with better smelting-works. Yet, impressive though the engineering advances were, until after 1460 mints still went short of silver, improved furnaces still left thirty per cent of the iron in the slag and stood cold much of the time for lack of fuel. Rolf Sprandel estimates that Europe at the close of the fifteenth century was producing no more than 40,000 tons of iron a year and that twenty-five per cent of the continuing high cost of any form of iron to a manufacturing craftsman was due to commercial and transport charges.

One only has to compare the first little guns coming out of Edward III's experimental foundry at the Tower of London in the 1340s—twenty-four inches long—with the Duke of Burgundy's three-ton darling made in the 1460s and named Catherine, which with care could be hauled five miles in a day, to see that the increased output of metals was going largely into the game of war. Rulers (although this particular ruler was reduced to borrowing at twenty-five per cent) once committed to artillery could not afford to argue about prices. Roger Lejeune, who in writing the history of the principality of Liège made a special study of its arms industry and metallurgy through the sixteenth century, when more of the work around forges was being mechanised, described even that century as industrially an age of wood.

Profits in ferrous metallurgy must undoubtedly have been highest in Sweden, where the 'bog' ore was unusually rich and there was extreme skill in refining it; the quality of the 'osmund' product fetched top prices wherever it was exported. Elsewhere the profits of ironworks were not high enough to attract the capital for really satisfactory solution of the technological problems that surrounded the industry. Nor were the annual wages enough, where fuel shortages broke the working year, to support all of the various types of labour that were needed, unless some of the men had a little land or other auxiliary employment. For example, it has been calculated that in 1475 about a quarter of the population of the upper Rhineland territory of the Oberpfalz worked in the iron industry. Including 750 miners, more than 3,000 transport men, 5,180 woodcutters and charcoal-burners, and other skilled and unskilled groups, the labour figure totals over 11,000. Yet a probably overgenerous estimate sets the iron produced at less than 10,000 tons in the year. If the 1,638 forge-workers were grouped in 3-man teams—each having one smith at the main furnace, one to tend the powered hammer, and a helper—the output of each team would then have been around 17 tons a year, well below that of the Bishop of Durham's less mechanised Weardale forge in 1410, where two smiths with irregular help from a 'forman' and from their wives turned out 27, of which all but 5.8 tons had gone through the second heating and been cut into pieces for carting to other workshops. There is no means of comparing this Weardale iron with the later Oberpfalz iron in respect of quality or value. Comparison of the physical output of the forge teams indicates only that organisation of the German work must have been hindered by frequent stoppages. In the English case, for which we have weekly accounts, there were no interruptions save for holy days; the bishop's administrative staff handled the supplying of ore and of fuel very efficiently. The workshops were open 267 days in the year covering Saturdays, which were pay-days. The smith treating the ore, the best-paid man, was absent for only one week. His co-worker at the second hearth seems to have appeared only when he felt like it; a third of the time he did not. Possibly he and the 'forman' worked irregularly also at another forge, or on family holdings of land.

The problems of the textile industry were simpler in calling for little or no entrepreneurial investment in fixed plant. After 1300, however, they called for more adaptability to changes in the character of demand than the skilled workers in the Flemish towns, absorbed in forcing reform on their town governments and fighting the French, could muster. For more was at issue in the decline of the Flemish industry than Edward III's 'Buy English cloth' policy and its equivalent in Spain. The Italian taste for lighter clothing that could be fur-lined for warmth, as it spread northward, was bound to reduce the market for the heavy cloth that had for two centuries been regarded as the height of luxury. Even if their supply of fine wool had not become capricious many of the Flemish, like some Yorkshire mill-owners in our own century who went on making flannel shirting while men were ceasing to wear flannel shirts, would ultimately have been in difficulty, left with no customers outside the cold old-fashioned Baltic world and few even there who would appreciate lavishly finished cloth. True, the Flemish had always been flexible enough to sell cloth straight from the loom if that was what customers wanted. It would be a great mistake to think of them as stupid. Agriculturally, they were the leading innovators of the fourteenth century. If social relations within the towns and between towns and countryside had not been so embittered by misgovernment and by French and English intervention, and if the Burgundian effort to unify the territories around them with Bruges as a court capital had come sooner, the Flemish might have been able to switch mercantile funds into a wider organisation of lower grade manufacturing with non-English wool, compensating for lower prices by quicker turn-over.

Actually, we have statistics of the decline of their own manufactures only for Ypres, where it had dwindled by the 1370s to fifteen per cent of its peak for the early fourteenth century. Since Ypres shrank in size more than any of the other textile towns, this over-measures the decline.

Yet throughout the century thousands of Flemish workers either retreated to the villages or emigrated.

The most brilliant recovery of labour-intensive manufacture in the regions flattened by English competition came in Arras, through a patrician draper's invention of the art industry of woven tapestry. Perfectly timed, this was able from the 1320s on to re-employ hundreds of poor weavers in Arras and many later in other towns: it set the dream-world of chivalric romance blooming in colour on the bed-chamber and dining-hall walls of all the rich who loved it.

Elsewhere in north-eastern France and the territories of the Low Countries textile skill reverted to rustic levels, to cloth known by a variety of names coming under the generic heading of 'little cloths'. This signifies reversion to the single-weaver narrow loom and to production of short lengths from the clip of a few sheep perhaps mixed with flax. With slightly smoother finishing than had been traditional in villages this simplified industry came to be heralded for sales purposes, as it generated some mercantile capital, as 'the new drapery'. There were some quaint efforts to simulate the older urban industry by giving rustic centres regulative codes. The Count of Hainault chartered the little town of Ath in this fashion in 1328. The regulations included a prohibition of weaving for sale during the month of August, in order that all servants be available as harvest hands. The count paid for work-sheds and fulling-troughs. Indeed, he thought of everything except the provision of working capital. Brabant towns managed to hold textile work at the cost, in the early fifteenth century, of using municipal funds to guarantee sales and subsidise food for the poor. Yet the population of Brabant declined, by mortality and emigration, between 1437 and 1472. The most successful of the Low Countries towns to urbanise light-weight rural weaving was Hondschoote. The town was five times larger in 1485 than in 1400; its export of cloth then accelerated and went on accelerating into the sixteenth century.

The English industry wandered in and out of the towns,

becoming more rural as provincial merchant capital organised the putting-out of work to cottagers. E. M. Carus-Wilson has attributed its gravitation to the villages to their advantages in water power for fulling. Yet this was only one of the cost factors involved and one of probably lessened significance as business in light-weight narrow cloth that needed less finishing found more favour.

Italians compensated for fall in demand for heavy cloth by planting mulberry trees to feed silkworms and with superb artistry producing expensive silk, brocade and velvet that no effort elsewhere could match. Luccans had already in the thirteenth century cut their labour cost in this by automating the process of twisting the silk before it went to the weaver. Their larger water-powered throwing mills, as they were called, carried two hundred spindles; Florentine silk shops used a machine with half this capacity, operated manually.

Italian account-books, the best clue that we have to profits in general commerce and to entrepreneurial profit from manufacturing, confirm the impression that the latter was generally lower. Detailed analysis of the accounts of Francesco Datini and his Florentine partners in having Spanish wool made into cloth in the 1390s, a period when general commercial profits ran at twelve per cent and higher, show that on the manufacturing the profit was 8.9 per cent. The actual work, which was put out, took seven months, but the interval between payment for the wool in Spain and sale of the cloth in Venice was nearer nine months; arrangements for buying the wool, which was grown on Balearic island sheep, had been made more than three years in advance. A Florentine silk entrepreneur over the next two decades made eight per cent on the output of about thirty looms. One of the Strozzi family over part of this period made 17.6 per cent from woollen-making but his profit later sank to little more than ten per cent. The Medici averaged fifteen per cent for silk-making over the 1430s and '40s but only six per cent from two woollen workshops. These were small enterprises, but Raymond De Roover is certain that had there been any advantage in enlarging the scale of production the Medici would have done so.

North of the Alps, if one were to believe all the stories of 'utter decay' laid before public authorities in pleas for protective legislation of one kind or another, the industrial population in the last quarter of the fifteenth century was in a very bad way. For example, cloth-makers at Rouen complained in 1480 that recent mill construction had thrown five hundred men out of work and was destroying demand for cloth by putting badly made stuff on the market. Yet Michel Mollat on investigating this complaint discovered ample positive evidence that mill construction and other entrepreneurial activity had for some years been steadily increasing total employment in textiles in and around the city and also in a number of other industries; among them was the exciting new one of book-printing. The only people in trouble were a small number who were resisting all innovation. The example is typical. The whole economic climate was changing. English trade statistics from export duties, like the production figures from Hondschoote, show a steadily accelerating rise in cloth business that is all the more striking in the English case by contrast with a long period of arrest on a mediocre plateau earlier in the century and because the new growth was not, as late fourteenth-century growth had been, a mere matter of kidnapping Flemish business.

The change is less marked in the Mediterranean world, where only Milan really stands out as notably advancing. But here the advance had never been stopped. Milan had only lately adopted a silk industry, and only in keeping with its traditional policy of diversification of interests. Florence, on the other hand, had too many of its industrial eggs in luxury manufacturing with a slow turnover; the new economic climate favoured cheaper goods and quicker turnover. Another foreshadowing of future trends is seen in the fact that Venetian shipbuilding was feeling the pinch of approaching deforestation of its territory. The state, in the last years of the century, had to take over this industry, private shipbuilding having retreated across the Adriatic.

The economic malaise that had been spreading over the Islamic side of the Mediterranean was due in part to depletion of all but its mountain woods. Although wood supply presented cost problems in northern Europe, it was already a more serious problem even in northern Italy.

EXPLANATIONS OF THE TRENDS

This bird's-eye survey of medieval industrial effort has only incidentally illustrated the explanatory theories that can be applied to it. Examples have been given of the more obvious kinds of interplay between population growth, money supply and technology, with stress always on the level of agricultural techniques as a limiting factor. Flanders and north Italy are by far the most interesting areas because the fertility of their soil and the ease with which they could import extra food from nearby 'breadbasket' regions had favoured high density of population. This gave them not only a large reservoir of part-time peasant labour free for country industrial work but enabled them also to urbanise a greater proportion of the population. As against a probable maximum of fifteen per cent in any other regions, Flanders and north Italy urbanised at least twenty-five per cent of their people; more than half of this proportion could normally put most of a medieval full-time year into actually producing goods.

The problem of gauging the effectiveness of medieval industrial effort is especially challenging between the 1280s and the 1470s. From the point of view of demographic research this stretch of time falls into three phases: (1) a continuance of population growth but at a declining rate and interrupted in 1293–94 and in 1315–17 by serious general famine; (2) the Black Death years and their immediate aftermath; (3) a century of vagrant epidemics of various diseases constantly checking growth in numbers.

In the first of these phases it is clear that up to forty per cent of the peasantry had already been reduced to small holdings incapable of full support of a family and that although in some regions these people were getting more auxiliary industrial work, in Flanders they were getting less. Productive power was certainly not fully utilised either in the towns nor in the countryside. On the other hand, skilled masters who succeeded in making extra money by trade in the materials of their craft and by money-lending were thriving. One meets such men everywhere, buying bits of land around the towns and carrying on several trades at once. Several in the rather poor little provincial town of Montbrison in the Forez in the early fourteenth century had incomes several times as large as those of professional men of landed families. One, starting as a butcher, had expanded first into making tallow and leather and then into trading in cloth and metal, and was besides a large money-lender.

Debate usually centres on the second phase, when plague suddenly cut population by close to one third. It has been argued that this should have raised productivity among the survivors, since the same amount of fixed equipment as had served the pre-plague population was still there. So far as industry is concerned this is largely illusory. The fixed equipment was mostly housing; empty, it was useless, though counted as an asset for the time being in hopeful accounting and in tax assessment on speculators who bought it. The same was true of unneeded fractions of the capacity of mills. Some craftsmen presumably gained through the tools of the dead coming on the market, and by a fall in the price of food as against a rise in industrial prices. Employers had to pay more for skilled labour. Skilled wage-earners were able to eat more white bread, in Germany butchers sold more sausages and every town boasted of its beer, there was concern over bad salting of fish, and doctors advised the rich that distilled drink, in moderation, was good for their health. Yet it was not until the third quarter of the fifteenth century that nutrition was adequate to build up resistance to epidemic disease. Every serious epidemic that struck a town had disrupted all its business for weeks or months because so many people fled to the countryside.

EMPLOYMENT RELATIONS

Wage-earning at piece rates and at daily, weekly or annual rates was more typical of medieval industry as a whole than the quasi-familial relation between master and apprentice. In mining and metallurgy and in many branches of metal fabrication, in all construction work except among groups of masons settling in late medieval towns, in the technical operation of mills and salt-works, in the rural textile and leather industries and also in new or unusual lines of specialisation in town industries and in rapidly expanding ones, skill was developed and rewarded simply by differential rates of pay. The apprenticeship of children and adolescents was feasible only in work not requiring much muscular strength.

Given the prevalence of wage-earning, there was in a sense always a labour market with some of the features of the modern labour market: wages were related to productivity, were pushed up or down according as employers or employees were the better organised and in response to changes in supply and demand, and there were purely customary ceilings on the wages of women. However, there were several important differences in the way the system worked, some operating in the employer's favour, some in the wage-earner's favour. Big builders, as has been seen, had always the right of impressment, and in any work that had the character of an essential public service—all victualling trades and in towns all building trades—public authority held masters' charges so far as possible at fixed levels, making for severe downward pressure on the wages they could pay their helpers. Again, gild organisation was sanctioned only on condition that masters did not 'conspire' to raise prices, but whether they were known to be doing so or not, they could always have servants who combined to demand higher wages committed to gaol. Again, shortages in money supply gave excuses for paying workers in kind at arbitrary valuations, and in the confusion that accompanied recoinages wage-earners were always the losers. But above all, what kept the poorer workers in poverty was their poverty itself, which put them at the mercy of usurers and perpetuated among artisans the ancient willingness of small peasant tenantry to exploit themselves mercilessly while they had small children to support and at other times to be improvidently slack.

This culture of hopelessness was gradually modified, both in towns and in villages, as it became possible for women's work to eke out a family's money income by more than pennies. Behind Chaucer's skit on his woman entrepreneur, the wife of Bath, is a long history that has been too little investigated. The frequent prohibition, in the rules of the composite groupings of skilled gild workers and merchant entrepreneurs in the textile industries of Italy and France, of advancing money to women spinners has usually been read as a sign of their subjection through usury. But it may also be read as an inevitable trend to differential reward for higher skill. Yarn can be spun irregularly and lumpily; perfectly smooth skeins were worth more. Working on time rates, women were paid hardly more than children; producing good work by the piece, they could break into the rational system of differential rewards. Several of some forty people who received belated payment from the executors of Jehen Boinebroke, a wealthy draper of Douai, of small sums owing for odd pieces of work done for him in the 1290s were women weavers and dyers. Women can be found in many other trades, working on their own. That they played an important role in the ethic of hopeful thrift in the many religious fraternities that doubled as sick benefit societies in the towns is a certainty.

Another circumstance that worked against degradation of the town wage-earner was the permeation of wage contracts by a variety of rights that a purely impersonal labour market later jettisoned. Analysing these in the trades of Paris, Bronislaw Geremek concludes that it is misleading to speak of a proletariat. He raises, however, another point that has been overlooked in historical studies. A building worker, for example, who was repeatedly assigned a particular kind of task, could become 'typed' as having too limited experience to try his hand at a more highly paid task. An extreme division of labour can in this way deprive a man of opportunity to rise.

Geremek's discussion of this leads him to point to an aspect of apprenticeship that has also been overlooked. What were the secrets of the trade that an apprentice was supposedly taught, that his parents were paying to have him taught? He suggests that these were not the manual skills of the trade so much as the art of managing a little business, of doing the buying and selling in a prudent manner. One need add only that the custom of apprenticeship struck root best in gild-organised trades in which the 'secrets' that a member would be punished for betraying were the details of agreements about holding a common line on prices and wages.

The mere fact that masters, apprentices and servants worked side by side did not eliminate discord if their interests diverged. However strong the common dedication to good craftsmanship, it could not prevent young men whose prospects of becoming masters themselves were poor from becoming restive. Yet until the masters' gild associations won official recognition, servants were unable to organise effectively, and during any struggle for recognition their interest lay in supporting the masters. This continued to be the case in export industries where wages depended directly and openly on the piece rates for finished work that masters received from merchants. The same was true where any finished product was assembled from parts made separately in different types of workshop, as for example in the saddlery trade, in which the wooden frames, the leather covering and straps, and metal stirrups, were made by separately organised masters who, along with the painters who decorated the leather, were all dependent for work on the master saddlers.

But in other trades, discord between masters and servants became endemic in the fourteenth century, for a variety of reasons. Servants were naturally the first to suffer from any decline in demand. Masters' agreements to restrict production inevitably created a sense of injustice. The best-documented instance of abuse of gild power in this direction is from London, where for a generation, beginning in the 1290s, the weavers systematically destroyed the looms of any member who died. They overdid this, raising their rates for piece work and stirring public indignation. In their case, servants thrown out of work would sooner or later have been able to find work in the countryside, where merchants disgusted with gild power were already advancing new producers the money to buy looms. A more discreet means of restricting production was to block the admission of young men to mastership by turning the customary examination of their skill by gild officers into the requirement that they produce a costly 'masterpiece'. Many gilds managed to institutionalise this, professing that in doing so they were protecting the public against bad workmanship.

It was not hardship that drove servants to organise in defence of their interest, however, so much as the experience of better conditions on the labour market in the generation following the Black Death. This and succeeding epidemics made for such erratic imbalances in the supply of young workmen that in spite of all governmental efforts to keep wages down, both skilled and unskilled rates of pay rose almost universally. Servants attached to gilds then formed their own separate fraternities to try to hold their advantage and ask for more. The custom of wandering from place to place in search of better working conditions became more common. The peak of all this agitation came in the 1370s and 1380s, when town discontent often merged with peasant discontent in a more or less revolutionary ideology. Many of the insurgents in the so-called Peasants' Revolt of 1381 in England were young artisans.

The upward trend of wages levelled off in the 1390s, the gain to servants being reflected in increased demand for meat, wheat bread, drink and cheaper grades of shoes and clothing. Reduction of population pressure on the land enabled agriculture to provide the first at lower price levels; cost-cutting by shortening the time taken in processing such

materials as leather helped to meet shifts in industrial demand. Cost-cutting of this kind accounts for much of the
petulance of contemporary complaints of bad workmanship. New skills replaced old ones, the migration of artisans
helping to spread innovations.

To many people it is puzzling that the late Middle Ages
did not, in these circumstances, make more of a shift to
mechanisation. They see small masters and their servants
alike as irrationally obstructionist, above all in Flanders,
where they had always opposed mechanical fulling. Yet the
reason given for this, that the mills damaged the cloth,
may well have been true on their first introduction, when
they were equipped with wooden blocks which could
roughen with wear. This problem was later solved by
shoeing the blocks with a smooth coat of iron, but the
solution added to the capital cost of mill construction.
Opposition to mills in late fifteenth-century Normandy was
on different grounds: the small urban masters there admitted their efficiency and objected only that they were
kept for the private use of the richer manufacturers who
had found the capital to erect them. Mills, they protested,
should be open to use by any master. They were not
Luddites, seeing the machine as an enemy; they simply
wanted it to be somehow incorporated into their own mode
of small-scale operation without altering the existing distribution of economic power. This idea was actually put
into practice in some small communities on the lower
northern slopes of the Alpine region, through communal
ownership of water-mills just large enough to full cloth
for local needs and to produce flour.

Yet so far as attitudes towards private advantage through
enterprise were concerned, the views that counted were
those of the men who had access to mercantile credit.
These attitudes depended on their expectations of profit,
which were higher in trade, and more secure through
acquisition of land and house property, than through expanding any single industrial enterprise or launching into
new lines of manufacture. The first printers had great
difficulty in finding backers. Another problem was the

general shortage of skilled mechanics. Still another, over long periods of the late Middle Ages, was the vulnerability of investment in mills in northern river valleys and coastal areas, and also in the Danube valley, to high wastage by floods, which repeatedly washed away their earthwork canals and foundations. One response to this, however, was to hitch horses to geared mills. This made it possible to generalise the use of power on a small scale in any locality. Prosperous town brewers often had a horse mill in their yard for grinding malt. Constructive reactions of this kind became more common as demand picked up with late fifteenth-century increases in population.

The great economic achievement of the centuries since 1000 A.D. had been to widen the scope of market economy and of incentives to train and use productive skill. But the disciplined organisation of an industrial society was far beyond the horizons of imagination of any citizen or rural worker of 1500. Leisure and a modest security were the prevailing values. Industry was still the Cinderella of the economy.

BIBLIOGRAPHY

BIBLIOGRAPHICAL NOTES on some books and articles of interest and importance that are more recent in date than those listed in *The Cambridge Economic History of Europe*, Vol. II, *Trade and Industry*, Cambridge University Press, 1952.

GENERAL

Harry A. Miskimin, *The Economy of Early Renaissance Europe, 1300–1460* (Prentice-Hall, 1969), puts key information into graphs and offers an explanation of differences between northern and eastern Europe and Italy in this period, in terms of imbalances in money supply.

REGIONAL STUDIES AND THE ROLE OF PARTICULAR CITIES

H. Van Der Wee, *The Growth of the Antwerp Market and the European Economy* (The Hague, 1963) displays the extreme sensitivity of industry in late medieval Brabant to monetary factors. A recent addition to the many Belgian studies of the role of industry in the history of a particular town is J. L. Charles, *La ville de Saint-Trond au moyen âge*, Liège, 1965. Some of the best descriptions in English of investment in Italian town industries, and on their management, are to be· found in Raymond de Roover, *The Rise and Decline of the Medici Bank, 1397–1464* (Harvard University Press, 1963), David Herlihy, *Pisa in the Early Renaissance* (Yale University Press, 1958), David Herlihy Robert S. Lopez and Vsevolod Slessarev, eds., *Economy, Society and Government in Early Medieval Italy*, Essays in Memory of Robert L. Reynolds (University of Wisconsin Press, 1969), and Richard A. Goldthwaite *Private Wealth in Renaissance Florence*, Princeton, 1968. The extent of the movement of rural industry to towns is well and fully described in E. Fournial, *Les villes et l'économie d'échange en Forez, XIIIe et XIVe siècles*, Paris, 1967. One of the best pictures of industry in a forest district in England, is Jean

R. Birrell, 'The Forest Economy of the Honour of
Tutbury in the 14th and 15th centuries,' *The University of
Birmingham Historical Journal*, VIII (1962).

NATIONAL AND INTER-REGIONAL

A balanced discussion of developmental issues relating to
England, brief and to the point, is Edward Miller, 'The
English Economy in the Thirteenth Century,' *Past and
Present* (July 1964). On earlier experience in Poland see
Karol Modzelewski, 'L'organisation ministériale en Pologne
médiévale', *Annales, Economies, Sociétés, Civilisations* (Nov.–
Dec. 1964) and on relations between development in
eastern and western Europe see Herbert Ludat, *Vorstufen
und Enstehung des Stadtwesens in Osteuropa*, Cologne, 1955.

PARTICULAR INDUSTRIES

The best general surveys of medieval building and mining,
along with E. M. Carus-Wilson's survey of the woollen
industry in Flanders, Italy and England, are in the *Cambridge Economic History of Europe*, II, *Trade and Industry* (1952).
On the Flemish and French cloth industry see also E.
Perroy, *Le travail dans les regions du Nord; l'industrie
drapière*, Sorbonne lectures, mimeographed, 1961. On cloth
and leather in Catalonia see Ch. E. Dafourcq, 'Prix et
niveaux de vie dans les pays catalans et maghribins à la
fin du XIIIe siècle et au debut du XIVe siècle', *Le Moyen
Age*, t. LXXI (1965). On Italian silk see Florence E. de
Roover, 'Andrea Banchi, Florentine Silk Manufacturer
and Merchant in the 15th century', in *Studies in Medieval
and Renaissance History*, ed. W. M. Bowsky, III (1966).
Rolf Sprandel summarises extensive research on the iron
industry in 'La production du fer au moyen âge', *Annales,
Economies, Sociétés et Civilisations* (1969). Germain Sicard
Les moulins de Toulouse au moyen âge (1953), is a definitive
study of the financing and management of milling at
Toulouse. A. R. Bridbury, *England and the Salt Trade in
the Later Middle Ages* (Oxford, 1955), describes the tech-

niques and cost problems of producing salt in Brittany, the Low Countries, Lünebourg and England. Elspeth M. Veale, *The English Fur Trade in the Later Middle Ages* (Oxford, 1966) describes techniques and fashion in the London skin-dressing industry. J. T. Tinniswood, 'English Galleys, 1272–1307', *The Mariners' Mirror*, Vol. 35 (1949) describes shipbuilding methods at that period and gives a list of surviving accounts of costs. For some new views of the commercialisation of the English rural cloth industry see Edward Miller, 'The English Cloth Industry in the Thirteenth Century', *Economic History Review*, XVIII, 1965. One of the most interesting of the numerous books on the rise of book-printing is L. Febvre and H. J. Martin, *L'apparition du Livre* (Paris, 1958).

EMPLOYMENT CONDITIONS AND THE INFLUENCE OF GILDS

By far the best analysis of employment relationships is Bronislaw Geremek, *Le salariat dans l'artisanat parisien du XIIIe au XVe siècle* (Paris, 1968), translated from the original Polish edition of 1962. On gilds see Sylvia L. Thrupp in the *Cambridge Economic History of Europe*, III (1963) and in *The International Encyclopaedia of the Social Sciences* (New York, 1968) for a briefer survey. For a comparative survey of medieval working conditions, with reproductions of contemporary drawings of men at work, see Philippe Wolff, *Histoire générale du Travail. Le Moyen Age*, Paris, n.d. For a case study on migrations of labour see Sylvia L. Thrupp 'Aliens in and around London in the Fifteenth century', in *Studies in London History*, ed. A. E. J. Hollander and W. Kellaway (London, 1970).

7. Trade and Finance in the Middle Ages 900-1500

Jacques Bernard

TRADE ROUTES AND COMMODITIES

In the middle ages only trade, and the financial activity which was closely allied to it, could offer a man the opportunity for enrichment and for rapid social promotion. In this way, it introduced change and movement into an economy and a society which were above all rural, and as such endowed with a great force of inertia. Links with the outside world moreover, the very essence of commerce, were in themselves powerful contributors to progress. In Western Europe neither climate nor relief nor long distances put any great obstacle in the way of the circulation of people and goods. On the contrary, it was favoured by the variety of its resources, by a network of water communications, and by the length of its indented coastline.

Nonetheless, like all the other mutually dependent elements of the economy, major commerce and finance experienced in the ten centuries of the middle ages those major fluctuations which are of the essence of economic history.

After the stagnation of the dark ages, marked by a slackening of foreign trade in western Europe, the period which extends roughly from the eleventh century to the middle of the fourteenth was by contrast a period of growth on all fronts. The colonisation of the plains of eastern Europe and the coastal areas of the Baltic, and the Crusades in the Mediterranean, all signs of the vitality of the Christian west, considerably enlarged the geographical scope of exchanges, which were also stimulated by increases in population and in production. A continuing rise in prices — of around 30 per cent between 1150 and the beginning of the fourteenth century — the growth of profits and the consequent accumulation of capital, sustained and stimulated all who engaged in trade. Notable among them

were the members of the great Italian commercial and
banking houses. Italy on the one hand and Flanders on the
other were closely linked together by means of the fairs held
in Champagne.

In the 1330s this tendency was reversed. An over-
burdening of population as a result of previous prosperity,
harvest failures, the crushing fiscal policies and currency
disturbances which the now endemic warfare imposed on
rulers, and finally the Black Death of 1348 to 1350, all
contributed to a long contraction in the economy, which
lasted up to the middle of the fifteenth century. The Turkish
offensive and the final check to the Crusades marked the end
of the great Christian enterprises, which henceforth drew
back to the island outposts of the eastern Mediterranean and
the Aegean. But, to compensate for this, the progress made
in commercial and financial techniques and in the concentration of capital during the previous age, became more
widely diffused. This more sophisticated organisation
precipitated the decline of the Champagne fairs, which
moreover now suffered competition from the opening of a
direct sea link between Italy and Bruges. Bruges became
then a commercial and financial centre of prime importance.
The German Hansa, born of a need for protection and
security which was foreign to the true spirit of enterprise,
reached its peak at this time, while England, beginning to
weave her wool into cloth, started on her first industrial
revolution.

In delivering the world 'from the spectre of over-
population and famine',[1] the demographic and monetary
catastrophes of the fourteenth century prepared the way for
a new equilibrium. In the second half of the fifteenth
century Europe recaptured that economic vigour and super-
abundance of life which had once been expressed in the
Crusades, and which now in the great voyages of discovery
were seen on the wider stage of the world's oceans.

Large-scale trade in the middle ages was closely associated
with two areas, which at first developed fairly independently,

1. E. Perroy, Les crises du XIV⁰ siècle, *Annales, E.S.C.*, 1949.

but which soon began to cross-fertilise: the Mediterranean, in which Italy held an unrivalled position, and the narrow seas of northern Europe, dominated economically by the Low Countries. The Mediterranean, scene both of the conflicts and of the continual interchanges between Europe and Asia, was first of all the route of the spice trade. This magical word, laden with all the prestige of the 'glamorous East', included in fact practically all exotic goods and some others. Their high value, the enormous gains they offered, and the universal demand for them, were alone capable of balancing the risks of distant and dangerous enterprise. These factors made spices the most highly valued international commodity, and one which itself contributed to the rebirth of international trade.

The greater part of these treasures came from farthest Asia; from India, Ceylon, Java ('the greatest and richest island in the world', according to Marco Polo), from Moluccas, the great area of flavouring spices, and finally from China, where the port of Canton was the distribution centre for pepper, raw silk, jasper and porcelain.

The Arabs were necessary intermediaries in this traffic, for they controlled both its land and sea routes. In the Indian Ocean they would sometimes equip huge ships, which had three or four masts, two or three hundred sailors, and fifty or sixty cabins holding a large number of merchants. But the Arab navigators also used smaller craft, lateen-rigged or square-rigged according to the weather, ancestors of the 'booms', 'sabouks', 'zarougs' and 'baghlas' which still sail in the same seas. Their pilots, checking their reckoning against the stars, brought them, with the aid of the monsoon winds, as far as the Persian Gulf or the Red Sea. In the upper part of the Red Sea, at the risk of being scattered by the fierce northerly winds which prevail in that region, the precious freight finally reached the port of Alexandria, where it was transferred to Christian galleys.

Meanwhile, tireless men led caravans of beasts of burden and camels along the transcontinental routes which were an extension of the sea routes of the Persian Gulf, or crossed the steppes of central Asia, Turkestan and the plateau of Iran.

These routes finished at Baghdad, and then went either to the '*scali*' of the Levant (Jaffa, Acre, Beirut, Tripoli and Antioch), or across Anatolia to Byzantium.

The substitution of the Turks for the Arab caliphs, and the loss of Syria and Palestine by the Christians, made these communications more difficult. But for a century — from *c.* 1250 to *c.* 1350 — 'the Mongolian peace' opened new routes across Asia to European commerce, and enabled it to escape the chicanery and the monetary and commercial levies of 'the Muslim middleman',[2] who controlled the exits from Egypt and Syria. This Mongolian route started from Tana on the north of the Sea of Azov, penetrated through Turkestan to the heart of the deserts and steppes of central Asia, and finished at Quinsai and Khambalik (Peking) the capital of the Great Khan. The chief staging points on this journey were Sarai and Astrakhan, Ourgendj, Otrar and Almaligh. A more southernly route was that used by Marco Polo, starting at Trebizond or Lazzaio on the Gulf of Alexandria, going through Tabriz and Astrabad, with possible variants towards Ormuz and the Persian Gulf, and reaching Bokhara, Samarkand, Kokand and the pass of Kashgar.

To the slow rhythm of the horses, asses, camels and oxen and the great wagons which took from 6 to 30 Genoese cantars (each representing around 47 kg, 103 lbs), the 'viaggio del Gattaio' took at least a year. But this was broken up by halts, major staging posts and great international markets, where Italian money was current and Italian weights and measures in force. The adventures of Marco Polo, which were later to inspire Christopher Columbus with the idea of reaching the empire of the Great Khan from the west, were met by some at that time (1271–1295) with incredulity, but the manual of Pegolotti, undoubtedly composed between 1310 and 1340, already presents the codification of a practice and experience quite without mystery.

The Sea of Azov and the Black Sea, encircled with Venetian and Genoese colonies, were not only starting-

2. J. Heers, *L'occident aux XIVe et XVe Siècles*, 1963, p. 142.

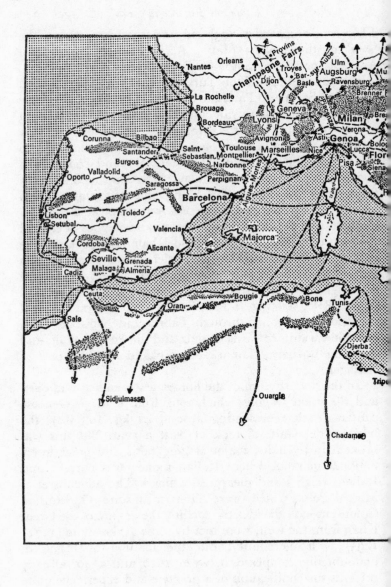

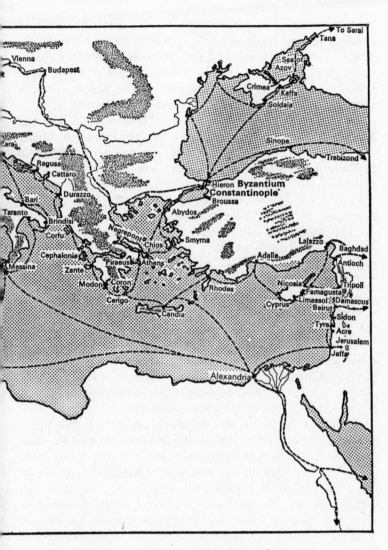

The Mediterranean showing the main trade routes.

point and terminus for the Asia traffic; they also received everything that came down the great rivers from the depths of the Ukraine, Russia, and the countries of the Danube — slaves, furs, grain, wood and precious metals. These were added to the other goods carried on the Bosphorus, the spices and silks which came from India and Cathay.

The offensive of the Ottoman Turks and the fall of the Mongolian hegemony ruined this fine organisation during the fifteenth century, and brought a greater number of Italian ships than ever back to the ports of Syria and Egypt, to Beirut and Alexandria. The Europeans were forced by this to look for another way of avoiding the obstacle presented by the Muslims; having by-passed them to the north by the Mongolian route which ran across the whole width of the continent, they now looked to go south, by sea.

These difficulties in the course of the fifteenth century had also prompted the Christians to produce for themselves — in Cyprus, Sicily and Calabria, in Valencia, Andalusia and the archipelagos of the Atlantic — some part of what they bought at Alexandria and the seaports of the Levant: silk, sugar, cochineal and wax. The discovery of alum at Tolfa in the Papal States in 1462 was described as 'our finest victory against the Turks', who held the mines of Phocea, for it freed the textile industry from a heavy servitude.

But this measure of emancipation came late. For practically all of the period studied it was necessary that the flow of goods from the east be compensated for by exports from the west. The agricultural products of the Christian side of the Mediterranean — grain, oil, fruit, wine, salt, and also textiles, timber, iron and arms, and later paper — sustained an active coastal trade, and left some surplus for export. This was nothing in comparison with the textile industry of Catalonia, Languedoc, Lombardy and above all Florence, but the development of the latter was closely linked with the economic rise of northern countries which decisively contributed to restoring the European balance of payments.

The Mediterranean did not produce only spices, and north-west Europe was not entirely given over to the production of coarse goods. But it is still a possible simplification to say that, by contrast with the south, the north produced rather the necessities than the luxuries of life. Under a windy and rainy sky, in which the sun rarely shone, a heavy earth, meadowland, mines, forests, and shallow seas which teemed with life, all produced inexhaustible supplies of the raw materials which the Mediterranean regions in general were badly provided with. The first of these heavy weight, low price goods in order of necessity was grain, which a broad usage referred to as 'wheat'. It ripened in the warmth of continental summers, all along the great alluvial plains which stretched from the Ukraine to the Paris Basin. France, the country of 'bread, wine and joy', was one of the granaries of Europe, and in some years England also had an exportable surplus. The grains of Picardy passed through Le Crotoy (a poor site for the port of so fertile a region), those of the 'Ile de France' through Rouen, those of the Loire and Aquitaine through Nantes and Bordeaux. The lands they went to were those such as Spain and Flanders, which were short of such products, either through natural conditions or by excessive urban concentration. To these anciently settled regions, where the soil had been turned by the hoe or swing or heavy plough continuously from Neolithic times, German colonisation east of the Elbe had added a vast new patrimony whose grain production was one of the basic ingredients of the Baltic trade.

In the realm of human nourishment, scene of the debate between 'Carnival and Lent', the sea was no less important than arable or meadow land. Both rich and poor consumed huge quantities of fish, salted and put in barrels, smoked or dried — as much from necessity as from religious conviction. Herrings were fished from spring to winter in the cold seas of the Baltic, the Sound, the North Sea and the eastern parts of the Channel; hake and conger-eels came from the drying-grounds of Cornwall, the Channel Islands and Brittany. So common a freight were they that the 'last' of fish (around two tons' weight) was the measure of a ship's tonnage in northern ports.

In the Atlantic this joined another standard measure; the wine-cask became the nautical ton, and thus the symbol and vehicle of another important traffic. The wines of Burgundy and the Rhineland came down the great rivers to the sea, rivalling those of south-west France, which the men of La Rochelle or the Bordeaux merchants of La Rousselle gladly exchanged for fish or cloth. This gave a decisive stimulus to sea traffic, as the sea custom which is known as 'les Rôles d'Oléron' testifies. The wine of Aunis, loaded at La Rochelle, had a steady market in Flanders and the Hanseatic countries. Gascon wine, by virtue of the political union of England and Gascony, found its best market in England. From the Bordelais and the *Haut Pays*, the annual vintage and the 'rake' (in autumn and winter), could easily be transported down the Gironde and the Garonne, and by sea; in good years at the beginning of the fourteenth century 80 to 100,000 tons a year were shipped. Resins, honey, quills, woad, and the 'bois brussin' from which combs were made for the textile industry, provided further cargoes for the ships of the wine trade.

The ports from which wine was shipped were not far removed from the coastal salt-pans, which the sunny climate enabled to stretch as far north as the marshland of Guérande, and from the roadsteads where they loaded up with salt from 'the Bay'. 'The Bay' referred in a general sense to the whole Bay of Biscay, but more precisely to the Bay of Bourgneuf, between the island of Noirmoutier and the southern coast of Poitou, and to the Bay of Brouage, on either side of the mouth of the Charente and sheltered by the island of Oléron. As assiduous as the wine traders, the salt fleet came year after year, primarily from England and the Hanseatic countries.

Agricultural and other food products formed the basis of trade in north and north-west Europe, from the Bay of Biscay to the Baltic, and were largely confined to this region. The mining and industrial production of England and central Europe remained small in scope. Neither of these sufficed to link their vast regions with the Mediterranean and thence with world trade. What did so was English wool and above all cloth. These were the only industrial products sustained by a universal demand and capable of being sold in the most distant markets.[3] The great manufacturing region was Flanders, which included Artois (Arras, St Omer), southern Flanders (Douai, Lille and Tournai), and the great cloth towns of the north (Ypres, Ghent and Bruges). In this whole area industrial activity was closely connected with an ancient tradition, a dense population, intensive agriculture and the general vigour of exchanges. In the fourteenth century the textile industry was extended further, when Brabant — Brussels, Louvain, Malines — developed, as the Flemish cloth industry ran into difficulties.

The cloth trade of Flanders and Brabant was linked with England in a close economic alliance, which had considerable political repercussions. For from England came the raw material, wool, which was the most ancient and had long been the most important English export, and which brought in customs dues that formed a basic part of the crown's financial resources. By the beginning of the fourteenth century, the organisation of 'the Staple' and the privileged company of Merchant Staplers had gained control of this trade for the English. Closely organised fleets took the wool from Hull, Boston, Ipswich and London to a single continental outlet, the Staple, which was moved from Antwerp to Bruges, to St Omer, and finally settled at Calais in 1390.

Yet in the fourteenth century the great Flemish textile industry declined, through a combination of domestic troubles and English competition. England had started on her 'first industrial revolution'[4] in the thirteenth century, thanks to an increase in the number of fulling mills. By the mid-fifteenth century her exports of cloth had caught up and passed those of wool: 54,000 cloths (the equivalent of 12,500 sacks of wool), as against 8,000 sacks of wool. The hardy Merchant Adventurers, who exported cloth to the Low Countries and elsewhere, slowly eclipsed the Staplers of Calais, who continued their unadventurous trade in wool. From the Baltic to Spain and even into the Mediterranean,

3. Renouard, 1968.   4. Carus-Wilson, E., 1967.

packs or bales of cloth were the standard freight of English ships, and guaranteed a large profit.

The luxury cloths of Flanders — 'Flanders cloth and fine cloth were for a long time synonymous'[5] — later replaced by those of Brabant and England, were the counter-balance to the trade in spices and other luxury goods. Between them they formed part of the basis of the great network of exchanges set up between the two poles of European commerce, Flanders and Italy.

Merchants from Artois and Flanders crossed the mountains into Italy, bearing cloth from northern Europe. It appeared at Genoa, Marseilles and Montpellier at the end of the twelfth century, at Milan, Piacenza, Bologna and Florence early in the next, and is recorded at Venice in 1265. It was also sold at Paris, in Poitou and Guienne, and in Spain. Trading in the opposite direction, Lombard merchants — from Novara, Vercelli, and above all Asti — had long been accustomed to journeying north. They are found at Paris by 1034, and at the fairs of Ypres as early as 1127. By the end of the twelfth century the Genoese also were travelling north.

The Flemings and Italians, some of them money-changers and some of them traders in cloth and spices, all found it convenient to save a part of the journey and meet in the Champagne fairs. In their great days of the thirteenth century there were fairs at Provins, Troyes, Lagny and Bar-sur-Aube, which between them lasted most of the year. For these were towns well placed on the routes which led, either by sea and up the Rhône valley via St Gilles, or across the Alpine passes of Mont-Cenis, St Bernard or Mont Genèvre, then up the Saône and Seine valleys, through the toll at Bapaume, to the cities and fairs of Artois and Flanders.

The steady decline of the Champagne fairs was caused partly by the policy of the French kings, but far more by the advanced commercial techniques which the Italians set up

in Flanders and England. Also, the land routes upon which
the fairs depended lost a good deal of their traffic to sea
travel. In 1277 a Genoese galley may be said to have
inaugurated the direct sea route between the Mediterranean
and Flanders. It was soon followed by those of the Venetians
(by 1317 at the very latest), the Florentines and the
Catalans. In the fourteenth and fifteenth centuries Italian
galleys or carracks came each year to the outer ports of
Bruges, Antwerp, Sandwich and Southampton, after a long
voyage lasting several months, with only rare — perhaps
between five and fifteen — ports of call. They brought not
only cargoes of spices, aromatics and fruit, but also textile
fibres and alum, and their normal return cargo was English
wool.

These regular sea links certainly rivalled the great land
routes across the continent, but they did not destroy them.
Transport by land usually cost more, but it was quicker, and
thus well suited to specialist traffic in goods of high value.
It also suited those merchants who did not fancy a long and
dangerous journey by sea. The fairs of Lyons and Geneva
replaced those of Champagne: they were on different
routes, and performed different functions. To the east of the
Roman route to France (the *Strata Francigena*), the Genoese
and above all the Germans and Venetians regularly used
the St Gotthard, Septimer and Brenner passes across the
Alps. These linked the plains of Padua and Venice to the
world of 'Oltralpe', notably southern Germany — Nuremberg, Augsburg, Munich, Ratisbon and Ravensburg —
where commerce, banking, mining, and the textile and
metallurgical industries created an area of intense economic
life in the fifteenth century.

The cloth which came from the north, and was linked in
this way to the markets of the Mediterranean, gave life to
the Italian industry, especially that of Florence. There were
two aspects to this. Firstly there was the finishing of cloth,
the 'Arte di Calimala', whose red band assured the product
of a prestige at least equal to that of the sealed and bordered
Flemish cloth; secondly there was cloth manufacture, the
'Arte della Lana', which received its raw material from

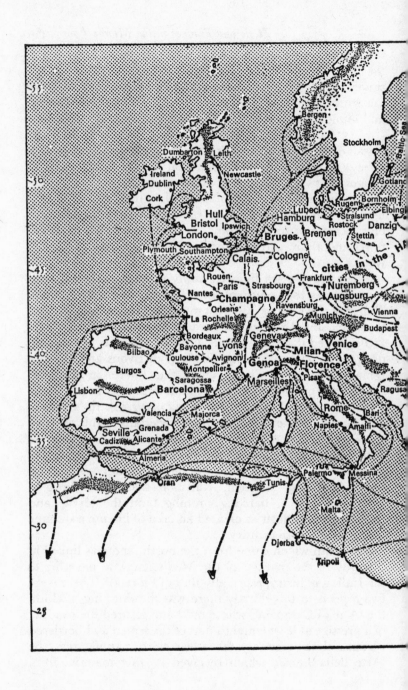

Bergen

Stockholm

Dumbarton Leith

Ireland
Dublin Newcastle

Cork

Gotland

Bornholm
Rugen Elbing
Lubeck Stralsund Danzig
Hull Hamburg Rostock Stettin
Bristol Ipswich Bremen
London Bruges
Plymouth Southampton cities in the HA
Calais. Cologne

Rouen Frankfurt Nuremberg
Paris Strasbourg Augsburg
Nantes Champagne Ravensburg Vienna
Orleans Munich Budapest
La Rochelle Geneva

Bordeaux Milan Venice
Bilbao Bayonne Lyons Genoa Florence
Burgos Toulouse Avignon Pisa Ragusa
Montpellier Marseilles
Saragossa
Lisbon Barcelona Rome Bari

Valencia Majorca Naples Amalfi
Seville Grenada
Cadiz Alicante
Almeria Palermo Messina

Oran Tunis
Malta

Djerba Tripoli

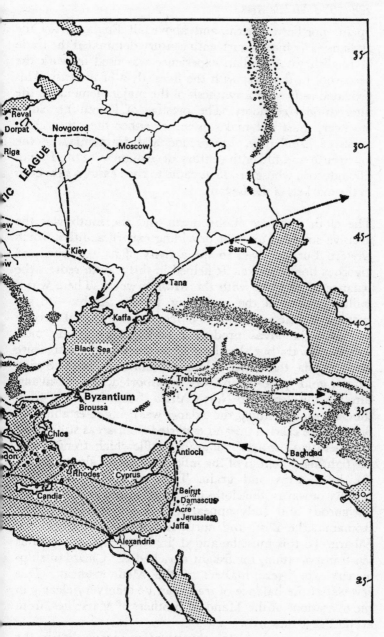

Europe showing the main trade routes.

Spain, northern Africa, and above all England, for the Italians early in the fourteenth century dominated the trade in English wool. Italian experience was used to work the best wool in the west with the finest dyes of the east. This provided as it were a synthesis of the major elements of the international economy. The prestige of Florentine cloth, however, must not make us forget either the other cloth areas of Lombardy, Languedoc and Catalonia, or the fourteenth and fifteenth century development of the Italian silk industry, whose products came to rival eastern silks even in the markets of the Levant.

The cloth industry of the north and the south was the decisive stimulus towards providing export facilities, which western Europe owed to the activity of its extensive and vigorous home market. It helped in this way to redress the balance of its trade with the Muslim world. There was a built-in deficit at the beginning, for the Arabs — to say nothing of their actual stocks of metal — controlled directly not only the areas producing and conveying the most valuable goods, but also the gold production of the treasure areas of Asia, the Urals, Ethiopia, Nubia, and of the Sudan whose gold production was transported, by caravans, through the desert, to North Africa. Soon, however, from the early ninth century, the balance was being re-established. Slaves were carried off and exported from areas still pagan and there was also a dishonourable traffic which strengthened the fighting potential of the infidel: wood for shipbuilding, tin, iron, arms and grain. Then, from the thirteenth century onwards, the cloths of Flanders (sold as far north as Novgorod) and Italy appeared in every market; in the Romania, the East, and north Africa as far south as the Sahara. To this must be added 'invisible exports', such as sea transportation, for freight enriched the Christian ship-owners who were masters of the Mediterranean. This reversal of the balance of trade can be seen very clearly in the operations of the Manduel brothers of Marseilles, from around 1230 onwards.

In the monetary realm, this situation meant that in the

thirteenth century western countries began to strike gold coins once again. Since the time of Charlemagne they had been tied to a silver currency alone, for exchanges were limited and the output of gold insignificant. In fact, from the tenth century, with a new growth of exports, gold had circulated more abundantly, in the form of Byzantine bezants (hyperperes) or Arab dinars (mangons, marabotins), or western imitations of these coins. The new course of trade brought this Muslim gold into the great circuits of European commerce, and in turn brought it back to its country of origin — either directly or via Byzantium, which was a creditor to the West, but in debt to the East. A new milestone was passed in the thirteenth century. Genoa coined the 'genovino' and Florence its first gold florins (*fiorini d'auro*) which carried an emblematic pattern of lilies. Their example was followed by Perugia, Lucca, Venice (in 1284), and the other countries of Europe. This established the financial autonomy of Europe, but not, for all that, the abundance of money, which is indispensable to a rapidly expanding commerce. In the last two centuries of the middle ages, however fast the circulation of specie, Europe suffered from a dearth of currency. A shaky bimetallism only made this worse, for it could not adapt to fluctuations in the real value of the two materials, and these were themselves tied to variable production and often far-distant exchanges. Only late in the fifteenth century did technical progress significantly increase the silver production of the mines of central Europe, at just the moment when the great gold hunger — 'auri sacra fames' — had become one of the most powerful factors behind the great voyages of discovery.

THE GREAT COMMERCIAL AND FINANCIAL CENTRES

A trade as sophisticated as this was necessarily based on a whole battery of towns. But it was a few really privileged cities which became the chosen centres of world commerce.

Byzantium. This was the city of cities, the second Rome. At the beginning of the thirteenth century it still continued the traditions of the ancient world with real panache, and it exercised a powerful hold over western imaginations. The magnificence of the site struck men first of all — 'none was so bold as not to tremble at it' (Villehardouin). It seemed impregnable — on an isthmus, protected on land by a formidable wall, and to the east by the sea defences of the Bosphorus and the Golden Horn. The latter, sheltered by a ridge and fortified by towers, formed a huge, deep natural harbour, in which the largest ships could come almost to the city walls. The general situation was no less impressive. Constantinople lay at the junction of Europe and Asia, mythological names which were at first applied to the narrow' coastal stretches on either side of Hellespont, but came later to refer to the whole continents. At two tolls at Hieron and Abydos, the imperial administration took its tithe from all the commerce which came via the Aegean and the Black Sea. The scope and variety of its trade gave the city, above all in its thriving bazaars, a cosmopolitan flavour quite without parallel in Europe. Already in 1180 there was an Italian colony of some 60,000, and in the fourteenth century the suburb of Pera was in effect a Genoese town.

As well as being a centre of commerce, Constantinople was an industrial centre of the first rank. Its guilds and the town governor subjected its industry to the authority of the state. This tended to keep prices up by keeping production down, for Byzantine industry produced above all luxury goods: silks, arms, goldsmiths' work, enamels, ivories, and also the somewhat less valuable cotton and linen goods. This export industry served for a long time to keep the city's economy balanced. But it became more and more threatened. Byzantium was obliged to settle in cash for its imports of oriental goods, especially the raw materials for its workshops; and it took back from the west, which bought its luxury goods, only some of the cash which the latter took from the goods it was beginning to export to the Muslim world. In this way Byzantine gold currency, the *nomisma* (later called 'hyperpere' or 'bezant'), remained a strong international currency until the eleventh century. Thereafter it steadily fell away.

Yet the Romania remained a flimsy construction of the Greek intellect, and its territorial base was steadily eroded by the Arab and then the Turkish conquests. Further, the eastern empire suffered economic eviction at the hands of the Italians. The germ of this can already be seen in the privileges Venice obtained at the end of the tenth century. And after the Fourth Crusade in 1204, the history of Byzantine trade becomes intermingled with the commercial and maritime expansion of the great Italian cities.

Italy. The 'Italian mastery' (Renaudet) long precedes the Renaissance. In all realms, especially the economic, Italy was far ahead of the rest of Europe. This dominance came partly from the persistence, even though they were diffused, of the techniques and superior forms of organisation of classical tradition — both Roman and Byzantine. In large measure also, it was the result of the exceptional geographical position of the peninsula. But all these advantages would have counted for nothing without the efforts of individuals. Trading and fighting with the Arabs along a contested maritime frontier, the necessity of self-defence and the hope of booty, all made for daring and initiative. The abundant population of a fragmented, mountainous and often arid land, found neither within nor outside the country any great space to colonise, to compare with those available to the peoples of western and northern Europe. 'Commerce was the frontier of the Italians.'[6]

The economic revolution whose pattern emerged in the eleventh century was closely linked to the birth of the communes and the economy of the cities, and this arose in turn from an agrarian, agricultural and demographic evolution which created capital and services. Between 1100 and 1250 a number of Italian cities grew from 5,000–6,000 to 30,000–40,000 people. The city lost its character as a collective rural lordship, to some degree self-sufficient, and the merchants finished up by gaining political control; for it

6. Lopez, R. S., in *The Cambridge Economic History*, 11, p. 304.

found a new raison d'être in the outside world, in commerce, finance and industry.

Italian colonisation. The tenth century saw the growth of the first generation of mercantile towns: the cities of southern Italy, notably Bari and Amalfi, which fostered contacts with Byzantium, the Levant, Egypt, Spain and Barbary. But the prosperity of the ports of Apulia and Campania did not survive their conquest by the Normans. By contrast, the Crusades offered huge possibilities of expansion to the great maritime cities of northern Italy — Venice, Pisa and Genoa. At the end of the eleventh century these already had sufficient capital in men, money and ships to sustain the great enterprises of the western aristocracy.

The conquest, and then the concessions, of the Christian princes of the East, combined with the ready tolerance of the Muslim potentates of Egypt and Barbary, allowed the establishment of Italian colonies. Such colonies were founded at Jerusalem, Jaffa, Caesarea, Acre, Laodicea, Arzouf, Gibelet, Beirut, Tripoli, Antioch, Alexandria, and along the whole coast of northern Africa, from Ceuta to Gabes. Their power consisted of anything from full sovereignty to a simple tolerance. The Fourth Crusade of 1204, and then the restoration of the Paleologi in 1261, opened the coastal regions and islands of the Greek empire to the Venetians and Genoese, and gave them access to the Black Sea. There Kaffa, Tana and Trebizond became the first stopping places in the continental routes across Asia.

Like that of the Phoenicians and the Greeks of antiquity, this Italian colonisation which fringed the world of Islam with a Latin coastline, was reduced to a discontinuous border of maritime and commercial centres, often juxtaposed or incorporated with long established and flourishing cities. In certain parts of the Greek empire, notably in Crete, the Venetians ruled the area, but the great majority of the Italian colonies of the Levant and Africa existed on a different basis. In whatever was granted to them — houses, a street, a neighbourhood, an entrepôt, an area round the port or simply a single building (*funduk, fondaco*) — sailors,

merchants and permanent residents could go freely about
their business. They were under the authority of their own
'bailiffs', 'viscounts' or 'consuls'; they had important judicial,
fiscal and customs privileges; they could worship freely. In
short, they were free citizens and privileged merchants, just
as they were in their home cities.

These adventurous colonies, on the outskirts of a hostile
world which pressed in on them from all sides, could only
survive and prosper by maintaining close sea links, each
with its 'Metropolis' or Mother City. The dangers of sea
travel, as much the outcome of rivalry between Christian
cities as of Muslim piracy, certainly meant that sailing
became a collective activity, and made imperative a system
of flotillas and convoys. But from the time of the First
Crusade, Italian navies had been able to gather considerable
forces, and sail without hindrance. They were masters of the
Mediterranean until the fifteenth century; and for the
benefit of the infidel their Trafego convoy guaranteed
contact between north Africa and the ports of Syria and
Egypt.

Venice and Genoa. After the Genoese naval victory at
La Meloria in 1284, Pisa was in decay, and this was
completed by its annexation by Florence in 1406. This left
only Venice and Genoa, whose rivalry — culminating in
the wars of Chioggia, 1376–1381 — was a feature of the
entire middle ages.

These were two huge cities for their age; around 1330
Genoa had perhaps 100,000 inhabitants, and Venice more
than that. Their prosperity was founded on large-scale
international trade, which was their predominant activity;
but each maintained a powerful originality. There was an
immediate contrast in their sites, for few places are less like
the spongy islands of the archipelago of Rialto than the deep
harbour and sharp shoulder of the Ligurian city. Genoa's
domination over the Tyrrhenian Sea, where the infidel
operated and there was the rivalry of Pisa also, was neither
as early nor as complete as that of Venice over the Adriatic,
From its site, by tradition, and because of its naval
expansion, Venice was further much more 'Byzantine' and

Levantine than Genoa. The Fourth Crusade brought Venice an acknowledged mastery over the eastern empire, but this was the culmination of a long-term effort, one already marked by the privileges of 992. In the ports of Syria, above all in Alexandria, Genoa was less strongly established than her rival, who was firmly based on the great trade routes of Asia. The Venetians remained the spice traders of Europe. On the other hand, the Black Sea turned into a Genoese lake after the restoration of the Greek empire in 1261. From the counting-houses of Gothia, all along the Mongolian route, Genoese weights and measures were those most frequently used. After the great retreat in the fifteenth century, the Genoese maintained at Brousse, in Turkish Anatolia, a similar position to that of the Venetians at Alexandria. The Genoese suburb of Pera in Constantinople, and above all the island of Chios, became 'the centres of an immense distributive trade'.[7] This was founded not so much on spices as on grain, wine, slaves and wood, and still more on silk, cotton and alum, which were taken from there, sometimes direct, to Flanders and England.

Genoa, less 'eastern' than Venice, had the advantage over her rival in the western basin of the Mediterranean, where she held Corsica and Sardinia and had bases all along the Barbary coast. This orientation and these sites pulled the Genoese towards the Atlantic. In 1277 they were establishing the first direct sea links with Flanders and England. Their spirit of adventure also took them southwards, in search of the gold of the Sudan, for explorers adventuring as far as Sidjulmassa and Touat had seen it being transported across the Sahara. In 1290 the Vivaldi had disappeared in the 'shadowy sea' beyond Morocco, but in the fifteenth century Lanzarotto Malocello rediscovered one of the Canary islands. The Genoese, great numbers of whom were in Seville, Sanlucar, Cadiz and Lisbon, then found themselves associated with the new enterprises of the Iberian peninsula. The career of Columbus in Lusitania and Andalusia merely reproduced more dramatically that of many of his compatriots.

7. Heers, J., 1961.

Within Europe also, Venice and Genoa were clearly differentiated. From both, merchants frequented the fairs of Champagne, and then founded at Bruges identical and adjacent *loges*. But the city of the Rialto had unobstructed links with a large and prosperous hinterland in the plains of Lombardy, while Genoa was more or less cut off from it. And so Venice had easier contacts with the commercial, financial and industrial centres of southern Germany; witness the famous entrepôt, the 'Fondaco dei Tedeschi', reconstructed in 1318 and 1505.

The mercantile activity of these two cities forced a complementary development of commercial and financial techniques. While Venice created the first proper banks, which grew from the tables of money-changers on the Rialto, it is to the inventive spirit of the Genoese that we owe the growth of maritime insurance, and the great joint-stock companies (or *maone*). Their fusion led to the creation of those pre-eminently original institutions, the Casa and the Bank of St George.

The Venetians and Genoese, though merchants first and foremost, were not thereby prevented from creating a number of export industries producing either luxury or utility goods. Both cities developed a strong industry in ship-building and allied trades. At Genoa this, like navigation and sea-trading, was a matter for private enterprise, while at Venice the state exercised a strict control.

All Genoese enterprise, in fact, was marked by a profound individualism, while that of Venice had to bend to civic judgment and the pressures of state. Certainly this contrast partly explains the differing political fates of the two republics. The former, torn apart by factions and deprived of a territorial base, lost its independence in stages between 1396 and 1541, while between 1404 and 1422 the latter quickly established a state on land, which was to last more than three centuries.

The Inland Cities. The reputation of the money-lenders and bankers of Asti, Piacenza, Lucca and Siena — known in general as 'Lombards' — paled before that of the

Florentines. The city on the Arno, which had 100,000
inhabitants at the beginning of the fourteenth century, was
favoured by its situation. It lay on a river crossing, and at a
crossroads which gave it easy links with Milan, Venice,
Genoa and the sea; it was also rich in the agricultural
resources of the largest hinterland in Tuscany, with a
population of around 350,000.

But the prosperity of Florence was based above all on the
foundation of three complementary activities, commerce,
industry and banking. Their great men, the flower of the
popolo grosso and of the higher arts, were the aristocracy of
the city. The commerce of Florence was essentially a trade
by land, at least until after the conquest of Pisa (1405) and
Leghorn (1421), when the Florentines took over from their
rivals at Porto Pisano and sent their own galleys to the
Levant and Alexandria, to Barbary and Catalonia, Flanders
and England. But it was the textile industry and banking,
partners in a commerce that had for long been safer and
more regular than trade by sea, which gave the Florentine
economy its special character. Its cloth exports reached a
total of 90,000 pieces in 1338, and its international banking
network represented a large-scale export of services. They
had branches in all the great centres, among them Milan,
Avignon, Lyons, Paris, Bruges and London.

The victorious crusade of Charles of Anjou (1265–8),
incited by the Pope and financed by Tuscan businessmen,
and the political alliance which tied together the Florentines,
the princes of Anjou, the Pope and the Guelf, gave the
decisive impetus to these societies in commerce, banking and
industry. The fourteenth and fifteenth centuries saw the
most famous of them at their apogee, and then in resounding
but not permanent bankruptcy. Such were the Frescobaldi,
the Bardi, the Peruzzi (bankrupt in 1343 and 1346), and
then from 1397 to 1494 the Medici. The greatest of the
Medici, Cosimo and Lorenzo ('the Magnificent'), became
the political masters of the city and the most discriminating
patrons of art of their day. One of their agents, Amerigo
Vespucci, was the 'discoverer' of America, which after his
day was reckoned a continental mainland. He epitomises

the alliance of Florentine science, and the arts of commerce and banking.[8]

Milan, whose economic activity can be traced back as far as the twelfth century, greatly benefited from the opening of the Alpine passes, above all the St Gotthard in 1230. This enabled the capital of Lombardy to take advantage of its incomparable position at the junction of all the routes across the Alps and the peninsula. But the growth of this commercial network resulted also from the wide extent and richness of the state of Milan. Still more, it came from the development of a great textile industry — wool, cotton fustian, velvet and silk. This in turn animated the satellite cities of Lombardy, and some others, in particular Verona whose urban and industrial growth probably came before that of Florence, Prato and Bologna. To this were added in the fifteenth century the stylish products of its metallurgical industry; its arms and armour were developed to perfection. In the first quarter of the fifteenth century, exports to Venice from all the cities of Lombardy (48,000 pieces of cloth and 40,000 pieces of fustian), far exceeded those of Florence. The value of Lombard exports to Venice was three million ducats, which was almost balanced by its imports of cotton, wool, dyestuffs, spices, and gold and silk cloths. This is a measure of the importance of the movements of currency and merchandise, which Milan and Lombardy carried out.

Whatever their superiority, the Italians had formidable competition in the western Mediterranean. This came from the ports of Languedoc and Provence, Montpellier and Marseilles, which were reinvigorated in the fifteenth century by the enterprises of Jacques Coeur; and above all from the Catalans. The latter built a vast territorial and commercial empire, headed by Barcelona, which reached its zenith between 1282 and 1348. But at the same time it was rivalled by the seamen and merchants of the independent kingdom of Majorca (1276 to 1343), whose port became a frequent stopping point on the international sea-routes. Barcelona

8. Renouard, Y., 1968.

found itself relegated to a dead corner of the Mediterranean, weighed down by monetary disorders and fiscal and financial burdens, and in 1348 it started its 'period of difficulties'.

The North. North and west Europe had been a well-articulated economic unity since early in the thirteenth century, integrated with the countries of the Mediterranean, but its commercial development remained very uneven.

The Hansa, Southern Germany, France and Spain. The most coherent and solidly based organisation, though its methods were far more rudimentary than those of the Italian cities, was the German Hansa. Born around 1230 of the alliance of Lübeck and Hamburg, it reached its zenith in the following century, when the peace of Stralsund gave it complete mastery over the Baltic and the Danish straits. The Hansa, with Lübeck as its capital, then formed a confederacy of merchant cities, whose ports existed both for shipbuilding and for trade. Cologne, Hamburg, Bremen, Rostock, Stralsund, Stettin, Danzig, Elbing, Wismar, Riga, Dorpat, Reval and Visby. Their *koggen* sailed from the Bay of Biscay, where they took on wine and salt, as far as the Baltic and Scandinavia, where they loaded grain, wood, furs, fish, mineral ores and metals. This great trade was founded on a network of branches which stretched from Novgorod, Stockholm and Bergen, to Bruges, the central staple of the Easterlings, and London, where in the protection of their 'Steelyard' they enjoyed privileges which the English thought exorbitant.

At the end of the fourteenth century a powerful economic life also blazed up in southern Germany. Its force came from the exploitation of the silver, copper, tin and zinc mines of Thuringia, the Harz, Bohemia and Hungary; from the metallurgical and textile industry (in linen and fustian); and from the flourishing commercial traffic which linked it with Venice and Bruges at the fairs of Frankfurt, Nordlingen and Leipzig. Its great cities — Augsburg, Nuremberg, Constance, St Gall and Ravensburg — became in commerce, banking and industry the centres of a powerful capitalism, the only ones in Europe comparable with the companies of Italy. The most remarkable of these was the *Grosse Gesellschaft* of Ravensburg, founded by Joseph Hompys in 1380, the same year that Hans Fugger, ancestor of the financial princes of the sixteenth century, established himself in a small way at Augsburg.

The commerce of the west was a good deal less advanced. In England, however, the fourteenth century industrial revolution was accompanied by the progressive emancipation of British commerce. Until this time it had largely been in the hands of the Flemings, the Hansa, the Italian financiers and wool-dealers, and even the Gascon wine-merchants. The new geographical distribution of industry, combined with the trade in goods from Aquitaine and Iberia, made Bristol into a great port. London, the greatest of all, Hull, Southampton, Bristol, Chester, then found themselves alongside fitting-out ports such as Dartmouth, Yarmouth and Ipswich, which were scattered along the coast of the Channel and the North Sea, and supplied most of the equipment, ships and crews.

France was a peasant nation, rather cut off from large-scale commerce. The prestige of Paris, a city of 100,000 in the fourteenth century, was due mainly to its university and to its political rôle. The Italian houses established branches there, however, and the origins of the Paris guild — 'The Society of the "Marchands de l'Eau"' — serves to prove its importance as a river port, and the importance of the Seine navigation. Nonetheless, the fair of Lendit cannot be compared with the great international fairs, and the economic life of the city was primarily directed to satisfying the needs of its own population. But the abundance of agricultural products (grain, wine, woad, salt) and some industry (linen and other cloth) did at least support the activity of some major ports: Bordeaux, La Rochelle, Nantes, Rouen, Le Crotoy (the outlet for the grain of Picardy), as well as the small coastal ports of Normandy and Brittany, which sent a host of smaller craft to the large estuaries.

Castile made contact with the sea through the ports of the Bay of Biscay and Cantabria — Bilbao, St Sebastian,

Santander — the nurseries of fishermen and sea traders. On the other hand, the growth of navigation between the Mediterranean and the Atlantic, and then the discovery and exploitation of the Atlantic archipelagos and of the African coast, gave a new stimulus to the ports of Andalusia (Seville, Sanlucar, Cadiz) and Portugal. In the fifteenth century the Basques and the Portuguese regularly sent large ships into the Channel and the North Sea, loaded with goods from the south.

Bruges. Inevitably, this great international trade became attracted towards Flanders, for this was the most densely populated, most industrialised and best situated region in northern Europe. It was inevitable also that Bruges, having eclipsed the rival ports of St Omer-Gravelines and Dordrecht, should become a focal point of land and sea commerce.

The merit of the site, which was slowly lessened by the silting-up of the Zwin, was saved by the foundation of outports at Damme (1180) and Ecluse (1290), where ships of more than six foot draught were forced to unload. But the lighters which relieved them of their cargo then went on up the Reie as far as Bruges, where they could make use of vertical wharves and a famous crane, and were next to huge entrepôts — the wool market, the water market, the cloth market. The last-named, topped by a magnificent pointed belfry, also contained the shops of the money-changers. Around the square where the Exchange stood, there grew up in the course of time the houses of the Genoese and Florentines, and the *loge* of the Venetians. Not far away were the buildings of the Castilians, the English and the Hansa, founded at Oosterlingplein in 1478. The Hansa were very much at their ease in the midst of a people whose language differed little from their own, and they made 'the Staple of the Zwin' one of the pillars of their commercial organisation, frequenting it assiduously despite a number of controversies. But the Zwin also attracted sailors and merchants from France, ships from Normandy, Brittany, Poitou and Bayonne. The 'Rôles d'Oléron' passed fully fledged into the naval customs of Damme.

This influx of foreigners into Bruges compensated for the retreat of the Flemings. In their active period, which ended around 1300, the latter had prospected and traded in all the markets of Europe, sometimes joined together in large associations, such as the 'hanse' of London, and the 'hanse' of the seventeen towns. By contrast, the citizens of Bruges in the fourteenth century abandoned navigation and commercial voyages, and let the foreigners whose initiative they had originally awakened come to them. Far more than the old fairs of Flanders, the five fairs whose decline made her fortune, the 'Venice of the North' which was in itself a very important regional and national market, became a genuine 'world market',[9] even more than Venice herself ever was. Its men were intermediaries and traders in the goods of northern and southern Europe: English cloth and wool (for the latter Bruges was a staple town only spasmodically); heavy goods from the Baltic; salt from Bourgneuf and Brouage; wines from the south-west; spices certainly, but also alum, woad, textile fibres and dyestuffs, all of them indispensable to a great industrial region. This movement of money, goods and men caused the spontaneous growth of a *Bourse* of commerce, both in the city's main square and in the house of the Van der Beurze (1257–1457), who left it its name. It made Bruges equally a financial centre, for receiving, changing and borrowing money. The Italians, of whom there were a great number by the banks of the Zwin, were past masters here, but there were also native money-changers, as the accounts of Collard de Marke and William Ruyelle (which survive from 1366 to 1370) testify.

At the end of the fifteenth century, however, the ports of Zeeland, above all Middelburg and Arnemuiden (the rendezvous of Breton shipping), often took the place of Sluys in bills of lading. But they were to be eclipsed by Antwerp, and became its outports for particular trade. The growth of Antwerp, already noticeable in the fourteenth century, finally in the sixteenth century ruined the time-honoured dominance of Bruges. To point to the silting-up of the Zwin, the opening of the western Scheldt to navigation,

9. Van Werveke, H., 1944. Van Houtte, J. A., 1952.

the richness of the hinterland of Brabant, and political accidents such as the patronage of Maximilian, who was an enemy of Bruges, will not explain this triumph. For it was above all the triumph of liberalism over the old economic restrictions of the middle ages. The men of Bruges were impregnated with the corporate, restrictionist and regimented spirit of that age. They clung obstinately to their rights of staple, brokerage and toll, and to all the commercial prohibitions with which they weighed down visiting merchants. They finally prohibited the import of English cloth, while Antwerp welcomed it. The port on the Scheldt attracted not only the Merchant Adventurers, but also all the foreign colonies, notably the Italians and the great firms of south Germany, such as the Fugger who established an agency there in 1508. The port became a staple for alum in 1491; and 1501 saw the landing of the first Portuguese spice ship. Antwerp took the place of Bruges, the medieval port of European commerce. In the same divinely ordained region, it became during the Renaissance the chief financial and commercial centre of a vastly bigger world, and its *Bourse* (1485–1531) was 'at the disposal of merchants of every nation and every language'.

The glamour of major international commerce should not lead us to forget the importance of local and regional trade, about which much less is known. Since it is less exciting and since further there is a shortage of sources, it has attracted less research. Small scale daily transactions either for cash or by barter, or the more important ones which even so operated only by verbal contract, necessarily left no traces in the archives. Lists of the tariffs charged at tolls, a good many of which survive, are no substitute for their accounts. Generally speaking, administrative records giving statistical data on local trade are not abundant. Where these exist, however, the records of notaries provide a sample of informative documents.

Trade of a purely local kind has always been associated with towns. The towns attracted to themselves agricultural products or raw materials from the flat countryside around, and offered in exchange their manufactured goods. Such modest objectives, attuned to moderate needs, gave rise to direct exchanges between consumer and producer. These could take place in the streets and the squares, in front of the benches of the tradespeople and craftsmen; and thus the whole town became a 'forum'. But the chief exchanges were concentrated on the 'market', held once a week or more in the open air or in a hall built for the purpose. The town and urban privileges did not originate with the market, but certainly this was one of the most important elements of the basic urban framework.

After the Hundred Years' War, the kings of France not only founded fairs but also granted a great number of markets, which they considered the best means of re-invigorating an economic life which was either enfeebled or ruined. The preambles to these royal grants, which allude to the quality of the site and its general situation ('a town . . . standing on a fine spot in a fertile countryside'; 'a fine, large borough, set and situated in a fair and fertile countryside') show very clearly the network of exchanges which united the small towns and boroughs with their rural environment. Thus in the second half of the fifteenth century, we see recur the process which in the early middle ages gave birth to the first rudimentary local and regional exchanges.

Early on, the regalian right of establishing fairs and markets had been usurped by the local lords, who drew appreciable sums from them in the form of taxes and various dues. This control was later transferred, in whole or in part, to the town authorities, and came to be extended to all the town's economic activities. The spirit of this regimentation, which arose from the authoritarian and protectionist attitudes of the corporations and guilds, tended to centralise as many dealings as possible in the market place, above all those in basic commodities. In this way they could prevent forestalling, monopoly, competition and speculation, and cut down on the rôle of middlemen. Local trade always remained to a greater or lesser degree subject to these constraints, while international trade by contrast sought to liberate itself from them.

In the towns which developed and which saw the field of their economic activity widen out in front of them, trade could not remain at this elementary level. Alongside the chief figures, the agricultural producers and the artisans, there appeared intermediaries, true merchants, such as the mercers, who soon formed themselves into guilds.

There were, further, any number of links between local and regional trade in basic commodities, and the great long-distance international trade. Pirenne observed that 'the trade of the middle ages from the beginning developed not from local trade but from export trade'. It is nonetheless true that the growth of exports was tied to the activity of the internal markets, just as we see this in our day on a larger scale. As it grew, so local trade stimulated the production of exportable surpluses, and attracted imports from far away. The merchants and master craftsmen in raw materials, when they did not themselves embark on trading voyages, became true sedentary entrepreneurs, 'merchant staplers'. The economic privileges which they drew from being townsmen and from their roots in the locality, often set them against the magnates of international trade and all foreign merchants. But by force of circumstance, they nonetheless became auxiliaries in an international trade which needed to import and export, by means of the avenues of distribution and purveyance which the local townspeople controlled.

For this reason local and regional trade, which developed around small and middle-sized towns a little away from the main lines of traffic, also played an important part in the great metropolitan economies, such as those of the Italian cities which were united to the *contado* around them. This was especially true of France. In Paris itself an economy chiefly based on local exchange to satisfy the needs of a large population was strengthened by the vigour and versatility of the skilled workforce and by the natural riches of the surrounding countryside. Before the great days of the woad trade, Toulouse was primarily supported by its links with the fields and the countryside which surrounded it.

The example of Bordeaux is no less revealing. The great growth of the wine trade dates from no earlier than the thirteenth century. Until that time, its exchanges were organised within the framework of a whole system of diversified food production and a manufacturing activity which remained modest. Economic life was centred on the old market ('lou Mercat') of the Faubourg Saint-Eloi and on the tiny adjacent port of Peugue. The development of the wine industry and its large-scale export never completely superseded the cornfields and meadows, orchards and woodlands, fresh-water fishing, and the complex of local exchanges which for a long time alone guaranteed the stability of the local and regional economy. Right up to the end of the Middle Ages, hosts of small craft, carts drawn by oxen, and beasts of burden, continued to bring to the warehouses on the wharves of the great city and the riverside towns, many other cargoes besides barrels of wine for export or bales of cloth and casks of salted fish for import. Alongside these they would load and unload grain from the Bordelais and the *Haut Pays*, salt from Saintonge and Médoc, hay from the marshes, cattle on the hoof, salted food, honey, game, fresh fish, oysters and shellfish, the cheaper furs, building materials, millstones, wood for building or fuel, resinous products, hemp from the valleys and wool from the surrounding countryside. The area of the production and consumption of all these goods might extend upstream over practically the whole of the Aquitanian basin, but downstream it rarely went beyond the bar of the Gironde and the 'Pertuis' of Aunis and Saintonge. Meanwhile the tradesmen of the great city, carpenters, blacksmiths, coopers, rope and net makers, made it possible to equip and provision ships, sailors and travelling merchants, so that they became the auxiliaries of large-scale trade. But a large amount of their production was designed to satisfy the needs of the local population, and many Bordeaux merchants, who never ventured beyond the river, drew a large part of their profits from trade with the inland regions.

THE MACHINERY OF TRADE
AND FINANCE

THE GENERAL CHARACTERISTICS OF MEDIEVAL TRADE

While in its volume, goods and methods a huge gulf
separated international wholesale trade from retail trade,
many merchants and firms combined the two. Their
trading-centre was often no more than a shop, with a store
on one side which looked rather like a bazaar, for merchants,
even when they appeared to some degree specialised, traded
in everything. On a trip to Bordeaux an English draper
could turn himself into a vintner with ease.

Every trading enterprise carried major risks, from the sea,
from men, and from the uncertainties of economic
conditions. Each voyage was an 'adventure', and its dangers
did nothing to raise the social standard of the men engaged
in it. In the earlier period the dubious origins both of their
profits and of some traders — adventurers in the pejorative
sense — the unfortunate connexion between piracy and
trade, the rural and seignorial models of the church, and her
long-standing distrust of all monetary transactions: for a
long time all this surrounded sea-trading with the darkest
suspicions. The moralists of antiquity themselves looked
back to a rustic golden age, and so they also had considered
it impious. In the course of time, however, this attitude gave
way before economic progress. The trader, who could only
rarely find grace with God, found the paths of an honourable
trade open in front of him. But the great money-lenders,
such as Italian businessmen in the fourteenth and fifteenth
centuries, still had something of a bad conscience deep
down, and this led them to increase their works of piety, to
open an account in the name of 'the Lord God' (*messer
Domeneddio*), and to enrich the Franciscans, servants of 'the
Lady Poverty'.

Whether the merchant class and the first creations of
capital originated in adventuring (Pirenne) or landed
property (Sombart), large-scale trade was first of all casual
and seasonal and the merchants involved were, first of all,

of a wandering type. The 'piepowders' of the land became 'merchants frequenting the rivers' and 'merchants by sea'. These were universal categories; they appear in the 'Rôles d'Oléron' as well as the 'Consolado del Mar', in the Atlantic and in the narrow seas of the Mediterranean. They appear on land as well as at sea: as the merchants in Flemish cloth who in the period of their active trade travelled towards Genoa, and as their Italian colleagues who climbed up towards the north and the fairs by the Alpine passes; as Gascon wine-traders, as English Staplers, and as the 'seefahrender Kaufmann' of the Baltic (Vogel). But these are anonymous figures. A more dashing historical figure is cut by particular travelling merchants, the Venetian Romano Mairano in the twelfth century, and the Genoese Benedetto Zaccaria in the thirteenth.

This kind of trade could be carried on with only elementary forms of organisation. The great ships came together in convoys for a common endeavour, and sometimes housed whole troops of merchants; but the smaller ships had only a few, sometimes only one. These were lonely adventurers, rich only through a hazardous credit, with goods which they could barter without ever opening their purses, or with a ballast of crowns and ducats which they locked in chests along with their notarised and sealed deeds. They were merchants and shippers at one and the same time. They took ship with their cargoes for a winding voyage, whose stages, main direction and ultimate destination were often made up as they went along, or changed at some foreign port according to any 'news' which came to hand.

This trade, however hazardous and nomadic, obviously could not manage without meeting places. It found them first in towns, 'the daughters of trade and industry' (Pirenne). The merchant quarter ('*suburbium*', '*faubourg*'), the *portus* of the northern towns (in the original sense of the word) and the market place were the first economic requirements. And so the terms 'bourgeois' and 'poorter' became synonymous for merchant, even for ship-owner. But before the fourteenth century only a few of the great cities of the Mediterranean could claim to be commercial and financial centres of international standing, and that only imperfectly. For this was the rôle of the fairs. Those of Flanders came before and prepared the way for the rule of Bruges. Those of Lyons and Geneva were financial rather than mercantile, and they belonged in the fifteenth century to a new age of methods and exchanges. From the twelfth century to the end of the thirteenth the meeting places par excellence of a travelling and still seasonal commerce were the six fairs of the four cities of Champagne (Lagny, Bar, Provins, Troyes). They stretched out between January and October. The ritual of those fairs, their spice and cloth trade, the dealings of their Italian and Flemish customers, the protection, franchises and legal guarantees they gave to merchants, the progress they encouraged in credit operations, in transferring funds, in exchanges, compensation for debt and backing for loans, all this is by now well known.

The decline of the Champagne fairs around 1300 is one facet of the 'commercial revolution' of the period 1275 to 1325 (Edler de Roover). It shows itself, among other things, in the relative decline of travelling, in favour of what has been called 'sedentary', trade (N.S.B. Gras). This was an entirely natural development. The adventurous merchant who had been lucky in his early undertakings, or the descendants whom he had enriched, tended to cut back on their travels. They confided to others — proctors, agents, attorneys, clerks, servants, and even to ships' masters — the job of transporting, accompanying, looking after and negotiating about their goods and their returns. Such agents could be either itinerant or resident, general dealers or specialists, and act on a permanent or temporary basis. A number of these sedentary merchants were content to work on a commission basis, as brokers, importers and distributors within their city or its rich hinterland of goods purchased at the landing port and brought there at the seller's risk. Their capital was invested in long-term loans or simply in loans for consumption. More often, however, especially in France where there was a passion for land and office, instead of the profits of 30 to 40 per cent which could

be hoped for from sea adventuring, men preferred the return
of 5 to 10 per cent which came from land or real estate. For
its possession led to responsibility, and to the ranks of the
noblesse.

Such was the history in the fourteenth and fifteenth
centuries of the Eyquem family of Bordeaux, who were the
ancestors of Montaigne. At the same time English merchants
engaged representatives abroad more and more often, the
Hanseatic merchant left his counting-house less and less, and
the great Venetian merchant Guglielmo Querini (1400–
1468) was rich in landed wealth and never set foot outside
Venice. But the most important development in this respect
was certainly the establishment of permanent branches of
the great Italian trading and banking companies in all the
major centres. In the fourteenth century this began a truly
new era in the organisation of large-scale trade.

Closely tied to this was the use of a number of more
sophisticated techniques, in methods of association, representation and communication, in insurance, methods of
payment, exchanges, credit, banking and accounting. The
Italians were the inventors and the chief users of each of
these.

At this level, the capitalistic nature of major commerce
and international finance becomes clearly apparent in the
fourteenth and fifteenth centuries. The volume of medieval
trade and the amount of business conducted was negligible
by comparison with present-day trade, but this means very
little. It was substantial considering the size of the population, and the relative importance of other sectors of the
economy. To say nothing of the local and regional trade,
the 120,000 tons of salted fish which came from Skania with
the help of 24,000 tons of imported salt, is nonetheless
equivalent to the annual catch of a great modern fishing
port such as Boulogne. 102,000 casks of wine were exported
from Bordeaux in 1308–1309, which looks quite respectable
alongside the 270,000 tons of various goods which the same
port sent to England in 1961. Some clues also make it
possible to see how important the grain trade was. In the
first half of the fourteenth century, further, the total value

of English exports was around £250,000, and she exported between 35,000 and 40,000 sacks of wool (weighing 15 million pounds) and 50,000 cloths (each 28 yards long); and this latter figure represents only perhaps one-third of Flemish cloth production at its peak. The taxable value of the goods exported from the principal Hanseatic towns in the 1370s reached 3 million Lübeck marks. At the beginning of the fourteenth century the production of woollen cloth at Florence had reached 100,000 *pezze*, worth 1,200,000 *fiorini d'auro*. In the fifteenth century trade with Lombardy brought Venice 2,800,000 ducats, and through Venice the Lombard cities imported 300,000 ducats-worth of pepper alone. Venice received 10,000 metric tons of goods from the East. And this was less than the combined total of 13,000 to 15,000 metric tons which the big Mediterranean ports sent into the Atlantic and the English Channel. Admittedly some of this was in heavy goods such as alum, but other cargo was precious and light in weight. In tonnage, these figures surpass those of Seville's trade with America in the first half of the sixteenth century.[10]

The amount of capital invested in trade and banking was proportionate to the size of this movement of goods. In 1310 the capital (*corpo*) of the Peruzzi was £149,000 affiorino. In 1451 the capital of the Medici banking-house was nearly 88,300 florins. In 1318 the capital of the Bardi was 875,638 florins, worth about £130,000, at a time when the ordinary income of the English crown was only £30,000. When the Bardi and the Peruzzi went bankrupt the King of England owed them almost 1,400,000 florins.

The return on capital, while never as high as is sometimes stated, was still considerable. Since it varied according to the amount of risk on the one hand and the degree of organisation on the other, it varied from one type of operation to another, and was in general less in the fourteenth and fifteenth centuries than in the eleventh and twelfth. A simple loan, running satisfactorily to its full term, might bring in 30 per cent or more; shipping shares might produce 100 per cent or more, as would the sale of certain

10. Heers, 1961

exotic goods. But in the fourteenth century associates of the Florentine companies who made additional deposits (*fuori del corpo*: in addition to the capital) received a fixed interest of 7 to 8 per cent, while non-associates received between 6 and 10 per cent. The same Florentine companies then charged from 7 to 15 per cent on their loans, although in the case of foreign borrowers this could rise to up to 30 per cent. Between 1318 and 1324 the profits of the house of Peruzzi fluctuated between 14·3 and 20 per cent a year on capital invested, and was much less than that after the deduction of expenses.

In this society the volume of trade and of financial transactions was then relatively important; there was the spreading out and rationalising of enterprises, the cult of figures, and the development of credit and speculation. The rôle of finance was basic, and dealing in money went on to some degree apart from other economic activities. · Men strove continuously to maximise profits, and business expanded without set limits in cut-throat economic competition. As most historians have recognised, as against Sombart, these are traits of a commercial and financial system which was capitalistic.

Now the development of capitalism, the cult of money, the frenzied search for profit which considered nothing save cold reason, ran up against both moral and material obstacles. This was particularly true of the ruthless capitalism typified by Jehen Boinebroke of Douai, a merchant draper who died in 1286, or William Servat of Cahors (1280–1320). For these things ran clean contrary to the Christian ethic, and to its practical applications — the idea of the just price, and the prohibition against lending money at interest, which was called usury. But the canonists admitted that prices were linked to the laws of supply and demand; and with regard to interest they tempered the rigour of their doctrine with considerations based on the idea of risk, of injury to the creditor, and even of missed opportunities for profit (*damnum emergens, lucrum cessans*). On the other hand, many tricks made it possible to conceal interest, and thus obey the letter of the canons but not their spirit. Such were

fictitious exchanges or sales, dry exchange,[11] the acknow-
ledging of a greater debt than the sum actually borrowed,
etc.

Free capitalist enterprise in the fourteenth and fifteenth
centuries also ran up against the regulations and economic
protectionism of cities and of groups of workers. For they
aimed to exorcise the effects of economic recession by means
of associations, prohibitions, privileges and monopoly. But
the high dams they erected had any number of cracks in
them. The countryside became industrialised, and the great
manufacturing cities produced for export. Ports and
commercial and financial centres could not cut themselves
off from the activities by which they lived, and these were
international of their very nature. And far from the
madding crowd, banking and the availability of credit to
princes and the aristocracy opened the horizon to huge
profits, although this prospect was tempered by the
terrifying risks involved.

All these changes, and the progress made in organisation
and in financial and commercial techniques during the last
two centuries of the middle ages, should not obscure the fact
that this evolution was not generalised, and that it did not
all take place at once. Italy was far ahead of the rest of
Europe, including the Hanseatic towns, and was only slowly
caught up by the great cities of southern Germany. In the
age of the Italian companies and the famous sedentary
trade, most of the merchants of western Europe still directed
their business on their own, or else traded in small-scale and
ephemeral associations. At the beginning of the sixteenth
century, in the French ports of the Atlantic, marine
insurance and double-entry book-keeping were almost
unknown, and bills of exchange were hardly ever used.
From the fourteenth to the sixteenth centuries there were
travelling merchants everywhere, sailing with their cargoes
— Hanseatic, English, French, Spanish, even Italians such
as the young Venetian, Andrea Barbarigo. If they were
sedentary it was thanks to the mobility of their attorneys,
agents, clerks and servants. They often carried on trade with

11. See p. 323.

very small resources and rudimentary methods. They did not aim to make their fortunes like the great money-dealers, but rather hoped to achieve the honest and quiet competence of 'an honourable man'. This mixture of very different men and methods provides the justification for the global study of goods and finance which we have attempted. But the various nuances in the time-scale must never be forgotten.

TECHNIQUES

The Political and Legal Environment. Lords, cities and kings all subjected trade to heavy burdens, which were either mercantilist or simply fiscal in origin. Foreign merchants came up against privileges and prohibitions which protected the city's inhabitants, or all citizens. There were staples, brokerage dues, monopolies of retail trade, and English navigation acts in 1381 and 1485. Trade was subjected to numerous levies in the way of customs and tolls, both national and local in character: royal customs in England, the *Pfundzoll* of the Hansa, aids and customs duties in France, the *gabelle* at Genoa, purchase tax at Venice, and tolls of every kind. Tolls were in origin regalian rights, which were often usurped by local lords and by the cities. Every route contained a great number of them, and some, such as those at Bapaume, Péronne and the passes of the Alps and the Jura (e.g. Jougne), were almost inescapable. In the fourteenth century there were about 50 tolls on the Rhine, more than 30 on the Elbe and on the Weser, 40 on the Garonne between Toulouse and Bordeaux, and more than 70 on the Loire between Rouanne and Nantes. Ships paid dues at essential passages (in the 'Ras' of Brittany — the *Brefs de Bretagne* — at the tolls of the Sound and the Straits of Messina), and paid anchorage, cranage and keelage in the estuaries, ports and roadsteads. These taxes were usually small, but there were so many of them that they were a heavy charge on the price of goods, often adding 20 per cent, and on the Seine and the Rhine 50 per cent and more.

There were many exceptions to this rule, and this indeed

was part of the raison d'être of fairs. Privileges and exemptions were granted to foreign merchants (to the Gascons and the German Hansa at London, for example), and the burden of tolls could be alleviated by choosing the most advantageous route. Ships which were only stopping-over would anchor outside a port, 'beyond customs and franchises', and by going via the open sea they could escape the *Brefs de Bretagne*.

While it took a heavy toll from trade, government by means of its 'peace' did at least offer a minimum of security; and it extended throughout its territory during the whole year that protection over men and goods which had initially been a feature of the fairs alone. On the coasts they endeavoured to limit rights of wreck and flotsam, which had been condemned by councils of the eleventh and twelfth centuries. They strictly controlled all 'letters of mark' and reprisals against foreign merchants, and in their place substituted due process of law, or agreed procedures. By means of registered obligation they also tried to guarantee the authenticity, validity and execution of trading agreements. In lands ruled by custom the contracts were enforced by the affixing of public seals, and in the lands of written law by the signs manual of papal, imperial, royal, episcopal or municipal notaries. Then in the course of the fourteenth century, because of new needs and the progress in trade and finance, business was partly freed from its subjection to the notary, by means of acts which were privately sealed and guaranteed solely by the signature of the parties, notably letters of exchange.

The specific needs of trade had also led to the creation of an international trading law (*Lex Mercatoria, Jus Mercatorum*; Law Merchant), and regulations for sea traffic (*Rôles d'Oléron, Consolado del Mar*). Along with them there were specific trading and maritime jurisdictions: in England the piepowder court or, later, the Chancery; the Admiralty courts and merchant tribunals of Venice, Genoa, Florence, Pisa and Barcelona; the provost of the Ombrière at Bordeaux. They often judged the cases of pilgrims, merchants and sailors by highly expeditious procedures: 'from day to day', 'between one tide and the next', 'in the space of three tides'.

Transport and the Risks Involved. Tolls and other factors could well lessen the economic attractiveness of river transport, but its capacity was much greater (a wagon carried less than a ton, while a barge could carry from 15 to 100 tons, or even more), and overall it remained cheaper than using beasts of burden or carts. Transport by sea, where the capacity was yet far greater and which was frequently the only means possible, had, save in some commodities, an even more striking advantage. This can be seen by a couple of comparisons. In the middle of the fourteenth century the annual traffic registered at the toll of Jougne (3,000 bundles or 4,500 cantars) was according to Professor Heers scarcely a quarter of the possible load of a single, large Genoese ship. In the fifteenth century the cost of transport from Geneva to Asti was 45 sous per cantar, while from Genoa to Southampton by water it was only 10 sous.

Now the great Genoese carrack of the mid-fifteenth century, with its rigging already well divided among its three masts, came at the end of an evolution in which naval progress had allowed the construction of larger and more manoeuvrable ships. The Mediterranean peoples remained loyal to their galleys, the largest of which, the merchant galley, *galeazza de mercanzia*, which travelled to the Romania, the Levant and Flanders, carried between 200 and 250 tons. Those of Venice were equipped by the state, went on organised and relatively safe journeys (the *mude*), and carried precious cargoes. But both the Venetians and the Genoese left free trading (*navigazione libera*) and ordinary traffic to the round ships, such as the lateen-rigged ships of the thirteenth century — the cogs, carracks and *naves*. With the exception of the large galleys which the Genoese (who replaced them by carracks), the Venetians, the Florentines and the Catalans sent to Flanders and England, it was those 'square-rigged' or 'round ships', under the names of *nefs*, *koggen* and hulks, which reigned without rivalry over the Atlantic and the neighbouring seas. In the

fourteenth century the great merchant ships were adapted
to the larger cargoes necessitated by economic expansion,
and carried from 100 to 200 tons. The Hanseatic *kogge* was
the prototype of these, and the Genoese ships of the fifteenth
century went as high as 800 or 1,000 tons. Yet all the time
these massive hulls never replaced the small craft of less than
50 tons, which technically and economically were more
flexible, and for certain trades were irreplaceable.

The freight rates reflected in general the movements of
prices and services, and also varied according to numerous
technical, economic and political contingencies, notably
risks from the sea and from men. The cost of transporting
wool from London to Calais in the fourteenth century was
only 2 per cent of the price at which it was bought. But for
transporting Gascon wine to England in the fourteenth and
fifteenth centuries the proportion varied from 10 to 50 per
cent. It was 50 per cent of the cost of transporting salt from
'the Bay', from Bourgneuf to Danzig in 1449. At Genoa in
1462 the freight of the big ships bound for Mediterranean
or northern ports varied from 0·4 for silk and 1·8 for spices,
to 13 for lead and 16 per cent (of the selling price in this
case) for alum. 'These were the tremendous results of the
policy of bulk transportation practised by the Genoese'
(Heers).

The fitting-out of ships, when it was not controlled by the
state (as it was in Venice, for galleys only), usually brought
together the holders of shares (*carati*, *loca*) in a ship. The
ship owner, whether a share holder or not, was first and
foremost a merchant who interested himself in shipping.
But the ship's master, who frequently held shares in the
ownership of the vessel, made money out of his own private
cargo, and thus could become either an occasional or
confirmed merchant in his own right: *mercator et nauta*.
Genoa, Venice, the Hanseatic cities, London, Hull and
Bristol were at one and the same time both trading-centres
and fitting-out ports. Nonetheless a spontaneous division of
function emerged, which to some extent grouped together
on the one hand the great trading ports, which supplied
freight and capital, and on the other the small coastal ports

which provided ships and sailors. In the latter category were the ports of Zeeland, Norfolk, Suffolk, Cornwall and Devon, Brittany, Bas Poitou, Saintonge and Bayonne, and the ports of the Basque country and Cantabria. In any case, both cargo and ship owners seem well established in the contracts relating to sea transport: chartering bills, bills of lading, and the two combined.

Closely associated with sea transport was the notion of risk; risks of the sea and above all of men — 'risicus et fortuna Dei, maris et gentium'. An effort was made to diminish these by empirical methods, founded directly or indirectly on the idea of association. Along with the grouping of ship-owners went the separation of cargoes, which were distributed over several ships in different fleets. 'My ventures are not in one bottom trusted' (Shakespeare, *The Merchant of Venice*, I, i). And it is well known that ships sailed in convoys; the *mude* of Venice, wool fleets, wine fleets with their hundreds of sails, and the 'Bay fleets' (*Baienflotten*). But 'free sailing' remained, and there were always those bold enough to risk individual voyages. The wind, however, and currents, necessary routes and passages, and the seasonal nature of much of the economy, still brought these ships together in groups.

An attempt was also made, in accordance with the customs of the sea, to lessen risks by making all the interested parties, cargo and ship owners, take a share of major losses (*avaries-dommages*). Then, in return for a heavy consideration, one of the participants or sometimes a third party would become responsible for the risks run by the other or several others. This applied to several kinds of practice; with commands, with sales of goods at sea which became effective on landing and which travelled at the seller's risk (this resembles the modern notion of C.I.F. — cost, insurance, freight), with sea loans where a considerable risk was involved, loans of marine exchange or insurance, artificial sales, or sales with the right to repurchase the ship or its goods (*emptio venditio*). These procedures were the forerunners of marine premium insurance by a third party, either of the ship itself or of its cargo. This development seems to have been the work of the Genoese, and the first examples date from 1350, but their model was perhaps the overland insurance of the Florentines. The cost varied a lot. At Genoa in the mid-fifteenth century it was usually less than 10 per cent for a single voyage; it was sometimes as low as 7 per cent, and even 5½ per cent for a journey from Genoa to England. These figures are a reflexion of the progress made by marine insurance in covering risks, as well as of the progress in naval skills and navigation.

Commercial and Financial Techniques. The lessening, transference or better still elimination of risk was only one of the factors, admittedly prejudicial, influencing trading operations of any scope. These were also under a number of other fundamental constraints: the forms taken by capital, the development of credit, the ease and speed of transactions whatever the distances involved, the types of regulation and ease of payment, the rational management of undertakings. The ingenuity of merchants and businessmen was able to discover procedures which, whether well or ill, were adapted to these conditions. They were relatively imperfect, however, and this made all the more important personal relationships founded on confidence, a good reputation, an honourable nature, and even 'courtesy'. All these were included among the qualities of the epithet 'worthy' or 'honourable' man, as it was applied to townsmen — citizens 'of good repute and unblemished reputation' (*bonae famae et illesae reputationis*). For these men oaths taken on the gospels or on relics were at least a subsidiary method of contract and of proof.

Associations of men were widely prevalent in the middle ages, and in the commercial and financial realm they provided capital, credit and security. The simplest form of this was a combination of two men who had equal shares (*societas vera*), sometimes for a single journey or operation but sometimes more permanently. Sometimes one partner provided the capital or the greater part of the capital, and the other the services and sometimes the smaller part of the capital. This type of association, or variants of it, was in use everywhere throughout the middle ages and long after. In Italy it was known as *commenda, societas maris* or *colleganza*;

in France as a *commande*; in Gascony as *Cabau*, and in the Hanseatic cities as *Sendeve*, *Wederlegginge* or *gegenseitige Ferngesellschaft*. They were adapted to a rudimentary kind of trade and credit, involving great risks and considerable profits, one which was prevalent until the thirteenth century and did not disappear for some time thereafter.

The great trading and banking companies of Piacenza, Lucca, Siena, Pisa and above all Florence in the fourteenth and fifteenth centuries were on a quite different level both chronologically and technically. Numbered among these were those of the Alberti, Scali, Acciaiuoli, Frescobaldi, Bardi, Peruzzi and Medici, and with them may be compared the *Grosse Gesellschaft* of Ravensburg (1380–1530). Some of these firms, like the Medici or that of Francesco di Marco Datini of Prato (who left abundant archives, with which we associate the name of Professor Melis) were groupings of almost independent associations, in which the dominant family held the greatest share. This form of organisation to a degree split up the risks which had led to the downfall of the centralised Florentine companies in the fourteenth century.

Yet these powerful companies still retained some of the characteristics of more elementary forms of association. There was nothing gigantic about them, since they joined together no more than 25 or 30 associates. They dissolved and reformed at very brief intervals, at each accounting session. Their essential continuity was assured, since they were based on the family, and the continuity of the family which dominated the company provided it with its social raison d'être. Nonetheless, they brought together a considerable group capital, known as the *corpo*, to which was added an additional capital (*sopracorpo* or *fuori del corpo*), composed of reinvested profits, and also deposits from their associates and from third parties, all of whom received back a fixed interest. These companies, which had no judicial personality as distinct from that of each of their associates, were what we would call unlimited companies, the partners being 'responsible towards third parties for their own goods, and having unlimited responsibility for any of the company's debts' (Renouard). With the limited companies recognised by legislation at Florence in 1408, the company's passive associates ceased to have unlimited responsibility, and with this their numbers grew considerably.

More modern still is the look of the groupings of men commissioning ships, whose ownership was divided into shares (*partes, loca, carati, sortes*), above all the 'compere' and 'maone' of Genoa in the fourteenth and fifteenth centuries. These two institutions, which joined together in 1407 to form the *Casa di San Giorgio*, were groupings of the state's creditors. Some of the public revenue was granted to them as security and in return for interest, and in the case of the 'maone' this income might come from the exploitation of foreign lands. The documents issued to subscribers (*loca, luoghi*) were negotiable personal property, and were not strictly speaking shares, and the interest accruing was not a proper dividend. Yet these societies do show several of the features of modern joint-stock companies.

In some ways also the 'maone' resemble the colonial companies of modern times. Certain of the latter, however, the 'regulated companies', grew from another model, of which also the middle ages offers numerous precedents. The German Hansa arose as a grouping of merchants, as did the Staplers and Merchant Adventurers, or even, at a humbler level, the *societas navium baiocensium* and the river 'hanses' such as the 'water merchants' of Paris and the merchants frequenting the rivers Loire (fourteenth century) and Garonne (*c.* 1470). These were all created on the model of the guilds, hanses, corporations, fellowships and fraternities of merchants; like associations of work-people they met the need for economic and material protection. This was assured them by privileges and monopolies. These companies, sometimes either created or confirmed by royal charters, were groupings not of capital but of individual traders, who submitted themselves to certain common rules with regard to prices, quantities, chartering and lading, the organisation of convoys and disputes between members of the group. They came to enjoy a monopoly in the area of influence and the kind of traffic granted to them.

In some cases also, associations offered the means of securing commercial representation, an idea which in the middle ages ran up against any number of legal obstacles. Here the travelling partner stood in the place of the sleeping partner. A sedentary merchant could also delegate from afar, on board ship or on land, an agent, clerk, servant or simply a colleague for a given operation (*quant a ce*). The power of such men came from a procuration, which for want of a better was the fundamental and solemn title of commercial representation. With the progress in organisation and trading techniques, sedentary representatives and correspondents were substituted for these occasional mobile agents — agents of the *Ferngesellschaft*, innkeepers and brokers (for the two functions were often combined), who necessarily acted for foreign merchants and were therefore predisposed to this kind of work. The most rational and at the same time the most modern solution was that of the permanent branches and agencies set up in major centres by the commercial and banking companies. In the fourteenth century the principal companies of Florence were thus represented at Barletta, Bologna, Genoa, Naples, Perugia, Venice, Avignon, Bruges, London and Paris — and many of them also had branches elsewhere. Between 1440 and 1450 the Medici opened branches at Rome, Naples, Venice, Geneva, Pisa, London, Avignon, Milan and Lyons. Offices of the *Grosse Gesellschaft* of Ravensburg were scattered throughout Germany, Switzerland, Flanders, France, Italy and Spain. The Hanseatic towns had nothing comparable, but they had offices (*Kontore*) with permanent delegations, at Novgorod, Bergen, Bruges, and London (the Steelyard), which had comparable results in the area of representation.

The conduct of trade at a distance and the existence of a true international market, presuppose the development of business correspondence and a network of information. Here again the Italians provide the model, with their private letters (*lettere private*), company letters (*lettere di compagnia*) and their couriers, for example the *Scarsella* of the Florentine companies in the second half of the fourteenth century.

Everywhere to some extent, letters came to take the place of direct contact and notarised agreements.

This belated triumph of private correspondence over public instruments was achieved among other ways by the use of bills of exchange, which brought fresh solutions to the irritating problems caused by the transference of cash, and by methods of payment, exchange and credit.

Barter, by which for example Gascon wine might be exchanged for English cloth, fish or tin, was a means of avoiding the difficulties of transporting and exchanging specie. But this rudimentary procedure could be of only limited use, and the great majority of business dealings suffered to some extent from the imperfections of the monetary system. Among these may be listed counterfeiting, the instability of currencies because of the mutations inflicted on them by rulers, the extraordinary variety in them which arose from the fragmentation of the feudal order and the usurpation of rights of moneying, the inadequate exchange relationship between gold and silver, and the shortage of specie, at times more noticeable than at others, but which was almost endemic in Europe.

There were some currencies, however, above all in gold which was the agency par excellence of international trade, which were of sound value and universally accepted, and these were used as international currency. Such were the gros Venetian, the gros tournois of St Louis, the gros of Flanders and the groat of Edward III among silver currencies; among the gold were Florentine and Genoan florins, the Venetian ducat, the French écu d'or, and in England the noble of Edward III and then the rose-noble and the angel.

The fluctuations in the exchange rate between gold and silver, the very different rates of depreciation of the various currencies, and the need for a common denominator currency, necessitated the use of money of account. Among these were the French and English pounds, the German *Pfund*, Venetian *lira di ducato*, Genoan *lira di buona moneta*, Florentine *fiorino di fiorino* or *lira a fiorino*, the *écu* of Flanders — and their lesser multiples, sous and deniers. These accounting moneys were in fact pegged to real currencies which either were or had been in circulation — deniers, groats, florins and ducats. Many transactions could thus be carried out in account books, without the need for cash.

The system used for compensating debtors and creditors at the fairs of Champagne, and still more the use of banking clearances (*giro di partita*) and bankers' granting of overdraft facilities to their clients, led in the thirteenth century to the creation of a true banking currency. And then by the first quarter of the fourteenth century paper money was being used, in the form of cheques and bills of exchange.

The origins, evolution and characteristics of these bills are by now well known, thanks to the work of Professor Raymond de Roover. Their general basis is certainly a contract for the exchange and transference of funds, and their more precise character comes from the effect of re-exchange (*contra-cambium*) as a credit dealing, in which the interest was concealed in the rate of exchange, and this ran at a higher level in places which kept the 'head of the exchange' and quoted the 'certain' (fixed quotation) than in those which quoted the 'uncertain'. The currency of the former was the standard and was exchanged against a variable number of currencies of the places which quoted the uncertain. Thus at Bruges the ducat stood for a variable number of Flanders groats, but on the other hand it gave the certain (the écu) at London and Barcelona. These operations found favour with the theologians, who did not notice the interest concealed in the rate of exchange. But to compensate for this they severely condemned dry exchange (or *ricorsa*), where the future exchange rate was predetermined by the parties in an arbitrary fashion.

The practice of endorsement came late in the day to give the bill of exchange all the features of a paper money. This probably goes back later than was once thought, perhaps to the mid-fifteenth century, for an example has been quoted from 1430. On the other hand the obligatory writs were not proper promissory notes, for they were payable to the bearer or his representative and to them alone.

Credit also fed on many other sources, using procedures

often older and more summary than bills of exchange. The 'Commenda' represented the opening of a credit relationship between the man who gave the order and the man who received it. Most of the sales of those goods which formed part of the network of international trade were made on credit. Sometimes credit was granted from the buyer to the seller, as with the Italians' purchases of English wool, but more often it was the other way round. The trade in English wool as it was practised by the Cely family in the mid-fifteenth century was based on a whole chain of credit operations. The sale at sea of a cargo which travelled at the seller's risk was dependent both on insurance and credit. This was related to the maritime loan 'at major risk', which derived from the *foenus nauticum antique* and which combined insurance with credit; and then payment was dependent on the safe arrival of a ship (*sana eunte nave*) or the successful completion of a journey. This form of loan was in use in the Mediterranean from the twelfth century, and it has survived on every coast of Europe up to the present day. It had numerous variants: bottomry loans granted to the master of a ship for its provisioning, fitting-out and repair; the loan of marine exchange (*cambium maritimum, cambium traiectitium*), in which the interest was concealed in the exchange rate; the insurance loan, usually granted by the ship-owner to the owner of the cargo, where this did not have to be paid for until after the ship had arrived (21 days after according to the Rôles d'Oléron), which thus amounted to a granting of credit. On the other hand it does not appear that sales of rent, which it is tempting to identify as loans concealing the interest, were in fact credit instruments.

As Professor Postan has shown, using the rolls and inventories which record the credit operations of English merchants, the relative part played by credit in the total volume of medieval trade was very considerable. At the end of the thirteenth century the loans of one Lombard firm in England came to as much as £1100, as against the £1400 which comprised the rest of their capital; and in 1424 the estate of William Lynn, a merchant stapler, contained outstanding loans of £3027 out of a total of £4842 7s. 2d.

The same point could be made with regard to several Gascon merchants of the same period; and at a higher level we can note that, in the estate of doge Rinieri Zeno (when he died in 1268) which amounted to 50,000 *lire di piccioli* the loans accounted for about one half of the total.

This development of credit postulates a corresponding development in banking. The death-knell of the Jews, who had been the great money-lenders of the early middle ages, was tolled in many quarters: in the general economic progress, in the commercial and financial success of the Italians, the indirect practice of usury (money being lent at interest) by Christians, the persecution and finally the expulsions (in 1182 and 1306 in France, in 1290 in England and in 1370 in the Low Countries). The suspicion which attached to them was transferred to the 'loan tables' of the Lombards and Cahorsins, who loaned on surety, using their own capital, and specialised in loans for consumption. These money-changers were citizens of the place where they did business, not strangers like their precursors, and by contrast to them they raised the level of their business from simple manual exchange to proper banking operations. They received deposits from private individuals, and worked on verbal authority by means of transferences and compensatory movements in day-books and ledgers. These books had the same authority as notarial records, and like them were guaranteed by the care and oversight of the public authority. Operating according to the principle of the fractional reserve, and using the surplus of their deposits on various sorts of investment, these bankers-cum-moneylenders allowed their clients overdrafts, and in this way as with their clearances they created the 'fiduciary' money of banking. With some variants, this was the way the money-changers of the *banchi di scritta* of Venice worked, along with those of the new and old markets of Florence, and the *bancarii* of the Piazza Bianchi at Genoa. Notable among the last-named were the Lomellini, whose books show several analogies with those of the bankers and money-changers of the Halle d'Eau at Bruges, Collard de Marke and Guillaume de Ruyelle (1366–1370), made familiar to all by the classic work of Prof. R. de Roover.

At a different level from that of these local banks, banking was also carried on by the merchant bankers of the great Italian firms, who added this form of activity to their commercial and industrial undertakings.

Thanks to the branches these companies had in all the major centres, and to the fairs of Lyons and Geneva, their operations were international in character. These great bankers guaranteed exchange, not just by hand to hand dealings but by a market in bills of exchange. At the same time, in return for a double profit ('pro portagio et cambio'), and without any movement of cash, they transferred money for their clients and made adjustments between place and place. In the first rank of their clients in the fourteenth century was the papal court at Avignon, whose transference of funds complemented that of the companies, as Yves Renouard has clearly shown.

It has been said that the *sopracorpo* of the companies welcomed the funds of a crowd of depositors. Thanks to this amount of capital these companies became powerful credit concerns.

Occupying first place among their customers and consumers of credit were popes, kings and magnates, who were importunate and often could not be denied. Genoese firms advanced some 80,000 Paris livres to Louis IX for his Egyptian crusade, and their debts were underwritten by the men of Piacenza. Guelf bankers, exiled from Florence and Siena, financed the crusade of Charles of Anjou in 1265, lending around 250,000 livres tournois at considerable risks. Between 1372 and 1376 the Alberti Antichi lent more than 400,000 florins to Pope Gregory XI. The Riccardi, Frescobaldi, Bardi and Peruzzi lent huge sums to the kings of England. At the time the two latter companies went bankrupt, Edward III owed them 900,000 and 600,000 florins respectively. According to Villani these debts were worth a kingdom, and this was no figure of speech. Later the loans of Portinari to Charles the Bold, Mary of Burgundy and Maximilian contributed to the liquidation of the Bruges branch of the Medici bank, an everyday misfortune. On balance, their legal privileges and exemption from export duties, the mortgaging of customs to them and the profits from rights of moneying, and even an occasional repayment, did not always compensate for what was owed them, or save them from the bankruptcy which was the normal fate of these great operations, which were as dangerous as they were unavoidable. The numerous creditors of the state, many of them men of small means, were better protected at Genoa, where in the fifteenth century the repayment of a debt was guaranteed by the Casa and the Bank of St George, founded in 1408. Venice, Florence (in 'the Mount') and Milan had each their equivalent.

But the great merchant bankers still did the bulk of their business with the merchants and industrialists to whom they allowed credit, either by book entries or by the purchase of their bills of exchange. The staple trade of major international banking was the market in these means of credit and speculation.

In the fourteenth and fifteenth centuries there was, then, a genuine money-market. This comprised, geographically, the major centres (listed above on p. 321) where the banking and trading companies had branches which dealt in paper currency. Like every market governed by the laws of supply and demand, the money market was subject to various seasonal and perhaps cyclical fluctuations. These were linked to the abundance or scarcity of money, which made for the alternation of periods of scarcity (*strettezza*) and plenty (*larghezza*), the contraction and expansion of credit, and cheap or dear money. The movement of exchanges reflected these fluctuations, and was governed also by the rate of concealed interest, and by a number of other factors — by monetary fluctuations, the balance of account between two different places, and speculation.

The money market was not in any strict sense dependent on trade, for in the accounts of the great merchant bankers the amount of exchange business was greater than that of strictly trading business. Much of the business done through bills of exchange — loans in which the interest was concealed

in the rates of exchange and re-exchange, and speculation —
was purely financial, and designed to show a return on
capital. The banking work of these companies, with the
profits it brought, came to take precedence over their strictly
trading activities. This point can be seen in the career of
Jacques Coeur, a trader, ship-owner and industrialist, but
above all a financier and 'the great money-lender' of a
kingdom. By borrowing money himself, he advanced to the
French king 100,000 écus (150,000 livres tournois) for the
reconquest of Normandy. A world in which the directors of
operations are no longer industrialists and traders but
bankers already has a very modern look about it.

The development of this complex business organisation
involved the perfection of accounting techniques, and in
this realm as in so many others the Italians were the great
innovators. On the basis of a register of the Massari of
Genoa in 1340, the Genoese were once credited with the
invention of double-entry book-keeping, which Sombart
considered the touchstone of modern capitalism. But now
Professor Melis has discovered a double-entry account from
1336 in the archives of a bank at Pisa. In this way he has
been able to trace back the appearance of this technique to
Florence in the first third of the fourteenth century, and
show the steps by which it developed from the fairs of
Champagne and the account book of Rinieri Fini (1296–
1305).

Alongside the new arts of business and banking, there
came in the fourteenth and fifteenth centuries methods of
instructing the men who practised them. Business apprenticeship took the form of a practical training in the service
of a merchant (sometimes a member of the same family) or
a firm. Manuals such as the famous 'Pratica della mercatura'
of Francesco di Balduccio Pegolotti (1310–1342) or that of
Giovanni di Antonio di Uzzano (1442), tried to collect
together and present this experience. But business practice
came to rest more and more on theoretical knowledge, on
arithmetic and calculation. The latter had gained in the
thirteenth century from the use of the number nought, from
the use of Arabic numerals, and from the arrangement of

figures in a set position. The simplification of accounting which came in the fourteenth century from the use of 'modern' dating (the 1st January, etc.), and the precise measurement of time by the division of days and of clocks into 12 or 24 equal hours, also witness to a new spirit. It is the spirit of number and precision, which appears in the chronicle of Giovanni Villani, the spirit of planning, accounting and the scientific conduct of business. These are the devotions allied to the modern worship of Mammon, a world removed from the religious ideals of the Christian middle ages.

BIBLIOGRAPHY

The range of this subject is so wide that only an introduction can be provided here. There are full bibliographies in most of the works cited, most notably in the *Cambridge Economic History*, and to these bibliographies the reader is referred for general works. And since finance and trade of their nature involve exchanges, every area and every part of the subject are inextricably bound up one with another. Outside their particular subject, therefore, almost all specialised works make points of more general importance. Without exception these works are to be recommended and in particular the classic works of Henri Pirenne, Italian historians such as A. Sapori and G. Luzzatto, and the French historian Y. Renouard which have inspired research into commerce and finance in the Middle Ages.

1. COMMODITIES AND TRADE ROUTES

THE MEDITERRANEAN WORLD
W. Heyd, *Geschichte des Levantehandels im Mittelalter* (Stuttgart, 1879).
A. Schaure, *Handelsgeschichte der romanischen Völker des Mittelmeergebiets bis zum Ende der Kreuzzüge* (Munich-Berlin, 1906); these two old works remain important for their factual information.
C. M. Cipolla, *Money, prices and civilisation in the Mediterranean World* (Princeton, 1956); this work lives up superbly to the promise of its title.
R. S. Lopez and I. W. Raymond, *Medieval Trade in the Mediterranean World. Illustrative documents translated with introductions and notes* (New York, 1955); the choice of texts, commentary, notes and bibliography make this an indispensable work.
R. H. Bautier, 'Les grands problèmes politiques et économiques de la Méditerranée médiévale', *Revue Historique*, 1965. See also, *Les navigations mediterranéennes et leurs liaisons continentales XIe-XVIe siècles* (Proceedings of the 11th

International Conference of Maritime History, Bari, 1969).

i. Italy and the Diaspora
The economic pre-eminence of Italy and the ubiquity of the Italians give works relating to them a general importance. Even on their own, the works of Cipolla, De Roover, Doehaerd, Lopez, Luzzatto, Melis, Renouard and Sapori make a fundamental contribution to the history of European trade and finance in the middle ages.

F. Carli, *Storia del commercio italiano*, 2 vols (Padua, 1934–6).

R. Cessi, *Le colonie medievali in oriente* (Bologna, 1942).

G. Luzzatto, *An Economic History of Italy from the Fall of the Roman Empire to the beginning of the Sixteenth Century*, trans. P. J. Jones (London, 1961).

A. Sapori, *Le Marchand Italien au Moyen Age* (Paris, 1952); this indispensable work comprises four lectures, and an outstanding bibliography. Along with this should be mentioned Y. Renouard, *Les hommes d'affaires Italiens du moyen âge*, new edn., prepared from the author's notes by B. Guillemain (Paris, 1968).

C. M. Cipolla, *Storia dell'economia italiana. Saggi di storia economica*, Vol. I (Turin, 1959).

ii. The great Italian cities
Venice: G. Luzzatto, *Storia economica di Venezia, dall'XI al XVI secolo* (Venice, 1961).

Genoa: E. H. Byrne, *Genoese shipping in the 12th and 13th centuries* (Cambridge, Mass., 1930).

R. Doehaerd, *Les relations commerciales entre Gênes, la Belgique et l'Outremont d'après les archives notoriales génoises, aux XIIIe et XIVe siècles*, 3 vols (Brussels-Rome, 1941); this selection of documents has a very important introduction.

J. Heers, *Gênes au XVe siècle: activité économique et problèmes sociaux* (Paris, 1961). This book, with its maps and its graphs, contains a great deal of quantitative information on the volume and fluctuations in Genoese trade. It corrects many preconceived ideas on late medieval trade, and is fundamental for the period.

Florence: A Doren, *Studien aus der florentiner Wirtschaftsgeschichte*, 2 vols (Stuttgart-Berlin, 1901–8); R. Davidsohn, 'Der florentiner Welthandel des Mittelalters', *Weltwirtschaftliches Archiv*, 1929.
Milan: G. Franceschini, *Storia di Milano*, 4 vols (Milan, 1954); C. M. Cipolla, *L'economia milanese. I movimenti economici generali, 1350-1500* (Milan, 1957).

iii Byzantium

Among recent works are the following: F. Thiriet, *La Romanie vénitienne au moyen âge. Le dévéloppement de l'exploitation du domaine colonial vénitien (XIIe–XVe siècle)* (Paris, 1959); H. Ahrweiler, *Byzance et la mer* (Paris, 1966).

iv. Provence, Languedoc

G. Rambert (dir.), *Histoire du commerce de Marseille*, Vols I & II (Paris, 1949–51); L. J. Thomas, *Montpellier, ville marchande. Histoire économique et sociale* (Montpellier, 1936).

v. The Iberian Peninsula

J. Vicens Vives, *Historia social y económica de España y América*, 4 vols (Barcelona, 1957–9); *An Economic History of Spain*, 3rd edn., trans. F. M. López-Morillas (Princeton, N.J., 1969).
Catalonia: C. Verlinden, 'La place de la Catalogne dans l'histoire commerciale du monde méditerranéen', *Revue des cours et conferénces*, 1937–8; 'The Rise of Spanish Trade in the Middle Ages', *Econ. H.R.*, 1940.
C. Carrere, *Barcelone, centre économique à l'époque des difficultés, 1380-1482*, 2 vols (Paris-The Hague, 1967).
Portugal: A. Castro, *A evolução económica de Portugal dos séculos XII a XV* (Lisbon, 1964).

THE NORTH

A. R. Lewis, *The Northern Seas: shipping and commerce in Northern Europe, A.D. 300-1100* (Princeton, 1958).

i. Flanders, the Low Countries, Bruges and Antwerp

L. Genicot, *et al.*, *Histoire de Belgique* (Tournai, 1961).

R. Haepke, *Brugges Entwicklung zum mittelalterlichen Welt-markt* (Berlin, 1908).

J. A. van Houtte, 'La genèse du grand marché international d'Anvers à la fin du Moyen Age', *Revue Belge de Philologie et d'Histoire*, 1940; and 'Bruges et Anvers, marchés "nation-aux" ou "internationaux", du XIVe au XVIe siècle', *Revue du Nord*, 1952.

H. van Werveke, *Bruges et Anvers. Huit siècles de commerce flamand* (Brussels, 1944).

ii. *The Hansa, and The East*

E. Daenell, *Die Blütezeit der Deutschen Hanse* . . . , 2 vols (Berlin, 1905–6).

K. Pagel, *Die Hansa* (Berlin, 1942).

P. Dollinger, *The German Hansa*, trans. D. S. Ault and S. H. Steinberg (London, 1970).

These two works handle the topic with great skill.

L. K. Goetz, *Deutsch-Russische Handelsverträge des Mittelalters* (Lübeck, 1922); M. Malowist, 'Poland, Russia, and Western Trade in the Fifteenth and Sixteenth Centuries', *Past and Present* (1958).

iii. *England*

As well as the *Cambridge Economic History* see the following:

E. Lipson, *Economic History of England*, Vol I, 11th edn. (London, 1956); the continued reprinting of this work shows that it meets a real need.

E. Carus-Wilson and O. Coleman, *England's Export Trade, 1275–1547* (Oxford, 1963).

E. Power and M. M. Postan, *Studies in English Trade in the Fifteenth Century* (London, 1933).

E. Carus-Wilson, *The Overseas Trade of Bristol in the later Middle Ages* (Bristol, 1937).

The last three works cited rest in large measure on a masterly use of the unique evidence of the customs accounts. Their statistical information is of cardinal importance for the later middle ages. See further the collected essays of E. Carus-Wilson, *Medieval Merchant Venturers*, 2nd edn. (London, 1967).

iv. France

F. Levasseur. *Histoire du commerce de la France*, Vol I (Paris, 1911). Apart from this now old work, there are no general studies of French trade. But for the later middle ages there is a series of good monographs, and between them they cover a large part of the subject. For example M. Mollat — Normandy; H. Touchard — Brittany; C. Higounet and J. Bernard — Bordeaux; P. Wolff — Toulouse; and J. Schneider — Metz.

The fairs of Champagne were also part of France's links with the great international trading routes:

v. The fairs and trade routes

F. Bourquelot, *Etudes sur les foires de Champagne aux XIIe, XIIIe et XIVe siècles* (Paris, 1865).

G. Bourquelot, *Les Foires de Champagne* (Memoires de l'Académie des Sciences et Belles Lettres, Paris, 1938).

R.-H. Bautier, 'Les foires de Champagne', in *La Foire* (Société Jean Bodin, Brussels, 1953); and his 'Les registres des foires de Champagne', *Bulletin Philologique et Historique*, 1942-5 (also published separately).

M. Brésard, *Les foires de Lyon aux XVe at XVIe siècles* (Paris, 1914).

A Schulte, *Geschichte des mittelalterlichen Handels und Verkehrs zwischen Westdeutschland und Italien mit Auschluss von Venedig* (Leipzig, 1900).

J. T. Tyler, *The Alpine Passes in the Middle Ages* (Oxford, 1930).

V. Chomel and J. Ebersolt, *Cinq siècles de circulation internationale vue de Jougne: un péage jurassien du XIIIe aux XVIIIe siècle* (Paris, 1951).

THE MAJOR TRADING COMMODITIES

A. Sapori, *I beni del commercio internazionale*, in *Studi di storia economica* . . . (Florence, 1955).

E. Power, *The Wool Trade in English Medieval History* (Oxford, 1941).

H. Laurent, *Un grand commerce d'exportation au moyen âge. La draperie des Pays-Bas en France et dans les pays méditerranéens: XIIe–XVe siècle* (Paris, 1935).

A. P. Usher, *The History of the Grain Trade in France, 1400–1710* (Cambridge, Mass., 1913).

P. Wolff, 'Un grand commerce médiéval: les céréales dans le bassin de la Méditerranée occidentale', in *VIe Congresso de Historia de la Corona de Aragon* (Madrid, 1959).

Among a whole host of articles on the wine trade see those of Y. Renouard in *Etudes d'Histoire Médiévale*, and also the following:

J. Craeybeckx, *Un grand commerce d'importation: les vins de France aux anciens Pays-Bas: XIIIe–XVIe siècle* (Paris, 1958). On the Gascon wine trade with England the fundamental work is the unpublished thesis of M. K. James, 'The Non-Sweet Wine Trade of England during the Fourteenth and Fifteenth Centuries' (Oxford University, D.Phil. thesis, 1952).

These works show clearly that the staple products of international trade were heavy goods, aimed at a large market.

2. ORGANISATION, TRADING AND FINANCIAL TECHNIQUES

METHODS OF TRANSPORT

J. F. Willard, 'Inland Transportation in England during the Fourteenth Century', *Speculum*, 1926.

P. M. Mantellier, *Histoire de la communauté des marchands frequentant la rivière de Loire*, 3 vols (Orléans, 1854–1869).

R. Dion, 'Orléans et l'ancienne navigation de la Loire', *Annales de Géographie*, 1938.

G. Fourquin, 'La batellerie à Paris au temps des Anglo-Bourguignons (1418–1436), *Le Moyen Age*, 1963.

F. Lane, *Venetian Ships and Shipbuilders of the Renaissance* (London, 1934); partly outside the period, but indispensable.

T. Sottas, *Les messageries maritimes de Venise aux XIVe et XVe siècles* (Paris, 1938).

J. Bernard, *Navires et gens de mer à Bordeaux (vers 1400–vers 1550)*, 3 vols (Paris, 1968).

There is a real mine of information on ships in a fine periodical, the *Mariner's Mirror*. This has articles and references to the works of the great English specialists, in particular those of R. C. Anderson. See also the Proceedings of the International Conference of Marine History, first held in 1956, and published under the direction of M. Mollat. On the Kogge, the prototype of the big trading-ships of the fourteenth and fifteenth centuries, see P. Heinsius, *Das Schiff der Hansischen Frühzeit* (Weimar, 1956). In 1962 came the major discovery of a kogge buried in the mud of the Weser, and a fine study has been produced, *Die Bremer Hanse-Kogge* (Bremen, 1969).

COMMERCIAL AND FINANCIAL TECHNIQUES

i. General
On notaries and notarial practice, and on commercial dealings in general, see several of the works already mentioned: Doehaerd (1941), Sapori (1952), Lopez and Raymond (1955), and Renouard (1968). See further: A. E. Sayous, 'Le transformations des methodes commerciales dans l'Italie médiévale', *Annales*, 1929.

ii. Money and Prices
M. Bloch, 'The problem of gold in the middle ages', in *Land and Work in Medieval Europe*, trans. J. E. Anderson (London, 1967); also 'Esquisse d'une histoire monétaire de l'Europe', *Cahiers des Annales*, 1954.
M. Lombard, 'L'or musulman du VIIe au XIe siècle', *Annales*, *E.S.C.*, 1947.
H. van Werveke, 'Monnaie de compte et monnaie réelle', in his collected papers, *Miscellanea Mediaevalia* (Ghent, 1968).
E. J. Hamilton, *Money, Prices and Wages in Valencia, Aragon and Navarre, 1351–1500* (Cambridge, Mass., 1936).
R. Romano, 'Les prix au Moyen Age; dans le Proche-Orient et dans l'Occident Chrétien', *Annales*, *E.S.C.*, 1963.

iii. Finance and Banking
G. Unwin, *Finance and Trade under Edward III* (Manchester, 1918).
M. M. Postan, 'Credit in Medieval Trade', in *Essays in*

Economic History, ed. E. Carus-Wilson, Vol I (London, 1954).
J. G. Dillen, *et al.*, *History of the Principal Public Banks accompanied by Extensive Bibliographies of the History of Banking and Credit* (The Hague, 1934).
R. de Roover, *Money, Banking and Credit in Medieval Bruges* (Cambridge, 1948).
C. M. Cipolla, *I movimenti dei cambi in Italia del secolo XIII al XV* (Pavia, 1948); R. de Roover, *L'évolution de la lettre de change* (*XIVe–XVIIIe siècle*) (Paris, 1952–3).
M. Mollat, *Les affaires de Jacques Coeur: Journal du procureur Dauvet*, 2 vols (Paris, 1952–3).

iv. The commercial and banking companies
A. Sapori, *La crisi delle compagnie mercantili dei Bardi e dei peruzzi* (Florence, 1936).
Y. Renouard, *Les relations des Papes d'Avignon et des compagnies commerciales et bancaires de 1316 à 1378* (Paris, 1941).
R. de Roover, 'The Story of the Alberti Company of Florence, 1302–1348', *Business History Review*, 1958; and his book, *The Rise and Decline of the Medici Bank: 1397–1494* (Cambridge, Mass., 1963).
A. Schulte, *Geschichte der grossen Ravensburger Handelsgesellschaft 1380–1530*, 3 vols (Stuttgart-Berlin, 1923).

v. Insurance
E. de Roover, 'Early Examples of Marine Insurance', *Journal of Economic History*, 1945; F. Melis, *I primi secoli delle assicurazioni: secoli XIII–XVI* (Rome, 1965).

vi. Accounting
F. Melis, *Storia della ragioneria. Contributo alla conoscenza e interpretazione delle fonti più significative della storia economica* (Bologna, 1950).
T. Zerbi, *Le origini della partita doppia: Gestioni aziendali e situazioni di mercato nei secoli XIVe XV* (Milan, 1952).

This bibliography shows up a number of twilight areas, in the realms of the geography of the Byzantine Empire and the countries of Eastern Europe, for which there are no general books available to those who are not either Byzantinists or Slavonic scholars. Then there are the gaps in our knowledge of local and regional trade which have already been stressed. But here the studies of individual towns mentioned above, along with the bibliography in Vol. III of the *Cambridge Economic History* (under 'Markets and Fairs'), enable us to fill the gap at least in part. And finally there is what may be called statistical history, money and prices, and the questions which concern the volume and fluctuations of trade. Here we enter a vast field of research, where Professor Cipolla in particular has paved the way quite brilliantly.

8. Government Economic Policies and Public Finance 1000-1500

Edward Miller

A general review of the fiscal and economic policies of medieval governments is no easy undertaking. During the five centuries after the millennium 'states' were being made out of very diverse constituents: the debris of earlier empires, feudal and tribal groupings, and the fragmented societies of the Scandinavian north and the Slav east. The reintegration of these elements created communities different in character and organisation according to a chronology which was not everywhere the same. For this reason the study of government policies can be based upon no straightforward progression through time; and it is also difficult to lay down hard and fast criteria defining what was and what was not a 'state'. At all times during the middle ages 'infra-state' agencies enjoyed a wide freedom to frame fiscal and economic policies, amounting in certain circumstances to virtual independence. The real policy makers may well be the Italian city, the feudal principality or the federation of Baltic towns in the Hanseatic north rather than the kingdom or the empire. It is necessary to accept the fact that public authorities were more diverse than in our own day.

It is not less necessary to accept the fact that medieval governments were precluded from prosecuting many of the policies falling within the competence of modern governments by their limited administrative resources and their imperfect political control over their territories. More than that, it is clear that many of the social and economic objectives underlying modern government policies were either absent in the middle ages or appear with a very different emphasis, that fiscal policies can be viewed in terms of opportunism in the face of budgetary stringency and that economic policies frequently represent tactical

concessions to political interests. To admit that much,
however, is not necessarily to deny the existence of medieval
economic and fiscal policies provided they are considered
in terms of medieval objectives pursued in medieval conditions with medieval resources. Viewed from this angle,
moreover, a measure of progress over time is discernible,
even if it was by no means uniform. Most governments of
the later middle ages were expected to intervene in the
economic field and some of them were capable of mobilising
considerable resources for major projects. The situation in
the eleventh century was very different. The Carolingian
empire and the caliphate of Cordoba had disintegrated;
England was a comparatively recent federation of king-
doms and the German empire a federation of duchies
already exhibiting symptoms of a new feudal instability.
Political evolution amongst the Slavs and in Scandinavia
was still in its infancy and government institutions everywhere were still more or less primitive. Public authorities,
even where they conceived of themselves as possessing a
properly public character, had capacities which were
necessarily limited.

PUBLIC FINANCE

GOVERNMENT AS LORDSHIP

These authorities also possessed limited resources, arising
principally from the profits of lordship. Rulers, as well as
being lords of a territory, were also normally landlords of
certain estates within it. From these estates they drew
revenues of the same sort as other landlords drew from
their land, including demesne produce and liveries in kind
from tenants which were either consumed *in situ* or sent
to the ruler's principal residences. This natural economy of
the state was disappearing rapidly in Norman and possibly
late Saxon England; but revenues in kind were prominent
in the receipts of the count of Flanders in 1187, discernible
amongst the assets of the French crown in 1227 and diminished rapidly in the duchy of Burgundy during the four-

teenth rather than the thirteenth century. Even in the later middle ages, moreover, Scandinavian rulers continued to rely heavily upon the produce of scattered royal estates. Early, and in peripheral areas even later, medieval governments stood literally upon feet of clay.

In general, however, from the eleventh century onwards rulers like other landlords increasingly demanded cash rather than produce from their lands. Manors which were not alienated were leased for money rents; and the most was made of more or less arbitrary imposts on manorial tenants and of charges for using seignorial monopolies like mills, wine-presses or ovens. In addition, rulers normally enjoyed powers of lordship in excess of those conferred by direct landownership. As lords of territories they could command the services of their inhabitants—in war or to build fortresses, bridges and roads—which satisfied some of the needs of the state. Within these territories, too, they might supplement their domanial revenues with receipts from judicial penalties, market dues, tolls on goods in transit, succession duties payable by feudal tenants and 'gracious aids' conceded by those tenants in time of special need. Many of them, too, inherited from the feudal age, when the church fell captive to laymen, claims to hospitality and financial contributions from ecclesiastical establishments and to occupy episcopal and abbatial lands during vacancies. These rights over the church were still being exploited vigorously in England by Edward I and they were vital to the German monarchy until the Investiture Contest undermined them.

This structure of revenues determined the nature of fiscal policies. To expand lordship—by war, marriage, purchase or the resumption of fiefs and administrative powers granted away in time past—was one method of expanding resources. One consequence of the Norman Conquest of England was an increase in the number of royal manors; and the history of France, from the conquests of Philip Augustus to the acquisition of Champagne through marriage by Philip the Fair, saw rapid progress towards that coincidence of the royal domain with the nation which was ultimately achieved when Gascony, Burgundy and Brittany were absorbed at the end of the middle ages. Policies of domanial expansion continued to be one feature of state formation right down to the dawn of modern times: in the German principalities, Queen Margaret's abortive Scandinavian empire, the Sweden of Sten Sture, the Spain united by Ferdinand and Isabella. Perhaps Henry VIII's dissolution of the English monasteries can be regarded as a belated but dramatic assertion of this venerable medieval tradition.

Revenues could be maximized, however, by a more intensive exploitation of resources as well as by expanding them, particularly as specialised financial offices, written financial records and more sophisticated methods of accounting and audit were developed. Administrative progress in this direction was very uneven, precocious in England, northern and central Italy, and Sicily and retarded in most of Germany; but the general tendency was for most governments to make better use of their assets. Louis VI of France and the twelfth-century counts of Flanders and Holland were patrons of agricultural colonisation; and the fortunes of many German princes were founded on participation in the great colonising movement within and beyond the frontiers of Germany. Exploitation of regalian rights over silver mines provided vital revenues for the margraves of Meissen in the thirteenth century and the dukes of Saxony in the fifteenth; Tolfa alum was worth 100,000 florins a year to Pope Pius II; and control over the mines of Tyrol enabled the Emperor Maximilian to bargain for financial backing from the Fuggers. Encouragement of urban development was another branch of intensified domanial exploitation; for, if rulers abated some of the charges borne by townsmen, in the long run they might draw a larger profit from the presence in their lands of more active centres of economic activity. The patrons of towns therefore, were very diverse: the Emperor Frederick Barbarossa and archbishops of Cologne, dukes of Meissen and counts of Champagne, English and French and Spanish kings, and those German and Slav princes who developed the virgin lands of eastern Europe.

The wider attributes of lordship were likewise exploited more intensively. Expanded administrative activity and public jurisdiction yielded greater emolument. Feudal duties and services were commuted for cash payments. Tolls and market dues became more profitable as trade increased. Jews and other vulnerable groups were subjected to arbitrary imposts. Subsidies were exacted in lieu of military service in Northern Italy in the twelfth century and from thirteenth-century French towns; and tallages were negotiated with the towns of England. Even so, from the twelfth century onwards, the limited potentialities of traditional sources of revenue became increasingly evident at a time when the scope of governmental activities was being enlarged, when mercenaries were replacing men who served gratuitously, and when prices were rising and the value of money was falling. Inflation of government expenditure coincided with tendencies making for stability or even a reduction of established revenues: the limitation of feudal dues to specific occasions and customary norms, resistance to fiscal exploitation of administrative processes, the fixing of the charges paid by urban and some rural communities and the winning of exemption from traditional taxes like the English Danegeld by the church and the military classes. Finally, while domains and regalian rights were eagerly expanded, they were as easily granted away to subjects in return for loyalty and service or alienated to secure a quick return in a time of need.

THE RECOURSE TO CREDIT

Expanded sources of credit, which general economic expansion made available to rulers, might also be a temptation to disperse their assets. This was especially the case when they exploited these sources of credit in an unsystematic and sporadic manner. Henry III of England, for example, borrowed from his brother, bishops and religious orders, Jews and English townsmen and some members of the baronage; and this form of dispersed borrowing was typical of German and east European governments for most of the rest of the middle ages. Many of their creditors were in a position to demand security for their advances in the form of pledges of princely property and rights, with the result that present needs were only met at the expense of future income. When Frederick I became margrave of Brandenburg in 1415 nine-tenths of his sources of income were either pledged or alienated; and France at the beginning of the fifteenth century and Lancastrian England were driven back upon similar hand-to-mouth methods of supporting government expenditure. The availability of credit was sometimes a direct cause of fiscal and political instability.

This was not, however, the necessary outcome, especially with the emergence of the Italian merchant bankers as international financiers first of the papacy and ultimately of most of the governments of southern and north-western Europe. At least down to the crisis of confidence following Edward III's repudiation of his debts in the 1340's their advances, made in return for interest payments and commercial privileges, enlarged the scope and increased the flexibility of government action. By the end of the middle ages south German bankers had reinforced the Italians and other methods of securing credit had been devised. Philip the Good of Burgundy developed the practice, already pioneered in Brabant and Hainault, of selling hereditary and life annuities through the intermediacy of the towns; and earlier still the Italian cities, in which forced or voluntary loans had long been a device of fiscal policy, had created their funded debts. Loans to the Venetian government were consolidated into a fixed interest-bearing debt in 1262; Florence consolidated its floating debt in 1347; and an association of state creditors, the *Casa di San Giorgio*, was established at Genoa in 1405 and soon became something like the financial agency of the Genoese state.

The mode of operations of the *Casa*, however, is indicative of the conditions required by a successful public credit system. To secure the payment of interest charges on the public debt it had, by the mid-fifteenth century, assumed responsibility for the collection of direct and indirect taxes and the proceeds of the mints and the salt-monopoly. Similarly, in contemporary Venice and Florence funded debts needed the backing of direct taxation, charges on trade or the profits of state monopolies; and it was the lesson of English public finance in the reigns of Edward I and Edward III, of Burgundy under Philip the Good, of Naples under Charles the Wise and of France under Louis XI that recourse to credit without disaster depended upon the availability of tax revenues to meet interest charges and periodically to repay the principal borrowed. In Brandenburg, for example, signs of progress towards a stable financial system based on credit only became evident when Albrecht Achilles persuaded the Estates of his electorate to assume responsibility for his accumulated debts and thereby forced them into contributions towards their reduction.

THE DEVELOPMENT OF TAXATION

The availability of credit, therefore, played a part in the development of new sources of revenue which ultimately assumed a prominence far exceeding that of the old. Powers of general direct taxation, largely dormant since the collapse of the Roman empire, were revived. They appeared prematurely in England around the millennium in the form of the geld to buy off the Danes; but exemptions so reduced the profitability of this tax that it was abandoned by the mid-twelfth century. A more continuous development began with the papal crusading taxes of the twelfth century and those imposts upon the whole western church which thirteenth-century popes levied, often by decree, to alleviate 'the burdens and necessities of the Roman church'. Other rulers, too, were soon tapping the resources which an expanding economy placed in the hands of their subjects. Frederick II took a 'general subvention' almost annually in Sicily and this right passed to his Angevin successors in the kingdom of Naples, where it provided nearly half the revenue of Charles the Wise. Direct taxation also made an early appearance in most of the northern Italian city states (at Pisa, for example, it was imposed first upon rural property in the surrounding countryside and later also upon town property and movable wealth). In the thirteenth century Theobald IV of Champagne converted fixed payments from his towns into variable property taxes; Alphonse of Poitiers multiplied hearth taxes in Toulouse; and the kings of England, Aragon and Castile succeeded in obtaining periodic contributions from their subjects. During the fourteenth and fifteenth centuries, after many vicissitudes, a direct tax (the *taille*) was established in France which provided up to 83 per cent of Louis XI's revenue; and similar imposts became more frequent in Bavaria in the fourteenth century, although in Cleves and Württemberg their history hardly began before the fifteenth century and in Sweden Karl Knutsson's attempt to introduce extraordinary taxation led to his deposition in 1457.

If popes in the plenitude of their power could tax by decree and, by the thirteenth century, a capacity of tax was an attribute of public authority in the Italian city states, the ability to impose more or less general taxes was seldom achieved easily. For most rulers extraordinary taxation was not a right: taxes had to be prayed for from those who would pay them. The attempt to establish general direct taxation, therefore, was one of the principal influences behind the appearance from the thirteenth century onwards of representative assemblies bringing together the various groups of taxpayers in the persons of their proctors or delegates. At the same time the fortunes of these assemblies were governed in part by trends in the incidence of taxation. While at Pisa the nobility and clergy were deprived of an earlier immunity from taxation and these classes never secured this immunity in England, in other places (in France, Bavaria and Spain, for example) they did become exempt. Where this happened, taxation rested upon the shoulders of the peasantry and bourgeoisie and the nobility and clergy had little incentive to unite with the third estate to limit the incidence of taxation or even to defend the principle of consent. By the end of the middle ages, therefore, the French *taille* was coming to be a charge imposed by government edict and the way of development towards the financial systems of the Ancien Régime was open.

Normally, however, direct taxes even at the end of the middle ages were still occasional imposts which had to be supplemented by indirect charges. Customs duties on trade crossing their frontiers were developed as sources of revenue by Frederick II in Sicily and by Charles Robert in Hungary; duties on trade in the Sound were valuable to the Danish kings and import and export duties contributed to the resources of the fifteenth-century dukes of Brittany. England most of all, however, relied on the customs to supplement traditional revenues and intermittent windfalls from direct taxation. Export duties on wool were established in 1275 and charges on other exports and imports were subsequently added. This branch of revenue was expanded to meet the costs of war in the 1290's and on the outbreak of the Hundred Years' War; Edward I used assignments on the customs as security for his debts; and these duties provided nearly half the public revenue in the early years of Henry VI. In a very real sense the fiscal policy of late medieval England was geared to the fortunes of English trade.

Even more typical than the taxation of foreign trade, however, was exploitation of tolls on internal trade. This was above all a 'German madness' which provided part of the exiguous revenues of the imperial crown in the later middle ages, a quarter of the income of the dukes of Austria in the thirteenth century and the counts of Tyrol in the fourteenth, and no less than half the resources of the counts of Cleves in 1481. Germany, on the other hand, had no monopoly of toll-takers. These charges appeared almost everywhere amongst the revenues of rulers, although sometimes (as in Hungary) they had fallen to such an extent into the hands of the provincial nobility that they provided an inadequate basis for fiscal reconstruction. Tolls did, however, contribute to Casimir the Great's attempts to provide financial foundations for the Polish monarchy in the fourteenth century; and, from an even earlier date, in the special form of charges upon sheep moving between winter and summer pastures (transhumance), they were a vital source of revenue for the Castilian kings. In some places, on the other hand, receipts from tolls were overshadowed by profits from government monopolies, especially of the sale of salt. Established in Sicily in the twelfth century, this regalian right made its appearance somewhat later in Pisa, Venice, the Papal States and elsewhere in Italy. During the fourteenth century it was introduced into Poland and France, and, in the latter country, it provided four per cent or more of royal revenues in the late fifteenth century. These *gabelles* were not so much onerous as vexatious; but they were by no means unprofitable to governments.

Among indirect taxes, however, excises levied in the towns and especially upon the sale of alcoholic drinks were often more productive than customs duties or government monpolies. 'Aids' of this sort provided between 15 and 30 per cent of the French royal revenue in the second half of the fifteenth century; they were the principal source from which the dukes of Austria expanded their revenues during the later middle ages; and they were always basically important to civic finance in Italy. In many places excises, like direct taxes, were established with the consent of representative assemblies; but there was a tendency, evident alike in Saxony and Castile, for this control to disappear. Like the turning of the French *taille* into a tax by decree the liberation of excises from the shackles of popular consent was symptomatic of developing fiscal independence as a prerogative of princes.

Diverse sources, therefore, contributed to public revenues during the later middle ages; but normally one or two of them were of special importance in a particular country at a particular time. Which those sources were depended upon economic and political circumstances. Customs duties on external trade were prominent where commerce was dominated by a staple export like English wool. Excises on domestic sales had a natural attraction for centres of intensive exchanges like the Italian city states and for regimes exercising close control over their towns like those of Angevin Naples, fifteenth-century Austria or the France of Louis XI. They were, too, an expedient form of taxation for the city fathers of Genoa in 1490 desirous of relieving town property-owners from the burden of direct taxation and for the kings of Castile after they had freed themselves from the need to seek consent for them. Direct taxation, on the other hand, was more attractive still when, as in England, all classes could be persuaded to contribute to it; when, as in France, the tacit acquiescence of the nobility and clergy to taxation of the peasantry and bourgeoisie was assured; or when, as in fifteenth-century Florence, a city government wished to relieve the burden upon urban trade and industry by shifting it to the rural *contado*. Methods and motives were diverse; but the general feature of the times was an expansion of government revenues and the diverse ways by which that expansion was achieved.

LIMITS OF FINANCIAL STABILITY

At the same time the history of revenue expansion is one which reveals many inequalities of development. New taxes accounted for more than 90 per cent of royal income in France during the later fifteenth century; but in Norway and Sweden the development of taxation lay mainly in the future, the control of representative assemblies over direct taxation in Castile made the poverty of its kings 'a jest in the mouths of their subjects', and most German princes had only begun to tap new sources of revenue and to administer them effectively. The assumption, moreover, that public revenues were the private income of the ruler, which he could dispense according to his caprice, was one which died hard. Financial efficiency, therefore, depended to no small degree upon the accident of a prince's personality; and even the most efficient princes found revenues adequate for normality insufficient for crises. In such circumstances internal and external stresses had exaggerated effects upon financial stability. In England there were periods of acute financial difficulty occasioned by war and political discontents under rulers as strong as Edward I at the end of his reign or as weak as Henry VI during most of his reign; and France plumbed financial depths under the incompetent Charles VI at the beginning of the fifteenth century. It should also be added that the new sources of revenue which rulers were tapping were less than securely gained in the eyes of subjects. The deputies to the French Estates General in 1484 denounced the tendency for the *taille* and other charges, 'instituted in the first place because of war', to become 'immortal' in time of peace and persuaded Charles VIII to profess unwillingness to compel his subjects to put their hands into their purses. It was, however, consonant with new realities that he reserved a claim to their money 'for the king to be able, as he ought to be, to undertake great things and to defend the kingdom'.

The inequalities of fiscal development and the precariousness of those new resources which were so painfully won also help to explain why the history of medieval government finance is so often a tale of more or less desperate expedients. Borrowing often outran foreseeable prospects of repayment. Vulnerable groups—Jews, townsmen, alien merchants—were plundered by forced loans or arbitrary imposts. Tolls were raised beyond reason and without counting the cost to trade. Currencies were manipulated by the long line of 'false moneyers' in positions of power. The English wool trade was taxed purely to raise revenue and heavily enough to have far-reaching consequences. Measures of this sort arose out of critical financial needs and they vitally affected economic development and prosperity. In that sense they represent the frontier where economic and fiscal policies intersected and upon which economic well-being often appeared as a victim of financial advantage.

GOVERNMENT ECONOMIC POLICIES

THE PROVISION OF GOODS

The economic policies of medieval governments, however,

have dimensions transcending those of fiscal expedients even if some of the most characteristic of them are, to modern western eyes, elementary in their character. Men prayed in the later middle ages: 'from famine, war and plague, spare us, O Lord'. War might be the fate kings visited on their subjects and plague a divine punishment; but famine was a common and recurrent experience for many of the people during most of the middle ages. It was direct consequence of harvest fluctuations in an environment in which the transport of bulk commodities was never easy and in which there were many barriers to the free flow of goods. In consequence the problem of the supply of basic foodstuffs was universal and perennial. It was particularly acute when medieval population density was highest in the generations around 1300 or in periods of dislocation occasioned by war and pestilence. It concerned every government, directly or indirectly; but it was a preoccupation above all of the governments of highly urbanised areas and those in which or over which townsmen were most influential.

Methods of tackling the problem were very various. Particularly in northern and central Italy and to a lesser extent in Spain efforts were made to increase food supplies by organising the reclamation of new land and by offering incentives to men who brought back derelict land to cultivation; while in the fifteenth century the dukes of Milan tried to stablise the acreage under grass in order to preserve the area under arable crops and to ensure an abundance of wheat. Again, principally in the territories of the Italian city states, concern about food supplies lay behind the drive of civic authorities to extend their control over the surrounding countryside. Bologna in 1305 deemed it 'more useful to have wheat from one's own possessions than ... from the possessions of another', echoing Aquinas's dictum that 'the city is worthier if it has abundance of goods from its own territories than if that abundance derives from merchants'. To the same end the countryside and countrymen were strictly controlled. Exports of grain from the *contado* other than to its urban 'capital' were forbidden; the city authorities saw that all available land was cultivated and sometimes prescribed specific quotas of grain to be delivered to the town markets; and selling prices were fixed or carefully regulated. These measures had their successes. They helped to limit to 25 per cent the rise in grain prices at Pisa between 1266 and 1322 during a period when the value of money fell by 66 per cent.

Restraints on the export of grain, at least temporarily in time of dearth, were common during the middle ages (for example in France from the thirteenth century onwards); but the idea of self-sufficiency was easier to proclaim than to realise. There were regions of chronic deficiency in certain foodstuffs: it was for this reason that Norway in 1315-16 banned the export of fish by alien merchants unless they brought in grain, malt and flour and the archbishops of Salzburg encouraged salt production in their territories because they ruled over a 'sterile place' which needed the services of merchants 'taking away salt . . . and leaving behind victuals'. In northern Italy, too, urban growth soon outran the productive resources of town hinterlands and deliberate attempts were made to stimulate an inflow of foodstuffs by import premiums, customs rebates and bulk purchases especially from Naples and Sicily. Sometimes, as at Venice, the grain trade was largely placed under government control and at Pisa reserve supplies were stock-piled in municipal granaries for sale in lean times at fixed and often subsidised prices.

It was more normal, however, to leave to private enterprise the provision of imports to offset temporary shortages like those of early fourteenth-century England or the more regular deficits of the late medieval Low Countries. Measures to regulate the terms of the food trade in internal markets, on the other hand, were far more generally adopted. Almost every western land throughout the middle ages viewed with suspicion the formation of rings or associations by food traders. Banned at Pavia in the twelfth century, similar prohibitions were reiterated by dukes of Brittany in the fifteenth. With the same ends in view Edward III of England opened the retail trade in foodstuffs to all; middleman and speculative dealings of fore-stallers and regrators were everywhere forbidden; and the sale of necessities was confined to the full publicity of public markets. In the difficult times following the Black Death, too, the cost of consumer goods was a matter of acute concern. English labour legislation sought to stabilise soaring prices as well as wages and in France price regulations bulked larger than wage controls. These policies, moreover, were new only in their scope and urgency. Regulation of food prices goes back in the Mediterranean lands to Carolingian times and was a consistent feature of communal legislation. Even in England from the twelfth and thirteenth centuries onwards the prices and quality of bread, ale and wine were controlled by a series of 'assizes' administered by the local authorities and by judicial commissions sent out by the central government.

NECESSITIES AND LUXURIES

At the same time, these English assizes indicate that a concern for goods went beyond the provision of necessities, for if bread and ale were fare for the ordinary man his betters also had a taste for wine. The goods which men desired, in fact, included 'luxuries' as well as basic commodities and the political structure of medieval states made these desires effective. Kings and princes, noblemen and town patricians, and the dignitaries of the church were not only the ruling circles of their day: they were also the consumers par excellence of goods which were dear because they were rich and rare. Their consumption preferences played a basic part in shaping many of the commercial policies of the middle ages; and they did so all the more effectively because the policies they dictated coincided with the fiscal interests of princes. The purveyors of desirable goods were in a position to pay for commercial privileges and might well be potential government bankers. A policy for consumers could be brought into line with a policy of power.

One outcome of these pressures in many countries, because initally economic development in the different regions of the medieval west was very uneven, was to give alien merchants a highly favoured position in their commerce. Advanced industrial enterprises and merchants with the techniques and capital resources needed for long-range commerce were found only in certain areas. The Hanseatic purveyors of Baltic furs, the men of Cologne and Flanders, the wine merchants of Bordeaux and above all the Italians, distributors at once of the products of northern and central Italian industry and of the trade goods of the Levant and further east, were representatives of developed economic regions for which the rest of Europe was, to one degree or another, colonial territory. The less advanced provinces of the west, on the other hand, tried to draw to themselves the merchants of the more developed centres. In Rudolph of Habsburg's eyes the Venetians provided useful and necessary things for many peoples and he sought to attract them by privileges to his territories, just as Charles of Anjou sought to bring Florentines to Naples and Charles Robert Italians to Hungary. The policy of Edward I of England and his successors followed similar lines. The *Carta Mercatoria* of 1303, in return for augmented customs duties, codified the privileges of stranger merchants in English trade; a series of statutes between 1335 and 1435 gave them freedom to deal even in some sectors of the retail market; and Hanseatic merchants during the later middle ages enjoyed terms of trade better even than those of denizens. In this way effect was given to the proposition Edward I advanced: 'the king understands that foreign merchants are valuable and useful to the magnates'.

Their utility was perhaps chiefly seen to lie in the fact that they brought in desirable goods and contributed on the side to the fiscal resources of the crown; but in some circumstances government patronage of alien merchants drew support from producer or commercial interests within the country with which they traded. Alien merchants were customers for the wool and other agricultural surpluses of English magnates; and in Castile, right down to the fifteenth century, royal subservience to the Genoese and other foreign wool exporters reflected the interests of the monopolistic association of sheep-owners, the *Mesta*, from which a significant part of royal revenues was derived. In the Low Countries, on the other hand, industrial interests and mercantile entrepreneurs favoured a not dissimilar policy, particularly after the decline of direct Flemish overseas trade and the spread of textile manufacture in Holland and Brabant. As early as the mid-thirteenth century Margaret of Constantinople offered inducements to foreign merchants to seek the ports of Flanders and, at the end of the century, the counts of Holland and Flanders engaged in bitter competition to draw English and German traders to Dordrecht and Bruges respectively. The basic character of policies had not fundamentally changed but the reasons for pursuing them gained in diversity.

THE PROVISION OF COMMERCIAL FACILITIES

In order to give effect to policies designed to secure an inflow of luxuries or necessities, the provision of commercial facilities within states was recognised to be necessary; and ultimately it came to be appreciated, however imprecisely, that such provision also contributed to more general economic development. This appreciation was sharpened by fiscal preoccupations, for when Lewis of Bavaria propounded the view that 'it is expedient that the state should have rich subjects' his mind was probably dwelling mainly upon their tax-paying capacity. On the other hand, the count of Holstein in 1253 regarded the protection which he accorded to traders to be for the 'profit and advantage' of merchants as well as of himself; and to an increasing extent rulers at least professed to have in view 'common utility' in the measures which they adopted. The initiative behind these measures often came from mercantile or other private interests; but the very pressure of these interests more and more influenced notions about what a ruler's duties and capacity were. Those notions in turn helped to determine the character of government economic policies.

In medieval conditions of life the first desirable commercial facility was a framework of order for economic activity. In this fact lay the significance of the special peace which English kings granted to traders, towns and markets, the patient negotiations of thirteenth-century dukes of Brabant for the protection of their subjects from spoliation by the petty princes of the Rhineland and the concern of Lübeck and its Baltic associates for security along the land and sea routes of the north. Order was most necessary of all in a fragmented and disorderly Germany. Emperors like Frederick Barbarossa and Frederick II proclaimed a general 'land-peace' to safeguard the 'happy estate' of their subjects and with the collapse of the monarchy individual princes, in isolation or by agreement, pursued similar ends within a more restricted context. In John of Viterbo's eyes, in the mid-thirteenth century, it was a positive duty of rulers to establish such order in their lands that 'cities are ruled and held peacefully, grow, become rich and receive great increment'. In this sense peace clearly served a 'common utility' in addition to creating wealth which princes could tap by taxation.

Making peace prevail, therefore, served a variety of interests: those of merchants, the fiscal advantage of princes and the presumed obligation of the latter to pursue the common good. Similarly, when rulers established or authorised the establishment of markets and fairs they might simply be responding to the demands of lords or towns or merchants. On the other hand, Philip of Alsace in Flanders and the counts of Champagne demonstrated that the institution and development of fairs could yield notable accretions of revenue; while Frederick II considered that his concession of a fair to Lübeck brought profit to his loyal subjects and the grant of a fair to Troppau in 1247 was designed to raise the burgesses from their poverty following the Mongol invasions. The attitude of princes to the great movement of town foundation and urban emancipation during the twelfth and thirteenth centuries can be viewed in a similar light. To a very considerable extent this movement was an outcome of bourgeois initiative operating in an atmosphere of economic expansion. Princely patronage, on the other hand, was a positive factor in the equation. If concessions were sometimes won by insurrection or if the authorisation of liberties was even more frequently bought for cash down, many rulers also played a deliberate and positive role in the foundation of towns. Doubtless their motives were mixed. They were concerned to establish administrative centres for the exercise of their authority, to expand their domanial resources and to raise up a political counterweight to the overmighty nobility. The idea that they were contributing to economic development, however, was not quite absent from the minds of some of them and, even where political and fiscal motives predominated in their counsels, their patronage evidently played its part in the expansion of the medieval economy.

The establishment of towns, markets and fairs as the principal centres of exchanges in the medieval west went part way only to easing the flow of commodities and the passage of merchants; for on the land routes and waterways between them lay obstacles to trade. In the Europe which emerged from the era of feudal disintegration roads and bridges were scarcely maintained and rivers were choked by obstructions. By the mid-fourteenth century, on the other hand, Philip of Leyden was able to assume that the oversight of means of communication was a responsibility of the public authority. Already the counts of Flanders had made some contribution to the equipment of their territory with canals and to the improvement of natural waterways, the English kings and Charles of Anjou in Naples had tried to ensure that internal routes were better maintained and even in Germany during the fourteenth century the provision of roads and bridges was deemed 'useful to the land and helpful to merchants'. Public authorities, of course, often lacked the financial and administrative resources to give effect to these good intentions and very frequently they were less successful still in reducing or abolishing the internal tolls which cluttered all the routes of the west. In England, it is true, 'outrageous tolls' were prohibited by statute in 1275 and the authorisation of new tolls was made subject to royal licence; and in Flanders, after a long struggle, the level of tolls was embodied in fixed schedules in the mid-thirteenth century. In France, on the other hand, the Loire tolls continued to divide the kingdom into two long after the close of the middle ages and in Germany periodic attempts to reduce the tolls on the Rhine, often by princes in combination, were equally regularly frustrated by a princely penury which drove them to raise charges to new heights. Something was done to mitigate the internal burdens upon trade, but probably these endeavours did less to reduce the costs of transporting goods than the expansion of trade by sea.

Merchants and especially stranger merchants made other demands upon governments within whose territories they traded. They needed access to rapid legal processes in order to enforce contracts without excessive delays and to machinery which would assist them to recover debts from those with whom they had dealings. These were facilities offered, among others, by Charles of Anjou in Naples and Edward I in England with a special eye to the alien traders whom they sought to attract to their lands. Desirable, too, were stable currencies of consistent value, an object not easily achieved in a Europe in which minting rights were dispersed almost as widely as the right to take tolls. Attempts to centralise minting were made at an early date in England and with almost complete success; but in France they had hardly begun before the thirteenth century and reached fruition only in the sixteenth. If the dispersal of minting rights made for currency chaos the expansion of mercantile transactions called for larger denominations than the little silver pennies and their like which had become almost the sole issues during the feudal age. An endeavour to satisfy this need appeared first, naturally enough, in the trading centres of Italy. Larger silver coins were issued in Venice in 1203 and in Florence in 1237 before the practice spread to other lands; and a gold coinage was struck in Florence and Genoa in 1252, in Venice in 1254, and by 1350 a similar provision was being made in England, France, Hungary and Bohemia. By that time, moreover, Nicholas Oresme had clearly stated that it was a ruler's duty to preserve good coin in his dominion; but like the principle that tolls ought to be reduced in order to serve the common utility this was a prescription all too frequently sacrificed to fiscal expediency. Princes could make quick profits by debasement or by manipulating monetary values. The temptation for them to do so was enhanced during the later middle ages when a shortage of bullion to maintain currencies disturbed the values of the precious metals; and this fact, in association with disequilibria between currencies arising from manipulations, also forced governments into measures of exchange control to preserve their own bullion stocks. From around 1300 there was something like a 'monetary war' in the medieval west which generated policies for the regulation of overseas payments and those bullionist preconceptions which haunted the mercantilist future.

Over and above the provision of commercial facilities some rulers sought to draw trade and traders to their territory by more positive and deliberate economic diplomacy or economic regulation. Their reasons were frequently fiscal, for any trade (even transit trade) could be taxed by the public authorities. This possibility may well have been the principal inspiration of attempts by the Habsburgs in the late thirteenth and fourteenth centuries to promote Italian trade to the Champagne fairs via the St. Gotthard pass, the nothern approaches of which they controlled, and to route through their lands the Alsace wine trade via the Black Forest to upper Swabia and Bavaria. The more ambitious schemes of Charles IV in Bohemia, too, probably did not neglect revenue considerations. He tried to divert the trade of Flanders and the Rhineland with eastern Europe from the Vienna route to his own kingdom, to develop direct trade between Venice and Bohemia and even to establish a route between Venice and Flanders via Prague, the Elbe and the North Sea. Even though his success was less than complete his concern for the trade of his land was evident.

Charles IV went about this work by patient economic diplomacy and, apart from his own profit, appears to have had a genuine concern for the economic development of his Bohemian principality. Such a concern, or a concern to exploit economic advantages already gained, was by no means unique. As early as the mid-twelfth century the archbishops of Cologne supported the merchants of their capital city in their ambition to be the sole intermediaries between southern Germany and north-west Europe by preventing ships proceeding further up the Rhine than Cologne. Soon afterwards Hamburg, too, under the patronage of the counts of Holstein was pursuing a 'staple' policy by somewhat different methods. Traffic through the city was subjected to heavy charges but goods bought in it were toll-free, a policy contributing to Hamburg's emergence as a focus of the east-west trade with Lübeck and the north-south trade along the Elbe. Later still the counts of Holland tried by similar methods to make Dordrecht the staple for all goods coming down the Rhine to the sea, not only for the benefit of their revenues but also as part of a policy designed to further the economic development of their territory. In that sense the patronage of trade by princes might serve 'common utility'.

INDUSTRIAL REGULATION

In most medieval countries during most of the middle ages economic policies were first and foremost commercial policies since these best served a ruler's fiscal interest and the consumption needs of society, but also because industrial interests capable of making their voices effectively heard normally emerged only at a relatively late date. Furthermore, control over industry organised on a small-scale craft basis was beyond the capacity of most medieval governments. The field was generally left, therefore, to infra-state agencies like towns or industrial corporations within towns. To this general rule, inevitably, there are some exceptions. These naturally included the Italian city states where, until the hold of the merchants upon civic governments was shaken during the last two medieval centuries, they used their political authority to frame policies designed to keep down manufacturing costs: indirectly by a cheap food policy and more directly, while permitting the formation of merchant associations, by restricting the development of industrial craft guilds which might have raised wages by collective action. In the short run these measures raised the levels of mercantile profits; but in the longer run they sharpened social antagonisms, and, like the similar policies of industrial towns in Flanders and elsewhere, provoked the craft revolutions which undermined the political and economic predominance enjoyed by the commercial patriciate in thirteenth-century towns. Elsewhere, consumer or commercial interests occasionally secured government backing for industrial policies. In England, for example, the 'assize' of 1196, regulating the quality of and fixing standard dimensions for cloth, seems first to have been designed to protect buyers and perhaps export merchants against the frauds of English weavers; but during most of the thirteenth century it was used principally to control (or to seek to control) the market in imported cloth. Only when native manufacture expanded rapidly during the fourteenth century was it used extensively to ensure that English exporters could expect to buy goods which would not deceive their overseas customers.

By the thirteenth century, however, for a variety of reasons a more positive attitude towards industrial production had appeared in some places. The archbishops of Salzburg encouraged salt production in their territories mainly as part of a traditionalist provisioning policy. Rather later, Edward III of England encouraged Flemish textile workers to settle in his kingdom as part of an assemblage of political and economic measures designed to apply diplomatic pressure to Flanders in preparation for war with France. On the other hand, both in northern and southern Europe, some rulers did appear to display a concern for the development of their dominions on the model of more advanced adjacent regions. When Charles of Anjou authorised entrepreneurs to exploit mines and set up forges he was probably only making the most of his domanial assets; but Charles II's invitation to Florentine silk and woollen workers to settle in Naples suggests a desire to further economic progress there on the north Italian pattern. The contemporary counts of Holland found their exemplar in Flanders. In competition with Flemish industry and with Bruges, they tried to make Dordrecht not only an international staple port but also a centre of textile manufacture by drawing to it English wool and granting to foreign weavers who settled there exemption from imposts for ten years. In this way they endeavoured to make available return freights especially for the German merchants who might be persuaded to frequent the Dordrecht staple.

Dutch and Angevin policies at the end of the thirteenth century, however, merely gave conscious direction to general economic tendencies. Down to that time the European economy had been dominated by certain advanced areas—industrial Italy, the Rhineland and Flanders in particular; and the trade routes of the western world had been no less dominated by north Germans and above all by north Italians. Even within the major regions there were marked economic disparities: between advanced northern and central Italy and the other lands of the western Mediterranean and between Flanders and the other lands of north-western Europe. In the later middle ages these disparities became less marked. The Angevin kings did something for the economic development of Naples, the Spanish textile industry became more active, Barcelona joined Venice and Genoa on the Mediterranean seaways, France under Louis XI sought to break into the commerce of that sea, and Portuguese and Castilians began to explore African and Atlantic horizons. Further north textile manufacture in England, Holland and Brabant undermined the old supremacy of Flemish weavers; Dutch and English merchants appeared on the sea-routes which Germans and Italians had frequented: and south German, Bohemian and even Hungarian traders were asserting a claim to some part of the gains of commerce. The emergence of new interests intensified competition at a time of economic dislocation and contracting markets caused by endemic plague. In a real sense the fourteenth century opened a new phase in the history of the western economy.

GOVERNMENT POLICIES AND THE INTERPLAY OF INTERESTS

The new economic phase brought new developments in economic policy. Kings and princes had no less need than in the past to expand their own resources and, to this end, they had increasingly to appeal to representative tax-granting assemblies through which economic interests could make their demands explicit and bargain for them to be met. For this reason, government economic policies were apt to reflect a broader spectrum of initiatives than in earlier generations, a tendency aided and abetted by developments in the structure of governments. Bureaucratic elements assumed an increasing role in administration, spreading from the more advanced political communities of the thirteenth century towards the peripheries of the west. These elements were recruited to no small extent from the ranks of the bourgeoisie and helped to implant bourgeois attitudes and aspirations in the very heart of the governmental machine. The administrative personnel who served him, as well as political calculations and personal predilection, helped to make Louis XI of France a 'king of merchants'.

The appearance of new interests, of course, did not push completely into the background the traditional political influence exercised by the landowning nobility. That influence contributed, right down to the end of the middle ages, to the persistence often in uneasy juxtaposition to other policies of time-honoured policies of provision. Governments still backed price and quality regulations for consumer goods and were often persuaded to favour the inflow of goods even if aliens carried them. Sometimes, on the other hand, they adopted measures which served the cause of landowners as agricultural entrepreneurs or recipients of agricultural rents. The interests of the *Mesta* and the payments it made to the crown long preserved the

privileged position of Italian wool merchants in Castile
and owners continued to be able to move sheep freely
between winter and summer pastures despite the damage
they did to arable farming. In England, on the other hand,
it was the arable farmer who secured government support.
A series of statutes between 1394 and 1455 permitted free
export of grain provided domestic prices did not rise above
specified levels and an act of 1463 forbade imports when
home prices were below a certain level. In the eastern
Baltic, too, Dutch merchants were welcomed in the
fifteenth century not only because they brought in cloth
and beer and herrings but because they were customers
for Prussian grain. Here, policies serving the agricultural
interest undermined the Hanseatic monopoly of northern
trade and furthered the development of the great Junker
estate as a characteristic economic institution of the German
east.

Mercantile interests were sacrificed in some parts of Italy
as well as in East Germany. The development of industrial
craft associations was favoured in some of the city states
which fell into the hands of 'tyrants' in order to undermine
the political position of the merchant patricians; and, in
Florence at the end of the fifteenth century, industrial
interests secured the opening of the port of Pisa to English
merchants in order to secure supplies of wool. In many
other places, however, the financial dependence of princes
upon towns and native merchants enabled the latter to
demand protection against their competitors. Protective
commercial policies, of course, were most thorough-going
where merchants themselves were the makers of policy.
Preservation of a monopoly of the Baltic trade and its
outlets in north-western Europe was the very raison d'être
of the Hanseatic League and, if Dutch competition broke
that monopoly, the English were more successfully ex-
cluded from Baltic markets without serious detriment to
Hanseatic privileges in England. Venice was even more
literally a mercantile state. From the late thirteenth century
its commerce was largely under state direction. Public
yards built a large part of the merchant marine; the

government laid down rules for voyages and organised convoys and overseas stations; and some commodities had to be bought in common to keep down purchase prices and improve the bargaining position of Venetian merchants in the distributive trade.

Venice and the Hanse were extreme phenomena but they were not the only patrons of mercantile interests. The dependence of the French monarchy on bourgeois loans and taxes and upon the towns as instruments of administration, especially in the age of reconstruction following the Hundred Years' War, made for a marriage of convenience between the crown and urban merchants which issued in royal intervention directed against restrictive craft policies. In Spain in the second half of the fifteenth century native shipping and exporting interests were served by navigation acts designed to give native vessels preference in overseas trade and in England, too, merchants secured intermittent government backing. Town prohibitions excluding alien merchants from the domestic retail trade were reproduced in national legislation; foreigners were obliged to stay with an English 'host' who would supervise their dealings and curtail their stay; and government agents scrutinised the quality of English textiles in the interest of exporters. Financial expediency, however, was even more the mother of protection. From the mid-fourteenth century onwards most English wool exports were channelled through a monopolistic association of English merchants, the Company of the Staple, to facilitate royal taxation of the trade and royal borrowing from traders. Taxation ultimately reduced the volume of the wool trade but, in conjunction with the private enterprise of English traders out of which the Company of Merchant Adventurers was born, the methods devised to secure taxes from the wool trade also helped to augment the share of English trade in English hands.

Industrial interests as well as landowners and merchants won protection in some places, if only in the form of government backing for town policies directed against a competing country industry. In some of the more advanced regions the success of the crafts in winning a place in urban governments in the generations around 1300 improved their bargaining position; and the financial and political dependence of princes upon the towns made them receptive to craft demands. The dukes of Milan in the fifteenth century and the counts of Flanders in the first half of the fourteenth were, therefore, persuaded to adopt measures restricting the development of rural industry. In Flanders, however, this surrender to pressure from the great towns carried with it the danger that their drive towards independence of the princely authority would be strengthened and the interests of cloth merchants were perhaps better served by permitting the growth of low-cost rural manufacture which they could profitably exploit. In an age of intensified international competition an alliance between the count and the merchants to sacrifice urban industry to its country rivals was almost inevitable and was consummated under Louis de Male and his Burgundian successors.

In Flanders, therefore, domestic circumstances made for domestic laissez faire; but a more unanimous support lay behind periodic attempts to exclude foreign (and especially English) textiles from Flemish markets. Similar protective policies are found in Italy, where infant industries growing in previously 'under-developed' centres needed nurturing and the industries of old 'advanced' centres called for support in the face of new rivals. The former encouraged the immigration of skilled artisans and restricted the export of raw materials; the latter, like Lucca when its silk industry met competition from Bologna, Genoa and elsewhere, retaliated with import tariffs or prohibitions. In Spain, too, Catalonian interests secured a ban on the import of foreign textiles into Aragon as early as 1422; a protective tariff for the Catalan industry was instituted in 1481; and Ferdinand and Isabella extended this policy to Castile and prohibited the export of more than two-thirds of the native wool-clip. These measures were perhaps more honoured in the breach than the observance but, at the least, industrial protection had become a legitimate sector of government policies.

England as well as Spain was one of the developing regions of the later middle ages and the statute book in 1463 carries a declaration that 'the chief and principal commodity of the realm of England consisteth in the wools growing in the said realm' and of these sufficient plenty 'should continually abide and remain in the said realm as may competently and reasonably serve for the occupation of clothmakers'. In fact, the growth of a native textile industry was furthered by government action in various ways: by a fiscal policy which without regard for economic consequences taxed wool exports heavily and cloth exports lightly; and by periodic embargoes on wool exports and cloth imports imposed for purely diplomatic reasons. By the fifteenth century, however, the economic utility of such measures was perceived, especially by the powerful groups of cloth exporters who increasingly sought government action to improve their competitive position. Where woollen interests led others followed, procuring the statutory prohibition of a wide range of imports competing with native products and in particular of imports brought in by aliens who were the competitors of English merchants. It was all the more convenient that alien activities could be stigmatised as contrary to the national interest.in so far as they involved draining from the realm those supplies of the precious metals which were always scarce, which were needed to support the national currency and which were seen increasingly to be the measure of the nation's wealth.

THE SCOPE AND LIMITATIONS OF GOVERNMENT POLICIES

The more sophisticated economic policies appearing during the later middle ages were not of universal application. They were adopted only to a limited extent, if at all, in Germany, the Slav east and Scandinavia; and even in more western lands there were many variations of emphasis. Their scope and limitations are well illustrated by France in the period of reconstruction under Louis XI. Royal policy furthered recovery of the textile industry at Poitiers and its establishment at Montpellier. A silk industry was implanted at Lyons and Tours. Louis welcomed to France foreign artisans with special skills: miners, armament makers, German glassworkers, Dinant coppersmiths, printers. In these ways he was the patron of French economic development and the protector of industrial growth. Many of his policies, however, had a much more traditional appearance. He welcomed Hansards and even his late enemy, the English, into his ports; and his attempt to create a Mediterranean trading company was principally designed to draw imports into the land, though admittedly through French rather than Italian enterprise. He linked this endeavour, in turn, with plans for revitalising markets and fairs, and above all the fairs of Lyons, as distributing centres for the whole of the west after the pattern of the fairs of Champagne in the good days of St. Louis. The growth of maritime trade during the later middle ages made such a policy in many ways anachronistic.

A variety of motives lay behind the measures of Louis XI. To traditional policies of provision were added policies aiming at industrial development, forerunners of those policies of plenty of a subsequent age. By supporting trade in French rather than alien hands and re-establishing on French soil the principal distributing centres of the west, he sought both to magnify the wealth of his land and to prevent the outflow from it of the outward and visible sign of that wealth, the precious metals—one of many examples of the medieval origins of bullionism. Louis was, however, concerned with power as well as plenty. The wealth he hoped to create for his subjects also represented assets which could be taxed or borrowed. His commercial policy in the Mediterranean was a means of putting pressure on Venice and of creating a Mediterranean merchant marine capable of supporting French strategic ambitions in that theatre. The establishment of fairs at Rouen and royal patronage of the Hansards subserved schemes for undermining Burgundian power in the Low Countries. Support for the urban mercantile élite strengthened his hold over a class from which he drew much revenue and upon which he

depended to rule the towns in his interests and to provide
a political counterpoise to the nobility which had en-
dangered the stability of France in the long time of troubles
following the death of Charles V. Indeed, by making it
easier for bourgeois to become noblemen and by permitting
noblemen to desert their traditional economic idleness for
commerce he threatened to erase deeply marked lines of
social distinction, leaving the monarchy in the lonely
isolation of incontestable authority.

The history of France under Louis XI makes clear how
impossible it is to separate economic policies from the other
policies of medieval governments and how professed
economic ends might be distorted by other objectives.
Except in a purely commerical federation (and as such
scarcely a 'state' at all) like the Hanseatic League or to
a lesser extent in the Italian city states before they capitu-
lated to 'tyrants', economic aims had to compete with
other desiderata and were often sacrificed to them. What
common utility demanded was often at war with financial
necessity. A ban on the export of Sicilian grain enabled
kings to sell licences to evade it; manipulation of the currency it was a ruler's duty to support undermined commercial confidence, disrupted exchange parities and nullified
the basis of contracts; schemes to reduce tolls were buried
because to raise them was a way of raising the wind; and
privileges designed to attract merchants were often rendered
nugatory by the temptation to plunder them. Diplomacy,
too, often involved a sacrifice of economic interests. The
prosperity of English industry might call for restraints on the
export of English wool and that of Flemish industry for a
ban on imports of English cloth; but the rhythm of controls
was more apt to be governed during the generations of
intermittent Anglo-French war by political or strategic
considerations. The widening scope of economic regulation
during the later middle ages, moreover, frequently represented an accommodation of government policies to the
insistent demands of special interests in order to secure some
short-term advantage. When this was the case, the policies a
government accepted might well be jettisoned with no

great qualms of conscience once that advantage had been secured.

To admit the many limitations, both in scope and in effectiveness, of medieval government economic policies is not completely to decry the progress which had been made during the centuries which separate feudal Europe from the Europe of the late middle ages. The period begins in a time when the fiscal and economic policies of governments were little more than policies of domanial exploitation; but with the passage of the generations much was added to them. How much can be read in John of Viterbo and Thomas Aquinas in the thirteenth century, Philip of Leyden and Nicholas Oresme in the fourteenth and English poets and parliamentary petitioners in the fifteenth. The conviction grew that governments did have extensive responsibilities in the economic field as well as a duty 'to undertake great things and to defend the kingdom'. To ensure the supply of goods, to encourage trade and nurture industry, to protect native interests, to provide good money, to sustain the 'common wealth' if only in the tangible form of stocks of bullion—all came to be regarded as contributions to that common utility of which rulers were the defenders and the guardians. Their guardianship was often imperfect, inconsistent and exercised with inadequate insight; but it would also be less than just to deny to these ideas about the responsibility of governments some part in that process of economic development which transformed feudal Europe into the far more advanced society which was the groundwork of the early modern world.

BIBLIOGRAPHY

Much material for medieval economic policies is scattered
through the pages of E. F. Hecksher's classic, *Mercantilism*,
trans. M. Shapiro, 2 volumes (London, 1935). There is a
more recent general survey in the *Cambridge Economic History*,
iii (Cambridge, 1965), ed. M. M. Postan. E. E. Rich and
E. Miller (chapter VI is a co-operative survey of government policies in England, France, the Low Countries, the
Baltic states and southern Europe and chapter VII draws
together a mass of evidence concerning public credit,
especially in north-western Europe). The principal omission
in this volume is any treatment of German economic
policies. This gap can be filled in part by H. Spangenberg's
discussion of the problem, admittedly somewhat schematic,
in *Territorialwirtschaft und Stadtwirtschaft* (Munich/Berlin,
1932); and more satisfactorily by U. Dirlmeier's *Mittelalter-
lische Hoheitsträger im wirtschaftlichen Wettbewerb* (Wiesbaden,
1966), which, as well as treating fully many facets of
German economic policy, contains a penetrating critique
of earlier literature.

A good deal of the information about medieval economic
and fiscal policies must be dug out of general histories or
general economic histories. H. A. Miskimin, *The Economy
of Early Renaissance Europe, 1300-1460* (Englewood Cliffs,
N.J., 1969) is a perceptive study of the later medieval
economy, including the new developments in economic
policy. E. G. Léonard's *Les Angevins de Naples* (Paris, 1954)
devotes considerable space to public finance and economic
regulation and P. Dollinger's *La Hanse (XIIe-XVIIe siècles)*
(Paris, 1964) is a masterly digest of the immense volume
of research on this northern commercial federation. W.
Cunningham's *Growth of English Industry and Commerce*, i (5th
ed., Cambridge, 1915) is now out of date in certain respects,
but it approaches economic development very much from
the angle of governmental regulation; and useful studies of
the Italian and Spanish economies during the middle ages
are G. Luzzatto, *Economic History of Italy from the Fall of the
Roman Empire to the Sixteenth Century*, trans. P. Jones (London,

1961) and J. Vicens Vives, *An Economic History of Spain*, trans. F. M. Lopez-Morillas (Princeton, N.J., 1969).

A number of more restricted studies can be used to fill out the general outlines. The character of English commercial policies under Edward III is sceptically assessed by G. Unwin in his *Finance and Trade under Edward III* (Manchester, 1918) and placed in a broader context by E. Power, *The Wool Trade in Medieval English History* (Oxford, 1941). D. Herlihy's *Pisa in the Early Renaissance: a Study of Urban Growth* (New Haven, 1958) contains a penetrating assessment of some of the policies of one Italian town; H. C. Peyer's *Zur Getreidepolitik oberitalienischer Städte im 13. Jahrhundert* (Vienna, 1950) draws together the evidence for the provisioning policies of the Italian communes; and in *Venice and History* (Baltimore, 1966), chapters VI, IX and XIII, F. C. Lane discusses Venice's funded debt and the organisation of Venetian commercial voyages. J. Klein, *The Mesta: a Study in Spanish Economic History* (Cambridge, Mass., 1920) is a pioneer work which provides an essential part of the background for Castilian policies and, for France at the end of the middle ages, R. Gandilhon's *Politique économique de Louis XI* (Rennes, 1941) is indispensable even though some of his conclusions have given rise to debate.

For the study of public finance in Germany there is an excellent summary of current knowledge by T. Mayer, 'Geschichte der Finanzwissenschaft vom Mittelalter bis zum Ende des 18. Jahrhundert', in *Handbuch der Finanzwissenschaft*, ed. W. Gerloff and F. Neumark, i (Tubingen, 1952); and M. M. Fryde began a review of the credit operations of German princes, unhappily curtailed by his death, in the University of Nebraska's *Studies in Medieval and Early Renaissance History*, i (1964). A vast amount of material for France is contained in *Histoire des institutions françaises au moyen âge*, ed. F. Lot and R. Fawtier, i-ii (Paris (1957-8), the first volume dealing somewhat unevenly with the feudal principalities and the second digesting in masterly fashion the present learning about royal finances and financial administration. Recently B. Lyon and A.

Verhulst, in *Medieval Finance: a Comparison of Financial Institutions in Northwestern Europe* (Bruges, 1967) have treated comparatively the crucial transitional period of the twelfth and early thirteenth centuries in England, Flanders, Normandy and the Capetian kingdom. Finally, the first four chapters of C. Stephenson's *Medieval Institutions: Selected Essays*, ed. B. Lyon (Ithaca, N.Y., 1954) deal with the interrelated developments of taxation and representation and the story is carried on by A. Marongiu, *Medieval Parliaments: a Comparative Study*, trans. S. J. Woolf (London, 1968).

There are extensive bibliographies appended to the chapters in the *Cambridge Economic History*, iii and a detailed guide to the German literature in Dirlmeier's book referred to above.

Notes on the Authors

C. M. CIPOLLA
is professor of economic history at the University of Pavia and at the University of California at Berkeley. Born in 1922 at Pavia *Italy*, he graduated from Pavia University, then proceeded to Paris and London where he continued his studies from 1945 to 1948. Since 1949 he has lectured at various European and American Universities on economic history. His publications in English include *Money, Prices and Civilisation* (1956), *The Economic History of World Population* (1962), *Guns and Sails in the Early Phase of European Expansion* (1965), *Clocks and Culture* (1967) and *Literacy and Development in the West* (1969).

J. C. RUSSELL
is Professor of History at Texas A & I University, Kingsville, Texas. Amongst his best known publications on medieval demography are *British Medieval Population* (1948) and *Late Ancient and Medieval Population* (1958).

JACQUES LE GOFF
was born at Toulon in 1924. He attended the Ecole Normale Superieure at Paris and the French School at Rome before becoming a Director of Studies at the Ecole Pratique des Hautes Etudes (VIth Section) and a Lecturer at the Ecole Normale Superieure and a co-director of the review *Annales*. Among his publications are *Marchands et Banquiers du Moyen Age* (1956), *Les Intellectuels due Moyen Age* (1957), *La Civilisation de l'Occident Medieval* (1964) and *Das Hochmittelalter*, vol. 11 of *Fischer Weltgeschichte* (1965).

RICHARD ROEHL
studied at Columbia University, receiving his B.A. in History in 1963. He obtained his Ph.D. in 1968 from the University of California at Berkeley, where he is presently Assistant Professor of Economics and has spent two years

engaged on research work in England, France and Germany. His thesis on *Plan and Reality in a Medieval Monastic Economy—The Cistercians* is to be published shortly in a revised form.

LYNN WHITE JR.

is Professor of History at the University of California, Los Angeles, and Director of the UCLA Center for Medieval and Renaissance Studies. He has taught at the Universities of Princeton and Stanford and was President of Mills College, 1943–1958. He has published a number of books and articles on the history of technology amongst which is *Medieval Technology and Social Change* (Oxford 1962).

GEORGES DUBY

is Professor at the University of Aix Marseilles and has written a number of books and articles on medieval agriculture, amongst which the most important is his *L'economie rurale et la vie des campagnes dans l'occident Medieval* (2 vols. Paris 1962), which has recently been published in an English translation by Lady Cynthia Postan under the title *Rural Economy and Country Life in the Medieval West*.

SYLVIA THRUPP

is the Alice Freeman Palmer Professor of History at the University of Michigan. Among her publications on gild and city history are *The Worshipful Company of Bakers*, London, 1933; *The Merchant Class of Medieval London*, Ann Arbor Paperbacks 1961; 'The Gilds' in *The Cambridge Economic History of Europe III*, 1963; 'Gilds' in *The New Encyclopaedia of the Social Sciences*, 1968; 'The City as the Idea of Social Order' in Handlin and Burchard, eds., *Historians and the City*, M.I.T. and Harvard University Press 1963.

JACQUES BERNARD

is Professor at the University of Bordeaux and has written several works on the history of Bordeaux and on the naval history of the fourteenth to the sixteenth century. The chief of these is *Navires et gens de mer à Bordeaux (vers 1400-vers 1550)*, 3 vols. (Paris 1968).

EDWARD MILLER
is Professor of Medieval History at the University of Sheffield. He was educated at King Edward VI School, Morpeth, Northumberland and St. John's College, Cambridge. From 1939 to 1965 he was a Fellow of St. John's College and from 1946 to 1965 University Lecturer in History. He has held his present position since 1965.

Index of Persons

Index of Places

General Index